Nassau
Plantation

Nassau Plantation

The Evolution of a
Texas-German Slave Plantation

James C. Kearney

©2010 James C. Kearney

All rights reserved.
Printed in the United States of America.

10 9 8 7 6 5 4 3 2

Permissions:
University of North Texas Press
1155 Union Circle #311336
Denton, TX 76203-5017

The paper used in this book meets the minimum requirements of the American National Standard for Permanence of Paper for Printed Library Materials, z39.48.1984. Binding materials have been chosen for durability.

Library of Congress Cataloging-in-Publication Data

Kearney, James C., 1946-
 Nassau Plantation : the evolution of a Texas-German slave plantation / by James C. Kearney.
   p. cm.
 Includes bibliographical references and index.
 ISBN 978-1-57441-286-4 (cloth : alk. paper)
 ISBN 978-1-57441-326-7 (paper : alk. paper)
 1. Nassau Plantation (Tex.)—History. 2. German Americans—Texas—History—19th century. 3. Adelsverein—History. 4. Texas—Colonization—History—19th century. 5. Texas—Emigration and immigration—History—19th century. 6. Germany—Emigration and immigration—History—19th century. 7. Fayette County (Tex.)—History—19th century. 8. Slavery—Texas—History—19th century. I. Title.
 F395.G3K436 2010
 976.4'251—dc22

2009047703

Publication of this book has been made possible by a generous grant from the Colorado County Texas German Society.

In Memory of
Anders Saustrup (1935-2008)
Historian, Naturalist, Eccentric
and
Bill Stein (1954-2008)
Historian, Renaissance Man, Friend

CONTENTS

List of Illustrations	ix
Acknowledgments	xi
Introduction	1
Chapter 1 *The* Adelsverein	11
Chapter 2 *Joseph Count of Boos-Waldeck*	25
Chapter 3 *The Plantation*	39
Chapter 4 *Germany and Texas in 1843 and 1844*	53
Chapter 5 *The Runaways*	63
Chapter 6 *Carl Prince of Solms-Braunfels*	75
Chapter 7 *Friedrich von Wrede*	93
Chapter 8 Das Herrenhaus	103
Chapter 9 *The Plantation and Agriculture in Fayette County*	109
Chapter 10 Die Katastrophe	123
Chapter 11 *Otto von Roeder*	153
Chapter 12 *Nassau-Rosenberg*	165
Chapter 13 *The* Adelsverein, *the Plantation, and Slavery*	183
Chapter 14 *A Clouded Title*	207
Postscript	219
Appendix A *Boos-Waldeck Purchases*	233
Appendix B *Bourgeois d'Orvanne Inventory*	237
Appendix C *Inventory, December 1847*	243
Appendix D *Slave Inventories*	245

Appendix E *Proclamation Concerning Slavery* 247
Appendix F *Descriptions of the* Herrenhaus 249
A Note on Sources and Abbreviations 255
Notes 263
Select Bibliography 319
Index 337

ILLUSTRATIONS

Texas Beaver Scene, by Conrad Caspar Rohrdorf, 1847	xii
Der Verein zum Schutze deutscher Einwanderer in Texas	10
The Jack League, Northern Fayette County	25
Count Boos-Waldeck Surveys the Jack League	39
Enchanted Rock, North to the Fischer-Miller Grant, by Conrad Caspar Rohrdorf	52
Butler Surrenders	63
Prince Solms Recites Schiller	75
Horse Races at the Plantation	91
Friedrich von Wrede, Sr.	93
Das Herrenhaus	103
Breaking the Prairie	109
Die Katastrophe	123
Armand (Dr. Schubert), Trust, and Czar, by Friedrich Armand Strubberg	152
Meusebach Enters the Comanche Camp	152
Otto von Roeder Supplies New Braunfels and Fredericksburg with Corn	153
Nassau-Rosenberg	165
Heel Flies	183
Sheriff Sells the Plantation	207
Barns of Nassau Plantation	219

Acknowledgments

My thanks first of all to the late Bill Stein, librarian, historian, and archivist of the Nesbitt Memorial Library in Columbus, Texas. Bill's command of the names and dates of Texas history was humbling; his knowledge of the techniques and resources of research, indispensable. Bill followed this study from the beginning until his recent, untimely death. He was always willing to give freely of his time, energy, and talents.

Thanks also to the late Anders Saustrup, who called everyone to a higher standard.

Thanks to Jean Howze for assistance with the manuscript and thanks to the library staff at San Antonio College for assistance with the Strubberg illustrations.

Thanks to Randolph and Mary Belle Rather, present-day owners of Nassau Plantation, who were always willing to share their knowledge and to allow me to explore freely.

Thanks to both the Colorado County Chapter of the Texas German Society and the Department of Germanic Studies at the University of Texas at Austin for their endorsements and financial support.

Finally, thanks to my wife Paulina for patiently putting up with stacks of books and documents cluttering her house and yet another trip to the State Archives or the Center for American History.

INTRODUCTION

The idealistic and delusionary attempt by the Society for the Protection of German Emigrants in Texas to settle thousands of German emigrants on the Texas frontier in the 1840s is a story of epic proportions, which one scholar characterized as the greatest tragedy of German emigration to the New World in the nineteenth century, but ultimately the greatest triumph.[1] The nineteenth century witnessed many schemes for promoting immigration in the New World; in scope and audacity, however, their program stands alone.

This organization, which often goes by the shorthand name *Adelsverein*, or Society of Noblemen, managed to effectively settle many thousands of Germans on the Texas frontier in 1845, 1846, and 1847, emigrants who eventually made the transition to and created community in their new home in Texas. Viewed from this perspective, the *Adelsverein*'s program has to be considered a monumental and unparalleled success. But for the organization itself, its efforts in Texas—as judged by the goals it had set for itself, which were to reap financial reward and to gain prestige for the organization—can only be considered a catastrophic failure.

Nassau Plantation, located in northern Fayette County near Round Top, Texas, was the first possession of these noblemen in Texas and was an important possession for them from beginning to end. Nassau Plantation failed miserably as an experiment in slavery by German noblemen in Texas, yet it ultimately succeeded in solidifying and enriching the German presence in South Central Texas. It did this by attracting fresh emigrants who likewise were successful in creating a new home and community in the New World. In this, the plantation reflected the larger success of the *Adelsverein* in Texas.

The main significance of the plantation, however, has been almost completely overlooked in the extensive literature about German emigration to Texas. The plantation played an absolutely essential role in supporting the thousands of emigrants introduced by the *Adelsverein* into the Texas Hill Country in the years 1845, 1846, and 1847. Through the plantation's supportive role in these critical years, the newcomers gained breathing room in which to plant gardens, to fence in and cultivate their fields, and to erect rudimentary housing. Without this support, surely hundreds more would have perished, and the whole venture would have collapsed in complete chaos and disorder, leading most likely to a large withdrawal of the German settlers from the area. Disillusioned and embittered, many would have chosen to return to Germany, but for those who remained, a retrenchment to more settled areas of the state would have been necessary.[2]

The sheer grittiness of the *Adelsverein*'s program has led to much speculation: were these men simply idealistic and naïve, or was something more disturbing at play here?[3] Not surprisingly, a large literature has grown up about the history of the German settlements in Texas. Indeed, fascination about it has spawned a cottage industry of Texas—German nostalgia to go along with the many solid works of historical research on the subject. The continued output led one scholar to remark that he could not read one more book about Germans in Texas.[4]

This is unfortunate because a wealth of original source material, largely underutilized, is available to scholars to document the *Adelsverein* and the plantation. This study has relied heavily on the thousands of documents in the Solms-Braunfels Archives (and related collections) to offer a fresh perspective on the formative period of the Society for the Protection of German Emigrants in Texas.[5] These documents reveal significant contradictions and divisions in concept and purpose within the Society, both in Texas and in Germany, which the plantation came to symbolize. This material also deepens our appreciation for the role played by the

Adelsverein and the plantation in the contemporary debate about slavery and immigration.

The plantation represented an organized attempt to set up a slave plantation by German noblemen in the 1840s. This fact alone renders the conventional belief that the Germans in Texas were uniformly opposed to slavery problematic. Yet, the extensive and sometimes contentious debates on this subject have uniformly ignored the role of the plantation. The path to successful assimilation for Germans of this period led unavoidably through the minefield of slavery, a challenge which lay dormant until the Civil War brought it dramatically and violently to the forefront. The anomaly of Nassau Plantation, a German slave plantation in Texas, provides a convenient forum for discussing this painful journey.

This book, however, is not just about slavery. It is primarily about a particular place, Nassau Plantation, and how the plantation evolved from a German slave plantation on a league of land in northern Fayette County to a collection of over twenty small farms and homesteads, characteristic of the present. Several dramatic events took place at the plantation during this transformation, providing stories that are compelling in their own right, even as they exemplify larger themes. There is also an important biographical contour to the story. Friedrich Armand Strubberg, Otto von Roeder, and Peter Carl von Rosenberg were all associated with the plantation and all come in for fresh interpretation based on new research.

The story of Nassau Plantation begins with the arrival in Texas in the summer of 1842 of the middle-aged Joseph Count of Boos-Waldeck and the younger Viktor Count of Alt-Leiningen-Westerburg with their servants as the first representatives of the *Adelsverein* in Texas. They spent the remainder of the year 1842 familiarizing themselves with the social, political, and economic realities of the young republic.[6] They also scouted for a suitable location to establish a slave plantation. Their conversations and observations during their travels reinforced their belief, apparently already formed in Germany, that investment in a slave plantation or, possibly, even in a string of them, would be a wise move for the Society.

Count Boos-Waldeck's observations and experiences led him to doubt seriously the wisdom of the Society becoming overly ambitious. He cautioned especially against any program of colonization based on a land grant contract with the Republic of Texas.[7] Later, he became quite certain that such a plan would lead to disastrous consequences, both for the settlers and for the Society. He expressed this gathering conviction in a series of letters and reports to the leadership in Germany. Toward the end, this correspondence became strikingly blunt and frank in tone. He resigned from the Society in the spring of 1844 when he was not able to convince the leadership in Germany to abandon their plans to colonize a land grant.

The count pleaded instead for a more modest program based on clustering limited numbers of immigrants around the Society's plantation(s).[8] Here, in the company of their countrymen, the fresh immigrants would be able to seek guidance in agriculture, find comfort and safety in the stability and strength of the plantation, and stimulate trade with the fatherland through their natural desire for German finished goods. The settlers, in turn, would be contractually obligated to render certain services to the plantation as recompense for the help they had received from the Society in their move to the New World. Presumably, they would also be motivated out of a sense of fidelity and gratitude. All the while, the plantations were expected to return a solid profit to their owners, the noblemen, in Germany.

The medieval stamp to this plan is obvious: the plantation replaces the castle, the German settlers take the place of the yeomen and tradesmen of the Middle Ages, the Negro slaves the place of medieval serfs and bondsmen, while the German noblemen at the top of this hierarchy bask in a life of leisure and privilege. It is not surprising that more than one commentator has asserted that something like the reestablishment of feudalism was the Society's secret agenda.[9]

This was doubtless an overstatement, but certainly it would have been a remarkable experiment had Boos-Waldeck been able to convince the leadership in Germany that colonization ought to proceed along these lines. Even as Count Boos-Waldeck preoccupied himself during the whole of 1843 with the task of establishing Nassau Plantation, the centerpiece of his program and vision, the leadership in Germany pressed stubbornly ahead with plans for a large-scale colonization project. These plans turned on a land grant contract with the Republic of Texas and reflected the strong influence of Carl Count of Castell with the close support of his friend, Carl Prince of Solms-Braunfels. Their ideas were utterly at variance with the advice they were receiving from their agent[10] in Texas and inconsistent with the course he was pursuing.

Boos-Waldeck's deep misgivings about settling a land grant proved prophetic, but the alternative he proposed was also deeply flawed. He completely underestimated the difficulties of setting up a plantation on the Texas frontier. What seemed a sure bet on paper was in practice bedeviled by false assumptions and costly mistakes. Boos-Waldeck arrived in Texas in the summer of 1842 optimistic and eager to act; he returned to Europe in December 1843 broken in health and spirit, leaving a Texas-German, Charles Fordtran, in temporary charge of the plantation.

No sooner had Boos-Waldeck departed than Charles Fordtran was confronted with a serious problem: three slaves ran away. In his reports back to Germany, Fordtran documents in an unprecedented way the attempt to recover the slaves.

Prince Solms-Braunfels, energetic, opinionated, and priggish, arrived on the scene to replace Boos-Waldeck in July 1844. He arrived knowing that the Society had committed firmly to the settlement of a land grant through its association with the Frenchman Bourgeois d'Orvanne. Upon inspecting the plantation for the first time, he immediately pronounced it unworthy of the Society. The incomplete and dilapidated condition of the plantation disturbed Solms-Braunfels, but the reality of slavery, when confronted firsthand, shocked the prince deeply,[11] demonstrating that even among the members of the Society, unanimity of opinion about slavery did not exist. The prince vented his spleen on Charles Fordtran, the man Count Boos-Waldeck had left in charge. The prince dismissed him as supervisor before returning to Germany in June

1845, replacing him with a former German officer, Friedrich von Wrede, Sr.

Despite his censure, the plantation served Prince Solms well as a convenient and comfortable home base from which to conduct the business of the Society. Solms-Braunfels hastily made preparations for the first boatloads of settlers who began arriving at Indianola and Galveston in the winter of 1844–45. His demeanor while staying at the plantation has given rise to the persistent legend of unbridled extravagance and high living with which the plantation has been associated in the popular imagination.[12] It was exciting news to the many Germans who were already in Texas that a real German prince had arrived with servants and attendants, a prince who had a large purse and even larger plans. Local German-Texans flocked to the plantation to meet the prince and offer their services.

The new supervisor, Friedrich von Wrede, Sr., attempted to reorganize the plantation and stem the continued financial loss. His detailed and perceptive reports, written from the perspective of a no-nonsense German officer, offer wonderful vignettes of life on the Texas frontier in the mid-1840s and complement nicely his previously published travelogue.[13] Von Wrede's untimely death at the hands of hostile Indians in the fall of 1846 put an end to his initiatives and left the plantation to drift. In an improbable twist, one of the slaves, Negro Jim, succeeded von Wrede as the temporary overseer of the plantation until other arrangements could be made.

The *Herrenhaus*, or manor house, had by this time been more or less completed. A crude and uncomfortable structure by European standards, in fit and finish it was certainly a step above the everyday crudity and shabbiness common to the Texas frontier. Many contemporary observers considered the *Herrenhaus* to be one of the finest houses on the Texas frontier. Peter Carl von Rosenberg later chose to settle at Nassau because of the house. A chapter has been devoted to its construction and continued refinement.

The imperious and idealistic Johann Otto *Freiherr*[14] von Meusebach succeeded Solms-Braunfels as commissioner-general[15] of the Society in Texas in the spring of 1845. In December 1846 he faced down a mob of angry colonists in New Braunfels. Partly as an escape and partly for convenience—proximity to Houston and Galveston—Meusebach spent the first months of 1846 at the plantation. Here, so his detractors maintained, he gave himself over to the pleasures of food and drink as an escape from his worries.[16] It was during this period that Meusebach made the fateful acquaintance of the cross-grained and wily Dr. Schubbert, whom he engaged to be the director of the Friedrichsburg (Fredericksburg) settlement.

Later, in the fall of 1847, Dr. Schubbert became involved in an ugly dispute with Meusebach, a dispute that eventually led to a deadly gun battle for control of the plantation. The official artist of the Society, Conrad Caspar Rohrdorf, died in the fight, and his valuable and irreplaceable portfolio, containing over forty drawings of the colonies, fell into the hands of Dr. Schubbert. This episode created a sensation, both in Texas and Germany.

Dr. Schubbert, whose real name was Friedrich Armand Strubberg, returned to Germany to take up a new career as a highly successful author of illustrated adventure novels based on his experiences in Texas. I argue that his first novel [17] contains illustrations by the slain artist Conrad Caspar Rohrdorf. Ironically, Strubberg is also generally credited as the author of the most strident anti-slavery novels written in German in the nineteenth century.[18]

By the fall of 1847, it had become painfully evident to the leadership in Germany that their grandiose plans in Texas had not worked out, and, in fact, had taken a disastrous turn, just as Count Boos-Waldeck had predicted. They then attempted to cut their losses by unloading their properties in Texas onto unwitting investors in Germany.[19] Their desperation was exacerbated by the outbreak of revolution in Germany in March 1848. The plantation always figured prominently in these negotiations, because it still appeared on the books in Germany as a substantial asset.

Officials in Texas, however, had parlayed a lien on the plantation into grain for the desperate colonists in New Braunfels and Friedrichsburg in 1846 and 1847. The important role of Otto von Roeder in this connection has been largely overlooked. This study attempts to complete this story by examining the complicated maneuvering by which Otto von Roeder eventually (but temporarily) gained control of the plantation in 1850 in exchange for the assistance he had provided.

Once under his control, Otto von Roeder immediately began parceling off the plantation and selling it to fresh immigrants from Germany, contributing to the process by which the region was transformed into one of the most exclusively Germanic areas of the state. Peter Carl von Rosenberg was the first and most prominent person to purchase land from Otto von Roeder, acquiring in February 1850 a substantial portion of the Nassau Plantation, including the *Herrenhaus*. Two of his grown children purchased land nearby. The von Rosenberg family is important because of their eminence and because they left a thorough and fascinating record of their move from Germany and their stay at "Nassau-Rosenberg" in the form of published correspondence.

In 1853 a young lawyer from Massachusetts, James A. Chandler, challenged Otto von Roeder's ownership of the plantation. This muddied the waters and led to a series of protracted legal entanglements. One case ended up in the Texas Supreme Court; another eventually made its way to the U.S. Supreme Court. Final resolution awaited the outcome of the Civil War because judgment was rendered in favor of James Chandler only shortly before the first shots were fired, a judgment that eventually compromised the purchases of the von Rosenbergs and twelve others who had purchased land from Otto von Roeder in the meantime.

Scholars have devoted a tremendous amount of discussion to anti-slavery and Unionist sentiments among the German element in Texas during the Civil War. The vote for secession and the declaration of war forced painful choices on the extended von Rosenberg family, as it did for most German immigrants in the state. On several occasions, in the western settlements, the festering tensions erupted in violent confrontations. This study addresses the anomaly of Nassau Plantation and the contradictory and hypocritical stance of the *Adelsverein* in the period leading up to the Civil War. The diversity of opinion among the cast of characters associated with the plantation illustrates that sweeping generalizations about Texas-Germans during the period often fall short.

The final story of the Society's activities in Texas—from roughly 1848 till 1855—has never been adequately explained and documented.[20] The plantation played an important role during this period even after it was handed over to Otto von Roeder for satisfaction of debt. The Society and its creditors took vigorous steps to try to regain possession of the farm, and the numerous financial and legal entanglements that ensued cast a troublesome shadow over the subsequent owners of land there.

Nassau Plantation is also the story of one particular tract of land, the 4,428 acres of the Jack League in northern Fayette County, and how this land became forever transformed by "progress" from virgin, untouched wilderness to the tamed, pastoral landscape of the present. In a sense, the plantation eventually accomplished in death what it could not achieve in life, namely, it attracted and held many fresh immigrants from Germany. It is a fascinating story, essential to the understanding of the rich history of South Central Texas and necessary to appreciating the complexity of its demographic makeup.

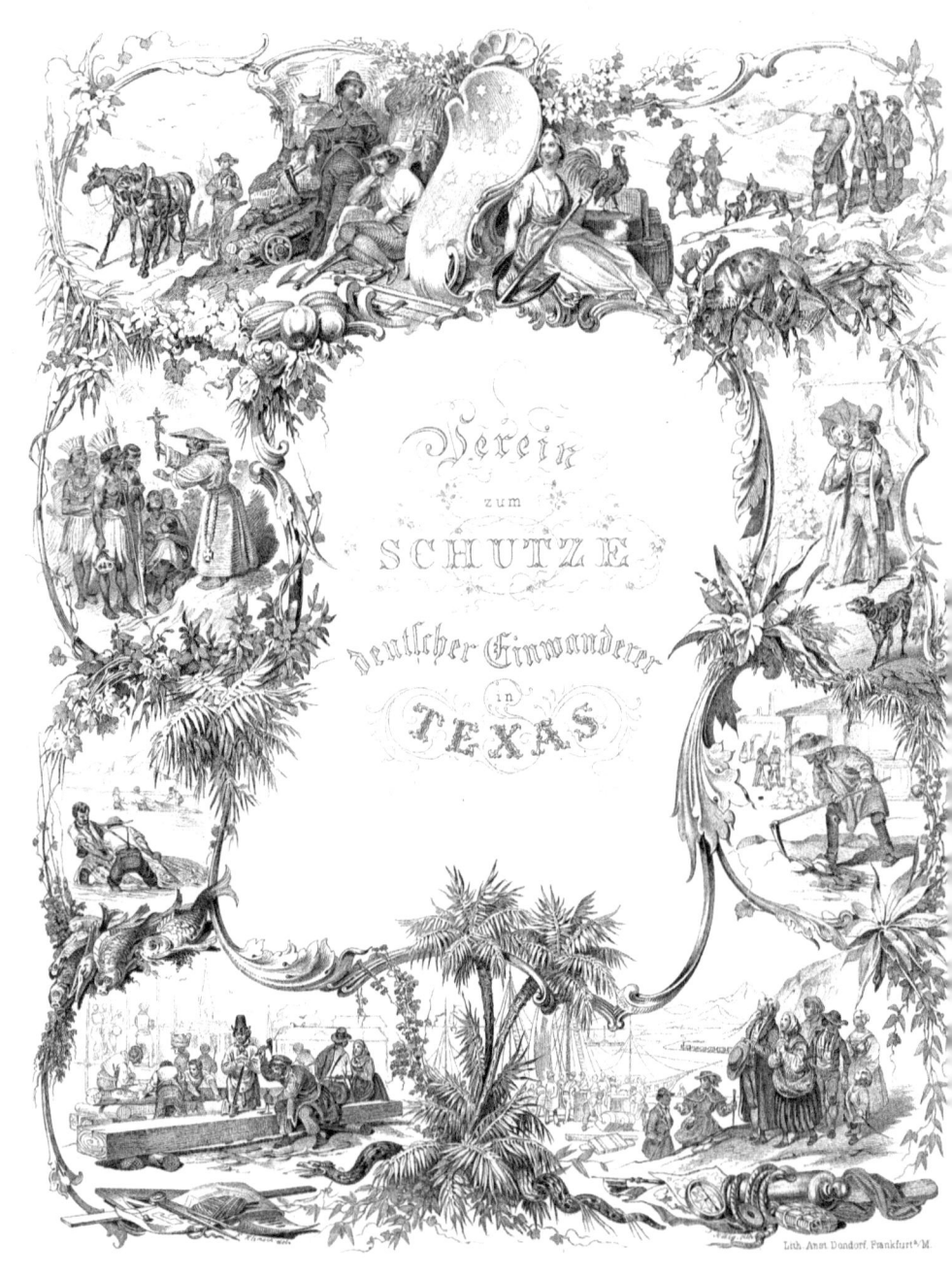

CHAPTER 1

The *Adelsverein*

Raus, raus und raus,
Aus Deutschland muß ich raus:
Ich schlag mir Deutschland aus dem Sinn
Und wand´re jetzt nach Texas hin.
Mein Glück will ich probieren, marschieren!

Out, out and out
From Germany I must out;
Germany I put you from my mind
My happiness in Texas to find.
Our fortune there to grow, let's go!

—*Hoffmann von Fallersleben*[1]

Fascination for Texas, despair about Germany—these factors, broadly speaking—motivated a group of German noblemen to fashion an ambitious program of emigration from Germany to Texas in the 1840s. To governments and to individuals alike, the young Republic of Texas suggested exciting possibilities. Britain, France, and Belgium hoped to see Texas develop into a viable nation, receptive to cross-Atlantic influence and poised to counterbalance the growing commercial and military dominance of the United States in the New World. Many individuals, likewise, pinned their hopes on the new republic: they dreamed of getting rich by speculating in cheap Texas lands or they aspired to create a fresh life in a wide open land frequently portrayed as a new Garden of Eden.

Germany, by contrast, appeared as a place of little or no opportunity. Its intelligent, vigorous, and growing population had no outlet for their energy; no possibility for betterment in their homeland. This brought about a frustration and despair that cut across class lines from peasant farmers to the upper nobility. A massive exodus from Central Europe resulted, and the destination was, in the main, North America.

In the spring of 1842, twenty German noblemen and one noblewoman met at the residence of Adolph Duke of Nassau in Biebrich on the Rhine.[2] They endeavored to fashion a program of important national significance whereby the opportunities of Texas would supply an antidote to the frustrations of Germany. In so doing they sought to enhance the prestige of the German nobility and also to increase their personal wealth by speculating in cheap Texas lands. In scope and audacity, the plan they eventually adopted holds a unique place in the history of emigration to the New World.

The German side of the story begins in the city of Mainz. Situated on the left bank of the Rhine across from the confluence of the Main River, Mainz keeps watch over one of the most fruitful and beautiful areas of Germany. The city is the gatekeeper, so to speak, to a long and picturesque stretch of the Rhine, which is the subject of so many postcards and travel guides. Since Roman times, geography has dictated its importance economically, culturally, and militarily. Thus, in the 1840s, in addition to housing the capitol of the Hessian Rhine Province and being a hub of trade and transportation, the city housed a *Bundesfestung*, a federal fortress of the first order of importance, manned by a combined force of Prussian and Austrian units. It was here that many of the titled officers came into contact with one another and began those speculations and discussions that eventually led to the formation of their Society.

With the final defeat of Napoleon at the battle of Waterloo in June

1815, the collective leadership of Europe convened in Vienna to establish peace. Under the strong leadership of Prince Metternich of Austria, a new order was given to the face of Europe. As part of this process, the Congress of Vienna restructured the political map of Germany. It set up a loose federation of forty-one states and free cities under the permanent presidency of Austria. This arrangement, referred to as the *Deutscher Bund*, or German Confederation, endured for over fifty years, until 1866. The Congress also provided for a common defense for the federation, anchored by a string of forts.

The officers who manned the common forts of the federation came from different states and were, by and large, of noble lineage. Only a few career paths were socially suitable, or *standesgemäss*, to the upper nobility in Germany during this period. Chief among these was a career in the army.[3] The relative stability and tranquility of Central Europe during the *Vormärz*[4], the period from 1815 until 1848, insured that those who had chosen to be officers had much free time on their hands. Out of idleness arose grandiose plans.

An hour's journey down the Rhine from Mainz one passes Biebrich. Located on the right side of the river, Biebrich served as one of the residences of the Dukes of Nassau until 1866. The castle, built in the Renaissance style in 1706, was a relative newcomer among the many castles and fortresses along the Rhine. It nevertheless impressed travelers along the river with its majestic grounds and well-groomed gardens.

It was here in April 1842 that the twenty-four-year-old Adolph, reigning Duke of Nassau, hosted the first general assembly of the association, which would later officially constitute itself as *Der Verein zum Schutze deutscher Einwanderer in Texas,* or The Society for the Protection of German Emigrants in Texas.[5] Of the men gathered here, two officers in the service of Austria stationed at the federal fortress at Mainz stand out: Christian Count of Neu-Leiningen-Westerburg and Carl Count of Castell-Castell.[6]

In a circular of March 8, 1842, the birth certificate of the Society, Christian Count of Neu-Leiningen-Westerburg outlined his conception for a society to promote German emigration to Texas and to speculate in land there.[7] He laid out in detail the reasons he regarded

Texas to be a land of exciting opportunity for investment and exceptional suitability for German emigration. He based his enthusiasm for Texas on recently published studies by the German G. A. Scherpf[8] and the Englishman William Kennedy[9] and on personal conversations with the celebrated traveler and naturalist Alexander von Humboldt.[10] A close reading suggests that both Scherpf and Kennedy had, in turn, drawn heavily from von Humboldt's earlier and influential study of the physical geography of Mexico, which, at the time, included Texas. Between 1799 and 1804, von Humboldt traveled to South and Central America, classifying and describing the plants and animals he encountered, as well as the geography and geology he observed. He did so with a heretofore unmatched scientific rigor and thoroughness. His descriptions and observations, published in many volumes over a twenty-one year span, represented a major scientific contribution to Europe's knowledge of the New World.[11]

In his letter, Count Leiningen proposed to fund a society to promote emigration to Texas by offering twenty shares at 5,000 florins[12] each, of which half was to be paid initially. This money would be dedicated to the purchase of land; the rest would be held in reserve to underwrite and support emigration. Upon a completed subscription to the initial twenty shares, Leiningen would call for a general assembly of the subscribers to settle on a program. Leiningen's request met with such enthusiasm that he quickly expanded the initial offering to twenty-four shares, and subsequently to fifty. The invitation for a gathering of shareholders soon went out. Twenty German noblemen and one German noblewoman, the Countess from Isenburg, responded.[13] The date was set for April 19, 1842, in Biebrich.[14]

The points Leiningen raises in his letter are worth a closer examination since he touches upon the whole complex of considerations and motivations behind the organization.[15] He begins by pointing out the favorable geography of Texas, which nicely combined characteristics of both the tropical and temperate zones. The political existence of Texas is assured because of the vigorous nature of the settlers, he writes.

The value of the lands in Texas, he maintains, will surely rise as settlers continue to flock to the country at the rate of 50,000 a year.

Those who are energetic are bound to improve their lot in life there. Germans, who enjoy a reputation as a diligent and energetic people, have no outlet for this energy in their overpopulated homeland. The destination of most emigrants from Germany is the United States where the immigrants become dispersed, which is neither to the benefit of them as individuals, nor to Germany as a nation. Would it not be better to locate and concentrate German emigrants in one area of the New World?

Very few speculations, he continues, have a greater certainty of success than capital invested in Texas lands. One can even recover the initial outlay by harvesting native plants of medicinal value such as sassafras or ipecac.[16]

The best approach, he suggests, would be to invest in a slave plantation. The situation in Texas is comparable to that in the United States twenty years before. Opportunity abounds. Although the temper of the times precludes the introduction of feudalism, Texas provides an outlet for the energetic genius of the noble class. Enduring fame and financial reward will come to those who have the will and means to fashion the above considerations into a workable program. Count Leiningen ends his letter with the admonition that time is of the essence.

Greed, glory, and patriotism—all these elements are present in Leiningen's letter. Present, too, is the idea that speculation in a slave plantation in Texas would be a sure windfall.

Several men associated with the Society had "Leiningen" in their names. They are often confused in the literature. We have been discussing Christian Count of Neu-Leiningen-Westerburg, whose very long name is usually reduced to Christian Leiningen. Christian Leiningen considered himself to be the father of the Society by virtue of his early enthusiasm for Texas, the above-mentioned circular, and his efforts at organizing the first general assembly at Biebrich.[17] When he began this effort, he was serving as an *Oberstleutnant,* lieutenant colonel, in the imperial Austrian army in Mainz.[18] He was appointed president of the first committee to organize the affairs of the Society, but from that point his importance to the Society waned. He rarely attended convocations of the Society; instead, he gave Carl Count of

Castell, his cousin, the power of attorney to act on his behalf, and he seemed to have deferred to his judgment in most matters.

A relative, Karl Emich Prince of Leiningen, was elected president of the Society. Karl Emich was an important man in Germany. He was the ruling patriarch of the ancient and prestigious house of Leiningen, a branch of German nobility that had ruled over possessions along the Rhine River since the eleventh century. As a *Fürst*, he ranked high, a weighty consideration among German noblemen.[19] In 1842, he was appointed to the Bavarian Council of Advisors. In 1848 Karl Emich also served briefly as the first Minister-President of the National Assembly in Frankfurt am Main.

Karl Emich von Leiningen's prestige as a man of connection and influence in Germany was certainly a feather in the cap for the Society. In addition he was also a half-brother to the future Queen Victoria of England. Another important player, Carl Prince of Solms-Braunfels, had family ties to the English throne as well, through his mother.[20] The English connection is one that has given rise to much speculation, and has led some to assert (and others to deny) that the English government might have been a silent partner in the Society's plans.[21]

There was one other Leiningen of note, namely Viktor Count of Alt-Leiningen-Westerburg. He accompanied Boos-Waldeck on the first expedition to Texas. After his return in January 1843, he dropped from the scene as an active participant although he remained a stockholder.

Count Castell's participation and importance, in contrast to Christian Leiningen's, steadily increased after the first general convention. A committee was set up to handle the day-to-day affairs of the Society. Although Christian Leiningen served as president and Count Castell as vice-president, Castell appears to have done most of the work.[22] This committee met on several occasions, especially from March through May of 1842. Among other things, it arranged for the "expedition" to Texas, corresponded with members of the Society, and continued to inform itself about the political, economic and physical facts of Texas.

Eventually (in March 1844), Count Castell's responsibilities would be formalized in the office of *Geschäftsführer,* or executive director of the Society.[23] From the first assembly in 1842 until his resignation in August 1848, Castell would sit at the center of the web, the most important man in the organization, the man whose vision set the tone and direction for the Society, often in the face of determined opposition.

Count Castell was close to Christian Leiningen[24] and also to Carl Prince of Solms-Braunfels. He signed his letters *Vetter*[25] (cousin) and addressed the prince with the informal "du" in his letters. The two appeared to be in close agreement in the early phases of the Society. Both enthusiastically supported the notion of a large and ambitious program of settlement rather than a modest, restricted one.[26] Thus, family ties, close friendships, and class-consciousness characterized the men gathered in Biebrich for the first general assembly. Family alliances also gave them access to most of the governments in Germany as well as the English court, as noted.

Of the twenty-one original members of the Society, four were ruling sovereigns and two were princes from sovereign houses. Sixteen of the members counted themselves members of a special caste of the upper German nobility that had come to be called the *Standesherren*, a term for which there is no exact English equivalent.

The *Standesherren* came from former ruling houses whose sovereign status had been reduced or eliminated during the turmoil accompanying the Napoleonic Wars and the breakup of the Holy Roman Empire. The process began with the Peace of Luneville in 1801 when Napoleon emerged victorious against the Second Coalition led by Austria. The left bank of the Rhine was ceded to France, dispossessing many smaller German ruling families. Later, by the so-called *Reichsdeputationshauptschluß* (Imperial Decree) of 1803, several of the ruling houses who had lost possessions were compensated using church properties that had been secularized by the same edict.

During this period, roughly 1801 until 1815, the number of political entities within the boundaries of the old Holy Roman Empire who claimed sovereign status shrank from approximately 300 to thirty. Many of the old ruling houses were "mediatized," that is, placed under the sovereignty of other rulers. These houses had lost much of their real power, but retained the prestige and late-feudal privileges associated with ruling sovereigns.

The story of the *Standesherren* is quite complex and beyond the scope of this history to explore in detail. But this much is certain: by virtue of their numbers and the pivotal role they played from the beginning, the *Standesherren* stood in the forefront of the Society. Nearly everyone of consequence in the Society (excluding certain officials in Texas) came from their ranks.[27]

It is also certain that they were conscious of their unique position in German society, and that this awareness goes a long way to explain their interest in underwriting a colonization scheme for Texas.[28]

By the 1840s, two thoughts appeared to preoccupy the *Standesherren* as a group: on the one hand, they sought to preserve the considerable privileges they still enjoyed; on the other hand, they felt driven to carve for themselves a new role that would justify these privileges. Apparently some saw in Texas a fertile field for a grand and magnificent endeavor which would help to revive the prestige of the *Standesherren* even as it served a pressing national need and remunerated its organizers handsomely. Count Castell put it succinctly when he wrote in July 1845 that "the Society wanted to create something grand in order to be able to say to itself, that is our work."[29]

The number of Germans leaving their homeland had grown steadily since the end of the Napoleonic wars. Indeed, the exodus had taken on such proportions that it rivaled the *Völkerwanderungszeit*, the great movement of Germanic peoples in the fifth through the ninth centuries, which had fundamentally altered the face of Europe. In 1845, for example, about 56,000 Germans left their homeland.[30] In the nineteenth century as a whole, nearly five million Germans came to the United States.[31]

Most of these emigrants came to North America, where the percentage of the population with German surnames increased daily. Here, due to their ignorance of the language and unfamiliarity of the culture, they fell prey in droves to the unscrupulous who profited from their vulnerability. Stories of disillusionment and despair regularly filtered back to the homeland.

The noblemen gathered at Biebrich in the spring of 1842 considered this a great national tragedy. They thought it desirable that their countrymen should be able to preserve their language and cultural identity in their new homeland. After considering the other possibilities, which ranged from Australia to Brazil, and with the encouragement of Christian Leiningen and Carl Castell, they settled on the young Republic of Texas as the place most suited for their purposes.[32]

Count Castell, in contrast to Christian Leiningen, pointedly emphasized the advantages a colonization project in Texas would hold for German trade. Just as the native Anglos leaned toward American and English products, Germans concentrated in Texas would prefer the German finished and manufactured goods with which they were familiar. This preference, he maintained, would stimulate a lively exchange between finished goods and raw materials, which would benefit both the colony and the homeland. The importance of trade became a basic tenet of the program, and was always emphasized in the Society's official pronouncements.

Texas had won its independence from Mexico in 1836. Idealists around the world hailed this as a triumph of the human spirit against tyranny and oppression and took heart from the fact that the Texans had conducted their revolt successfully without compromising their institutions of self-government. Many governments had also taken note of the new republic, but for less idealistic reasons. They realized the strategic implications of a young republic blessed with fertile soil, access to the sea, and a vigorous population strategically located between the United States and Latin America.

England, France, and Belgium initially took a wait-and-see attitude. Would the new republic be able to maintain its independence from Mexico? Would it be able to organize itself into a viable country? Had the revolt been truly spontaneous, or were imperialistic ambitions among certain elements in the United States really behind it? Was annexation inevitable?

France and England faced a foreign policy dilemma. On the one hand, they ardently hoped to see Texas grow into a prosperous, stable, and independent country; a country that could help check the growing power and domination of the United States in the Western Hemisphere; a country that would provide a market for the finished goods of Europe in exchange for raw materials and agricultural products, such as tobacco and cotton; and, finally, a country over which they could exert political influence. On the other hand, they did not want to alienate Mexico, a country with which they had already developed commercial and political ties and also a country to whom they had loaned a great deal of money.[33] Complicating matters, England had received 45,000,000 acres of Texas land as collateral to secure her loans. In the end it was a judgment: who in the long run would hold out the greatest promise, Mexico or Texas?

The noblemen in Germany found themselves in general agreement with the foreign policy objectives of England and France with respect to Texas. Thus, a sense of unified interest reinforced the close family ties that existed between several of the German noblemen in the Society and the ruling house of England.

To observers in the present, there seems something foreordained and inexorable about the eventual incorporation of Texas into the Union: it had to happen, sooner or later, because certain irresistible historical forces demanded such an outcome. To intelligent and knowledgeable observers of the day, however, such an outcome appeared neither foreordained nor inevitable.

William Kennedy, English consul in Texas and author of an influential book on Texas, had argued strongly that annexation was unlikely. To begin with, the people of Texas were by no means overwhelmingly in favor of statehood, and had, in fact, rejected initial overtures. Moreover, the free states of the Union would not easily welcome Texas, for to do so would upset the precarious balance between free and slave states. Also, annexation would very likely provoke a war with Mexico, which might open the door to an even greater expansion of slavery.

For its part, Mexico still considered Texas a Mexican state in revolt and fully intended to bring it back into the fold. To underscore this point, General Mariano Arista issued from Monterrey in January 1842 an address to the inhabitants of the "Department of Texas" in which he pointed out the hopelessness of their struggle for independence and promised amnesty.[34] During the first six years of the republic, there was a constant threat of reinvasion from Mexico. Indeed, in March 1842 the Mexican army briefly occupied Goliad, Refugio, Victoria, and San Antonio. But when Texan forces gathered in San Antonio, the Mexican army quickly retired.

European observers on the scene expressed confidence that Texas could, and would, maintain its independence against the claims of Mexico. Kennedy and Scherpf considered Mexico, despite her superior numbers and resources, to be moribund and corrupt. Both men contrasted the vigor and resourcefulness of the Anglo population with the supposed lethargy and disorganization of the Mexicans. There was undoubtedly an element of racism in this attitude, which was as widely believed then as it is now rejected.

France took the first step and recognized Texas in 1839. On November 13, 1840, England executed a reversal in its policy and concluded a treaty of friendship and commerce with Texas that was formally ratified in 1842. Thus, England signaled that she had faith in the new republic and intended to foster economic ties even if it meant a loss of trade with Mexico.

Above all, the new republic needed settlers. In recognition of this fact, in February 1842, the Texas Congress empowered the president to offer conditional title to vast tracts of land as a reward to entrepreneurs who would agree to settle specified numbers of colonists within a set time.[35] The law echoed the *empresario* system by which Stephen F. Austin had established the original Anglo colony in Texas.

The German noblemen gathered in Biebrich took note of these developments. Mexico did not have the means to subjugate Texas while the politics of slavery held the expansionist ambitions of the United States in check. Recognition of the young republic by France, England, and Belgium legitimized it on the international stage. Resurrection of the *empresario* system held out the possibility of enormous financial gain for those who could secure a colonization contract and who had the energy and resources to fulfill its terms, a fact quickly noted by entrepreneurs on both sides of the Atlantic.

Texas had been, and continued to be, the site of one of the world's great land giveaways, first through the *empresario* contracts of the Spanish (and later) Mexican governments, and then through a revival of a similar program by the Republic of Texas.[36] The hunger for land and the opportunities that Texas provided are a recurring and transforming theme in this story. Threat of invasion by Mexico, the German noblemen concluded, had temporarily created a panic within the republic, which could be turned to advantage in negotiations for land even as the possibility that Mexico could subjugate the fledgling republic receded.

The noblemen in Germany were ambivalent regarding the question of annexation. The Society anticipated in 1842 that Texas would maintain its independence, but continued independence was not a prerequisite for the success of their plans. Count Castell pointed out on several occasions that investment in lands in Texas was a win-win situation. In fact, it would yield an even greater return if Texas were to come into the Union, as this likely would lead to an overnight increase in land values. In this Count Boos-Waldeck concurred.

On the other side, Carl Prince of Solms-Braunfels passionately believed that Texas should remain independent. Certainly, the argument for a special trade relationship with attendant trade concessions turned on this point. Solms-Braunfels' attitude, however, clearly drew more from his strong nationalism than from practical considerations of trade or personal gain. One feature of the Society's program was for him uppermost, namely, to settle and concentrate German colonists in a place where they could preserve their linguistic and cultural identity. An independent Texas would better serve this goal. The thought that the Texans might voluntarily surrender their hard-won independence and join the Union infuriated the prince.

The Society, then, expected that Texas would remain independent; the importance attached to this expectation varied greatly among the members. This discrepancy would have implications for Nassau Plantation, and underscores the fact that the noblemen in Germany never were of one mind in regard to their hopes for Texas or their understanding of the goals of the Society. Hence, different observers over the years, through the fallacy of judging the whole by its parts, have ascribed widely divergent master motivations to the Society, motivations that range from purely altruistic to completely sinister. The truth of the matter is that different members understood the role and purpose of the Society differently.

Certainly, an infatuation with the possibility of a land grant contract animated the first convocation of the noblemen gathered at Biebrich in the spring of 1842. They felt that they needed to act quickly and decisively before the constellation of possibilities faded. Count Castell, in a committee report from May 4, 1842, suggested that the Society immediately dispatch an expedition to Texas composed of two members of the Society together with a technician and two hunters; that they give these members power of attorney and letters of credit so they could act in the Society's behalf; and that they raise the necessary funds by calling for payment of the first installment on subscribed shares in the organization.[37]

A sense of urgency dominated the first meeting of these noblemen in Biebrich. They felt that the window of opportunity might shut precipitously if they did not act quickly and decisively. Without formulating a clear plan of action, or arriving at a real consensus, they dispatched an expedition to Texas with the power to act in their name.

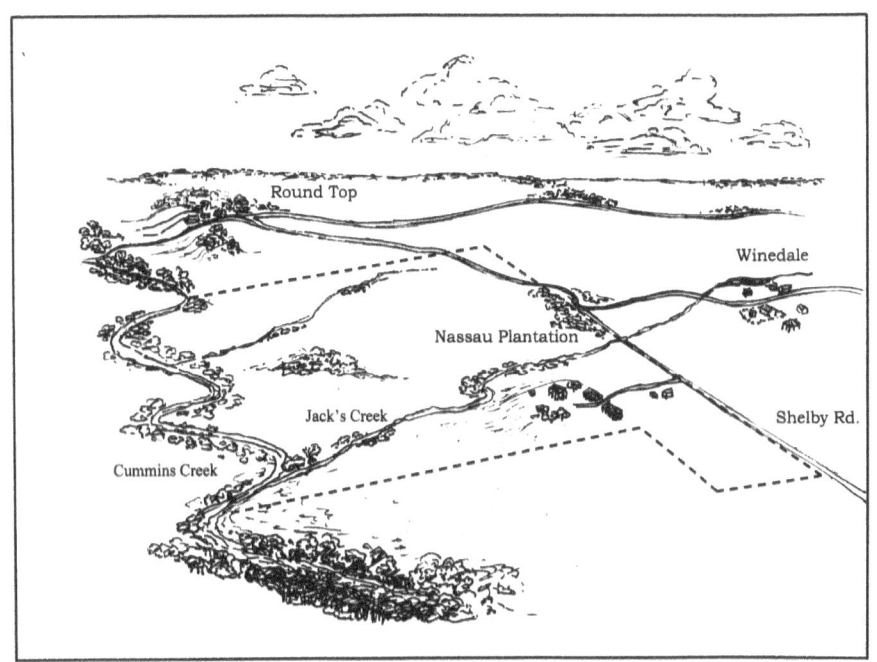

CHAPTER 2

Joseph Count of Boos-Waldeck

Joseph Count of Boos-Waldeck, the founding member of the organization most intrigued by slavery, volunteered for the expedition to Texas and was appointed leader. He was fifty years old, had the rank of major, and was the *aide-de-camp* to Adolph Duke of Nassau.[1] The organization agreed to cover all his expenses.

The younger Viktor Count of Alt-Leiningen-Westerberg also asked to go along. His request was granted on condition that he pay his own way to the first American port and back to Europe. Once in America, the Society agreed to cover all his expenses, as well as those of his servant, as long as they were engaged in the Society's business. He applied for and was granted a year's leave from his position as an officer in the garrison at Mainz.

A suitable technician could not be found, so the expedition was reduced to the two noblemen and their servants, Wilhelm Ötzel (Etzel)[2] and Johann Schwind.[3] The two were given the dignified title of *Jäger*, or "hunter," though it is not clear that either had ever done any hunting.

Power to act on the Society's behalf remained in Boos-Waldeck's hands, with one exception. Special instructions for the two, drawn up by Count Castell, stipulated that both men had to concur and sign should they decide to purchase land for the Society. Moreover, in any land deal, they were to deal only with the government of the republic and thereby avoid unscrupulous speculators. Land fraud in Texas, it seems, had already attained international notoriety. The men were to contact G. A. Scherpf,[4] whose book about Texas had helped shape Christian Leiningen's enthusiasm for Texas. He was thought to be in New York. Finally, they were to be prudent with their cash since American banks could balk at promissory notes. On June 10, 1842, Boos-Waldeck and his party shipped out of Le Havre, France,[5] on a three-master, the *Lorena*, and arrived in New York on July 18, 1842, after a thirty-eight-day passage.[6]

In New York, Boos-Waldeck bought maps and provisions and sought the acquaintance of men who were knowledgeable about Texas. In this regard three names stand out: the German consul Wilhelm A. Kobbé,[7] the New York businessman Morgan Smith,[8] and the German author G. A. Scherpf.[9] Kobbé impressed Boos-Waldeck as a sincere, intelligent, and congenial man whose company he enjoyed. Moreover, he introduced Boos-Waldeck to the rocking chair, which struck him as a marvelous contraption. Kobbé counseled extreme caution in any undertaking in Texas. He had himself been involved in a speculation there that had gone awry.[10]

The extent to which Texas had become the target of speculative and promotional schemes by the 1840s is extraordinary.[11] Most of these schemes centered on land even though the framers of the constitution in 1836 had taken steps to outlaw land speculation and had made the ownership of land by non-Texans difficult. There was a widespread disdain for those who withheld prime lands from the real users, the farmers and planters. Yet, most everyone who had access to credit or capital seems to have engaged in the practice to one degree or another, including the president of the republic, Sam Houston. A few were successful in their schemes; most were not.

Morgan Smith was one of the successful. He combined enthusiasm for Texas with facts and figures gleaned from firsthand experience. His business experience had acquainted him with the economics of slave plantations and the astounding returns on investment that some Texas plantations had provided. He suggested to Boos-Waldeck that these plantations could operate with minimal direct supervision. One needed only to engage the services of a professional overseer to manage and direct the everyday life of the plantation, and such men were readily available for hire. It is clear that Boos-Waldeck had brought his curiosity about slave plantations with him from Europe, but Morgan Smith's enthusiasm for the "peculiar institution" clearly gave this interest a lift. By the time Boos-Waldeck arrived in Texas, it had grown into an obsession, and he began to consider the best way to incorporate a slave plantation into a colonization plan.

Boos-Waldeck had to track down G. A. Scherpf. He had apparently run afoul of the law in the form of customs fraud and retreated with his family to a country house on Long Island, twelve miles from the city. Boos-Waldeck spoke with him for more than three hours. He found him to be a practical and sober man who confirmed the judgments about Texas that he had voiced in his book, namely that a colonization initiative in Texas could have splendid results but would be fraught with difficulties at every turn.[12]

Scherpf also reiterated his belief that certain areas in Texas suited the German emigrant better than others. That the poorly drained and mosquito infested coastal prairies were unsuitable for Central Europeans eventually became an article of faith among many Germans. Scherpf was one of the first to elaborate on this theme. It is clear that his ideas influenced Count Boos-Waldeck in his decision to locate Nassau Plantation away from the established plantation areas along the lower river bottoms of the Trinity, Brazos, and Colorado rivers and opt, instead, for the rolling landscape of northern Fayette County.

The opinions offered by these men foreshadowed eerily the career of Boos-Waldeck in Texas. Morgan Smith praised the plantation system, Scherpf confirmed in Boos-Waldeck the belief that Germans needed to settle away from the coastal lowlands, and Kobbé voiced doubts that proved to be prophetic.

Boos-Waldeck and his party departed New York on August 2, 1842, on the schooner *Ferry-not*, bound for Velasco, the fledgling Texas port at the mouth of the Brazos River. Morgan Smith accompanied them, as well as a young Swede, Swante Magnus Swenson,[13] who had set up a merchandising business in Houston. There was definite poignancy in this chance encounter. Swenson, who had begun his new life in America as a penniless Swedish immigrant in New York, would later become one of the largest private landholders in Texas. He founded the SMS Ranches in the panhandle, and by 1860, in addition to his West Texas holdings, which had increased to nearly 500,000 acres, he owned over 128,000 acres around Austin. Through business savvy, thrift, and uncompromising integrity, Swenson eventually accomplished as a private individual what the Society with all its resources would not be able to achieve.

A normal itinerary would have taken the travelers first to New Orleans. News of a severe outbreak of yellow fever, the dreaded "Yellow Jack," prompted them to take a less comfortable, but more direct passage to Texas. Considerations of disease and health emerged early as a constant companion to the story of German immigration in Texas.[14]

The *Ferry-not* arrived in Velasco[15] on August 27, 1842. James McNeill,[16] a friend of Morgan Smith and a rich plantation owner, invited the count and his party to spend a couple of days at his plantation. Boos-Waldeck judged his company to be excellent and especially enjoyed the ladies in his circle.

In a letter of September 5, he once again spoke of the importance he attached to his acquaintance with Morgan Smith. He praised Smith as "an educated and informed man, proud of his German heritage, of an open, upright character, in one word, a rare occurrence."[17]

On August 30, Counts Boos-Waldeck and Leiningen arrived in Galveston after an overland trip. By September 5, Waldeck had made up his mind. He wrote back to Germany that he intended to set up a plantation that would serve as a home base for the colony they intended to found, a plantation, he predicted, that would become, after the second year of its founding, a productive endeavor, yielding a solid return in hard currency for its owners.[18]

Boos-Waldeck had convinced himself that the Society should base its colonization plans on the plantation model. Leiningen concurred. For the next several months the two laid the groundwork for such a plantation. Boos-Waldeck's only departure from the above-stated intentions would be to buy land from a private individual rather than to receive or buy it directly from the government.

On September 9, the two men met with President Sam Houston in Houston. Boos-Waldeck was somewhat annoyed that his audience included the presence of the general's pretty young wife and niece and a couple of other men. Nonetheless, he reported that they were not disappointed in the personality and presence of Houston.[19]

They explained in detail their plans, which Houston received with the warmest interest. On October 15 they returned to Houston where they outfitted themselves for travel in the interior. They bought four horses and a mule. Boos-Waldeck bought himself a padded saddle, pistol holster, and cartridge belt. They departed Houston on October 22, 1842, for Columbia in order to visit once again with Colonel Morgan Smith. While there the count visited the property that Morgan Smith later developed into "Waldeck" Plantation.[20] They also obtained letters of introduction and made several interesting acquaintances, including that of Anson Jones, recently appointed secretary of state of the Republic of Texas.

On October 29 they left Columbia in the company of Anson Jones, headed ultimately for Washington-on-the-Brazos. They were obliged to leave *Jäger* Schwind behind in Columbia. He had shown himself to be completely unsuited to horseback travel through the countryside.[21]

In Columbia they engaged a young man who was well acquainted with the country to serve as their guide. Their trip took them first to San Felipe and then fifteen miles west to *Katzenquelle* (Cat Spring), the first German settlement of note that they encountered. About twenty German families had settled in the neighborhood in the years immediately prior to the Texas Revolution in 1836. The count characterized the region as not particularly fertile, but rolling and healthy.

Here the party met several members of the von Roeder family. The allure of cheap land and the promise of a new start had led the whole family to immigrate to Texas in 1834. The father and mother, six sons, and four daughters eventually made the move.[22] They had barely established themselves before war with Mexico broke out, enmeshing the whole family in turbulence and danger. Several of the brothers distinguished themselves in military service during the war.

Legend has it that at one point the young Otto von Roeder sat down to a high-stakes poker game with a young, rich, and freshly married Alabamian who had just arrived with a whole wagon train of supplies and slaves to set up a new plantation in Texas.[23] They played the night through. By the next morning von Roeder had won all of the man's earthly possessions. In one last hand, double or nothing, the Alabamian put up his wife against all that he had heretofore lost. The young bride was asked if she agreed to this arrangement. Disgusted with her husband's performance and impressed by the dashing young Prussian, she consented. The hand was played and von Roeder won all. The Alabamian pulled a pistol, but before he could pull the trigger, von Roeder ran him through with his rapier, the very one with which he had killed the Prince of Prussia in an earlier duel in Europe. This is the legend, but the facts concerning Otto von Roeder's subsequent relationship to Nassau Plantation are no less extraordinary.

The party traveled on to the settlement of Industry, only a few miles to the northwest. Industry is known as the earliest German settlement in Texas, and its founder, Friedrich Ernst, is sometimes referred to as the father of German emigration in Texas.[24] He enjoys this reputation by virtue of a letter he sent to a friend in Oldenburg in which he painted Texas as a veritable paradise. The letter circulated widely in North Germany, probably in unpublished form.[25] Whether printed or copied, it created a sensation, influencing many, including the von Roeder clan, to settle in Texas.[26]

Boos-Waldeck does not mention Ernst in his reports, but he does mention his former companion, Charles Fordtran. Fordtran had emigrated to New York from Westphalia in 1830. His family, originally of Huguenot stock, had been engaged in the manufacture of soaps and perfumes for several generations and apparently was quite well to do. The son, however, chose to make his life in the New World.[27]

Fordtran had met Ernst while in New York and was persuaded by him to come to Texas in 1831. But soon thereafter the two men, at one time such close companions, quarreled and their disagreement became bitter. Fordtran went so far as to name his nearby farm "The Castle of Indolence," presumably in parody of Industry, the community that Ernst had founded, and also, perhaps, in parody of the name "Ernst," which suggests seriousness and gravity in German.

Fordtran, forty-one years old in 1842, already had left his mark on the republic by the time he met the count. He surveyed Ernst's grant in Stephen F. Austin's colony for one-fourth of the land and purchased a half headright for himself in Austin County in 1833. He made a contract to secure 800 families for Austin's colony but became discouraged and gave up the idea. During the Texas War of Independence, he was a member of Captain James Bird's company of Spy Rangers and, as such, helped move Texas families out of reach of the Mexicans and protected the communities from Indian attacks.[28]

Why Ernst and Fordtran quarreled is not known, but their mutual dislike was intense. Perhaps Fordtran discovered the truth about Ernst: that his real name was Fritz Dirks (Dierks), and that he was wanted for postal theft in Oldenburg. Or perhaps jealousy played a role. Fordtran, a trained surveyor as well as a farmer, had generally prospered, whereas Ernst, though energetic and innovative, does not seem to have done as well.[29] It probably chagrined Ernst when he discovered that a German nobleman with ambitious plans and a large purse had employed Fordtran.

Fordtran had mastered the English language, and his work as a surveyor, a much sought-after and lucrative profession, had brought him into constant contact with the Anglo as well as the German settlers. He firmly solidified this relationship when he married the daughter of a prominent Anglo settler, William Brookfield. Fordtran was also a slaveholder. By 1850, with fourteen slaves, he was second only to Otto von Roeder as the largest Texas-German slaveholder in the area.[30]

Thus, Fordtran was a man who could move with equal ease in both the dominant Anglo culture and in the emerging German communities, and he was a Texas-German slaveholder. Perhaps Waldeck sensed this advantage in Fordtran. He recognized that he had a thorough knowledge of the area and was of a practical bent of mind, and, in addition, was "quite sociable."[31] He engaged Fordtran as a guide in the area between the two branches of Mill Creek as well as the area of Cummins Creek in northern Fayette County.

Boos-Waldeck left Industry with his party, which now included Fordtran, on November 7, 1842. He set for himself the goal of viewing all the land between the Brazos and Colorado rivers from San Felipe as far north as Captain Horatio Chriesman's settlement, Oak Valley.[32] From there, they traveled to Washington-on-the-Brazos, where a special session of the legislature had convened on November 16.

The noblemen had two purposes in mind for attending the legislative session: they wanted to inquire about the possibility of securing a land grant contract, and they wanted to have their Society chartered as a Texas corporation, an action which required the consent of the legislature. Boos-Waldeck was not able to have the organization registered as a Texas corporation because, at this time, no member of this Society was a citizen of Texas. This was to have serious ramifications for the plantation.

Several studies suggest that Waldeck and Leiningen tried, but failed, to secure a colonization grant at this time and that Leiningen's intransigence in insisting upon certain tax concessions caused this failure.[33] Boos-Waldeck's report paints a different picture of these events:

> *The president and secretary of state were and still are willing to offer us a grant, but after mature reflection we thought better of entering into such a contract since we had convinced ourselves that such a speculation required too much in the way of preparation.*[34]

This report makes it clear that Boos-Waldeck and Leiningen concluded that a land grant was simply too impractical: the lands still available in large unpopulated blocks were far removed from the settled and established areas of the republic, from the existing system of roads (such as they were), and from the coast. In addition, various tribes of plains Indians still roamed these areas at will and were in no mood to surrender their hunting grounds without a fight. Boos-Waldeck concluded it would be better to buy land outright and establish a slave plantation. Such an endeavor, he argued, offered the greatest promise of a good return. He proposed settling families of German farmers and artisans in small numbers around the plantation.[35]

This part of Texas, the upper reaches of the Cummins Creek watershed, pleased Boos-Waldeck. In a gently rolling landscape, reminiscent of many European landscapes, prairies alternated pleasantly and conveniently with wooded areas. The natural meadows provided ready-made fields for cultivation after the work of fencing and plowing had been completed. The woods, a mixture of various hardwoods and stands of cedar, provided the raw material for construction of homes and fences and the fuel for cooking and smoking. Several creeks watered the area, Cummins Creek, an important tributary of the Colorado River, being the most prominent.

The sandy soil of the Cat Spring area had given way to a darker, more promising loam. Also, the climate had improved—mild winters, summer breezes, an absence of the damp and smelly vapors associated with the lower coastal counties and universally believed to be the cause of fevers—all these things bespoke, as G. A. Scherpf had observed, a healthier area, better suited to the taste and disposition of the German immigrant. The Indian depredations, which had held back all but the most intrepid settlers for the past two decades, appeared to be over.

A smattering of German settlers had already found their way to the area. The region, however, was predominantly Anglo. Boos-Waldeck never exhibited the virulent anti-Anglo bias that characterized his successor, Carl Prince of Solms-Braunfels. His bias was one of class: in the Old World, the nobility formed the upper class. In the New World, plantation owners and successful businessmen formed the "better class," and he was willing to associate with them on an equal footing.

Colonel Sam Williams, an early associate of Stephen F. Austin, had two leagues of land for sale in the area. Boos-Waldeck opened negotiations for the leagues and sent Charles Fordtran to Galveston with an offer. The negotiations broke down, however, when Colonel Williams refused to budge from his asking price of one dollar per acre. The threatened Mexican invasion had created a temporary panic that had driven land prices down throughout the republic. Boos-Waldeck fancied himself a shrewd businessman who knew how to take advantage of a situation.[36]

Soon thereafter, Boos-Waldeck became aware of the Jack League on Cummins Creek owned by Robert Mills of Brazoria County.[37] Robert Mills was a plantation owner, a merchant, and a large-scale speculator in land. By the outbreak of the Civil War, he was reputedly the richest man in Texas and the largest slaveholder.[38] On the assumption that good land was bound to rise in value as settlers flocked to the new republic, he speculated in vacant Texas lands on a vast scale. The deed records of Fayette County show that throughout the 1840s he was constantly buying and selling large tracts of land. There are over ten such entries from this period in Fayette County alone.[39]

Mills had purchased the property on January 10, 1840, for $5,000 from William Jack, a prominent lawyer and author of the Turtle Bayou resolutions.[40] William Jack had received his patent for a league of land on March 19, 1833.[41] The evidence indicates that neither Robert Mills nor William Jack had made any improvements on the land. Certainly neither had established a plantation, as some studies have suggested.[42] When Boos-Waldeck viewed the land in the latter days of 1842, it was most certainly virgin and undeveloped.

Boos-Waldeck judged the Jack League to be superior in every respect to the land offered for sale by Colonel Williams. The soil was less fertile than the rich bottomlands of the Brazos, he opined, but he was willing to trade this for the more vigorous climate. The count concluded the deal on the January 9, 1843, for $3,321 or 75 cents per acre.[43]

Soon after acquiring the Jack League and before embarking on a planned trip to New Orleans to purchase supplies and slaves, Boos-Waldeck's wrote a lengthy "General Report," detailing his activities and observations in Texas up to that point.[44] Count Leiningen probably hand carried this document back to Europe where it was made available to the membership and read aloud at the second general assembly in the spring of 1843.

The extensive report is a more or less chronological exposition of the party's travels, detailing their activities from their departure from Europe until the purchase of the Jack League. The report is interspersed with many fascinating observations.

Boos-Waldeck points out, for instance, the shocking lack of education and religious instruction among the German settlers whom he has encountered in Texas.[45] Many of the children, he observes, have grown up to be complete heathens. He mentions, particularly, the sad plight of the German preacher Ludwig Cachand

Ervendberg,⁴⁶ who has been ministering to the communities of Cummins Creek and Mill Creek. He lives with his family in miserable circumstances, the count laments, and is forced to do hard physical labor to survive. He suggests the Society ought to do something to help him.

Boos-Waldeck concedes that he has deviated from his instructions in buying land from a private individual and in setting up a plantation with slaves, but he argues, this is preferable to a land grant. He casts doubt on the feasibility of introducing large numbers of emigrants.

Any colonization attempt, he avers, should begin with select emigrants—especially artisans such as potters, masons and carpenters—who will be settled around the plantation. It will be a symbiotic relationship: out of gratitude for the guidance and assistance they receive from the leadership of the plantation, the new settlers will remain loyal and devoted, and will perform useful services for the plantation. Once the first plantation has been organized and consolidated, another one can be set up, and then another, and colonization could proceed hand in hand with the Society's continued investment in slave plantations.

The hierarchical, aristocratic tint to Boos-Waldeck's vision for Texas is unmistakable. The plantation replaces the castle; the slave-holding plantation owner emerges as the new nobleman with the leisure necessary to pursue culture and to cultivate attitudes of honor and propriety. An energetic and grateful class of artisans and tradesmen, motivated by loyalty to their benevolent sponsors and willing to exchange their services for the guidance and protection they receive, takes the place of medieval yeoman bound by feudal ties to the overlord. African slaves, like medieval serfs, occupy the bottom of this pyramid.

Continuing with his report, the count next describes the land he has just purchased in glowing terms and details to what great lengths he has gone to insure the validity of the title. He has been ever vigilant against fraud. He brought a great mistrust with him from Europe, but, he assures his colleagues, he had only dealt with the better classes. He requests that more money be put at his disposal and that he be authorized to buy more land and more slaves. He will personally guarantee the title to any additional land he purchases.

In a final statement, Boos-Waldeck admonishes the young members of the German nobility who may find themselves in reduced means not to miss the opportunity that Texas affords for rebuilding their family fortunes and prestige.

Boos-Waldeck was confident that he had seized a favorable moment to buy a beautiful tract of land at a bargain price from a reputable man. For the next ten months, until October 1843, Boos-Waldeck would completely immerse himself in the task of setting up and equipping Nassau Plantation, the centerpiece of his vision.[47]

CHAPTER 3

The Plantation

In January 1843, Count Boos-Waldeck departed with Count Leiningen and Charles Fordtran for New Orleans to outfit his plantation with supplies and slaves.[1] Strategically located at the mouth of the Mississippi River, New Orleans had one of the largest slave auctions in the South. As a port city it also had many stores in which to find a great selection of the items needed to equip a plantation.

The city also had emerged as a regional center for credit and finance. The financial system in Texas at the time was embryonic and chaotic: banks were essentially outlawed and the official currency of the republic, the notorious "red backs," had been drastically discounted.[2]

The lack of close access to a bank or credit institution in Texas with European ties created problems for the Society. So Count Boos-Waldeck opened an account with Messrs. Schmidt & Co., one of several banking establishments in New Orleans with European correspondents. Later, officials did business with Lanfear & Co., another New Orleans firm with similar connections.

Finally, New Orleans continued to serve as one of the major ports of entry for German immigrants bound for the Midwest.[3] Consequently, there was a large German quarter where one could catch up on news from the homeland and be among native speakers.[4]

Boos-Waldeck and his party spent a couple of weeks in the city, and with the assistance of Charles Fordtran completed the initial purchases for the plantation. They departed New Orleans bound for Galveston on February 14, 1843, on the steamer *Neptune*.[5] The bill of lading listed eleven slaves, three wagons, and several thousand pounds of goods of all sorts.[6] The eleven slaves included six men and five women. Except for one older man, Richard (fifty), all the men were around twenty years old. The women also were young with one, Hanna, being only fourteen years old. The slaves cost about $6,000.[7]

The count's purchases reveal a curious blending of the practical and the elegant. Along with the saws, shovels, and axes necessary for transforming wilderness, we find a complete place setting for twelve, including plates, saucers, bowls and cups, and soup tureens. He also bought a brass candelabrum and lantern shades, as well as a feather mattress, a most unusual luxury on the Texas frontier. The manifest lists three wagons, one designated a "pleasure carriage."[8]

The practical goods of the bill of lading fall into several categories: tools (axes, shovels, saws, wagon wrenches, braces and bits, adzes, awls, blacksmithing tools); agricultural implements (plows, chains, hames); raw materials (iron and steel bars, nails, ore); household items (knives, forks, spoons, plates, coffee pots, slop bowls for the slaves, mattresses; transportation (two wagons and a pleasure carriage, a saddle and harness); and, finally, condiments, medicines, and dry goods (flour, salt, iodine, and calomel).

Later, in April, the count had a guitar shipped to him by the Houston merchant S. M. Swenson, whom he had first met on the boat from New York. He subscribed to several newspapers and periodicals and requested that a complete set of the collected works of Schiller be sent from Germany. Certain cultural standards needed to be upheld and social formalities observed, even on the frontier.

The transportation of all this merchandise turned out to be quite an undertaking.[9] Boos-Waldeck expected draft animals to be waiting for him in Houston, but when he arrived with his collection of goods and slaves, the draft animals were lacking. Knowledge of this dilemma spread quickly and led, to the count's chagrin, to an overnight inflation in the price of oxen.[10]

Morgan Smith and S. M. Swenson had explained to Boos-Waldeck that the usual way to organize and manage a slave plantation was to employ a paid "overseer" to see to the day-to-day operation of the plantation.[11] While in Houston, Boos-Waldeck hired William Bryan as his new overseer, characterizing him as "upright and honest" and a man who understood his profession. With such a person, the count maintained, the oversight and administration would be so easy that a capable member of the Society could easily manage four plantations.[12]

Bryan fit the profile of a typical overseer. He was young, about twenty-five years old, and single. He had grown up on a sugar plantation in Florida and had apparently worked for some time on the Perry plantation on the lower Colorado River.[13] His salary was set at $300 a year in addition to room and board.[14]

While in Houston and Galveston, Boos-Waldeck bought six more slaves. He purchased a blacksmith, Jim, plus his wife and two daughters, who were twelve and nine years old, for a total of $1,306. He also bought two more young females, the seventeen-year-old Emily for $375 and the sixteen-year-old Elisabeth for $252.[15] Boos-Waldeck judged these to be excellent purchases. The purchase of slaves, he observed, was cheaper in Texas than in New Orleans, and, in addition, one saved the cost of transportation. He now had purchased a total of seventeen slaves: seven men, eight women, and two children at a total cost of $7,883.

After procuring draft animals, Boos-Waldeck departed Houston with his caravan, which included two wagons, one carriage, seven yokes of oxen, several horses and mules, seventeen slaves, the overseer Bryan, Charles Fordtran, and Wilhelm Etzel. At one point Boos-Waldeck pulled ahead of the rest of the train in order to scout the best place to lay out the fields and structures of the plantation. The weather turned miserable. A "blue norther"[16] blew in with rain and sleet. The troop had to set up their tents deep in a thicket to help break the wind.

After five days' wait, the rest of the troop arrived during the first week of March. The count decided to locate the functional buildings of the plantation in an oak grove bordered to the east by Jack's Creek and to the west by a meadow that would be suitable for cultivation.

The slaves were put to work right away felling trees. It took eight days to put up the first building, a blacksmith's shed. The white men immediately took up temporary residence here. Upon completion of the smithy, a smokehouse was begun and then a house for the overseer. Boos-Waldeck entrusted his erstwhile servant, Wilhelm Etzel, with the construction of the preeminent building of the plantation, the so-called *Herrenhaus*, or manor house. He contracted two local German carpenters by the name of Stuesse and Nelson, to help him.[17]

The site chosen for the *Herrenhaus* stood apart from the other buildings about "two musket shots," or approximately a half a mile to the east, across Jack's Creek on the crown of a hill in a grove of magnificent live oaks. Though impractical from the standpoint of the day-to-day operation of the plantation, the location of the house reinforced class distinction through physical separation.

The *Herrenhaus* took the shape of a story-and-a-half "dog trot," a simple and straightforward plan common to many southern log homes on the frontier. It was a large house by the standards of the frontier, but not excessively so. The workers completed the basic structure of the house, amazingly, by the middle of July.[18]

Three houses stood by the end of April: the smithy, the smokehouse, and the overseer's house, all of log construction. As soon as the overseer's house was completed, the white men moved into it and turned over the smithy to the slaves. In the smokehouse, Boos-Waldeck laid in 5,000 pounds of bacon and hams (an extraordinary figure), as well as other provisions.[19] Most of the orders for supplies were placed with the firm of S.M. Swenson & Co. in Houston. If Mr. Swenson could not fill an order from his own establishment, he completed it from other stores in the city. The goods were then transported by wagon at the rate of one penny per hundredweight.

By the end of April, it was getting late in the planting season. In southern Texas, seed corn is usually in the ground by the middle of March. Local row crop farmers of the present day maintain that a bushel-to-the-acre yield is lost for every day of delay in planting after the fifteenth of March. But before Boos-Waldeck could plant the field to the west of the plantation buildings, the land had to be fenced and the native prairie turned under, both daunting tasks.[20]

Several systems for putting up a fence existed, but all required an enormous amount of labor. The usual method was to stack four or five posts in a zigzag fashion so that the ends meshed. This system avoided having to set posts in the ground. But whatever system one used, the amount of labor required was stupendous. As a rule of thumb, it took about 5,000 rails to fence in each twenty acres, and the value of this labor was pegged at two dollars a hundred rails or five dollars an acre. Thus, a fence more than doubled and, in some cases, quadrupled the value of the land.[21] Not surprisingly, many Germans in Texas found their own words for enclosing land, such as *einfrieden* or *einzaunen,* to be inadequate. The Anglicism, *die Fenz,* and its verbal equivalent, *fenzen,* quickly became standard Texas-German words.[22]

It was absolutely essential to fence in land before putting it into cultivation. Texas, as many observers noted, was a paradise for livestock who could run free the year round. Fences, therefore, served more at this stage to keep animals out than to keep them in.[23] Boos-Waldeck recognized this fact quite early.

Plowing the native prairie for the first time, likewise, was a formidable undertaking. The native grasses formed a thick mat that clogged a turning plow. Often four, six, or even eight oxen hitched together strained to pull the plow through. The usual practice was to wait until after the first frost in the fall had turned the grass dry and flammable. The top growth would then be burned off rendering the initial turning of the sod easier. After the first plowing, the soil would be left to mellow over the winter, then re-plowed prior to the spring planting. As with fencing, plowing was a big job, and the job completed often doubled the value of the land.[24]

It had become obvious to Boos-Waldeck that it would be impossible to fence and work up a field at Nassau in a timely way. It was all the count could do to get a twenty-acre garden fenced and plowed by the end of April. His solution was to rent, on March 22, an eighty-acre field known as the "Peach Orchard" from a neighbor, Sam Lewis. It had already been fenced and plowed. The count traded a road wagon valued at $100 for the field. In so doing, he followed the advice of Charles Fordtran and others experienced in such matters. Unfortunately, the land was eight miles away and occasioned much hardship in transporting the Negroes to and from the field.[25] Boos-Waldeck had the slaves stay there in tents during the week. They were allowed to return on Saturday, but had to go back on Sunday afternoons.

After the corn had been planted in the rented field, Boos-Waldeck continued the work of building quarters for the slaves who had been staying in the smithy or in tents at the rented land. At the end of a hard day's work, he wanted them to have at least a healthy place to spend the night with protection from the wind and rain. He declared that each couple should have a shelter of their own. By this point, six couples had paired, he noted, therefore six houses would be necessary.

We do not know the dimensions or the particulars of these dwellings. Nothing survives of their presence. According to an inventory of 1844, the value of the slave houses was pegged at twenty dollars each. In contrast, it assigned the *Herrenhaus* the value $1,200, the overseer's house $150, all the stalls $200, and the smithy $50. The total value of the six slave huts was less than that of the stalls and one tenth that of the *Herrenhaus*. A later observer characterized the slave quarters as "dreadful barracks."[26] We can assume, then, that they were very rudimentary single-room log houses with dirt floors.

Upon completion of the slave quarters, Boos-Waldeck had two more buildings constructed, a barn for the horses and a communal kitchen for the slaves. Hay was put up for the barn so that the workhorses could receive feed in the wintertime, a rare event in Texas.[27]

One slave woman, the seventeen-year-old Emily, probably a mulatto or quadroon, remained without a man. Boos-Waldeck praised her industriousness and orderliness, and remarked that she was the strongest and most energetic of the women.[28] She was quartered at the *Herrenhaus* once it became habitable. The evidence is quite strong that Boos-Waldeck took her for a mistress, and that his subsequent illness may have had something to do with this attraction.[29]

The end of April was the high-water mark for Count Boos-Waldeck in Texas. In a personal letter to Count Castell, he enthuses about the progress made and the decisions taken.[30] News of the death of his father, recently arrived, had certainly clouded his spirits, but his passion for the plantation remained undiminished. He writes of the indescribable charm of Texas in the spring, of the beauty of the Jack League, the fertility of the soil, and the salubriousness of the climate.

The count details what is lacking at the plantation in his letter. It will eventually require a gristmill and a cotton gin. The plantation needs sheep, cattle, Spanish mares, and pigs. He has already purchased fourteen pigs and intends to buy a large herd of cattle—three to four hundred head—since the upkeep on grazing livestock is so minimal. He plans to have two one-hundred-acre fields ready for next year's spring planting, one for cotton and the other for corn. He may need to plant sugar cane as well.

The principle of self-sufficiency, he emphasizes, must guide the plantation in all matters. The slaves and staff must make or grow everything possible in order to achieve the necessary economies to produce real growth in capital. The plantation cannot afford to lose a single year of production.

He concedes that he has exhausted his credit in New Orleans, but he still needs to buy several items in order for the plantation to become profitable by its second year. Above all, the plantation requires more slaves. An additional 15,000 or 20,000 florin will be necessary to accomplish these things.

He will have to think about returning to Germany. Were it not for the loyalty he felt for his overlord in Germany, he would remain in Texas to watch the growth of the plantation, and to pursue personal and family investments. He will, however, stay until a suitable replacement from the Society can be found.

The count repeats his plea that the Society not water down its efforts by doing too much too quickly. The time is not yet right to send colonists. Enough corn has not been planted to feed them and, besides, the Germans still need to learn from the Americans. The realities of the Texas frontier would doom such an undertaking to a disastrous outcome. Those safely ensconced in their libraries and studies in Europe should trust his insights and recommendations for they are grounded in firsthand experience. The Society needs to focus its energy and resources on developing and improving the plantation, he writes.

Perhaps the onset of spring contributed to the count's buoyant attitude. Spring can be delightful in Texas. The cold, wet, blustery northers of February and early March yield to the warmth and mildness of April. The slaves, still quartered in tents and the blacksmith shop, must have welcomed this change the most. Wildflower displays, which to the present day draw hordes of tourists to the area, reach their high point in April, perfuming the air and painting the landscape in exquisite hues of red, blue, and lavender. It is hard to be pessimistic in such a setting.

The count concluded his letter with the ambitious prediction that the plantation would be appealing by fall, exceptionally lovely by the following year, and the most beautiful plantation in Texas by the end of its third year.[31]

In a very short time, Boos-Waldeck had a rendezvous with reality, for his next two communications, a personal letter in May and a report in July, put forward a stunning counterpoint to the euphoria of the May letter. Boos-Waldeck is no longer deluding himself In the May letter, and even more so in the July report, experience replaces conjecture and enthusiasm gives way to sober self-reflection. His time in Texas, confessed the count, has not only given him insight into the true situation in Texas, but also into his own conduct and role.

He concedes that he has made mistakes. The slaves, with the exception of the blacksmith Jim, were not such a good buy after all. They have shown themselves totally inept in the use of axes. Apparently none had ever done this sort of work before.[32] One of the men was a cook and the other a bricklayer. Likewise, the "hog wallow prairie" proved unexpectedly difficult to plow, and the few oxen they had were insufficient to the task. The overseer Bryan, he now confesses, has also displayed a questionable side. He will do for the time being, but at some point he will need to be replaced.

The austerity of the frontier, explained the count, has been difficult. For the Anglos, this is not a problem, because they are accustomed to a Spartan way of life. But such deprivations fall hard on Europeans who have grown used to the finer pleasures of civilization. It falls especially hard on single people, such as himself, and he attributed his own sense of isolation and loneliness to this fact.

To Christian Leiningen he will give the honor of the authorship of the Society, but the responsibility has fallen to him to carry through its program, and, should things not turn out, the blame will rest on his shoulders. He came over as someone basically ignorant of agriculture, a fact he made perfectly clear. He admits that he now understands for the first time how difficult it will be, despite all the means at his disposal, to create a new homeland in the wilderness.[33]

Mistakes aside, the count mused, he is at peace with himself. He has left no stone unturned in setting a course that he regards as proper and correct. He is ready to return to Europe, but will stay on until a replacement arrives and is adequately briefed.[34]

The count reserved his most pointed observations for the subject of colonization. The tone of his comments suggests that he had begun to sense the ground was shifting, that he was now on the losing side of a political struggle based on different interpretations of the basic goals of the Society. Was the primary emphasis of the Society practical or idealistic? Was it to make money in Texas through investment in lands (and slaves), or to promote an ambitious and risky colonization scheme?

If it is still at all possible, the count pleaded, the Society should not send over even one colonist, even if it means throwing away money for preparations already undertaken, for it will be better to sacrifice some money in Europe, than to lose money and time here, and receive for it only ingratitude and aggravation.[35]

In a change, the count now recommended that if colonists are to be sent over they should be members of the German nobility, who would be welcomed and made to feel at home. He has observed how far humans can sink when they are not bolstered by religion or the principle of honor (*Ehre*), which survives best among the noble class. If he had had the funds, he would have bought an adjoining league of land in order to sell it cheaply to members of the German nobility. Unless our impoverished nobility is hopelessly blind, he observed, its young members must strive to make their fortunes here and by so doing restore the earlier prominence of their families, because the times are past where this could be accomplished by steel and iron.

Boos-Waldeck closed his report of July by reiterating that he still expected Nassau to develop into one of the finest plantations in Texas. Despite the exceptionally wet winter, spring, and summer, he has maintained his health and hopes to make it through his entire stay without ever having to resort to the services of a doctor.

Boos-Waldeck's desire for continued good health was not to be. He contracted a slight cold in late July that quickly grew into a serious fever. His efforts to find a treatment are a case study for the cure being worse than the disease. He began his treatment by taking liberal doses of rhubarb and other stomach remedies as a purgative. This provided little relief. An American advised him to take twenty-five grams of calomel, which produced a slight improvement. In a few days, however, he experienced a relapse with such a high fever that he sent for a doctor in Rutersville.[36] Before that, the overseer had bled him excessively. The doctor then gave him fifty-five grams of mercury in the space of twenty-four hours; a remedy, which poisoned him to the point that he felt more dead than alive. He could not shake the fever. It persisted through September and October. His teeth loosened and he could barely summon enough energy to answer his correspondence.[37]

The mysterious illness[38] led Boos-Waldeck to advance his timetable for departing Texas. In September he left the plantation for good and moved to Galveston to take advantage of the cool sea breezes. Doctors had suggested that the West Indies would be good for his recuperation and he resolved to go there as soon as he could book passage.

Boos-Waldeck had intended to remain at Nassau Plantation until a replacement had arrived and been made "*au courant.*" He seems to have expected one of the Leiningens (most likely Viktor) to return in the spring of 1844 and Count Castell to come over with his family in the fall of 1844.

Before departing for Galveston the count took several steps to tie up loose ends as best he could. He elevated Carl Fordtran to the position of supervisor of the plantation and set his salary at $250 a year, which, he remarked, would be cheaper for the Society than for him to remain there. He put $1,170 at Fordtran's disposal to cover immediate expenses and authorized him to draw on the funds in New Orleans.[39] Fordtran was given overall responsibility for the condition of the plantation and was made accountable for the expenses and income. He was required to submit regular reports to Boos-Waldeck in Germany. Bryan would continue as overseer and be responsible for the day-to-day work of plowing the fields, harvesting the crops, and supervising the slaves, but he would be under the authority of Fordtran.

In his penultimate letter to Count Castell, dated November 15, 1843, Boos-Waldeck praises Fordtran's honesty and reliability and states that they have become fast friends. In recognition of his service, Boos-Waldeck presented him with a gold watch and chain, which had been authorized by the second general assembly of the Society in June 1843, and sent over as the personal gift of Count Hermann zu Wied.[40]

It becomes clear from this letter that Boos-Waldeck had not yet received official notification of the decisions of the second general assembly, which had taken place in June, authorizing Count Castell to pursue a land grant. He had, however, recently received a letter from his brother, Eduard, who had informed him in general terms of the situation in Germany. His next-to-last communication from Castell, which he received in August, predated the second general assembly and other initiatives of Count Castell. Boos-Waldeck replied to this letter immediately, but his letters were lost to the waves when the steamship *Sara Barnes* sank.

Communication between Europe and Texas not only took a long time; it was precarious. It often took eight to ten weeks for a letter to travel across the ocean. A letter and response, therefore, could take as much as five months. Boos-Waldeck always had a delayed awareness of shifts in European attitudes; similarly, Europe remained ignorant of events in Texas until considerably after the fact. This problem plagued the undertaking from beginning to end, and was aggravated by the fact that the leadership in Germany always wanted to exercise more direct control, especially in financial decisions, than was feasible.

While not fully informed, Boos-Waldeck was obviously aware that something was afoot. Castell had written in May about the importance of concentrating Germany's emigrants so that a trade relationship between the colony and Germany could develop and flourish. Castell also had hinted—alluding to the anticipated subsidies—that the Society would soon be in a position to solve this problem.[41]

Boos-Waldeck undoubtedly also gleaned information from Henry Francis Fischer when the two met in Galveston. President Houston had granted Fischer and Burkhart Miller an extension of their land grant contract in September. Thereafter, Fischer had hurried to Galveston to meet with Boos-Waldeck. Boos-Waldeck acknowledges this meeting in his letter. He granted Fischer, who was soon to depart for Germany, a letter of introduction. As for Castell's plans, such as he knew, he offered this opinion:

> *I am too weak and incapable to write and think a lot or to immerse myself in details, so in respect to your colonization project, I will just offer my opinion, namely that I consider*

it to be completely unrealizable even if the governments give you monies for that purpose.[42]

He concedes that of all the land grants, the Fischer and Miller grant is probably the best, at least in respect to natural beauty and climate. But, he cautions, land can be had cheaply, and, above all, there is no need for haste. Boos-Waldeck is obviously unaware to what extent Castell has committed the Society. He believes there is still time once he returns to Europe to talk matters out.

Two days later, Boos-Waldeck was relieved of his innocence. A letter arrived from Castell laying out in great detail all that had been done in Germany in the spring and summer to further a large colonization project. With barely concealed anger and bitterness, Boos-Waldeck replied to Castell in a final act before leaving.

Receipts indicate that Boos-Waldeck departed New Orleans on the steamship *Alabama* on November 21, 1843, two days after the above letter was written. Prior to his departure Boos-Waldeck spent a couple of days in New Orleans to take care of business and to finish correspondence.

The count had not succeeded in registering the Society as a Texas corporation, and this created problems of ownership. Boos-Waldeck had originally registered the land, the slaves, and other purchases under his and Leiningen's names. He had also had the deed for the land, filed of record in Fayette County, made out to himself and Leiningen rather than to the Society. Before he left, he transferred his part to Castell and suggested that Leiningen needed do the same in Germany.

Passage to Havana via New Orleans cost forty dollars.[43] After spending a couple of weeks in Havana, Boos-Waldeck shipped out for Southampton, England, on December 11, 1843, on the steam packet *Clyde*. His ticket cost fifty pounds. He did not arrive in Germany in time for the third general assembly of the Society, which was held on January 13, 1844. By the middle of February, however, we can document that he is back in Germany in the town of Sayn.

CHAPTER 4

Germany and Texas in 1843 and 1844

Decisions reached in Germany in 1843 put the Society on a path that would lead to financial disaster and relegate the plantation to a supporting role. Carl Count of Castell had his sights set much higher than a plantation, or a string of them, and he set about to insure that the Society adopted his vision. The plantation encompassed a little more than four thousand acres; a land grant amounted to hundreds of thousands of acres. Like gold fever, this was a mighty temptation, which clouded his judgment. Several letters by various members of the nobility testify to the count's active involvement working behind the scenes to promote the Society. His friend, Carl Prince of Solms-Braunfels, supported him in his program.[1]

His efforts bore fruit in the second general assembly, which convened in Biebrich June 18 and 19, 1843, amidst an atmosphere of great optimism.[2] All the initial subscriptions had been covered. The program had, in fact, met with such enthusiasm that the list was expanded to thirty shares. Ten members attended, several with the power of attorney to act on behalf of others. Count Castell, for example, was empowered to vote for five other members.[3] In the absence of Christian Leiningen, the founder and nominal president, Count Castell also presided over the meeting.

Viktor Count of Leiningen had returned to Europe from Texas

early in June 1843 and reported his experiences to Count Castell.[4] He apparently hand-carried Boos-Waldeck's first "Comprehensive Report" from February back with him, and it was read aloud to the assembly.

The assembly also read and approved a revised draft of the statutes and formally constituted itself as a corporation.[5] The assembly also petitioned the Duke of Nassau to become the protector of the Society; he accepted. The authority of the executive committee was expanded so that it could make many decisions on its own with minimal consultation. Finally, several interesting motions were presented for consideration.

The assembly determined that Count Boos-Waldeck had strayed from his authority, especially in buying land from private individuals rather than from the government. Nevertheless, the plantation was retroactively approved. An additional 10,000 florins was made available to him in New Orleans.[6] The assembly requested, however, that Boos-Waldeck should redouble his efforts to secure a land grant from the Texas government.

Each member was asked to contribute one-pound sterling to alleviate the plight of the poor preacher Ervendberg[7] about whom Boos-Waldeck had written. The assembly went on to approve the gifts that Boos-Waldeck had requested for the plantation and for persons in Texas who had been of service to the Society. These included works of Schiller, two pistols, and, for Charles Fordtran, a pocket watch with a golden chain. In addition, various members of the Society wished to donate items:

1. from Adolph Duke of Nassau, a tin pot together with silverware for twelve persons;
2. from Carl Prince of Solms, two dozen porcelain pipes;
3. from Friedrich Count of Alt-Leiningen, two table cloths for twelve persons;
4. from Count Castell, glassware for twelve persons;
5. from Count Isenburg, a kitchen table and accessories;
6. from Collorado Count of Mansfeld, an encyclopedia;
7. from Viktor Count of Alt-Leiningen, a technological lexicon; and

8. from Eduard Count of Boos-Waldeck, a Meerschaum pipe.

The assembly drew up another list of suggestions for the members who were not present. It included linens, books (especially those concerning agriculture), and purebred sheep for breeding, two sheepdogs, and an assortment of wines, medicines, bandages, and containers.[8]

Boos-Waldeck needed a replacement since he had announced his intention to return to Europe. Count Castell indicated his willingness to go to Texas for an extended period of time, perhaps as long as ten years. Consequently, a legal document was drawn up defining the terms and conditions as well as the remuneration for his time in Texas.[9]

Most importantly, the second assembly affirmed the idea of a large colonization project based on a land grant contract, but this was a general affirmation, devoid of particulars. Count Castell worked throughout the summer and fall of 1844 to use the authority and discretion granted to him to put the pieces in place.

For all the pieces to fall in place, several things had to happen, and each conditioned the other. The three pieces to the puzzle were land grants, subsidies, and trade concessions. Count Castell wished for a land grant, but to make a land grant work, he needed subsides. In order to obtain subsidies, he needed some gesture of good will from the Texas government, and the preferred gesture would be the offer of generous trade subsidies on the part of the Republic of Texas to the Society.

Frustrated in the attempt to obtain a land grant directly, Count Castell entered into an agreement with Bourgeois d'Orvanne, who had traveled to Europe from Texas in the spring of 1843 with a land grant in hand. To receive trade concessions, he opened up discussions with Colonel Daingerfield,[10] the Texas *chargé d'affaires* in Hamburg, and he sent one last letter to Boos-Waldeck in Texas imploring him to lobby for this cause. To obtain subsidies, he continued to use his influence and connections to petition several German states, especially the Kingdom of Prussia.

The hope for financial subsidies was a determinative factor for the Society. Apparently, Castell had made overtures along these lines to several governments, with special emphasis on Prussia, and had received encouragement.[11] In his September letter to Boos-Waldeck, he still hoped for (and, indeed, expected) a million-florin allowance. The Prussian foreign office did not consider itself competent to evaluate the request, so it asked for a *Gutachtung*, or an official appraisal, from the renowned naturalist Alexander von Humboldt.[12]

Alexander Bourgeois d'Orvanne was a Frenchman who had moved to Texas sometime prior to 1840. One source has him running a store at San Felipe at this time.[13] He, along with his partner Armand Ducos, was one of the four parties to receive a land grant contract under the terms of the colonization law of 1841, as amended in February 1842. The others were Charles Mercer, Henri Castro, and Fischer and Miller.[14] D'Orvanne and Ducos had obtained their grant, located in the vicinity of the Medina River west of San Antonio, on June 3, 1842.[15] It was due to expire by limitation on December 3, 1843, if the requisite number of settlers had not been introduced by that time. D'Orvanne returned to Europe in the spring of 1843 to begin gathering settlers.

It is not known whether d'Orvanne made the initial contact with the Society or if the Society approached him. It is clear, however, that the leadership in Germany was frustrated with Boos-Waldeck's stubbornness, and when the opportunity appeared to negotiate directly, they seized upon it.[16]

The correspondence between Castell and d'Orvanne reveal d'Orvanne to be alert, sophisticated, and well connected. Moreover, he had a very good command of German (although he was ignorant of the proper forms of address due a German nobleman). The correspondence was conducted in German. D'Orvanne never concealed the fact that his land grant contract was due to expire by limitation in December 1843. He was confident, however, that he would be able to secure an extension, especially if he returned to Texas as an associate of a society with impressive credentials and important international connections.

The parties came to a quick agreement. By the terms of the contract, d'Orvanne was made a member of the Society. He was required to devote himself actively in its behalf for three years. In return for turning over ownership of the grant to the Society, he (and Ducos) would receive 47.5 percent of the profits from the future sale of land after the debt of the Society (estimated to be no less than one million francs) had been retired by amortization at 5 percent interest.[17]

The agreement with d'Orvanne was the first concrete step in Castell's plan. It suggests that by the fall of 1843, the possibility for the Society to obtain a land grant for itself had all but faded.

In Count Castell's final communication to Boos-Waldeck, mentioned in the last chapter, Castell explained to Boos-Waldeck at great length the decisions of the second general assembly, his dealings with d'Orvanne, and the necessity of obtaining trade concessions. He implored Boos-Waldeck to make one last attempt to speak with President Houston and other men of influence in this cause. He also included a document drawn up by the Society in Mainz, written in English, explaining the purposes of the Society and formally requesting certain concessions. This memorandum was put in the hands of William Henry Daingerfield when he visited Mainz in September 1843.[18]

In the document, Count Castell explained that of all the parties receiving land grants, only the German Society had the means to fulfill its terms. Since the principal concern of the Republic of Texas lay in securing settlers, it was in the interest of Texas to help the Society by providing land and by granting trade concessions.

From this memorandum, we can see that Count Castell was thinking very big: "upward to ten thousand German families," with donated land sufficient to accommodate them. It also spells out the exact nature of the trade concessions—reduction in import duties in the amount of $200,000 per year. Especially intriguing is the suggestion that the Society would seek to obtain a loan in Germany as a *quid pro quo* of one million dollars on behalf of the Republic of Texas.

Boos-Waldeck received Castell's letter with this memorandum two days prior to his departure from New Orleans. It obviously came as a shock. He knew that Count Castell was leaning toward the idea of an expanded colonization scheme, but he had no idea how far things had progressed until this letter arrived. He still believed, apparently, that he had time to return to Germany to face the membership and argue his case.

Gone are all the niceties. Boos-Waldeck replied in anger and bitterness to Castell's letter. He warns Castell in stark terms not to be deceived by all the books about Texas, which paint such a rosy picture, nor to place his trust in such men as d'Orvanne or Daingerfield, who will laugh behind his back at his guilelessness.[19] Above all, he cautions against entering into binding contracts out of a sense of urgency and haste, because the Society would come to regret it bitterly. He predicts that even if the subsidies are forthcoming, the project would end in disaster. The gentlemen sitting in their comfortable offices in Germany, he laments, have no idea of the harsh realities of the Texas frontier, and in their blindness and infatuation have chosen to ignore the wisdom of one who had experienced these realities firsthand.

Meanwhile in Germany in 1844, several events pointed at the coming social unrest. Karl Marx met Friedrich Engels in Paris. The weavers in Silesia rose up in revolt in a desperate attempt to bring attention to their plight, and, by extension, to the plight of traditional craftspeople, to farmers, and to the growing ranks of those who had nothing to offer but their labor, the proletariat. The festering contradictions in German society, which would erupt violently in 1848 and briefly hold out the promise of constitutional government, had come to the surface and could no longer be ignored. In such an ambience, the Society crystallized in shape, in purpose, and under the name for which it is generally recognized, *Der Verein zum Schutze deutscher Einwanderer in Texas* (The Society for the Protection of German Emigrants in Texas).[20]

Three general assemblies were held in 1844. The first took place in January. Boos-Waldeck had not yet arrived in Europe, and Count Castell had not heard from him since his July letters. Castell had not yet heard anything in regard to subsidies. The noblemen decided, as a matter of prudence, to open negotiations with the banking house of Flersheim to cover the additional costs of the d'Orvanne contract. They discussed the possibility of installing a second overseer at Nassau Plantation who would write monthly reports. Dr. Meyer announced his willingness to take the job.[21]

The Society held two back-to-back conventions in March and April. In the first of these gatherings, several resolutions were passed that affirmed the question of colonization and approved the contract with Bourgeois d'Orvanne.[22] They also elevated Count Castell to the position of *Geschäftsführer* (executive director).

In the broadest sense, these resolutions represent an attempt to adjust the structure of the Society to the reality of its commitment to a land grant. The plantation now becomes secondary but is not discarded. Item nine, the Special Register, formed the basis of the *"Gesammelte Akten,"* or the published statutes of the Society. These are often reproduced in discussions about the Society.

The second gathering, which followed immediately on the heels of the first, must have been dramatic and tense. Boos-Waldeck appeared before the assembly in person to deliver a comprehensive report of the results of his trip to Texas.[23] He declared himself against a large-scale emigration plan and predicted that such a plan, if enacted, would end in catastrophe. But the assembly had already voted against him, and it refused to reconsider. Boos-Waldeck, therefore, resigned from the Society and put his and his brother Anton's shares at the disposal of the Society in accordance with article seventeen of the statutes. Boos-Waldeck, it should be noted, did have the support of the Duke of Nassau in this disagreement. The Duke declared that he preferred the original plan of Boos-Waldeck, namely to start small around Nassau Plantation. Although outvoted, the Duke of Nassau announced that he would go along with the plan as long as the Society began modestly with only 150 families and awaited a favorable outcome from this before expanding its plans.

Thus the seeds of discord were present even as the Society published its first official proclamation and call for settlers on April 9, 1844.[24] They called for 150 families to depart in September 1844.[25] In June they set forth the conditions for the emigrants.[26]

There were other, more serious, storm clouds on the horizon. Would Bourgeois d'Orvanne be able to secure an extension or renewal of his contract with the Republic of Texas? Would the subsidies be forthcoming? Would the Republic of Texas offer any concessions or inducements that would signal to the governments in Germany and to the public in general that there was enthusiastic support for the endeavor across the ocean?

For d'Orvanne, the possibility of receiving an extension was becoming increasingly unlikely. Widespread abuse and fraud had accompanied the colonization act. The public was outraged, and political pressure mounted to redress the situation. The Eighth Legislature responded by passing a law in January 1844 repealing all other laws in force regarding colonization and relieving the president of his authority to make or extend contracts. The act also declared all contracts forfeited if the contractors had not complied strictly with terms of the contract, and allowed no extension of time to enable them to carry the contracts into effect.[27]

By the terms of d'Orvanne and Ducos' contract with Texas, they were obligated to introduce one third of the colonists, that is, either 200 single men or families, within one year, with the possibility of a six-month extension. Since this had not been done, and since the new law of 1844 took away the president's right to grant extensions, d'Orvanne's contract was essentially worthless.

Ignoring this, d'Orvanne pressed ahead with his plans. Was the leadership in Germany ignorant of the true state of affairs, or did they allow themselves to be swayed despite their better judgment? We do not know, but we do know that they moved forward as if all were well. The same general assembly designated Carl Prince of Solms-Braunfels as Commissioner-General and Bourgeois d'Orvanne as Colonial Director and authorized their travel to Texas to prepare for the arrival of colonists.[28]

Thus, the spring of 1844 was a pivotal period for the Society. The assembly had followed Count Castell's counsel and turned a deaf ear not only to Count Boos-Waldeck's words of warning, but also to the emerging faction, led by the Duke of Nassau and Count Wied, who counseled restraint. The assembly also took up the question of the plantation during their deliberations. They decided to retain the plantation even though they had, in effect, rejected the rationale for its existence, and rebuffed the man, Boos-Waldeck, who had set it up. They drew up a very curious contract with one Dr. Burkhardt to take over the care of the personnel of the plantation and to be a kind of watchdog for the Society, making sure that the slaves were not being mistreated and giving them medical attention if necessary. In return for these services, the doctor and his family were to receive free passage from Mainz to Texas and free room and board in the manor house. At the end of an unspecified period of time, the doctor could be given overall supervision of the plantation. This arrangement did not work out, however, because Dr. Burkhardt fell ill and died before he could depart from Germany.[29]

Henry Francis Fischer's arrival in Germany signaled another disturbing development. Fischer arrived in Bremen in April 1844, as the

Texas Consul and also as a holder of a land grant contract, one which, unlike d'Orvanne's, was still valid. It also offered a longer window of opportunity in which to introduce colonists.

Much of the literature paints Henry Francis Fischer as a villain. It portrays him as a wily but devious speculator willing to enrich himself at the expense of the suffering of others. Biggers, for instance, in *German Pioneers in Texas* refers to him as a "fakir."[30] Likewise Tiling, in *German Element in Texas,* castigates Fischer as one of the "evil spirits" of the Society.[31] Judgments, oft repeated, become articles of faith. These criticisms neglect one central fact: it was in Fischer's own self-interest that the endeavor should succeed, for it was only through success that he and his partner would receive full reward for the years of work given and for the personal sacrifices made. These criticisms also neglect the fact that their own agent in Texas, Count Boos-Waldeck, had clearly warned the gentlemen in Germany about the terms and pitfalls of a land grant contract. The charge then, that Henry Francis Fischer somehow pulled the wool over Count Castell's eyes, cannot be sustained.

Fischer set about organizing a stock company and began immediately advertising in Germany with some success for prospective emigrants to Texas. This became a cause of great consternation to Count Castell. He wrote Solms-Braunfels that, "since your departure the position of the Society has become more difficult due to the fact that we now have a competitor and none other than Henry Francis Fischer."[32]

Count Castell began to have doubts. An undertone of uncertainty, even fear, crept into his correspondence. He also mentioned the emerging faction within the Society, headed by the Duke of Nassau, who were less than enthusiastic about his program.

So, it is not surprising that Castell now voiced doubts about d'Orvanne's ability to obtain an extension of his contract, which, in any case, could not occur before December 1844, when the next Congress was scheduled to convene. This would leave the Society in the embarrassing position of having to purchase land for the colonists who had already subscribed to the program. Since this could be done for only a limited number of families, it would render the whole undertaking a small rather than a large affair, and this was never what Count Castell had in mind.[33]

Consequently, Count Castell responded favorably when Fisher approached the Society. On June 27, 1844, Castell and Fischer came to an understanding and signed a contract. This meant that the Society now had, theoretically at least, two contracts to fulfill, one with d'Orvanne and one with Fischer. Castell confided to Solms-Braunfels that this would be difficult, but he put a good face upon it and stated that the challenges this provided were preferable to the alternative because the Society could not pass by the certainty that it had gained through the contract with Fischer for an uncertainty. It was right to accept the offer of the grant if the Society were "to accomplish something that is grand, profitable and securely based."[34]

If we calculate the best scenario under the terms of the Fischer/Miller contract, The German Emigration Co., theoretically, could have received title to more than 2,200,000 acres of land from the Republic—a handsome payoff for their time and energy. Fischer and Miller would have been entitled to one third these profits. Subsequently, in 1849, Fischer and Miller calculated that they were due 250,000 acres of land.[35] One can understand, then, what was driving these men beyond the limits of better judgment, for the desire to accumulate land can be a master motivation.

The period of 1843-1844 is significant, then, because the leadership in Germany abandoned the idea of structuring their colonization plans around slavery in favor of a more ambitious program based on a land grant. They did not, however, divest themselves of their slave plantation.

CHAPTER 5

The Runaways

Meanwhile back in Texas, the first episode illustrating the incompetence of the German efforts to run a slave plantation by proxy was taking shape. Three slaves ran away from Nassau Plantation. Charles Fordtran, the Texas-German left in charge by Boos-Waldeck, documented his attempts to recover the slaves in a hitherto unprecedented way.

Charles Fordtran did not actually live at the plantation. His own farm was only a few miles away in the direction of Industry. It was his responsibility to stop by every few days and make sure that the activities of the plantation followed the general plan and concept of Count Boos-Waldeck. He seems also to have been directly responsible for supervising the work on the *Herrenhaus*. It was left to the overseer, William Bryan, who did live at the plantation, to take care of the day-to-day tasking of the slaves.

Judging from his reports and letters, Fordtran applied himself conscientiously to his duties. With fences to construct, fields to plow, and buildings to complete, both Bryan and Fordtran had full plates.

Fordtran had accompanied Boos-Waldeck to Galveston. He returned with a wagonload of supplies to Nassau Plantation on November 10, 1843. It had been a rather difficult trip due to wet weather and swollen streams. He detailed his return trip and the situation at the plantation in a long report sent to Boos-Waldeck, dated November 15, 1843.[1]

In the report, Fordtran mentioned that Wilhelm Etzel, the former servant of Boos-Waldeck, was happy and had big plans for the future. He continued to be diligent in his work on the manor house but did not get along well with his associate, a man named Stuesse. In consequence, Stuesse had collected his wages, twenty-eight dollars, and departed even though his work was not completed. Fordtran thought it would be best to contract outside labor for the completion of the stall, which was to be built next to the manor house with dimensions of twenty-two feet by fourteen feet by fourteen feet. Fordtran also expressed concern about the condition of the oxen, which were so indispensable for the work of breaking the fields and transporting the rails for the fences. They were in bad shape, he reported, and only three pairs remained to do the work. He suggested to Bryan, the overseer, that he make the rails, of which 4,000 had already been split, lighter and shorter, and, therefore, reduce the work for the oxen. One can detect in this letter a growing rift between the two.[2]

By this point, only forty acres had been broken for cultivation. Fordtran expressed disgust at the slow progress in plowing. He compared the work at Nassau to that on the Holman plantation[3] south of La Grange where 150 acres had been broken and fenced without losing a single ox.

On a more positive note, Fordtran reported that a mercantile store, Ward & Cazello,[4] had opened in La Grange. Now wares could be had as cheaply in La Grange as in Galveston. He also reported that there were plans to make the Colorado River navigable from La Grange to the coast, an important development, for it matters not how much corn you harvest, cotton you pick, or sugar cane you press if you do not have access to markets. The new mercantile establishment in La Grange was offering five to six cents per pound in gold or silver for cotton. The previous year, he noted, had seen a bumper harvest for the plantations along the Colorado River, with corn averaging around 400 pounds to the acre and cotton from 2,500 to 3,000 pounds to the acre.

Fordtran also investigated the feasibility of planting sugar cane. He rode up the river twenty miles to the farm of John Murchison[5] in order to get some sugar cane cuttings. Murchison wanted four dollars for one hundred cuttings and Fordtran estimated 500 cuttings would be necessary. From the 500 cuttings, he stated, one could get 14,000 to 16,000 stalks. From these, molasses and sugar could be made at the plantation the following year. It would cost five dollars to have the cuttings shipped, he observed, but it would be worth this for two reasons: the oxen were not up to the trip, and it would be unwise to take the slaves so far away from the plantation and let them get a feel for the lay of the land.

Soon, a much more serious crisis arose than the condition of the oxen, the disagreement with Bryan, or the quarrel between Etzel and Stuesse. About eleven o'clock on the night of November 29, 1843, three slaves ran away. Butler, Washington, and his younger brother, Joshua, stole three horses, an ax, and a brace-and-bit, and made their escape.[6] The alarm went out within fifteen minutes by two other slaves, Henry and Richard, but it was not until daybreak the next morning that the overseer Bryan, with the assistance of a neighbor, rode after them.

Bryan thought it would be easy to recapture them. It had rained in the night, making it easy to follow their tracks on the wet ground. Also, the slaves were thought to be generally unaware of the lay of the country and the paths to freedom. Indeed, they had been kept intentionally ignorant for this very reason. Mexico, realistically, offered the only hope for freedom, and this would require a journey of several hundred miles and the crossing of several rivers. We can infer from the fact that the slaves took along tools necessary to build rafts that they may have had a better idea of the lay of the land than their white masters supposed.

The escape represented a serious loss. All three slaves had been purchased in New Orleans for about $650 each, or a total of approximately $1,950.[7] Of the seventeen slaves brought to Nassau, only seven were men, and among these, only five were in the prime of their youth. The three who escaped fell into this category. This left only two young male slaves to do the heavy work of the plantation. Butler was twenty-four years old. The exact ages of Washington and his brother are not known, but it can be inferred from the prices paid at auction that they were also in their twenties.

Boos-Waldeck had assigned jobs to the seventeen slaves he brought to the plantation in the spring of 1843 in this way: for the heavy work of clearing, splitting and plowing, he used the five younger men and six of the younger women, not an uncommon practice. Two of the women he put to work as cooks: the sixteen-year-old Emily at the manor house and either Patience or Rachael as cook for the slaves and overseer.[8] The amount of labor that had been expected of the slaves, especially the younger men, must have been stupendous—a labor for which many of the slaves were unaccustomed and unsuited. The task of felling trees and splitting their trunks for the thousands of rails necessary to fence the fields was in itself gargantuan. In addition to this, the men had to plow the fields and do much of the construction of the buildings.

The usual place to buy slaves was at established auctions. (Steinert has given us a description of the New Orleans slave market.)[9] Although most slaves were warranted to be of sound health and mind, the practice of buying slaves, as with anything at public auctions, could be very tricky, especially for novices. According to Abigail Curlee, the practice of selling lazy or fractious slaves meant that one had to be very careful in the purchase. She makes the odd statement (at least to modern sensibilities) that the most commonly accepted test of good health in a Negro was a greasy hand after being rubbed over the Negro's body.[10]

In his early reports, Boos-Waldeck had written enthusiastically about the eleven slaves he had bought at the New Orleans market, which included the three slaves who ran away. Later, however, he conceded that he had not made such a good buy.[11] The slaves "had to be taught everything," he complained in his April report, and this increased the work of the overseer immeasurably. Only a few understood how to use an ax, so instead of 150 rails per day, they were able to finish only 90 or 100. One had been a cook who had never done hard work; another had laid stones for fifteen years. In short, lamented the count, "they were not trained farm Negroes."[12]

At $1,300, Jim and his family stood out as the most satisfactory purchase. The count claimed that Jim was more capable than any German smith. In addition to the usual work of the smith, the shoeing of horses, he could fashions locks, make chisels, and build the finest plows together with all the woodwork. He was, moreover, an exemplary person. His wife could cook and wash, fashion mattresses, and make soap, while his daughters, eleven and eight, could help with the sewing and the housework.[13] Luckily, the family had been sold as an intact unit.

The fact that the three runaway slaves were willing to undertake such great risks and uncertainties in a desperate bid to gain their freedom testifies to the harshness of their treatment and the conditions under which they had lived and worked since they had been brought to Nassau. The winter and spring of 1843 had been unusually wet and cold; the summer continued wet.[14] Until their rudimentary shelters had been completed, the slaves were forced to live in tents, but their houses, once completed, apparently were not much better.

Several observations suggest that their treatment at the hands of the overseer Bryan had been severe. Boos-Waldeck commented in his report of May 26, 1843, that the most difficult aspect of the plantation was the management of the slaves. The best approach, he wrote, was unyielding strictness coupled with a sense of fairness and compassion. He went on to say that due to the military strictness imposed, as well as the sufficiency in food, shelter, and clothing provided, one saw nothing but happy faces.[15]

But it was the overseer, Bryan, who enforced this "military discipline," and the evidence suggests that he applied more strictness than fairness, and, in fact, the way he treated the slaves, especially Washington, had been on occasion cruel and inhumane. Fordtran reported he had heard how on one occasion Bryan had whipped Washington in a very cruel way. First, he was stretched out on the earth between four stakes, then he was whipped first long ways and then cross ways, and thereafter salt and pepper were rubbed into the wound.[16] Hermann Spiess recounted later that, "One of the overseers, Brown [*sic*: Bryan], must have been a veritable beast. Several Negroes, male and female, showed me deep scars on their backs where they had been whipped." [17]

In a later report, Prince Solms-Braunfels was unequivocal in stating that the reason the slaves ran away was because of their mistreatment at the hands of Bryan.[18]

Upon hearing of the escape, Fordtran rode immediately to the plantation from his home. He stayed behind to keep watch and dispatched Bryan to search for the runaways. To his great surprise Bryan returned the next day without the slaves. He and another man who had joined in the pursuit, had been able to follow the tracks only as far as the Stevens farm.[19] From there, they had ridden to La Grange to spread the word. Fordtran then hurried back to his place to make ready to take up the chase himself. He left his house the next day at four in the morning riding his good white horse.

Bryan accompanied him and said he had expected something like this for a long time. He had not felt safe in his house; he slept with loaded guns at his side and kept the door bolted. He was certain that Butler had tried to poison him. Next, Bryan showed Fordtran his feet and chest. Both were swollen. One later commentator suspected that the slaves had indeed poisoned Bryan.[20] Fordtran, however, diagnosed his affliction as a severe case of dropsy[21] and sent him back to the plantation. In the course of the next four weeks, Bryan became so sick a doctor had to be summoned. The immediate consequence of this was that Bryan could be of only limited utility in the pursuit of the runaways.

Fordtran picked up the spur again near the Stevens place. He followed the trail easily until Rutersville,[22] where it disappeared. After a long search, he encountered it again two miles to the east. Bryan's mare was one of the horses stolen; her tracks were easy to spot as she had small hooves and was shod. A mile from the Colorado River bottom, Fordtran spotted the mare's prints again, and they were very fresh. He followed it for a couple of hours. Two miles from Biegel's farm,[23] he came across Bryan's mare. After searching the bushes and following the other track, he came upon a brown horse tied to a tree, a horse Boos-Waldeck had purchased from Bryan in the spring. Apparently the Negroes had abandoned the horses and taken to foot, which would make following their tracks much more difficult.

Fordtran wanted to take possession of the horse, but Mr. Holloway,[24] who had joined the search, was adamant that the horse belonged to him. This led to an unpleasant disagreement and an unfortunate delay. They had to wait until someone came along who could serve as a witness so that a justice of the peace could decide the matter the following day.

Darkness approached during the delay, so Fordtran rode back to Biegel's farm in order to get something to eat. Thereafter, he resumed the search with the help of Joseph Biegel. They searched fruitlessly until two in the morning. The following morning they rode to the justice of the peace for the hearing about the brown horse. The judgment went against Fordtran because Holloway brought several people to swear on his behalf. Angrily, Fordtran sent Biegel back to the plantation with the message for Bryan that if he did not take steps to get the horse back, its value would be deducted from his salary. At this, Bryan hired a lawyer for ten dollars, who succeeded in persuading Holloway to return the horse. All this cost Fordtran another two days' time.

This episode illustrates pointedly that on the Texas frontier good horses were, next to slaves, a man's most valuable possession—one did not give them up easily.

In the meantime, Fordtran had sent two people on foot into the dense brush of the river bottom to continue the search. They had instructions to rendezvous at a house six miles farther down the river, but Fordtran overtook them a mile from the house in a stand of post oaks.[25] They consulted and came to the conclusion that the runaways were probably aware of the fact that there were boat crossings between that point and Columbus, a distance of twenty miles. They believed that the runaways would most likely try to seize control of one of the boats to cross the river.

Thereafter, Fordtran parted company and followed the river downstream at a trot for twelve miles. Meanwhile, Mr. Coyer,[26] one of the two men with Fordtran, followed a track into a dense river bottom six miles long by two-to-three miles wide and so thick with underbrush, he maintained, a pig could not make his way through it. He agreed that the Negroes would probably try to steal a boat in the darkness and make their way across the river. Fordtran rode on to Columbus and waited at the crossing the entire night, but the Negroes did not show. The other two men went back into the river bottom on foot. They discovered a half-completed raft. Upon hearing of this, and fearing that the slaves might be successful in another attempt, Fordtran crossed the river to the south side and rode ten miles up the river to the point opposite the bottom, but here he found no sign of the runaways.[27]

Fordtran spent several days in the vicinity and notified all the surrounding farms of the situation. He finally returned to La Grange and inquired whether anyone had word of their whereabouts, but in vain. Fordtran feared that the runaways would attempt to steal more horses since they still had a bridle and bit. He had seen the imprint of it in the sand. It seemed best, therefore, to ride to San Antonio and spread the word. He spent two days in Gonzales and then traveled in the company of Mr. Higginbotham[28] to San Antonio. They spread the word in all the settlements along the way. They were compelled to camp out two nights in the cold and damp without the warmth of a fire due to the danger of hostile Indians.

There was no word of the runaways in San Antonio, but news of their escape had spread to the surrounding countryside including to the nearby missions. Fordtran was told to offer at a reward of at least fifty dollars for the runaways because otherwise the Mexicans would hide them; he did. During this time, he also heard from an acquaintance that a certain Mr. Leal,[29] leader of a band of robbers, had the means to get the slaves returned even if they should succeed in making their way across the border into Mexico. He listened to the man's proposition and sent a letter with two Mexicans containing an exact description of the runaways, but after six days' wait, he departed San Antonio with no news and in a sour mood. During this period, several horses had been stolen and fifteen to twenty head of cattle killed in the vicinity by hostile Indians.

Fordtran's journey to San Antonio was premature, because the slaves were still hiding out in the river bottom between Columbus and La Grange. Fordtran learned this upon returning to La Grange on January 22. Two days before, Mr. McDonald [30] had encountered the three slaves about two miles from where Fordtran had last seen their track. The slave Butler had confessed that they were the runaways from Nassau Plantation. Upon hearing this, McDonald drew his pistol and ordered them to march. But near Butler's farm[31] (not to be confused with the slave by that name), where a wooden fence ran alongside a creek, two of them made a break for their freedom. McDonald chased down one, but he refused to heed McDonald's warning and McDonald, reluctant to shoot someone else's slave, let him escape. The slave Butler, however, did not attempt to escape and returned with McDonald, who handed him over to Mr. Butler. He, in turn, delivered the slave to Mrs. Fordtran at the farm near Industry. She wanted to have him bound and tied, but Mr. Butler assured her that this would not be necessary.

Soon Bryan came from Nassau plantation with heavy irons, which he fastened to Butler in Fordtran's smithy. When he returned to Nassau, Butler had a large iron collar with spikes put around his neck to which ox chains were attached. In reporting this to Boos-Waldeck, Fordtran could not conceal his disgust with Bryan and the cruel way he treated the slaves. He remarked that many of his acquaintances, himself included, rarely, if ever, beat their slaves. They had much more success in the handling of slaves by using the word rather than the whip: a word of reproach, appealing to their innate sense of honor, usually had more effect than the blows of the overseer.

Butler never attempted to escape again and became, by later accounts, an exemplary servant. Before he was bought by Count Boos-Waldeck, he had worked as a cook in New Orleans and he was skilled in making cakes. When Prince Solms stayed at the plantation, Butler served as cook and confectioner to the prince. He later served in the same capacity for Otto von Roeder and earned the praise of Amanda Fallier von Rosenberg for his abilities.[32]

In the meantime, the search for the other two runaways continued along the Colorado from Columbus to La Grange. Four miles from La Grange Mr. Murkirson [*sic*: Murchison][33] spotted smoke rising about a quarter mile from his house. In a short period, a posse of eight men was assembled. They approached the fire from different directions, but one of their dogs chased a pig, and the resulting ruckus alerted the Negroes. They managed to escape, but in their haste left behind axes, a brace-and-bit, bridle, and other items. Because the weather was dry and the ground hard, the searchers were not able to pick up the slaves' tracks, and after six days of searching they returned to La Grange.

Soon thereafter, word came that Schneider's[34] Negro, who had run away ten weeks before, had been caught. It was suspected he had been keeping company with the other runaways, and when Fordtran learned of this, he rode to La Grange to interview him. Fordtran intended to offer the Negro a dollar for information, but was told that he would rather be beaten to death than betray his comrades, so after much questioning, Fordtran came away no smarter than before.

The Texas Congress adjourned on the fifth of February, and Fordtran thought it wise to ride to the capital, Washington-on-the-Brazos, and spread the word about the runaways. Congress adjourned three hours after his arrival, and the next day he was able to give a description of the Negroes. General Burleson, candidate for president, promised he would tell the Tonkawa Indians about the escape. They had often proved helpful in capturing runaways in the past. Fordtran also talked to a newspaper editor so as to get the story in print.[35]

Thereafter, Fordtran returned home on his mule after a seven-hour ride. He soon received hearsay news from a Columbus man that the runaways had stolen a boat and crossed the river and then stolen two horses from a Mr. Lewis[36] sixteen miles further up the river. The last week of February, Fordtran learned that the slaves had, in fact, returned to the plantation during the night to ask for food and to inquire how Butler had been treated after he gave himself up. Hockley told the other slaves he had gotten twenty-five lashes to which Washington replied, "Let's take it and stay; twenty-five is nothing." Joshua, however, was unwilling. They tried to persuade Hockley to go with them, but he refused. They rode off on a dapple-gray horse, promising to return the following night.

Upon hearing this, Bryan tried to set a trap. He gave Emily some food and instructed Jim and Henry to find a hiding place where they could nab the two when they dismounted to take the food. The plan did not work, and a dispute arose as to whether Washington and Joshua did or did not show up. Henry swore he spotted them from his hiding place in the fog; but Jim insisted he had only imagined it and had really seen two white cows. The two nearly came to blows over their differing interpretations.

Stephen Townsend, an Anglo neighbor to the north,[37] was of the opinion that the Negroes had to be somewhere in the settlement, that is, in the vicinity of Round Top. He intended to sneak up to the shack where two Negro women were staying and try to listen in on their conversation. When he did, he heard such a confused patois that he could make neither heads nor tails of it. Fordtran came to the conclusion that the two runaways must be getting support from other slaves in the area, and he suspected a slave belonging to Toni,[38] a neighbor. He took one of the plantation slaves to Toni's farm to observe whether Toni's slave, who was known to be a friend of runaways, was giving Washington and Joshua food, but to no avail. All these efforts led nowhere.

In the middle of March, Mr. Higginbotham[39] from San Antonio paid Fordtran a visit and informed him that he had heard that the slaves had been apprehended twenty miles from Gonzales and had been chained together, but after a day had escaped again. He had heard many rumors of this sort, but not been able to substantiate any of them. He still held out hope that one day the slaves would show up to receive the punishment they deserved.

This is the last official report available. Solms-Braunfels later suggested that they were killed while trying to break into a house near

San Antonio,[40] but this was hearsay and never confirmed. It seems, if the slaves had indeed been killed, that members of the Society eventually would have received more solid corroboration. This never happened. There is, therefore, at least a possibility that the two runaways eventually made their way to Mexico and freedom. If they succeeded in this, it was by any measure an epic escape. The two successfully eluded a determined search party for weeks in the bottomlands of the Colorado River between La Grange and Columbus. Many were on the lookout for them, either because of the possibility of a reward, or because they considered it to be in the general interest. Always suspicious and even paranoid, slaveholders were ever fearful of conspiracies, and they considered the successful escape of even one slave to be a threat to the whole edifice of slavery.

In the face of this determined effort, the runaways successfully eluded their pursuers, and, as we have seen, on at least one occasion became so brazen that they slipped back to visit the plantation, presumably to restock, to inquire about the chase, and to visit their womenfolk. But all the while they had to feed and shelter themselves with no firearms and only rudimentary tools, which they eventually abandoned. Then, with what we have to assume was only a partial and secondhand knowledge of the roads and topography, they made their way undetected to San Antonio through stretches of countryside that were still not completely safe from the threat of Indians, and, eventually, to the border with Mexico and freedom. Their escape represented a substantial loss to the plantation and a shock to the noblemen in Germany.

CHAPTER 6

Carl Prince of Solms-Braunfels

About the same time as the slaves were eluding capture in Texas, Hoffmann von Fallersleben,[1] a prominent German political lyricist of the forties, wrote a cycle of songs called the *Texanische Lieder* (Texas Songs). In them he gave eloquent voice to the frustrations and hopes that drove so many of his countrymen to forsake their homeland for the wilds of Texas. One of his songs, *Ein Guadalupelied* (Song of the Guadalupe), celebrated the freedom from rank and privilege awaiting German emigrants in Texas.

In the valley of the Guadalupe
Lives neither prince nor nobleman.
One knows not bond service,
The tithe, injustices,
*No rules, no bans.*²

A dashing, thirty-two-year-old German prince *was* traipsing across Texas in 1845, the year Hoffmann von Fallersleben wrote the song; and, ironically, it was this German prince who would set the stage, more than any other person, for the beautiful Guadalupe Valley to become a destination for German emigrants.

Of all the personalities associated with German emigration to Texas, Carl Prince of Solms-Braunfels is by far the most intriguing—a man who has captured and held the public's fascination. A 1930 article in the *Houston Chronicle* with the somewhat lurid title, "German Prince once made Whoopee on Texas Farm," illustrates this fascination. In it, Prince Solms is portrayed as a romantic and quixotic figure on the Texas frontier: dashing, haughty, extravagant.

*The quiet pastures and sturdy farm buildings of Nassau Plantation in Fayette County, near Round Top, if suddenly given tongue, would tell a stirring tale of days when German noblemen rode spirited horses to death and made royal whoopee that burned up thousands of dollars in one wild night of merrymaking.*³

The prince certainly left his mark on the state. Decisions he made and actions he initiated shaped patterns of German emigration leaving a demographic imprint that endured for generations. He also gave his name to a prominent town, New Braunfels, and he caused the beautiful Guadalupe Valley, among other areas of the Central Texas Hill Country, to become a primary destination for German emigrants. Here, they left a positive imprint that defines the area to this day. The prince also left his mark on Nassau Plantation.

Solms-Braunfels achieved notoriety in little less than one year—

from July 1844 until June 1845. His first responsibility in Texas was to make preparations for the boatloads of settlers who were scheduled to begin arriving in the winter of 1844–45 and to be on hand and assist them when they arrived. This task led him to crisscross Texas twice, for the most part on horseback, and usually at a trot, the most jarring and uncomfortable gait to sustain over long periods of time. An entourage of servants and attendants usually accompanied him on these travels, and they were often utterly depleted by the pace he kept. During these sojourns he habitually wore a regimental field uniform befitting an officer of the Austrian Imperial Cavalry, replete with feather in hat. He also made a habit of displaying the Austrian Imperial flag. The impression this created added to his mystique.

As the uniform and the flag suggest, Solms-Braunfels did not leave awareness of rank and social standing behind and insisted, even on the Texas frontier, that those around him behave in a way that was *standesgemäss,* or in accordance with the deference due a German prince. He generally refused, for instance, to be seated at a meal with anyone who was not of his rank.[4] Since there were no other princes on the Texas frontier, this meant that he usually ate alone.

Some found his rigid formality humorous: General Alexander Somervell,[5] who, upon seeing the prince being lifted into his riding boots and breeches by his servants, broke out into an uncontrollable fit of laughter.[6] Still, his stiffness did not sit well with many Anglos, or with many Germans for that matter.[7] For his part, Prince Solms-Braunfels could barely conceal his disdain for the Anglo population and their democratic proclivities, and this disdain was fueled by a very pronounced pro-German bias.[8] These prejudices conditioned all his decisions to one degree or another.

Prince Solms' presence on the Texas frontier in 1844 and 1845 would have been a mere curiosity but for one thing: the lives and fortunes of many rested utterly on how effectively he carried out his mission, and the prince was deadly serious about his purpose. He carried out his task with decisiveness, dedication, and vigor, and in all things he was motivated by a strong sense of duty.

During his year in Texas, Prince Solms and his party stayed at the plantation three times—for about a week in July 1844, for an extended period in September and November 1844, and for one day in May 1845. This study will concentrate on his stays at the plantation and focus on his reports that are pertinent to the plantation.

Prince Solms wrote eleven official reports and several letters and kept a diary while in Texas. When he returned to Germany, he wrote a guide for emigrants based on his observations and experiences. Bourgeois d'Orvanne, who accompanied Prince Solms from Europe and traveled with him as far as San Antonio, also kept a diary. These records, plus other material in the Solms-Braunfels Archives, paint a fairly comprehensive picture of the prince's itinerary and activities in Texas. Of the reports, numbers one, three, and six are especially helpful for understanding the plantation.

The prince departed from Liverpool in the company of Bourgeois d'Orvanne and their attendants on May 10, 1844, most certainly unaware of the fact that very soon Count Castell would open negotiations with another *empresario* for another land grant contract.[9] The pair made hay diplomatically and cut quite a path. While in England, they met with Prince Albert, who gave assurances (according to a subsequent letter to Castell from d'Orvanne) of the full support of the English government.[10]

The party arrived in Boston on May 31, 1844. From there, they made their way by train, steamer, and stage to Brownsville, Ohio, where they caught a riverboat for New Orleans.[11] From New Orleans, they took the steamer *Neptune* to Galveston. They arrived to the greeting of a twenty-one-gun salute on July 1, 1844.

The warm reception Solms-Braunfels and his party enjoyed upon their arrival in Galveston testified to the good will of most Texans.[12] In Houston the prince bought a horse for himself and two more for the servants. He also rented a wagon. The prince's purchases led d'Orvanne to observe that the princely title served nicely to inflate prices whenever the prince wished to buy something. Prince Solms split the party and sent the wagon with Armand Ducos[13] to Nassau Plantation while he and d'Orvanne rode to Washington-on-the-Brazos where they hoped to convince the government to grant an extension of the d'Orvanne land grant.

Here the party also was warmly received.[14] The prince brought up the matter of the extension of the d'Orvanne land grant contract with the secretary of state, Anson Jones. The secretary informed him, regretfully, that he was powerless; the matter would have to wait until the Congress convened in January.

Prince Solms and Bourgeois d'Orvanne arrived at Nassau Plantation on July 9, 1844, and spent a week. The wagon and the luggage, dispatched earlier from Houston, did not arrive until the following day. Boggy conditions and poor roads in the Brazos River bottom had delayed the progress of Armand Ducos and his party. They spent one night at the farm of Charles Fordtran along the way, and he accompanied them to the plantation.[15]

Once the party was together, the prince wasted little time in inspecting the plantation. The *Herrenhaus*, under the supervision of Wilhelm Etzel,[16] appeared to be in good order, and the general lay of the land pleased him. The house, he remarked, was substantial, but incomplete, with the cracks between the logs as yet unfilled, allowing the wind and rain to blow in.

Prince Solms was decidedly unimpressed with the rest of the plantation. He expressed clearly the dismay he felt in his report of July 15, the first sent back to the leadership in Germany. "I share the opinion," he stated, "which prevails uniformly in this land that this endeavor is unworthy of the Society and that any farmer could have achieved as much while spending less."[17] D'Orvanne seconded this opinion by observing in his diary that the plantation was poorly organized and poorly led, had a poor arrangement for the fieldwork, and horrible housing for the Negroes. "It was," he commented, "less than a stellar recommendation for a large landowner."[18]

Prince Solms was extremely annoyed that the German-Texan supervisor, Charles Fordtran, could not produce an inventory. He ordered d'Orvanne and Fordtran to begin one immediately, which the two undertook and completed.

Prince Solms' report gives us a very comprehensive (and unflattering) picture of the state of the plantation on its first anniversary. The overseer Bryan had been a poor choice; his reduced health and excessive drinking had finally led to his dismissal in the early part of the summer. His mistreatment of the slaves had caused three to run away, two of whom never returned. Their reputed death in San Antonio represented a substantial loss. He had failed to get the fields in shape in a timely fashion, while the cotton and corn he did succeed in planting did not fare well, promising a meager harvest. Mr. Denman, the new overseer hired by Charles Fordtran to take the place of Bryan, promised to bring more professional competence to the job, but he was already making unreasonable demands. The plantation encompassed 4,428 acres, of which to date only eighty acres, or less than 2 percent of the total, had been put into productive use. Considering the money spent, what a meager result this had been. Similarly, Boos-Waldeck's conviction that slave plantations could be made to operate profitably on their own with only one paid employee—an overseer—had been extremely naïve.

Above all, the prince was disgusted with the fact that the Society was now associated with slavery. The prince had been fully aware that Count Boos-Waldeck had set up a slave plantation in Texas, and there is no evidence that he had voiced any strong disapproval with this course of action while in Germany, but once he confronted the reality of slavery in Texas, he had a change of heart. The prince did not mince words. Slavery, he remarked, "is a true stain on human society, and something completely unworthy of our Society." [19] The prince recommended that the Society dispose of the plantation as a whole. In a later report, he suggested that it might be better to parcel it off.

Solms-Braunfels' dislike for Charles Fordtran was manifest from the beginning, and seemed to be an extension of his disapproval of the direction that Count Boos-Waldeck had set. For the time being, however, he was left with little choice but to leave Fordtran as provisional supervisor of the plantation and to give him power of attorney until a replacement could be located. He expected a new supervisor to be coming from Germany in six months or so, who not only would be knowledgeable in agriculture, but also would be a medical doctor.

One of the more interesting interactions concerned Wilhelm Etzel, Boos-Waldeck's former manservant, and the man most responsible for the building and furnishing of the *Herrenhaus*. Before he departed, Boos-Waldeck had promised to reward Etzel for his loyalty and conscientious devotion to duty. Etzel had worked on the house for over a year at a salary less than his talents and output warranted. His reward was to be a gift of fifty acres taken from that part of the Jack League that jutted out to the east.

Prince Solms refused to honor this part of the bargain on the grounds that he did not have the authority to sell or gift any part of the plantation. He proposed instead that Wilhelm Etzel come with him to the settlement area where he promised him a hundred acres. Etzel, however, steadfastly insisted on his fifty acres. When the prince refused to honor the bargain, Etzel became infuriated.

Prince Solms generally adopted a very measured tone in his reports with respect to Boos-Waldeck. He was extremely deferential, never attacking or criticizing him directly, but the whole thrust of his commentary can only be construed as a devastating critique. The criticism did not go unnoticed by Boos-Waldeck. Upon hearing of the situation with Etzel, he became very angry. He also was furious that Prince Solms (later) demanded Charles Fordtran give back the golden watch presented to him the previous year in the name of the Society by Count von Wied. Count Waldeck considered this to be an affront to his honor and challenged Prince Solms to a duel upon his return to Europe. The duel never took place.[20]

The prince attracted considerable attention during this and subsequent stays at the plantation, especially from his countrymen. For the most part, Germans who had already settled in Texas enjoyed a newfound sense of freedom in their adopted land. Still, they suffered from the deprivations of frontier life. The universal lack of cash exacerbated the situation. Credit was limited or nonexistent while much of the economy rested on barter. The appearance, then, of a real German prince with ambitious plans and a big purse created even more of a sensation in the German communities than had his predecessor, Boos-Waldeck. Many made the pilgrimage to Nassau to pay their respects and to see if there might be some place for them or chance for employment in the colonization project. Some even donned their German uniforms in a show of respect.[21]

Many were successful in this hope. During his first and second stays at the plantation, Prince Solms began to assemble a company of men, primarily as a security guard, to assist him and protect the settlers during the move from the coast to the interior. Ludwig Cachand Ervendberg, whom Boos-Waldeck had discovered ministering to the needs of the Cummins Creek community, was offered a position as Protestant pastor for the Society. The preacher held the first Christmas service for the incoming settlers on the banks of Lavaca Bay in December 1844. The prince considered it imperative that incoming German settlers should have access to both Catholic and Protestant services. He requested a priest from the district diocese, and when one was not forthcoming, he took an abbot along as a substitute.

Solms-Braunfels also discovered the botanist Friedrich Lindheimer at the Cummins Creek community and offered him a position with the Society. His subsequent contributions as scientist, newspaperman, and leader of the Germans during the difficult days of the Civil War are well documented.[22]

Several local craftsmen were given jobs. The Brune brothers, also from the Cummins Creek area, received a commission to work on saddles and tack.[23] Friedrich Ernst's son, Johann, obtained a position as guide and hunter in the prince's party as did Karl Jordt, the son of Detlev Dunt (Jordt), author of one of the earliest studies of Texas published in Germany.[24]

Otto von Roeder also made the pilgrimage. He did not impress the prince initially—Prince Solms likened him to a vagabond in his diary.[25] Still, it is possible that the significant business relationship that developed between Otto von Roeder and the Society had its roots at this meeting. Von Roeder, the owner of a gristmill at present-day Shelby, a few miles east of the plantation, soon would become the principal supplier of corn to the colonies of New Braunfels and Friederichsburg. By the September stay at the plantation, von Roeder obviously had become a part of the entourage, for he is often mentioned in the prince's diary.

Prince Solms-Braunfels and his party spent less than a week at the plantation during this first visit. Business was pressing—already a boatload of immigrants had arrived in Galveston—and Prince Solms was impatient to have a look at the grant area of d'Orvanne, which lay to the northwest of San Antonio in the upper reaches of the Medina and Sabinal rivers.

He and his party left for San Antonio on the evening of July 16 after a stay of seven days at the plantation. The ranks of his entourage had by this time swollen to include a young Swiss-German doctor by the name of Emil Meyer who became a close confidant of the prince.[26] The party also included, by Prince Solms' account, d'Orvanne and his partner Ducos, a friar, a cook, a guide, and two hunters.[27] The plantation lent two mules, an American horse and a pony, and also a buckboard wagon for the trip. The party was well armed. The two servants rode the wagon; the rest were mounted. Charles Fordtran accompanied them on the first leg of the trip. The party broke a wagon shaft while attempting to cross the creek at Rutersville. Fordtran helped with the repair and then returned to the plantation.

The party had an Indian scare but arrived safely in San Antonio on July 25. A few days later, with the escort of Texas Rangers, as well as a surveyor, the prince made an inspection of the grant area of Bourgeois d'Orvanne, which encompassed the upper reaches of the Medina, Frio, and Sabinal River valleys northwest of San Antonio.[28] In his second report, the prince noted that the Medina River had beautiful, clear-flowing waters, and that there were selected areas in the river bottom that were suitable for cultivation, but that the bulk of the grant was semi-arid, rocky, and only suited to free-ranging livestock. In general, his report was less than encouraging.

Prince Solms was extremely lucky not to have encountered any hostile Indians on these forays. The battle of Plum Creek (1840) had snipped the boldness of the Comanches and reduced the range of their raids, but they had regrouped enough to be an ever-present and formidable threat, especially to isolated settlers and travelers in the area that the prince and his party were reconnoitering. Prince Solms, moreover, underestimated the warlike abilities of the Comanches and overestimated the defensive capability of his party, which could have been disastrous. He scorned the presence of Captain Hays and the Texas Rangers, and at a later date ordered Fischer to make it clear that the help and presence of the Rangers was unwelcome.

Prince Solms received a personal letter from Sam Houston on August 11 that did not bode well for the enterprise, but which testified to President Sam Houston's goodwill concerning German colonization. The Congress had taken away the president's authority to issue any more land contracts, or to extend the terms of any already issued, and had done so over the president's veto.[29] This discouraging news, however, was soon offset by a letter from Germany, hand-carried by Lieutenant Friedrich von Wrede,[30] from Galveston, informing Prince Solms that the Society had signed a contract with Henry Francis Fischer and had abandoned the d'Orvanne contract. He was instructed to return to Nassau Plantation and there await the arrival of Fischer, who would be arriving from Germany.[31]

On August 24, 1844, Prince Solms dismissed Bourgeois d'Orvanne as Colonial Director and departed for Nassau. His party now included Lieutenant von Wrede, who from this point on was a constant companion.[32] He and his party arrived at the plantation on September 1 after a trip filled with many adventures and trials. They covered the 143 miles in five days, averaging nearly thirty miles a day,[33] a strenuous pace for man and beast.

Prince Solms' longest stay at the plantation followed, and he arrived to find that not all was in order. Wilhelm Etzel had deserted and, apparently as an expression of his disgust with the prince and what he took to be a breach of contract, had taken many effects belonging to the plantation, including the feather mattress, some of the porcelain ware, a shotgun, powder and shot, saddles and bridles, as well as a considerable amount of sawed lumber.[34] Driven by his sense of injustice, he had even threatened to shoot the prince on sight and had attempted to burn down the manor house. Negro Jim, the blacksmith who lived with his family in the shed next to the big house, had intervened and prevented this catastrophe. Equally disturbing, one of the slave women, Mary, had died, and another had deserted.[35] When Fordtran arrived, he seemed very pale with anxiety because he had to account for the bad news.

What was at the root of Wilhelm Etzel's violent reaction to the prince? Etzel had come over as the trusted and loyal manservant of Count Boos-Waldeck, and thus was a man intimately acquainted with the rigid class system of hereditary privileges and obligations still very much in play in Germany in the 1840s. The freedom he discovered in Texas must have proved intoxicating. He obviously had enjoyed a good rapport with his former master, but he had no desire to return to his former life as a servant to the wealthy and privileged. Boos-Waldeck, to his credit, had the good sense to accept Etzel's decision and to wish his former servant the best. His work on the manor house—laying the floors, building the furniture, constructing the chimneys, and working on other refinements—carried out with dogged dedication for over a year at sub-par pay was to be the last service, one gathers, to his former master, and, by extension, to the old order. He had carried out his end of the bargain, and he expected the noblemen from Germany to honor their word. Prince Solms, with his belief in the old system still very much intact, was not nearly as sympathetic to Etzel's aspirations. When the prince reneged on the fifty acres promised by Boos-Waldeck, it triggered an eruption of resentment in Etzel.

This interaction on the Texas frontier, curiously, foreshadows in microcosm the festering discontent and class hatred soon to break out in southern Germany in the March revolution of 1848.

Prince Solms really had two purposes for his extended stay at the plantation: to await the arrival of Henry Francis Fischer from Germany and to assemble and train a private military escort for the settlers once they began arriving. In line with this second purpose, Prince Solms dispatched Dr. Meyer and several of the servants to Houston for the purpose of acquiring supplies for his "army," and also for replacing the lost items—especially the coveted feather mattress.

Prince Solms noted in his diary that he was left alone with Lieutenant von Wrede at the plantation for several days. It was very hot, and the prince suffered from the heat and was troubled with chronic headaches. The overseer Denman paid a visit and later the prince rode down to the farm. The well, which had been dug for the slaves and the overseer at the farm, had gone dry. One of the slaves, Richard, brought stagnant water from the creek. Prince Solms was forced to get drinking water for his party at the farm of Captain Sutton[36] in the vicinity of Shelby. Consequently, he ordered a well dug for the *Herrenhaus*.

In a few days, Dr. Meyer and his party returned with the supplies including a new mattress as well as a wagon full of champagne and wine. With their arrival began the round of partying and drinking that has spun into the myth of Prince Solms' wild night of extravagance while at the plantation.[37] Actually, the events extended over several days, a fact that becomes clear in Prince Solms' diary, and most of the events were surely intended primarily as quasi-training exercises for his recruits, who were showing up daily, some in the uniform of their old regiments in Germany.

During the day, Prince Solms organized target shooting and also equestrian training, an understandable *sine qua non* for an Austrian cavalry officer. In the evenings, the prince arranged for choral singing and poetry readings for his troop, events lasting until the wee hours. While sipping generously from their "punch," a mixture of champagne and wine, they read poetry, sang songs, and took turns reading dramatic excerpts, especially from Schiller, for the prince exhibited a great partiality for Schiller's great dramatic work *Wallenstein*. These events may well have become rowdy as the effects of the alcohol took hold.[38] At one point, Dr. Meyer squabbled with another member of the party, and their disagreement led to a challenge. Otto von Roeder, no stranger to duels, agreed to be Dr. Meyer's second.[39] Fortunately, the doctor fell conveniently ill and the fight never took place.

It was during this time that Prince Solms composed several poems and *Lieder* (songs). For this reason, he is sometimes credited as the first Texas-German poet. In an ironic twist, Hoffmann von Fallersleben penned *Das Guadalupelied*, championing the frontier life free of German nobles and class privilege at roughly the same time that Prince Solms, from the vantage point of Nassau Plantation, composed one of the first Texas-German poems praising, in essence, the *status quo* of the glorious *Vaterland*.

There is some suggestion that Prince Solms may have challenged, or been challenged, to a horse race by the Townsend clan, who resided nearby.[40] If such a contest did in fact take place, pitting the proud equestrian prince and his Germans against the putative two—faced Texans, then we can only imagine the dramatic contour of the event.

How fascinating all this activity at the plantation must have appeared to the local frontier families, whose lives concentrated almost exclusively on the basics of a minimal existence. The coming and going of troops of men, the shooting, riding, singing, and drinking at the plantation—all these events, taken together and spread over several days, fueled the legend of an eccentric and extravagant German prince who made "whoopee" at Nassau Plantation.

By the end of September, the tension between the prince and Charles Fordtran came to a head. Much had gone wrong at the plantation between July and September, and the prince held Fordtran accountable for these problems. When Fordtran failed to produce an updated *Verzeichnis*, or list, by means of which the present inventory could be compared to the receipts of previous purchases, Prince Solms flew into a rage. When the comparison was updated, it turned out that much was missing, including several head of cattle. The prince suspected, as Friedrich Ernst had insinuated, that Fordtran had stolen, or eaten, the missing cattle. The prince dismissed Fordtran and also served notice to the overseer Denman that when his contract expired in December, it would not be renewed.

The perceived injustice of this action chagrined Fordtran deeply. He refused to surrender the power of attorney granted to him earlier, and he absconded with many documents from the archives that had been housed in the *Herrenhaus*. When the prince demanded that he hand over the gold watch presented to him by Boos-Waldeck from Count Wied as a token of appreciation for his service, he steadfastly refused, and the watch remains in the family to this day as a poignant memento of these events.

Although punctuated by several side trips—one to Washington-on-the-Brazos and another to Galveston—the period from the beginning of September 1844 through the end of November can be viewed as one continuous stay at the plantation by the prince. Prince Solms made the trip to the capital to have further discussions with Secretary of State Anson Jones concerning the land grant situation. When Henry Francis Fischer did not show up at the plantation at the designated time, October 20, the prince grew impatient and resolved to go to Galveston to meet him. The two must have crossed paths in the dark, for Henry Francis Fischer showed up at Nassau nine days later, October 29. The prince arrived back at the plantation November 5 and was much annoyed by the inconvenience of this delay.

The prince coordinated with Fischer and assembled his party of followers. He then departed on November 16 and reached the coast on November 22 to greet the first boatload of immigrants who arrived on the schooner *Johann Dethard* on Lavaca Bay. Over the next several months, Prince Solms' energies would be entirely consumed in providing for the boatloads of immigrants as they arrived, establishing an interim settlement (New Braunfels), and facilitating transportation of the new arrivals into the interior. This story has been sufficiently documented by Rudolph Biesele and other historians of the period.[41]

With respect to the plantation, the focus shifts to Friedrich von Wrede, Sr., the man chosen by Prince Solms to succeed Charles Fordtran, but a man unable to assume his duties at the plantation because of other jobs and tasks entrusted to him by the prince. Prince Solms was essentially finished with the plantation. Other than a brief stop for one night on his way back to New Orleans and Germany in May 1845, he had no more direct involvement.

Upon reflection, it is safe to say that Prince Solms' idiosyncrasies compromised his effectiveness and had serious ramifications for the success of the whole colonization venture. He was very quick to form judgments of people based on his biases, and these judgments, once formed, did not alter. He was contemptuous of Bourgeois d'Orvanne, who was French. D'Orvanne became quite put out with the prince and his condescending attitudes. This is clearly revealed in his diary. The prince, for his part, did not like the idea of a Frenchman at the center of an essentially German endeavor, and he could not see beyond this prejudice.[42]

As with d'Orvanne, so too with Fischer: once the d'Orvanne contract had been discarded, it was in everyone's interest that Prince Solms and Henry Francis Fischer should put aside their differences for the common good. But it was not to be.[43] Prince Solms distrusted

Fischer's plebeian background and his mercantile frame of mind. He wrote: "As soon as I saw that Fischer had become an American, I no longer counted on him."[44]

Prince Solms finally confronted Fischer at Agua Dulce, a few miles inland from the coast where the prince had purchased a tract of land to serve as a staging area for the boatloads of emigrants who begin arriving in December 1845. In a scene reminiscent of the episode with Wilhelm Etzel, the prince accused Fischer of harboring democratic ideas, spreading dissent among the settlers, and undercutting his authority. He recommended removing Fischer from an active management role in the venture based on accusations of business incompetence and neglect, charges that in retrospect appear unfounded. The costly buyout that ensued came at an inopportune time and was a bad deal for the Society.

Similarly, Prince Solms judged the plantation harshly from the moment he laid eyes on it. He had little or no sympathy for the rationale that had led Count Boos-Waldeck to set up the plantation, and, likewise, he was disdainful and suspicious of those whom Boos-Waldeck had left in charge, criticizing the course they had set and eventually terminating them all. Prince Solms recommended selling the plantation, but the leadership in Germany did not concur, and so the plantation drifted for the next few months, essentially leaderless, sometimes with a slave, the talented blacksmith Negro Jim, left to serve as *de facto* supervisor.[45]

For all his disgust, the plantation certainly served Prince Solms well as a home base and also as a place to assemble the people he needed for his various expeditions, and, yes, even as a place to relax and enjoy himself. Prince Solms, however, greatly resented the worry the plantation caused, considering it a distraction from the important job of orchestrating the bigger picture. In his report from Agua Dulce, he made the astonishing observation that the plantation had caused him more aggravation than all his other worries combined.

Although straight as an arrow in his beliefs, on one important point, the prince was grossly hypocritical: he did not impose upon himself the same standards of strict accounting that he had demanded of Charles Fordtran and others. As Solms-Braunfels crisscrossed the republic in 1844–45, he left a trail of IOUs, which, in the aggregate, had grown to be enormous. Yet, when the prince rendezvoused with his successor, Johann Otto *Freiherr* von Meusebach, in Gonzales in May 1845, he could not hand over a precise accounting of what he had spent or to whom the Society now owed money. Meusebach, understandably, was annoyed by this, for it put him in an exceptionally embarrassing and difficult position at the beginning of his tenure.

Prince Solms-Braunfels was blunt and uncompromising in his attitudes. As a result of this and other traits, he inspired fierce loyalty in some and hatred in others. But undeniably, he was a man who left his mark on Texas. The point to keep in mind, however, is that in the quixotic person of Solms-Braunfels, we find the personification of a fundamental contradiction in this story which rendered its success so improbable from the beginning: it was an aristocratic adventure in a democratic land.

CHAPTER 7

Friedrich von Wrede

There is no evidence of Prince Solms-Braunfels opposing slavery prior to his appearance in Texas in 1844. But after confronting it firsthand, his judgment about slavery is forceful and unequivocal: it is a "cause for shame,"[1] a stain on human society, and a matter "unworthy" of the *Adelsverein*. Because Charles Fordtran was so closely associated with Boos-Waldeck and with slavery, Prince Solms was prejudiced against him from the beginning and resolved to replace him as soon as a suitable candidate could be located.

In his second report from San Antonio, Prince Solms had stressed the importance of having dependable and trustworthy Germans in all important positions and agencies. He particularly preferred men of the officer class.

The von Wredes, both father and son, seemed to fit the bill. Count Castell most likely enlisted both in the service of the Society in Germany in response to Prince Solms' desires. Friedrich von Wrede, Jr., arrived in Texas from Germany in August 1844 carrying official documents for the prince and thereafter became his constant companion. Friedrich von Wrede Sr. arrived in Texas sometime in the late fall of the same year, also as an agent of the Society.

The elder von Wrede had earlier traveled extensively in the United States and Texas with his family and returned to Germany in June 1843. In 1844, he published a guidebook in Germany about the American frontier with emphasis on Texas.[2] In his earlier years, he had served as a cavalry officer in the Hessian army during the Napoleonic wars and had participated in the battle of Waterloo. During his first visit to America, he had often supported himself by giving lessons in equestrian dressage.

The senior von Wrede demonstrated an amazing vigor for a man of fifty-eight years. In February of 1845, he made his way to San Antonio from Galveston carrying dispatches from Europe for the prince, a good part of the way on a rented nag with a saddle that had only one stirrup. He then accompanied the prince on a journey back to Houston from San Antonio where the prince set such a furious pace over a distance of over two hundred miles that von Wrede compared the trip to the epic ride of King Charles XII of Sweden in 1718 from Hungary to Stralsund on the Baltic Sea, a story apparently well-known in aristocratic circles.[3]

The trip from San Antonio left behind a trail of lame horses and broken men. The prince's personal servant, Anton Kück, as well as the hunter, Johann Jordt, became so *"total durchgeritten* [utterly depleted through riding]" that they had to be diverted to Nassau Plantation to recuperate while the rest of the party pressed on to Houston from the Friedrich Ernst place at Industry where they had spent the night. The older von Wrede, however, was able to keep pace with the prince for the whole time until his horse gave out. He straggled in several hours later on the final leg of the ride.

Of all the reports to be found in the Solms-Braunfels Archives, none captures so deftly the flavor of frontier Texas as the report of Friedrich von Wrede of February 1845.[4] Friedrich von Wrede, Sr., comes across as a keen observer of human nature as well as a person of unquestionable integrity. His brief sketches of the various characters the prince and his party encountered—from the tobacco-chewing and whiskey-drinking "gentlemen" who crowded around the single stove in the City Hotel in Victoria, to the poor Irishman who put them up for the night along the way, to the castle-dwelling Scotsman in Columbus, to the *Gemütlichkeit* (comfortable German atmosphere) of Friedrich Ernst's place in Industry, to the assertive crudeness of a Texas senator, Judge Billburg,[5] in Washington—on-the-Brazos—all offer wonderful vignettes of life in Texas in 1845 as seen from the point of view of a sophisticated, no-nonsense, and hardy German aristocrat.

Friedrich von Wrede emerges in this and subsequent correspondence as someone extremely conscious of duty and responsibility, qualities which recommended him to the prince. As a former cavalry officer and member of the lesser aristocracy himself, the elder von Wrede felt a natural affinity and ease in his relationship with the prince. His admiration and respect for the character of the prince is unbounded. For his part, the prince found in both the father and son those qualities that he so admired: a strong sense of duty, reliability, and integrity, combined with a robust physical constitution.

Despite this mutual affection, the elder von Wrede always gave his honest and candid opinion in his assessments, even if these were not exactly in harmony with those of the prince. He counseled, for instance, that the prince should not be too radical in his desire to keep Americans out of the colony. To do so would arouse the hostility and suspicion of the Americans, while creating unnecessary costs and hardships in the implementation of the program. In this regard, he mentioned specifically the unnecessary costs associated with the prince's insistence on bringing in the settlers at Indian Point rather than allowing them to land at Tres Palacios,[6] where they would be able to follow the established trail along the Colorado River from its mouth. Prince Solms had vetoed these routes on the grounds that he did not want his colonists to come into close contact with the Anglos who had settled the Colorado River.[7]

After dismissing Charles Fordtran, the prince decided to appoint the elder von Wrede as supervisor of the plantation. His duties were scheduled to begin the first day of January 1845. With the dismissal of Denman, the plantation also needed a new overseer. Henry Francis Fischer arranged for an Anglo, S. A. Durand,[8] to succeed Denman, and drafted a contract for his service.[9] The two then drew up a plan for the plantation.[10] Durand assumed his duties on the first day of January 1845, and his contract ran for a year. His salary was set at $400 a year.

As the prince's confidence in von Wrede grew, he began assigning him other tasks, tasks that took precedence over his responsibilities at the plantation. Once immigrants began arriving by the boatload, it became necessary to have a permanent agent in New Orleans to procure needed supplies and to maintain contact with the Society's correspondent banker, Lanfear & Co. This responsibility fell to the senior von Wrede, and he spent the middle of January through the first week in March of 1845 in New Orleans.

In New Orleans, von Wrede encountered a general skepticism about the Society's plans. Many felt that the Indians, especially the Comanches, would create serious problems and that much of the land was unsuitable for cultivation. Von Wrede had planned to write a letter for publication in Germany highlighting the positive features of the colony, but in light of what he had heard, he decided to put off such a letter until he could view the grant area for himself. To give an accurate and truthful report he considered to be a matter of personal honor and a service of the utmost importance.

Von Wrede left New Orleans March 6, 1845, and accompanied a load of supplies to Indian Point (Carlshafen), where the boat ran aground. He managed to get the supplies unloaded and then shipped by wagon to the newly formed settlement at the "fountains," which eventually was christened "New Braunfels." He had hardly settled in from this journey when Prince Solms-Braunfels called for a volunteer to hand-carry reports and dispatches to Galveston. Von Wrede volunteered for the trip.

As a result of these added responsibilities and diversions, von Wrede was frustrated in his desire to visit the grant area. Also, he was not able to lay eyes on the plantation until May 1845, when he finally spent two weeks there. Von Wrede set down his observations and recommendations concerning the plantation in two reports to the administration in Germany dated from the end of May 1845.

Unfortunately, it did not take von Wrede long to get into an unpleasant disagreement with S. A. Durand, the new Anglo overseer who had taken up residence in January. Von Wrede arrived to find that Durand was absent, having taken the day off to visit a neighboring plantation. He discovered, moreover, upon inquiring of Negro Jim, that Durand's sister and two younger brothers also lived at the plantation. When von Wrede confronted Durand about this added expense, he became quite agitated and insisted that Henry Francis Fischer, who had hired him, had approved this arrangement.[11]

Durand claimed he now had 200 acres fenced and in cultivation, of which he had planted 60 in corn and 140 in cotton. Von Wrede suspected that this was an exaggeration and intended to measure the fields himself to obtain a precise size. He reported that the corn looked good, but not the cotton. The moist spring had worked to its disadvantage. He conceded, however, should the weather turn more favorable, the crop would turn out decently. Durand had estimated the yield at 100 bales weighing 400 pounds apiece.

The fruit trees, planted the previous year at the *Herrenhaus*, did not look healthy. This surprised von Wrede because the soil appeared rich and promising. He surmised (correctly) that the problem was poor drainage: the underlying clay had trapped the moisture, which was unhealthy for the trees. He proposed digging small ditches to drain off the excess moisture and improve the yield.

It is clear from the report that von Wrede disliked Durand intensely, almost from the moment he laid eyes upon him, saying he was prone to exaggerate and often smelled of whiskey. He was a "grober Amerikaner [crude American]." A visit to the Ernst farm on Mill Creek in Industry soon reinforced his suspicions.

Friedrich Ernst and Charles Fordtran, it will be remembered, had moved to Texas together in March 1831 from New York, where they had met. Once close friends, they had quarreled bitterly, and Ernst, it seemed, took every opportunity to slander his former companion with outrageous accusations. The previous year he had intimated to Prince Solms that Fordtran had stolen cattle from the plantation, an accusation that formed the basis, in part, for his dismissal. Similarly, he now accused Fordtran and the former overseer, Denman, of hatching a plot to encourage the slaves to run away and otherwise cause damage to the plantation. He suggested, moreover, that Durand was an accomplice in this scheme.[12]

Unaware of the malice behind these accusations, von Wrede took them seriously. He wrote to Prince Solms and suggested that it would be prudent to adopt measures to deal with this threat. He suggested that they hire some German workers to live at the plantation. He would then have some reliable backup to assist him should some situation arise.

During this stay, von Wrede undertook a thorough analysis of the plantation from a business standpoint and came up with several sensible suggestions. He proposed that the unused part of the league (over 4,000 acres) be split up in six to eight smaller farms, which could be rented out to reputable and well-to-do German farmers brought over by the Society. The slaves would then be free to concentrate on the developed part of the farm, whereby the farm could, with luck, recoup some of the losses of the previous years.

In any case, he continued, the present administration was simply too inefficient and expensive to reap the full benefit of the labor of fourteen slaves. The situation with two households was very wasteful. He proposed terminating Durand once his contract expired in January and replacing him with a married German, whose wife could take care of their household, thus freeing a female slave for fieldwork. For the time being, he would need to stay at the *Herrenhaus*, where the wife of Negro Jim could do his cooking and cleaning. For the next year, however, he proposed building a small house near the main compound, and thereby uniting the two households for a considerable savings.

As for the "beautiful" *Herrenhaus,* it should not sit empty, he wrote. Von Wrede proposed making it the site of a second large farm, which the Society could offer as a lease to a prosperous and respected (German) family, thus gaining in rent revenue while saving on upkeep. In the meantime, he intended to fence and plow a twenty-acre field in the vicinity of the *Herrenhaus*. This arrangement, he opined, held out the best prospect for a quick and sizeable appreciation in the value of the land should the Society decide at some point to sell it.

In concluding, von Wrede mentioned that on the way from New Braunfels he had seen several oat and wheat fields that were as nice as any he had ever seen in Germany. He speculated that such crops, as well as clover, might do well at Nassau. He intended to plant fifty pounds of red clover seed the following year. He hoped to reduce the plantation's need for corn by planting oats and also to increase the yield through the use of "green fertilizer," that is, clover.

Von Wrede wrote a quick follow-up to his report of May 20, 1845, in which he elaborated on his suggestions for the plantation.[13] The more he thought about it, he wrote, the more convinced he became of the need to divide the plantation into at least eight farms to be leased to German farmers brought over under the auspices of the Society. It could be structured in such a way that it would be a good deal for both the Society and the emigrant farmers. The Society would offer to each a twenty-foot square log cabin and a fenced-in field of twenty acres. All additional structures and improvements would come at the expense of the tenant. However, upon termination of the lease all improvements would remain with the farm.

There should be no problem with obtaining enough applicants, he contended. Several articles had appeared in newspapers concerning the troubles of the German emigrants at Indian Point. The fear this aroused had caused many settlers otherwise disposed to come to Texas to settle elsewhere. The certainty of this arrangement, as opposed to the uncertainty of the grant area, would be a powerful inducement.

Moreover, the tenants would still receive title to 320 acres of land in the grant area, just as the other emigrant heads of household. While tenants at Nassau, they could acclimatize, gather experience, and build up their assets. When it came time to sell, the plantation would benefit from the added improvements while the farmers would be in a better position to move to the grant area.

The tenants, for their part, would be obligated only to aid with the harvest of the cotton, corn, and (possibly) wheat and also to help in the transportation of the cotton to market. They would be required to pick 150 pounds of cotton a week during harvest and be responsible for transporting sixteen bales of cotton to market either to Houston or a suitable place.

This last requirement could result in great savings for the plantation. Even had the plantation produced bumper crops of cotton and corn, there was still the problem of transportation and undeveloped markets in the early 1840s. Local plantations, von Wrede pointed out, hauled their cotton to Houston, ninety miles distant. It took eight or more oxen to haul eight bales of cotton.[14] Under favorable conditions, a round trip required fifteen days. With an estimated crop of 100 bales, this meant that two wagons would have to make at least six trips, which would require a full three months under the best conditions. This obviously would cut into time and profits, and, in fact, the plantation would be forced to pay others to haul the cotton at the rate of four dollars per bale.

Von Wrede concluded his report by expressing the hope that his proposal would meet with the approval of the leadership. It was not to be. Von Wrede traveled to Galveston and on May 29, 1845, met with Prince Solms and his newly arrived replacement, Johann Otto *Freiherr* von Meusebach. Von Wrede presented his proposals to Meusebach, but he did not agree with them. Meusebach intended to return to Nassau with von Wrede. Von Wrede hoped that once there, he would be able to persuade Meusebach of the efficacy of his proposals.

It is not known why Meusebach did not accept von Wrede's recommendations. They appear very reasonable in retrospect. Meusebach never explained his decision, but perhaps he desired to keep the plantation whole so that it could be better used as collateral.

Indeed, the money problems of the Society, which had gathered on the horizon like a threatening storm during Prince Solms' tenure, soon broke over Meusebach, with all the fury of a high plains tempest even as more immigrants arrived by the hundreds and thousands in the fall and winter of 1845-1846. Meusebach scrambled to get a handle on the situation and to provide for the settlers under his care. The plantation represented an important asset for the Society in Texas, which Meusebach and subsequent officials could use as collateral when the need to borrow money became acute.

After the departure of Prince Solms in May 1845, Friedrich von Wrede, Sr. returned to the plantation and his role as supervisor. He also continued to serve as a courier and agent in the business of the Society. This business took him once again to New Orleans. Von Wrede's last correspondence dates from July 1845. In this letter he reports on progress at the plantation and also sets forth his salary and living requirements should he remain as supervisor of the plantation.

In late October 1845, von Wrede rode to Austin on business for the Society and headed from there to New Braunfels accompanied by Lieutenant Oskar von Claren, another young aristocrat of the officer class, who had come into the service of the Society. The two camped at Live Oak Springs near present-day Manchaca about twelve miles south of Austin, a well-known camping spot for sojourners of the day between Austin and San Antonio.

It was also well known to the Indians. Unsuspecting, the two German officers made camp where they were overwhelmed by a party of renegade Indians who scalped and killed them. Their bodies were discovered soon thereafter by a party of U.S. soldiers who buried them with full military honors.

The news of the massacre created a sensation in Germany even as hundreds were preparing to depart for the New World. Many had pointed out that the German immigrants would face the threat of hostile Indians, especially in the grant area. But up until October 1845, the Society and its officials had enjoyed a remarkable streak of luck in their avoidance of any major incident. The deaths of Oskar von Claren and Friedrich von Wrede underscored that the Indian threat was real and foreshadowed a full generation of conflict and bloodshed in the

Hill Country area of Texas despite admirable efforts at reconciliation and peace.

The death of the elder von Wrede left the plantation to drift leaderless once again throughout the fall and winter of 1845-46—a leaderless slave plantation with an empty manor house.

Das Herrenhaus

CHAPTER 8

Das Herrenhaus

The tragic and unexpected death of Friedrich von Wrede, Sr., left the manor house to stand empty for several months. By placing the house a half-mile from the center of operations, Count Boos-Waldeck had placed class-consciousness above functionality, and this contributed to the inefficient administration of the plantation, as Friedrich von Wrede had pointed out. The house had been under construction for a full year, and it was nearly finished by the time of von Wrede's death.

It came to be widely known and celebrated as one of the finest houses on the Texas frontier.

When, for example, the celebrated Dr. Ferdinand Roemer visited the house during his travels in Texas in 1846, he described the house as charming and a cut above the average Texas frontier house.[1] Friedrich von Wrede, Sr., never given to exaggeration, characterized the house as *"schön,"* or "lovely."[2] Later, in 1850, Amanda Fallier von Rosenberg, spoke in a similar vein: "You also have no idea of what one calls a house in Texas—a rectangular room, high and airy, with a good roof is called here a house. Among these a house like ours, six years ago the best and still one of the best, is called a fort, a castle, a prince's house, a manor house. Our house is called all these things in jest, but it is pretty and, I may add, romantic."[3]

Boos-Waldeck had located the house on the crown of the most prominent hill in the league where a magnificent panorama opened up for 360 degrees. He put it about a half mile distant from the other buildings of the plantation: impractical, but socially palatable to a German nobleman. It nestled in a large mott of stately live oak trees, which provided shade to the south and east.

At first appearance, the house resembled many on the frontier. It was a story-and-a-half dogtrot[4] constructed of planked oak logs that were carefully notched and fitted at the corners, in a half-dovetail configuration.[5] Well prior to the construction of the *Herrenhaus,* German craftsmen of the area had mastered and employed this technique.[6]

Both Boos-Waldeck and Fordtran had singled out Wilhelm Etzel for praise for his work on the house. A picture emerges of Etzel in regard to certain characteristics of temperament: he was a volatile perfectionist who did not mind offending people if that was what it took to do a good job. This is what Fordtran meant when he reported that Etzel had kept everything in "military order." Under his supervision, the fit and finish on the house was most certainly excellent and a cut above the usual. Etzel's singular dedication to his work insured quality, but it also created problems. Two local German carpenters, Stuesse and Nelson, eventually quit because of his demanding and overbearing ways.

To build a frontier house of this style required dressing the logs with an adze to form a flat surface on both sides. This presented a more refined look than a full log house. This method left a gap of two to four inches between the logs. These spaces needed to be filled in with stones and mud, or mortar, if available. A house thus "chinked" became a substantial structure and a solid barrier against wind and rain.

The planked logs were fitted to construct two pens, or rooms, separated by a breezeway, or "dog trot." These were raised to a height sufficient to make a story and a half so that two more rooms could be added above the bottom two. A narrow stairway in the breezeway led to the second story. Over these pens, a roof was fitted which extended to cover two full-length porches on the long axis of the house. This created what is sometimes referred to as a "Louisiana" style roof. Wilhelm Etzel enclosed the porches with a balustrade sufficient to make it childproof.[7] The house sat on live oak stumps about two feet off the ground. There is some disagreement on what was used for flooring.[8] Shipping receipts suggest pine, but Amanda Fallier von Rosenberg described the floors as cedar.[9] Whether cedar or pine, we know it was sawed planking, and this represented an uncommon refinement at this point: sawed planking was considerably more expensive, and had to be shipped in.

The chimneys—one at each end of the house—stood out as the most refined feature. According to Dr. Ferdinand Roemer, they were made of dressed ashlar stone, which could be quarried in the vicinity. Ashlar counts as a very beautiful stone, suitable for decorative facings. Amanda Fallier von Rosenberg remarked that the chimneys were attractive and they worked well, providing ample heat with little smoke. The multitalented Wilhelm Etzel also supervised the construction of the chimneys.

The fireplaces apparently were used mainly for heat and not for cooking. The inventory of 1845 describes the house as having four rooms and a kitchen.[10] It is not clear whether the kitchen was attached to the main structure or whether it was placed next to the house, with an intervening space—for reasons of fire prevention and summer comfort, a common practice of the period.

Each room had two cutouts serving as windows that faced the porches. The doors to the rooms opened to the breezeway. At first, the windows were only shuttered; later, the lower two rooms were fitted with frames for multi-paned windows. The windows to the north had fifteen panes while the windows to the south were slightly larger with twenty panes each.[11] Wilhelm Etzel built all the tables, chairs, cabinets and beds for the house. His woodworking skills were considerable, with examples of his handiwork still extant. The quality of workmanship and the sophistication in design are both excellent.[12]

Count Boos-Waldeck, during his stay, dedicated one ground-floor room for his office and archive and the other for a dining room. This arrangement continued until the von Rosenberg family took up residence. Guests slept upstairs, or, if so inclined, on the porches on mattresses or in hammocks to take advantage of the evening breezes.

The compound around the house continued to expand. Boos-Waldeck started another building immediately to the east of the house. It was a barn with two partitions, one for the Negro servants and one for the horses. To finish it, Charles Fordtran contracted the work out, and it was completed by the time Solms-Braunfels and his party arrived in the summer of 1844. This structure was fourteen feet deep, fourteen feet high, and twenty-two feet in length. Later, Negro Jim, the blacksmith, and his family took up residence here. They also had constructed a pigeon house, a chicken coop, and a rabbit hutch. The inventory of 1844 also notes that a fence enclosed the entire compound.

The lack of easily accessible drinking water was a real problem for the *Herrenhaus,* and for the farm in general. The slave compound sat close to Jack's Creek upon which they depended for their water until the first well could be dug. The *Herrenhaus* was over a half mile from Jack's Creek, a great inconvenience. With our modern knowledge of bacterial contamination, one can imagine that the creek, under the best circumstances, was not the healthiest place to obtain drinking water. As it was, the creek became stagnant at the dry periods of the year, compounding the difficulty.

To solve this problem, Boos-Waldeck decided to dig a well. A well-known local, Abner Kuykendall,[13] was given the contract for the well, which was completed in February.[14] It, however, turned out to be less than satisfactory. It was prone to run dry during the summer, and the water, though sanitary, had an unsavory taste, probably from dissolved sulfur—an unfortunate feature in many shallow wells of the area.[15] Solms-Braunfels had the well deepened when it ran dry in the summer of 1844, and he ordered another well started for the *Herrenhaus*.

Later inhabitants solved the problem of lack of readily accessible drinking water by having a large underground cistern dug for the collection of rainwater from the roof. Prior to the introduction of windmills, cisterns of this sort dotted the landscape. They also served as crude refrigerators. Since they were underground, they maintained a constant temperature, which at this latitude is approximately seventy degrees, or the average annual mean temperature. Meat or milk lowered into the cistern on a rope would hold its freshness longer.

The German carpenters had put up the rough structure of the house in an amazingly short period of time—three weeks.[16] Wilhelm Etzel and his helpers continued working throughout the summer and the fall of 1843 and through the spring and summer of the following year.

The amount of work put into the *Herrenhaus* attests to its refinement. The inventory ordered by Solms-Braunfels in July 1844 allows us to compare values. The *Herrenhaus*, still in an unfinished state, is set at $1,200.[17] The overseer's house, by comparison, is appraised at $150. The *Herrenhaus* is actually assigned a value greater than all the other structures of the plantation combined. Interestingly, the porcelain tableware of the *Herrenhaus* is worth more than the combined value of the slave houses.[18]

These refinements, rather than the size of the house, probably impressed many visitors. And then, there were those cultured objects of domestic life more readily associated with a European salon than a Texas frontier home: a guitar, a feather mattress, the complete works of Schiller, a silver place setting for twelve, reference books on agriculture, porcelain, and linen tablecloths.

Fit and finish, silver and linen, tasteful furniture, pretty chimneys, a high hill with patriarchal live oak trees—all these things combined to create a warm and inviting impression. It is understandable, then, that the house came to enjoy a reputation as one of the finer dwellings in the area.

As charming as it was, the *Herrenhaus* can be viewed as a metaphor for what was wrong with the plantation. It represented an enormous expenditure of time, energy, and money which could have been better applied.

CHAPTER 9

The Plantation and Agriculture in Fayette County

When Joseph Count of Boos-Waldeck viewed the Jack League for the first time in the fall of 1842, he found the area sparsely populated with nearly all the settlers engaged in rudimentary farming and animal husbandry in one way or another. Industry, such as existed, centered on a handful of sawmills and gristmills and a smattering of blacksmith shops and similar businesses playing a supportive role to agriculture. Economic activity of all forms was embryonic and disorganized. The intrepid pioneers prior to 1840 appeared to have spent as much collective energy fighting the Indians and organizing expeditions against the Mexicans as they did developing their farms and businesses.[1]

As the Indian threat waned and the pioneers gained confidence that they could successfully repulse any attempt by Mexico to reassert her authority, the situation began to change; slowly at first, then more rapidly, gathering steam in an almost logarithmic progression of growth and development. By 1850, scores had moved into the northern part of the county and established viable farms. The acreages were still large, on the average 427 acres, with, as a rough rule of thumb, about 12 percent of the land in cultivation and the rest reserved for grazing.[2]

In the county as a whole, there were slightly fewer than 10,000 acres in production, with about 80,000 acres in unimproved pasture. Fayette County, with a total area of 950 square miles (608,000 acres), had less than 15 percent of the land in use by 1850. Much vacant land remained upon which to settle fresh immigrants from Europe and to relocate Americans from other states.

The settlers planted cotton and corn almost exclusively, with cotton being the main cash crop. They planted corn to feed their horses and poultry, winter the milk cows, and fatten the swine. The excess they sold or bartered to advantage. In 1850, only seven farmers in Fayette County raised tobacco, and all but one of these were German.

The average farm kept several yoke of oxen for plowing, a couple of mules for pulling wagons, a large number of pigs and a few head of cattle for milking, for food and for hides. A large market for beef cattle had not yet developed. In addition every farmstead kept a large flock of chickens, and sometimes turkeys and geese.

The farms were largely self-sufficient. Nearly all had large gardens with potatoes, especially sweet potatoes, as mainstays. Peas were also important. All kept pigs, and the numbers, as revealed by the agricultural census, often astound: Otto von Roeder, for example, owned one hundred pigs in 1850, and this was not unusual.

This attests to the importance of this, the most versatile and adaptive of all farm animals.

Lured by the prospect of cheap, virgin land, most of the settlers in the area had moved from the southern United States. Of the 475 families in the county in 1850, 297, or 63 percent, came from the core states of the South, with the majority coming from Tennessee (14 percent), closely followed by Kentucky (11 percent), and Virginia (8 percent).

Cotton, corn, and tobacco, the staples of the South, are hungry crops, taking much from the soil and giving little back. In the days prior to commercial fertilizers, yields quickly went down as the soil was depleted. It would be time to move on. A pattern developed with a concomitant mentality: you used and then you moved. For many of the Anglo planters, the move to Texas represented the second or third translocation. The census shows that the majority of these farmers came from one state while their spouse came from another. The explanation: by the time children reached marrying age, the families often found themselves on another farm in another state.

The census reveals a smattering of fresh immigrants from the British Isles (sixteen families), but by far the majority of foreign-born in the area hail from the German-speaking areas of Europe with 106 families or 22 percent of the total number of families in the county. Already, by 1850, they had begun to concentrate in the Round Top and Fayetteville areas. By 1860, this trend is unmistakable, with German-surname farmers forming the majority in these areas. Czech-speaking immigrants did not begin appearing in significant numbers until after 1850, and even in 1860 their numbers are relatively small.

The 1840 tax rolls list 360 male taxpayers in Fayette County. Of these, fifty, or 14 percent, owned slaves. There were 206 slaves in the county. By 1850 for every four farmers in the county, three were slaveholders. Of the 210 farms in the county, 172 had slaves. The total slave population was 1,016 and the total free population was 2,760. Slaves made up 27 percent of the population. The average slaveholder owned about six slaves.

Many slaveholders were drawn to northern Fayette County in the 1840s by the same considerations that had led Boos-Waldeck to locate there: a well-watered region offering a favorable combination of open and wooded land; also, a black, virgin soil, which seemed promising for cotton and corn.

The largest of the Anglo slaveholders in the Round Top area in 1850 was C. H. (Kit) Taylor with thirty-three slaves. Other prominent slaveholders in the area were Isaac Lafayette Hill (fifteen slaves), J. R. Robison (eleven slaves), and Hamilton Ledbetter (eleven slaves). Otto von Roeder with twenty-seven slaves counted as one of the largest slaveholders in the county, but was in every other respect an anomaly. Very few Germans (about 4 percent) owned slaves. This pattern continued through the 1860 census.[3]

By 1860, the number of persons engaged in agriculture in the county had grown to over 1,200. Thus the number of farmers tripled from 1840 to 1850 (67 to 210) and quintupled from 1850 to 1860 (210 to 1,200). Likewise, the number of slaveholders almost tripled in the decade (172 to 499). Slave numbers increased even more in real numbers and as a proportion of the population (1,016 to 3,786 and 27 percent to 33 percent).

Nassau Plantation followed this general trend. Seventeen slaves—seven men, seven women and three children—were originally purchased. Two of them escaped—Washington and his brother Joshua—and in the summer of 1844 a female, Mary, died, so that in one year nearly 18 percent of the slaves disappeared—a significant loss, as Prince Solms had been quick to point out. Even so, by the inventory of 1848, solely through the addition of children born to the slaves, the slave count had risen to twenty-five, or a 41—percent increase in just three years. Despite violent dislocations, hard work and primitive living conditions, the slave women successfully gave birth to ten children.

All these facts and figures document an optimistic period, bringing prosperity to many and astounding increases in personal wealth to a few. Times were good until the upheavals of the Civil War brought slavery to an end and ushered in a period of painful transition to a new social and economic model. But certainly, throughout the 1840s and 1850s, the southern slave plantation was the dominant economic and social model for the county. The daunting job of clearing, fencing, plowing, and building had been accomplished in large part by the forced labor of Negro slaves.

Mindful of notable exceptions, such as Otto von Roeder, and a few others, the German settlers, in contrast, developed their modest holdings by their own or hired labor. Thus, for Fayette County (and also for the surrounding counties of Austin, Washington, and Colorado, whose demographic patterns reflect similar trends), a different model arose on a smaller scale simultaneously and coexistent with the slave plantation, namely the modest, free-labor farms of the German immigrants.[4]

The central role of slavery in the early development of Texas certainly illuminates why Count Boos-Waldeck leaned toward a slave plantation in the first place: the model made sense to him both economically and psychologically. Psychologically, it echoed the hierarchical social structure of Europe with which he was familiar and comfortable; economically, it held out the best hope for a quick return on investment, which he understood to be the chief goal of the Society.

But in the midst of this period of general prosperity, Nassau faltered. What went wrong? Boos-Waldeck, as it turned out, was a dilettante with respect to agriculture. After six months in 1843, sobered by events and experience, he confessed as much. He had bought slaves in New Orleans who had never worked in the fields and (with the exception of Negro Jim) were inept in the use of common farm tools such as axes and adzes.

This was a fundamental mistake, because the slaves, at over $7,000, represented the largest single capital outlay, costing even more than the land. Most of the Anglo plantation owners, in contrast, had brought their slaves with them. Moreover, they had been acquired (and paid for) over a long period of time, and their initial acquisitions had grown through natural increase. Then, as now, it is very difficult, if not impossible, to purchase an agricultural enterprise lock, stock, and barrel and expect it to pay for itself.

Next, Boos-Waldeck had insisted on placing a river-bottom

plantation with the traditional river-bottom crops of corn and cotton in an upland setting. The results were predictable. Boos-Waldeck had said that he was willing to trade a 5 percent reduction in fertility for the healthier setting. The reduction in yield, however, was more like 50 percent. The lessened fertility was compounded by the heavy clay soils where he located his fields, which made plowing much more tedious and demanding. Had they been asked, the overseers Bryan and (subsequently) Denman and Durand probably could have foretold these problems. As it was, they no doubt felt the pressure to produce results. This may have led, in the case of Bryan, to abuse of the slaves and to the loss of two of the youngest and ablest.

Even so, neighboring Anglo planters had been successful under the same conditions. It simply had required more in the way of labor and effort than Boos-Waldeck had anticipated, and thus his timetable for developing the plantation had been naively unrealistic.

Even if the plantation had produced bumper crops of cotton and corn, the problems of transportation and undeveloped markets in the early 1840s would have challenged its resources. Cash crops, especially cotton, would have to be hauled by wagon east along Gotier's Trace[5] to San Felipe, where steamboat service to the coast existed, or all the way to Houston. True, cotton brokers had set up shop in La Grange by 1844.[6] These, however, only negotiated prices for cotton; they did not accept shipment.

The ever-present tension between Anglo overseers and German supervisors also compromised the productivity of the farm. The German masters of Nassau were never quite comfortable with their Anglo help: Charles Fordtran quarreled with Bryan, Prince Solms did not like Denman, and Friedrich von Wrede did not trust Durand. The turnover in leadership, a natural result of these tensions, undercut the patterns of continuity and rhythm in the tasks of the plantation, which are prerequisites to success in any agricultural endeavor.

The location of the *Herrenhaus* so far away from the main compound of the plantation was inherently inefficient, causing problems of communication and coordination, as Friedrich von Wrede correctly pointed out.

The problem of divided purpose bedeviled the plantation from the beginning. Boos-Waldeck had contemplated the plantation primarily as an investment that would grow in value and provide a predictable return. Once Count Castell wedded the Society to a land grant, the role and purpose of the plantation necessarily changed: its primary role twisted to support the larger purpose which undercut the ability of the plantation to focus on its own needs.

Above all, the German noblemen lacked patience. Believing that time was running out, they had rushed into the venture. After one year, Prince Solms arrived and judged the situation severely. He lacked the perspective to realize that Fordtran and Bryan (and, of course, the slaves) had accomplished much in a short period of time. Despite various setbacks and distractions, the plantation was on track to become profitable and to participate in the great economic and agricultural boom of the 1850s. The worst mistake was to surrender the plantation for a pittance on the eve of its promise. In this, the plantation reflected in microcosm the larger failure of the Society in its colonization efforts.

While Nassau Plantation faltered, an Anglo neighbor to the north, Sam Lewis, prospered. Sam Lewis came from South Carolina to Texas with his family in 1838 where he received a patent for 640 acres in Brazoria County. He first appeared in Fayette County in the latter part of the 1840s. Later, in 1848, he became a neighbor to Nassau Plantation on the north when he acquired the homestead site of the William Townsend quarter league.[7] This site is now the center for the University of Texas' Winedale Historical Center. He also acquired additional acreages in the area.

The tax records and census reveal a steady growth in Sam Lewis' net worth. He was a shrewd businessman who often supplemented his farm income through activity as a surveyor, sometimes taking payment in land. The 1840 tax record, however, showed that he owned five slaves.[8] The 1850 census listed him as forty-three years old with a wife and eight children and an estate valued at $8,000. By the 1860 census his real estate had grown to a value of $60,000, his personal property to $28,000, and he owned thirteen slaves.

This represents an astonishing appreciation in wealth over a relatively short period of time. By the time of his death in 1867, his land holdings had grown to 2,356 acres in Fayette County and over 6,000 acres in ten other counties. Even with the steep depreciation in land values following the end of the Civil War, he died a wealthy man. This rise in personal wealth, acquired for the most part through agriculture, was accomplished next door to Nassau Plantation. What had Sam Lewis done so differently?

Certainly he was an astute dealmaker, as the trade for the "Peach Orchard" discussed in Chapter 2, suggests. He also was quick to seize opportunities. He is said to have set up a cotton gin at his farm.[9] It is not clear whether steam or mules powered it, but in addition to being a cotton planter himself, which is costly, labor intensive, and risky, he provided the service of ginning, thus an additional stream of cash.

Lewis diversified in several other profitable ways. He kept a large number of pigs—500 by the 1860 agricultural census—certainly a number in excess of his own needs, which leads to the conjecture that he either raised them for sale or cured and sold the excess meat.

He also raised and trained mules. This region of Texas, as Count Boos-Waldeck had realized, but failed to capitalize upon, was ideal for raising livestock, and of all forms of livestock (other than fine riding horses), mules were the most valuable. Mules were the diesel engines of the American West: durable, powerful and efficient.[10] Their great disadvantage, in addition to being willful and sometimes mean, is that they cannot reproduce on their own. For stagecoach operators and freighters, the mule was the preferred animal. When he died in 1867, Sam Lewis owned seventy-five jacks and jennies, more than anyone else in the county. They were used most certainly for the breeding of mules.

It is now taken as an article of faith that Lewis enlarged his house (now restored and open to the public as the Lewis-Wagner House at the University of Texas' Winedale Historical Center) to serve as a stage stop and to provide room and board to the wayfarers. The evidence for this is actually quite thin. More likely, he provided mules on a contract basis for the various stage lines and freighters that serviced the area, and through this association the idea arose that he operated an inn.

Whatever the truth may be, it is clear that even as Nassau Plantation sank deeper into debt, a neighbor prospered. This could lead to harsh judgment of the plantation and its masters, but this would not be entirely fair. It is not fair because the plantation had an importance for agriculture that perhaps transcends judgments based on immediate financial success.

The plantation became an unusual meeting ground of different practices and mentalities. Count Boos-Waldeck had patterned his plantation on the southern model, but he did so through the unmistakable filter of his European background. Subsequent directors, especially Friedrich von Wrede, continued experimenting with an eye toward giving the plantation a more European flavor, and these experiments, seen in the larger context, are significant.

The *Herrenhaus* and its compound hosted many of these innovations. Charles Fordtran laid out a sizeable garden to the north and fenced it. Here they planted many of the stock vegetables of the South: watermelons, sweet potatoes, peas, corn, etc. They put in an orchard, planting both fig and peach trees. But they also ordered seeds from Germany with which to experiment.

Friedrich von Wrede continued and expanded this idea. In the summer of 1845, he requested from Germany an extensive wish list of seeds, cuttings, and rootstock along with elaborate instructions on how to pack and ship them. The vegetables included different varieties of beans and peas, cauliflower, broccoli, savoy cabbage, beets, radishes, and several kinds of potatoes. He had ambitious plans to expand the orchard with apricot, mirabelle (French plum), and cherry trees. He also ordered different berries, including raspberries and currants, and rootstock for various varieties of grapes. All these items were packed and shipped to von Wrede in October 1845.[11] Unfortunately, he died at the hands of a renegade band of Indians before he could realize his plans.

Boos-Waldeck speculated that sheep could be a profitable endeavor, but the local race of Mexican sheep, in his opinion, needed to be upgraded by Saxon rams and he requested that some be sent over for this purpose.¹² Cattle, horses and pigs—these were the big three for livestock production for the average Anglo settler. Boos-Waldeck never received his Saxon rams, but Peter Carl von Rosenberg, upon buying the *Herrenhaus* and 800 acres in 1850, brought his idea to fruition with the purchase of 100 head of sheep. His son, Carl Wilhelm, reported that Otto von Roeder had imported rams from Germany with which to improve the local breed.¹³ Thus the German settlers at Nassau introduced sheep production to the area as the agriculture census of 1860 indicates.

The same held for viticulture.¹⁴ Many Germans had noticed right away that Texas hosted a vigorous native grape, the Mustang grape,¹⁵ which seems to have a symbiotic relationship with large live oak trees. The vines often grow to enormous size and reach a very old age, rising to intertwine and cover the crowns of the old patriarchal live oaks. They produce prodigious amounts of grapes year after year out with no intervention on the part of humans. There are resistant to drought, disease, and insects. The only problem was that these grapes are extremely acidic, and in order to mask the acidity one had to make the wine very sweet, too sweet for the average person's palate.¹⁶

Friedrich von Wrede received advice on how to pack European wine stock for the long trip overseas from a local German Texan, Johann Leyendecker,¹⁷ who had settled early north of Columbus in 1843, about twenty miles south of Nassau Plantation. Leyendecker apparently came from Europe with a sophisticated understanding of the intricate techniques of grafting and transplanting. His son, Johann Friedrich, subsequently founded a nursery and began experimenting on how to graft European varieties of grapes onto the local stock.¹⁸

The balance between wooded land and open prairie, so nicely displayed in the Jack League, had impressed Boos-Waldeck upon first sight. Later, he drew up a comprehensive plan for its proper management, and this plan was included in a subsequent lease agreement recorded in the Fayette County courthouse. Careful husbandry of woodland resources reflected a centuries-old German custom.¹⁹

The Meusebach-Schubbert lease is quite instructive. The document contains over fifteen provisions that specify in detail how the fields, the livestock, the buildings, and the forests of the plantation are to be managed. The contract also obligates the lessee to plant a vineyard and to maintain and expand the orchard and garden. There is a whole section devoted to the forests. All in all, the document confirms that the Germans were deeply dedicated to innovating, upgrading, and improving all aspects of the plantation in accordance with the most advanced agricultural practices of the period.

Small grains—wheat, barley, oats and rye—were crops not normally planted by the local Anglo farmers. They were certainly not staples of the traditional plantation, which concentrated on the big four: cotton, corn, tobacco, and sugar cane, which had been reduced for the most part to cotton and corn in this part of Fayette County. Boos-Waldeck had said that he thought the plantation was suitable for wheat.[20] Friedrich von Wrede was absolutely convinced that wheat and oats would do well at Nassau. He fully intended to plant wheat in the fall of 1845. Unfortunately, his untimely death precluded this experiment.

Many Germans associated with the Society also seemed keen to experiment with small grains. The German Protestant pastor Ervendberg, for instance, in a long article about the agricultural possibilities of Texas, forecast that one day winter wheat would become a major cash crop in Texas.[21] He was a visionary because his prediction, at least on this point, proved correct.[22] It was not an opinion widely shared at the time, and, indeed, the belief that Texas had a climate unsuitable to small grains possibly had serious consequences for the Society.

The world-renowned naturalist Alexander von Humboldt, as noted, had been commissioned to give an official assessment, or "*Gutachten*," concerning the feasibility of German immigration in Texas. Subsidies from the Prussian government depended largely on his conclusions. In the end Humboldt advised against subsidies.[23] Certain intriguing comments in the Solms-Braunfels Archives suggest that this judgment, at least in part, was based on his belief that Texas was unsuitable for the cultivation of small grains.[24]

Why was this so important? Many felt that "Germanic" culture, taken in the broadest sense to include groups as diverse as the Scandinavians and the English, was deeply wedded at all levels to the cultivation of small grains, and that Germanic culture could not be successfully transplanted and sustained in a climate unsuitable to them. To put it in the simplest terms, Germans could not stay Germanic without wheat, rye, and barley. Bread, beer, animal husbandry, village life—all depended on the cultivation of these grains, and the circle widened to embrace all aspects of life. We can appreciate, then, why the Germans at Nassau, and elsewhere in Texas, hoped to successfully cultivate wheat and other grains. Amanda Fallier von Rosenberg put it succinctly when she stated that she really did prefer wheat bread to the ubiquitous cornbread of frontier Texas.[25]

The positive German contributions to horticulture, animal husbandry, and agriculture in general in Texas have been well documented. The Agricultural Society at Cat Spring,[26] reputedly the earliest such organization in Texas, was certainly the most visible and enduring manifestation of this tendency in South Central Texas.

In Nassau Plantation, we sense the reflection of this: a desire to innovate, but to do so in a way that was lasting and sustainable. This experimentation no doubt contributed (at least in financial terms) to the eventual "failure" of the plantation, for many of its experiments did not work out, and, in any case, were undercut by the larger problems and uncertainties of the Society. Prince Solms complained about this very point. Nevertheless, it was important in a broader sense: it offered an alternative not only in technique, but also in attitude. The plantation did not survive, but many of the ideas and attitudes, for which it was one of the first in the area to give expression, did persist. In them, one senses a counterpoint to the "use and remove" mentality, and the genesis of what has grown into the modern sensibility for innovative and "sustainable" agriculture.

The central role of slavery in the early development of Texas certainly illuminates why Count Boos-Waldeck leaned toward a slave plantation in the first place: the model made sense to him both economically and psychologically. Psychologically, it echoed the hierarchical social structure of Europe with which he was familiar and comfortable; economically, it held out the best hope for a quick return on investment, which he understood to be the chief goal of the Society.

But the census figures clearly show that the great majority of Germans in South Central Texas rejected slavery. Why did so many German immigrants reject slavery? Was this rejection primarily ideological, or economic, or was it a visceral response conditioned by deep cultural differences? Prior to 1848-49, when many German intellectuals came to the United States and Texas, the great majority of immigrants were either farmers or tradesmen. Their rejection of slavery appears to lie in the tradition of skilled labor, which had roots in the medieval guild system. By this system, the so-called *Zunftwesen*, almost all jobs—even menial jobs—were done by people who were highly skilled and trained. Out of this tradition rose a reputation for quality that is still associated with German manufacturing today. The Germans could not reconcile this tradition with slavery, where work was done by illiterate, unskilled bondsmen.

They created a new kind of farm in the area—one sustained by free labor and embodying attitudes of permanence and continuity. Slavery, on the other hand, spawned a predatory attitude toward the land. Germans wanted to establish orchards, manage the forests, plant vineyards, import new strains of sheep, and cultivate fruit trees and vegetables. But a slave plantation meant cotton, corn, and tobacco—all crops which quickly depleted the soil—leading to a pattern, repeated throughout the South and clearly seen in Fayette and surrounding counties, of use, abuse, and move. It proved difficult, if not impossible, to reconcile slave plantations with notions of permanence and sustainability. The attempt to do this at Nassau Plantation contributed markedly to its failure as a profitable agricultural entity.

CHAPTER 10

Die Katastrophe

October 29, 1847: a crisp fall pre-dawn morning at the compound of the *Herrenhaus* at Nassau Plantation. The distinct sound of the cocking of guns disturbs the morning calm. A shotgun blast suddenly shatters the quiet, followed by an eruption of gunfire lasting several minutes. Captain Frederick Somers, an Anglo-American, who had just stepped out of the manor house at Nassau Plantation into the morning chill of the veranda, receives a deadly charge of buckshot to the body, staggers and falls to the ground. Dr. Schubert and the others in the house quickly rouse themselves and grab their weapons. Absalom

Bostick rushes out the door and, although fired upon several times, manages to discharge his shotgun. Conrad Caspar Rohrdorf, a Swiss-German artist and naturalist in the party of attackers, falls mortally wounded with three slugs in the cheek. Panicked by the unexpectedly vigorous defense and the mortal wounding of one of their own, the attackers withdraw in disorder, leaving their dying comrade behind. Word quickly goes out and creates a sensation, for Captain Somers, a prominent Freemason, is well known and respected in the county. A posse forms and apprehends Ernst Sörghel, whose farm adjoins the plantation, but Hermann Spiess, newly appointed commissioner-general of the German Emigration Co. in Texas and leader of the party of attackers, flees on the slain Rohrdorf's horse and eludes capture.[1]

Thus took place the most dramatic story associated with the plantation, an event that created an uproar both in Texas and in Europe. In Fayette County it provoked another shootout (and killing), led to a sensational trial, divided the county into factions, and prompted, according to one account, the formation of a secret vigilante committee composed of both Anglos and Texas-Germans. A future governor of Texas, A. J. Hamilton, served as an attorney for the Society while a former secretary of state, James S. Mayfield, emerged as a behind-the-scene conspirator on the Schubert side. Because of Mayfield's involvement, the shooting thrust the plantation (and the Society) into the forefront of the pro-slavery, anti-immigrant debate in the state, which had arisen prior to annexation, a heated debate in which Mayfield, a member of the legislature, had spoken vociferously in favor of limiting European immigration. Thus the affair had a significance that went well beyond any internal dispute within the German Emigration Co. Still, for the Society itself, the shootout was a disaster on several counts, for it exacerbated tensions, squandered time, money, and energy, and, in general, plunged the Society into disrepute at a time when it was desperate for favorable publicity. Little wonder then that the whole affair came to be known by the Germans as the *Katastrophe* (catastrophe).[2]

To unravel the history of this violent episode it will be necessary to examine the challenges that confronted Johann Otto *Freiherr* von Meusebach upon his arrival in Texas in the spring of 1845 as the designated replacement for Prince Solms-Braunfels. It is also necessary to review the considerations that led him to engage Dr. Schubbert to be the director of the Fredericksburg colony, for it was this association that set into motion the train of events that culminated in the shootout at the plantation.

By consensus, Meusebach is regarded as a bright spot in a sometimes-stained story—integrity, dedication, and courage—all these attributes apply. His presence commanded respect: a long flowing beard and flaming red hair seemed to accent an imposing stature and countenance. Buffalo Hump,[3] one of the Comanche war chiefs with whom he negotiated a treaty in the spring of 1847, dubbed him "El Sol Colorado," the flaming red sun.

Outwardly autocratic and aloof, inwardly he believed deeply in democracy and his adopted country. To drive this point home, he anglicized his name to John and dropped the aristocratic appellation "von." This attitude set him apart from nearly all others of importance in the Society and put him in tune with the spirit of his adopted country. History, therefore, generally regards him with a favorable eye. He has been the subject of numerous articles, a biography, and a historical novel.[4]

The challenges facing Meusebach were daunting. The bulk of the colonists arrived during his tenure. Upon assuming the reins of authority in 1845, he quickly grasped the magnitude of the colonists' dilemma and realized that the Society's financial and administrative resources were woefully inadequate to its obligations. Creditors hounded him with old bills to pay, the legacy of Nassau Plantation's expenses, Solms-Braunfels' extravagances, and the unforeseen costs of the immigrants.

The future promised even greater outlays. Still, there was hope for eventual success. The creaky machine teetered forward, but without lubrication it would soon fall dead in its tracks, and money was the lubricant it needed. Meusebach stressed in his first report that it was the financial mess which threatened the whole enterprise and that if timely and substantial infusions of capital were not forthcoming, the whole venture would collapse.[5]

The amount required, Meusebach quickly grasped, would exceed by a large margin anything that his naïve colleagues in Germany had anticipated. The fears that Boos-Waldeck had voiced in 1843 were coming true; the "Big Plan" was cascading toward financial disaster and human tragedy.

Meusebach needed to deal with the immediate crisis of feeding, housing, and transporting the hundreds of settlers who had already been deposited by the shipload on the beaches of Lavaca Bay at Indian Point and in Galveston even as he made preparations for the thousands still scheduled to arrive. The outbreak of the Mexican War had led to the requisition by the U.S. Army of most of the wagons which Henry Francis Fischer had hired to move the immigrants from Indian Point to New Braunfels. Horses, mules, and vehicles of any kind had become scarce and expensive commodities. Hundreds were stranded on the beach. An epidemic broke out, which carried away the weak, the old, and the young by the scores.[6] The first half of 1846 was a dreadful period for the immigrants.[7]

There was another, gathering threat. Throughout 1846 a wave of discontent spread among the settlers who had reached New Braunfels. The hardships, the lack of transportation, the epidemics, the mass deaths, the frustrations, and the failure of the Society to redeem monies it had collected from the emigrants in Germany all culminated in an unrest which threatened to break out into open rebellion. Meusebach's imperious nature clashed with the needs of the moment, which called for empathy and openness.[8] Still, in December 1846, he bravely faced down a mob threatening to lynch him, and by so doing, defused the situation.

In truth, as many letters and reports in the Solms-Braunfels bear witness, Meusebach could be a distant, difficult and untactful man. He was quick to criticize and slow to praise. By virtue of his education, he could usually carry the day when it came to words, but in practical knowledge, many found him deficient. He did not conceal his atheism, which alienated many of his colleagues and offended most colonists. He was also disorderly in his personal habits, which led to procrastination and a shuffling distractedness in his demeanor. Often, for instance, he would work late into the night but sleep until noon, or later. These habits stood in contradiction to the goal of imposing strict discipline on the bureaucracy in Texas, especially in financial matters.

Meusebach's relationship with the leadership in Germany had been strained from the beginning. They were suspicious of his democratic beliefs and uncomfortable with the fact that he came from the lower, rather than the upper, nobility. They felt that he was not diligent enough in accounting for the monies sent to him and deficient in reporting back to Germany.[9] They distrusted him; he came to scorn them.

In a move that exacerbated the mutual distrust, Count Castell dispatched a trained bureaucrat and accountant, Philip Cappes, to act as a kind of ombudsman in Texas. He arrived in July 1846 with a new line of credit. He was instructed by Count Castell to survey the situation, keep an eye on Meusebach, and send detailed and timely financial reports back to Germany. The presence of Cappes provided another source of friction as those settlers and bureaucrats who were disgruntled and disaffected intrigued with Cappes to further undermine Meusebach's authority.[10]

Throughout his tenure as commissioner-general, from the spring of 1845 to the summer of 1847, Meusebach struggled with these challenges. He reduced duplication, clarified lines of authority, and otherwise imposed a sense of discipline and order on the bureaucracy in Texas, resulting in a noticeable improvement from 1846 to 1847.[11] He attempted to communicate the seriousness of the situation in Texas to the leadership in Germany. When funds were not forthcoming, he went public with his accusations in an effort to shame the leadership in Germany into meeting its obligations.[12] He made arrangements to feed and house the settlers in New Braunfels and to expedite the transportation of those still stranded at Indian Point. He did what he could to keep the growing army of creditors at bay. He suffered the meddling of the unwelcome Cappes. He faced down the mob in New Braunfels whose frustrations and sufferings had led them to the point of open rebellion.

During this period more than any other, the resources of the plantation were used to support the larger mission of the Society. This great mass of people, who were deposited on the beaches near Indian

Point on Lavaca Bay, had to be supplied with food and shelter and then transported inland to New Braunfels and, a portion, thereafter, to Friedrichsburg (Fredericksburg).

The overseer Durand was borrowed from the plantation and put in charge of a wagon train possibly using slaves as teamsters. (Meusebach reported that he had engaged fourteen slaves as teamsters.[13]) Wagons and horses from the plantation were pressed into service to support this effort. Under the circumstances it was amazing that any work on the plantation was accomplished.

Meusebach spent the first part of 1846 in Galveston and New Orleans doing the best he could to raise new funds, forestall the collection of old debts, and assist the boatloads of immigrants who were beginning to arrive. In April he removed to Nassau Plantation where he stayed until the middle of July. Some have criticized him for his four-month stay at Nassau, saying that he fled to the plantation to escape the wrath of the settlers in New Braunfels and to otherwise avoid his responsibilities.[14] Rumors of gastronomical excesses while at the plantation, which may have had some basis in fact, did not help his reputation.[15] In truth, there were good reasons for his stay.[16] The plantation's intermediate location made it easier to coordinate among the merchants in Houston and Galveston, the bankers in New Orleans, the fresh immigrants at Indianola, and the settlement in New Braunfels.

It was during this stay that Meusebach made contact with Otto von Roeder, and through him, with many of the corn planters in the area to supply the immigrants with corn. Apparently, he also reached an agreement with Charles Fordtran to supply beef.[17]

In respect to the Fischer-Miller grant, Meusebach took several concrete steps, which must be examined in greater detail, since they tie directly into the story of the shootout at the plantation.

The land grants offered by the Republic of Texas in 1842 were not gifts; they were conditional contracts, and failure to satisfy the terms rendered the contracts void. The Fischer-Miller contract concluded with the Republic of Texas (and extended once Texas became a state), specified that 600 families, or single men over the age of seventeen, be settled within the limits of grant area by September

1847.[18] Failure to do so would constitute material breach and the Society would forfeit its claims to the hundreds of thousands of acres of bonus and premium lands.

It was upon these lands that the Society staked its hopes. Through the future sale of these parcels it hoped to recover its expenses and reap its reward. Time, however, was running out. By this point the plans of the Society were in a race with bankruptcy, which, by 1847, appeared imminent: if it could fulfill all the terms of the contract and gain title to the hundreds of thousands of acres to which it was entitled before collapsing into insolvency, then it could gain a second life by using these lands as collateral.

The Society had actually cleared the first hurdle by bringing over more than 2,000 families and single men into the republic by January 1, 1846. The second hurdle was to move 600 of these into the grant by September 1847. In order to ensure eventual success and to redeem the costs and sacrifices already made, then, Meusebach needed to expedite the movement of settlers into the Fischer-Miller grant. New Braunfels, where most of the settlers had concentrated, had only been contemplated as a kind of way station, and it was nearly a hundred miles removed from the grant area.

The Llano River formed the southern boundary of the Fischer-Miller grant and this was many scores of miles north of the settlement at New Braunfels. In consideration of this point, Meusebach contracted to buy a large block of land, 10,000 acres, on the Pedernales River about halfway between New Braunfels and the Llano River. Here in February 1846, an expedition of thirty-six men finished the survey of the settlement to be known as Friedrichsburg, later anglicized to Fredericksburg.[19] The idea was to establish this settlement as a final steppingstone into the grant.

Meusebach needed a director for this proposed settlement, someone who incorporated force of personality, administrative ability, and experience on the Texas frontier. He thought he had found such a man in the person of Dr. Schubbert, to whom he was introduced by Henry Francis Fischer in the spring of 1846.[20] Meusebach invited Schubbert to visit him at the plantation in April 1846, and it was here that he offered him the directorship of the Friedrichsburg settlement.

Initially, Schubbert balked at the offer. As an inducement, Meusebach offered to lease the plantation to Schubbert for six years once he had gotten the new settlement on its feet.[21] Meusebach hoped to kill two birds with one stone with this arrangement. On the one hand, he hoped to get a competent director for the new settlement of Friedrichsburg (at least in its formative stages); on the other hand, he hoped to relieve the Society of the administrative (and monetary) burden of the plantation.

One solid benefit of the plantation remained: it would continue to serve as a convenient home base between the colonies to the west and the populated centers to the east. By the terms of the extensive lease, drawn up by Meusebach and filed of record in La Grange, Dr. Schubbert was obliged to house and feed at his own cost officials of the Society who might be passing through. He also had to stable, feed, and shoe their horses.[22] Since the plantation would remain in the possession of the Society, it could also continue to be used as collateral, which emerged as a guiding consideration.

After completing the agreement in July 1846, Meusebach and Schubbert left the plantation together for New Braunfels. By now all but about 300 people had been transported from Indian Point on the coast to New Braunfels.[23] In October Schubbert proceeded with some of the colonists to Friedrichsburg.[24] In December he attempted a scouting expedition into the Fischer-Miller grant north of the Llano River, but turned back without making contact with the Indians, or accomplishing anything significant.[25]

Essentially leaderless since the death of Friedrich von Wrede in October 1845, the plantation had been left to drift. Meusebach had appointed Hermann Wilke, an official of the Society stationed at Indian Point, to be interim supervisor in January 1846. Wilke paid a visit to the plantation in January 1847, but as the Society's engineer, surveyor and mapmaker, he faced the same dilemma that had confronted von Wrede: he had other, more pressing responsibilities that left him little time to devote to the plantation and its needs.

Dr. Schubbert became aware of the situation, and with an eye toward his future lease did not want to see the plantation completely fall apart. He notified Philip Cappes that he had sent word to Charles

Fordtran and asked him to visit the plantation.[26] Fordtran responded, and in January 1847 wrote to Dr. Schubbert about a recent visit to the plantation.[27] He reported that he had been pleasantly surprised to see that the slaves, under the direction of Negro Jim, were going about the work of plowing and other tasks, as if they were pursuing their own interests. He impressed upon Jim the importance of this period for him and what trust and confidence he could gain by doing a good job. Fordtran stated that he needed the keys to the warehouse so that the slaves could be issued new clothing.

Fordtran suggested to Schubbert that an arrangement be reached whereby Negro Jim would in fact become the overseer under Fordtran's supervision. This arrangement was confirmed with the tacit approval of Meusebach,[28] and thus, in an improbable twist, a slave, by his devotion and competence, rose to become the overseer of Nassau Plantation for a good part of the year 1847.

Dr. Schubbert presided over the Friedrichsburg colony as its director from October 1846 to July 1847. For this reason, he is sometimes referred to as the "Father" of the city. But it was also during this period that serious questions came to the fore. His critics charged that he ruled by a combination of capriciousness, intimidation, and cronyism.[29] Meusebach later charged that he was extravagant in the supplies he purchased and deficient in the accounting of their use. He also intimated that Dr. Schubbert had profited personally from the sale of alcoholic spirits, which he had shipped in at the Society's expense in generous quantities. Apparently impressed by the industry and communal structure of a group of Mormons who had settled nearby,[30] Schubbert also had encouraged a communal approach to building the infrastructure of the town, such as the *Vereinskirche* (Society Church) and the mill. He insisted that the settlers farm their first crop communally in a field which he laid out for that purpose. Thereafter, the cultivated land would be divided by lot. Meusebach disagreed with this approach because he felt it made the settlers too dependent on the Society.[31]

Schubbert answered both these charges convincingly.[32] Yes, he conceded, he had sold the Society's liquor provisions, but only to Americans who were passing through, and with the profit from these sales, he had bought badly needed medicines and other provisions for the colonists in Friedrichsburg, which, according to Schubbert, Meusebach had failed to provide, even after an epidemic broke out. Even Meusebach conceded that Dr. Schubbert had acted conscientiously and effectively in his role as medical doctor.[33] As for the communal approach, Schubbert argued, even though it required more of the Society, it was the least the Society could do considering that the settlers had yet to receive their promised land in the grant area. Dr. Schubbert, in fact, had many supporters among the colonists in Friedrichsburg. In June 1847, sixty-eight supporters circulated a petition in which they expressed their strong support for the doctor.[34]

One charge Schubbert did not answer. Meusebach was upset that Schubbert had mounted an expensive expedition in October 1846 to make contact with the Comanche Indians and had accomplished nothing. In fact, Meusebach accused Schubbert of spreading alarmist rumors of upwards of 40,000 to 60,000 warlike Indians in the grant area ready to wipe out any settlers who dared to set foot in the area.[35]

In March, Meusebach came to Friedrichsburg to view the situation for himself, to mount once and for all an extensive exploratory expedition into the grant area, and also to try to make contact with the Comanche Indians. The Fischer–Miller grant area was, of course, the domain of the Comanches, and it was absolutely critical that Meusebach should reach some sort of accommodation with them. Against the advice of Major Neighbors, the American Indian agent, and others, Meusebach struck out into the territory north of the Llano River with a large expedition consisting of several wagons and forty-five men. Eventually they located a combined camp near present-day San Saba consisting of several thousand Indians.

In an act of astounding bravery (or complete foolhardiness) Meusebach ordered his men to ride into the village. The assembled Comanche warriors were dumbfounded but pleased when Meusebach ordered his men to discharge their weapons in the air, signaling that their intentions were peaceful, but also rendering themselves completely defenseless. After several rounds of negotiations over the course of two days, Meusebach succeeded in convincing the chiefs to sign a treaty of peace and cooperation, a treaty fundamentally novel in that it sought to integrate the two cultures rather than separate them. Meusebach's treaty, which by and large was honored for a generation, stands out as one of the bright spots in the otherwise sordid history of European/Native American relationships in Texas and was perhaps his greatest accomplishment.[36]

In July 1847, after concluding the treaty with the Comanches, Meusebach resigned as commissioner-general. He justified this step in an earlier communication to Cappes by stating that "I am tired of continuing in a position in which I am constantly exposed to criticism without being able to defend or justify myself."[37] In truth, Meusebach had by this point become almost completely isolated. He was scorned and ridiculed by most of the functionaries in Texas, distrusted by Count Castell in Germany, and reviled by many of the settlers, who had little appreciation for the challenges he had faced and the hurdles he had overcome.

By this point the rift between Meusebach and Schubbert had become open and ugly. Schubbert wrote a letter to Cappes (the man who had been sent over to keep an eye on Meusebach) accusing Meusebach of being an atheist and conspiring with the *Darmstädter* (to be discussed later) to take all the better land and perhaps the plantation.[38] For his part, Meusebach came to suspect that Schubbert was not only deficient as a leader, but that he was also a fraud who had completely misrepresented his person.[39] His last act was to dismiss Schubbert.[40] He turned over the reins of authority to Hermann Spiess, one of the *Darmstädter,* whom Schubbert and others had come to despise. This set the stage for the shootout.

Who was Dr. Schubbert and what is the truth about him? First, he certainly cut quite a figure. He was a very tall man who sported an ostentatiously long and twisted handlebar mustache. Later, he wore a patch over one eye. His later pictures suggest the quintessential stereotype of the villain in melodramas. He also rode a striking white horse and kept a large bloodhound as a companion.[41] To many his appearance reinforced the belief that he was no more than a con artist who used his sophistication, charm, and force of intellect, as well as his adroitness in the use of firearms, to intimidate, to deceive, and to promote himself shamelessly. To his friends, however, he was a competent and forceful leader whose very talents had aroused such envy in Meusebach that it led to his dismissal.

His real name was Friedrich Armand Strubberg. He was born into a prominent family in Kassel, Germany, in 1806. His father was a wealthy tobacco merchant. The son had a connection through his mother with the local aristocracy since he was supposedly the great-grandson of Count Friedrich I of Hessen, later King of Sweden, through a morganatic marriage.[42] This left him without an official title, but nonetheless acceptable to Hessian aristocratic society. He had been the recipient of a good education with an emphasis in business, but in the wake of a lover's duel in Hamburg in 1826 had found it prudent to remove himself to the United States. He lived the life of a dandy in the New York for several years until another duel in 1841 put him on the run again, this time with an arrest warrant for murder over his head.

Like many in his predicament, he looked to Texas. He boarded a steamer in Cincinnati with the intention of going to New Orleans and thence to Texas. The boat, however, ran aground and sank near Louisville, Kentucky. While waiting for the recovery of his luggage, Strubberg made the acquaintance of a German professor who ran a medical institute. Strubberg became his student under the name of Schubbert and, after two years of study, took the title of Doctor of Medicine.

Eventually, Dr. Schubbert came to Texas where he would be safe from the hangman's noose. Driven by the spirit of adventure, he founded a colony on the Texas frontier.[43] There were only a few families associated with this "colony," and after a short period it was abandoned. Henry Francis Fischer, who also hailed from Kassel, may have supported Schubbert in this venture. It was through Fischer that Meusebach learned of Schubbert. His first impressions must have been very favorable. Meusebach even referred to him enthusiastically at one point as the "Baron von Brückenau."[44]

The *Darmstädter* also played a part in this story. It will be remembered that Schubbert accused Meusebach of conspiring to turn over the plantation to this group and, otherwise, to show them favorable treatment. Who were they and what was their role?

In 1846 a group of intellectuals, students and professional men, many of whom were loosely or directly connected with an industrial school in Darmstadt, Germany, banded together to form an association. They also seemed to have been connected through the social activities of their university fraternities, several being members of the *Starkenburgia* Corps.[45]

There were about forty members in the group, so they are sometimes referred to as *die Vierziger*, or Society of Forty. In the beginning the circle was a debating society where many of the pressing issues of the day were discussed. The group had connections with many of the leading intellectuals of the period and they seemed to have been very much under the influence of the German philosopher Ludwig Feuerbach.[46] For this reason, they were sometimes referred to as "Feuerbachianer," or "Feuerbachytes."[47]

To sum up, the *Darmstädter* emerged as a group of educated and idealistic young men who were democratic in politics, communistic in economics, and freethinking in matters of religion. Seeing no future for themselves in Germany, they decided to immigrate as a group to the New World. Five men emerged as the guiding spirits of this organization: Gustav Schleicher, Ferdinand von Herff, Hermann Spiess, Friedrich Schenk and Julius Wagner.[48] Of these, Spiess, who had known Meusebach in Germany, is the most important to this story.

Count Castell was very much aware of the *Darmstädter*, and he feared that they would become competitors to his own project. He feared that they intended to move to Wisconsin, where their presence, once established, would attract the educated and disaffected. In consequence, Castell resolved to bring them into his organization.[49] After a vigorous debate, the Society offered the group a generous package, including substantial subsidies, as an inducement.[50] The group accepted. Hermann Spiess came over in February; most of the rest followed in July 1847. Their first act was to establish the commune known as "Bettina" on Elm Creek across the Llano River from the newly formed settlement of Castell. It was named for the wife of the German poet Achim von Arnim. Here Dr. Ferdinand Herff, who was related to Meusebach,[51] reputedly performed on a Comanche chieftain the first successful eye surgery in Texas.[52]

From the beginning the *Darmstädter's* presence created friction and resentment; friction due to their special treatment and resentment because of irreverent and unconventional attitudes, attitudes too extreme for many of the settlers.[53] This discontent extended to certain officials in Texas, especially Hans von Coll, who succeeded Schubbert as director in Friedrichsburg, and Lieutenant Bené, who later served as general agent in the period from 1849 to 1850. Philip Cappes, the official sent over in October 1846 to keep an eye on Meusebach, also shared this point of view. In a subsequent report Lieutenant Bené complained "that my education, sensibilities, and social standing are irreconcilable with the basic tenets and attitudes of a communistic connection."[54] This was a sentiment shared by many.

Meusebach, who hailed from a cultivated and open-minded family with close connections to many of the leading German intellectuals and writers of the day, sympathized with the *Darmstädter,* and so, by association, incurred the hostility of many. When he opted for the newcomer Hermann Spiess to be his successor over more established members of the bureaucracy, it seemed to confirm certain suspicions. Dr. Schubbert took exception to the reputed atheism of Meusebach, as the letter to Cappes shows, but he also suspected that Meusebach wished to turn over the plantation to the *Darmstädter,* which further inflamed the situation.

Here the story of the shootout resumes. Dr. Schubbert did not accept his dismissal in July 1847 graciously,[55] and he refused to concede that his lease on the plantation was invalid. By the terms of this lease, he was due to take over completely on January 1, 1848, but was allowed to take up residence and assume the administration of the plantation in August 1847.[56]

Dr. Schubbert left Friedrichsburg in August and made his way to La Grange. To his displeasure, two men were assigned to accompany him with whom he had quarreled in the past.[57] Once in La Grange he began plotting (according to a decidedly anti-Schubbert account) on how best to gain control of the plantation. The suspicion exists that Schubbert may have become a Freemason at some point and through this connection found support to put together a group of men to enforce his claim.[58] He decided to wait until October to make his move, so the anti-Schubbert report goes, so that the year's harvest would be in, which he could then sell.[59]

Hermann Spiess, the successor to Meusebach, apparently was inclined to compromise and allow Schubbert to have the plantation, but only if he posted a large security bond, by one account $15,000.[60] Spiess rode to the plantation in early October, preceding Dr. Schubbert's takeover by several days. He instructed Ernst Sörghel, cousin of Alwin Sörghel,[61] who farmed on Rocky Creek near Round Top, that the plantation was to be handed over only if the security bond were posted. Sörghel had been appointed caretaker of the plantation by Hermann Wilke the year before. Dr. Schubbert balked at this condition, arguing with some justification that the contract did not specify a security bond.

Hardly had Spiess departed for New Braunfels when Ernst Sörghel was confronted on October 19 by three men whom he took to be officers of the law. Sörghel did not speak English and the men knew no German. By one account Sörghel then acquiesced voluntarily to the takeover of the plantation and by other accounts he felt threatened to do so. That same day Dr. Schubbert arrived with a party of men and took up residence. On the following day, October 20, 1847, Sörghel apparently had second thoughts and in the company of a Texas-German by the name of Fehrmann, decided to ride back to the plantation with the purpose of dislodging Dr. Schubbert and his companions. On the way they met two riders. A heated argument ensued. One of the riders, Absalom Bostick, pulled his pistol and struck Fehrmann across the face, knocking him to the ground unconscious. They then pointed their pistols at Sörghel and ordered him to leave the plantation.[62]

This event set the stage for the shootout. Sörghel rode as quickly as he could to New Braunfels. Upon hearing his account, Hermann Spiess, the new commissioner-general, quickly gathered a party of seven men who were employees and officials of the Society in New Braunfels.[63] Spiess consulted with the Society's attorney, M.A. Dooley,[64] who advised that it should be possible to regain the plantation through legal means, and that the cost of such litigation would be less than the damage incurred by leaving the plantation in Schubbert's hands. Dooley also departed for La Grange to initiate legal proceedings.⁶⁵

Hermann Spiess had his men make their way individually to Fayette County so as not to arouse suspicion. They were instructed to rendezvous at Ernst Sörghel's house. Spiess came later by wagon. Dooley, who also travelled separately, lost his way in the dark and ended up at the Townsend homestead nearby.⁶⁶ Spiess' plan, according to the anonymous author of the *Galveston Zeitung* article, had been to first have Dooley confront Dr. Schubbert and his party with legal arguments and barring this to use force. Spiess later denied that he ever intended to use force and this denial became the basis of his subsequent legal defense.⁶⁷

Among the party put together by Spiess was a young and congenial Swiss-German artist and naturalist, Conrad Caspar Rohrdorf. He had come to Texas in January 1847 with three others—M. Gürth, A. Altstäder, and J. P. von Bauer—all self-appointed members of the *Naturforschender Verein*, or Society for the Research of Nature.⁶⁸ They left one member behind in Germany, Georg Schultz. They intended to make observations, write reports, collect and preserve specimens (especially birds), and make drawings. These they intended to market to museums and private collectors through their representative in Germany, and, by so doing, to finance their trip and earn money. There is some indication that they also either received, or were promised, some support by the Society in Germany.

They arrived in Galveston in January 1847 and succeeded in publishing one report about Dickinson Bayou, which was printed in *Der deutsche Auswanderer*, the leading German newspaper devoted solely to issues of emigration.⁶⁹ As a group, however, they seemed to have spent as much time singing and drinking as they did researching. Alwin Sörghel remarked, somewhat disdainfully, in his wonderfully irreverent and witty book about Texas, that they spent most of their time researching the nature of laziness.⁷⁰

Whatever the truth, Rohrdorf soon left the group and accepted a position as the official artist of the Society in Texas. He was commissioned to do a series of drawings of the colonies, with an emphasis on landscapes, which were to be used to publicize the endeavor in Germany. He was present when Meusebach concluded the treaty with the Comanche Indians in the summer of 1847. The treaty, executed by Rohrdorf, is a beautiful document, written in both English and German.[71] Eventually he completed over forty drawings[72] of the colonies, of which only one, *The Panorama of New Braunfels*, is known to survive.

Rohrdorf was present in New Braunfels when Ernst Sörghel arrived with news of the takeover, and, unfortunately, joined the party put together by Hermann Spiess to retake the plantation. Rohrdorf rode his own horse and took along in his saddlebags two sketchbooks containing the forty drawings he had completed.

Spiess and his men assembled at Sörghel's house, which was northwest of the plantation. Hermann Spiess wrote that he attempted to gain a better understanding of the situation by consulting with the nearest Anglo neighbor, the wealthy plantation owner Hamilton Ledbetter. Ledbetter related in confidence that Schubbert's had attracted people of the most dangerous sort, the leader of whom was Absalom Bostick, a known murderer who had escaped from Mississippi and who now wanted to exploit Schubbert for his own criminal purposes.[73] The district court was due to convene in La Grange in two days and both Dooley and Ledbetter counseled Spiess not to attempt anything in the meantime. Spiess, by his own account, feared that inaction would be interpreted as cowardice. Moreover, he was afraid that there was a plot underfoot to steal the slaves, and so, he decided to confront Schubbert, who was ensconced in the *Herrenhaus* with the party he had collected, and demand the surrender of the plantation.[74]

His plan was to first secure the slaves and then, just as breakfast was being prepared, to confront Schubbert and demand the surrender of the plantation. If Schubbert refused, so Spiess wrote, he intended to back out peacefully and pursue the matter legally, but, in the meantime to make sure that the slaves stayed out of the hands of Schubbert and his gang. Spiess, accordingly, roused his men early on the morning of October 29, 1847, and ordered them to make their way in the dark to the plantation. First, they went to the slave quarters and ordered the slaves to leave, an order with which they willingly obliged. Then they made their way to the *Herrenhaus*, which lay nearly a half-mile to the east across Jack's Creek. Four of the party, Spiess, Zobel, Krauskopf, and Rohrdorf entered the kitchen of the Negro cabin, which stood twenty-five paces to the east of the *Herrenhaus*. The others were to take up positions along the fence on the outside thirty paces from the mansion, where they were to serve as Spiess' riflemen.

With Schubbert in the house were Absalon Bostick, Benjamin Breeding, Captain Frederick Somers, another young American, and a man by the name of von Zabitsch together with his family.[75] Judging from the court records of the period, both Bostick and Breeding counted, to use the parlance of the period, as "rowdy loafers." Both had records for disorderly conduct, gambling, and public intoxication. Captain Somers, in contrast, was widely respected in the county. It is possible that he and Schubbert had become acquainted at an earlier date.

Captain Somers, unable to sleep and restless, had roused himself and came out on the gallery of the house. Most reports claim the attackers fired first,[76] but Hermann Spiess later disputed this.[77] Whatever the truth may be, shots were fired upon the appearance of Somers and he received a charge in the abdomen that lodged in his spinal cord. As he fell he called out for help, his last words. Absalom Bostick, clothed only in his underwear, quickly grabbed his shotgun and rushed to Somer's aid. As he emerged from the house he was fired on several times, but, incredibly, sustained only a scratch on his leg and a hole through his underwear. Noticing the flash of an attacker's weapon, he discharged his shotgun in that direction, striking the artist Rohrdorf with three slugs in the cheek and head.

In the meantime the others in the house had quickly roused themselves and grabbed their weapons. They stormed out of the house and captured one of the attackers, a man by the name of Hermann Krauskopf, who reputedly had been a member of the *Darmstädter* group. The unfortunate Rohrdorf lingered on several hours before death relieved him of his agony.

After the initial exchange of gunshots, which left Somers and Rohrdorf dead, the attackers dispersed, and, according to the official report of Lieutenant Bené, they did so in a panic, leaving behind their fallen comrade.[78] The man who was captured gave a complete confession and divulged all the names of the participants. He swore that Hermann Spiess had fired first and had fired the shot that killed Captain Somers. Hermann Spiess, who had driven from New Braunfels to Sörghel's house in a buckboard wagon, fled on Rohrdorf's horse and eventually made his way to the vicinity of the new settlement of Castell and over the Llano River to the safety of his colleagues at the Bettina commune. An arrest warrant for murder was issued against him the following day. Ernst Sörghel was arrested at his home and taken to the jail in La Grange where he was also charged with murder and attempted murder (against Absalom Bostick).

This episode, which came to be called the *Katastrophe* (catastrophe) among the Germans, set off a chain reaction of indictments, lawsuits, and countersuits, clogging several terms of the district court in La Grange and draining money, time, and energy at a critical period for the Society.

The grand jury, which convened on November 7, 1847, returned a true bill of murder for the death of Frederick Somers against all members of the attacking party, including Spiess and Sörghel.[79] Sörghel posted a $2,000 bond and was ordered to appear before the spring term of district court to face trial for murder. The grand jury also indicted Absalom Bostick for assault and battery for his part in the attack and injury of Fehrmann.[80] M. A. Dooley, the Society's lawyer in New Braunfels, travelled to La Grange in the name of the Society to prepare a defense for the indicted and to take legal steps to regain the plantation.

Feelings ran high, however, and as Dooley came down the stairs in the hotel where he had taken a room, he was accosted by James S. Mayfield and Absalom Bostick. Bostick grabbed him by the beard and pulled him to the floor while Mayfield took out his pistol, aimed it at Dooley, and snapped the trigger.[81] The pistol, however, did not discharge. Dooley interpreted the confrontation as an attempt to frighten and intimidate him. He continued, however, with his defense work.

The shootout at Nassau brought together an improbable cast of characters. To help sort out the legal issues the Society also retained the services of a La Grange lawyer, Andrew Jackson Hamilton. Hamilton (1815-1875) was a man of strong views that often went against the grain: he was staunchly anti-slavery and pro-Union. His pronounced views made him a hero in the North and subsequently led to his appointment as the first provisional governor of Texas during Reconstruction (1865, 1866) where he gained a reputation for being a political radical. At the time of the shootout, he was a lawyer in partnership with his brother in La Grange.

Another player, James S. Mayfield, who had served as Indian commissioner, postmaster general and secretary of state at various times, presented quite a counterpoint to Hamilton. He was radically pro-slavery and this conviction had led him to pronounced anti-immigration views. He was suspicious of foreigners, especially Germans and Englishmen. He suspected, with some justification, that there was a plot underfoot to flood Texas with immigrants from these two countries as a conscious effort to dilute pro-slavery sentiment.[82] In the period prior to annexation, the debate about immigration (from Europe as opposed to the United States) had become intense.[83] Mayfield, at this point a member of the legislature, delivered an impassioned speech on the floor of the Texas House in 1843 in which he opposed land grant contracts, because, he maintained, they would lead to the formation of "little petty dukedoms and principalities"[84] upon the state's frontiers, thereby eroding the extent of slave territory.

Mayfield, according to Hermann Spiess, was the one who convinced Schubbert to occupy the plantation by force and had helped Schubbert put together the party that was ensconced in the manor house when the shooting took place. Later, during the trial of Hermann Spiess for the murder of Captain Somers, he created a commotion in court by standing up and demanding that the prosecution examine the larger role and motivation of the German Emigration Co. in Texas, which, he maintained, was trying to impose an "aristocratic agenda" on the state and also attempting to undermine the institution of slavery.[85] Thus, through the Mayfield connection, the shootout at the plantation had the effect of placing the German Emigration Co. front and center in the debate about slavery and immigration in the state. And even though the Society owned and maintained a slave plantation in Fayette County, its wider program of colonization in the Hill Country came under greater scrutiny and suspicion, an unhelpful development politically.

Mayfield, apparently, was a man of passionate views and a violent temper. In 1842 he had shot David Kaufmann, former speaker of the house, after an acrimonious exchange on the floor of the House of Representatives.[86] In 1845 he challenged Edward Burleson, renowned Texas military figure and politician, in the wake of a disagreement about his military service in 1842.[87] A preventative arrest halted the duel.

Mayfield had moved to Fayette County in 1842 and set up practice as a lawyer in La Grange. By 1847, the year of the shootout at the plantation, he had become associated with Absalom Bostick, the man who had pistol-whipped the German Fehrmann and taken over the plantation for Schubbert. Hermann Spiess characterized Bostick as "a Texas ruffian, and of a class of men, dangerous and unpredictable, previously unknown to me." Bostick, Spiess claimed, did Mayfield's dirty work. From an examination of the court records of the period, it appears that Bostick might have even presented himself as a lawyer, for his name appears on several legal documents as co-counsel with Mayfield. On one occasion the court awarded him a sizeable piece of river bottom property for "services rendered."[88] In any case, documents from the period corroborate Spiess' contention that Bostick and Mayfield were associates at the time of the shootout and that Mayfield was a party to the Schubbert faction.

In December, the German Emigration Co. filed suit against Dr. Schubbert, Absalom Bostick, and Benjamin Breeding, asking the court to compel the defendants to vacate the plantation and requesting an order of sequestration in the interim, which was granted.[89] The administration of the plantation was turned over in the interim to Hamilton Ledbetter, a prosperous and well-respected Anglo neighbor to the plantation. Otto von Roeder was brought in as a middleman and consultant. Once the legal issues were sorted out, von Roeder took over as supervisor of the plantation[90] with August Vogelsang[91] as his assistant.

The order of sequestration is a very instructive document. It explains how Meusebach felt he had been duped by Schubbert and why his misrepresentations invalidated the lease. The order of sequestration included a detailed inventory of the plantation. It is reproduced as an appendix at the end of this book.

Schubbert's lawyer filed a countersuit and the issue was continued until the spring session. In April 1848 lawyers for both sides hammered out an agreement whereby Schubbert in exchange for $3,000 in damages, gave up all claims to the plantation. Both suits were then dismissed on motion of the plaintiffs.[92] The Order of Sequestration was lifted and the Society briefly resumed control of the plantation.[93] In July Otto von Roeder took over control of the plantation pending a final settlement to his claims against the Society.

Other litigation, however, continued in the spring and fall sessions of the district court. Hermann Wilke, who had served as an engineer and mapmaker for the Society, filed suit as administrator of Rohrdorf's estate to recover the forty drawings from Schubbert.[94] The suit maintained that in the wake of the shootout Schubbert came into unlawful possession of the two sketchbooks containing the drawings, and that these sketchbooks had a value of over $2,000.

This is an astonishing value—a reflection of both Rohrdorf's talents and the importance the Society attached to his drawings. Schubbert immediately filed a demurral to Wilke's suit based on technicalities.[95] He did not deny having possession of the drawings. The suit was continued to the fall session of the court. Wilke was ordered to post a bond to cover the court costs before this time. When he failed to post the bond, his suit to recover the drawings was ordered dismissed from the docket and Schubbert retained possession of the drawings.

Among the drawings was Rohrdorf's rendering of the "Treaty with the Comanches," a beautiful document written in German with a facing page in English. In a complicated series of transactions, this original document, but apparently none of the other drawings, made its way back to Texas where it is now housed in the State Archives in Austin.[96]

Meanwhile, in April both Hermann Spiess and Ernst Sörghel were put on trial for murder. Once again Spiess fled to avoid prosecution. This action prompted a denunciation of Spiess by Lieutenant Bené in a communication to Count Castell. He maintained that Spiess could no longer effectively serve as head of the Society in Texas and that, legal troubles aside, his communistic inclinations discredited him in the eyes of most colonists.[97] The leadership concurred and soon thereafter Lieutenant Bené assumed the leadership role of the Society in Texas.

Both trials were continued until the fall 1848 term of the court at which time Spiess decided to return voluntarily to La Grange to face the court. He did so in the face of vigorous opposition from his lawyers who felt that given the high state of emotion, a good chance existed for conviction and execution. But Spiess was adamant, and his appearance and the subsequent trial in September 1848 created a sensation in the county.

The night before the trial a man rode his horse into the saloon, located on the bottom floor of the hotel where Spiess was lodged. The rider discharged his pistol and called for Spiess to come down, but Otto von Roeder, who was staying with Spiess, refused to let him take the bait. During the trial itself, James Mayfield, who was seated in the crowd, stood up and demanded of the judge and the prosecution that they investigate the "hidden" agenda of the German Emigration Co. in Texas: its attempt to introduce an aristocratic program and to dilute pro-slavery sentiment and undercut the authority of slave owners.[98]

Once the trial got underway, Spiess maintained that he had never intended to take back the plantation by force and he cited the fact that two of the men from New Braunfels had brought along their wives and children. The jury apparently found his story believable; he and his co-conspirators were found not guilty of murder.[99] The verdict produced an uproar in La Grange, for the slain Captain Somers was highly regarded. Spiess remarked simply "that the better element in La Grange approved the verdict."[100] The state, however, continued to prosecute on lesser charges. The issue was not completely resolved until March 1851 when the state decided not to pursue the cases further.[101] In the meantime Absalom Bostick was found guilty of assault and assessed a fine of ten dollars in March 1849.[102] In the same term a jury ruled in favor of Absalom Bostick and Benjamin Breeding on the charge of forcible entry and unlawful occupation.[103]

Although acquitted of the murder, one has to question Spiess' judgment in creeping up to the plantation in the dark of dawn with a party of armed men, especially in consideration of the fact that district court was due to convene in two days and legal options were available. Hermann Spiess, however, insisted that the slaves were in imminent danger, and he used this concern as an added justification for his decision to approach the plantation with the armed men. In one of the strangest twists to this story, a subsequent altercation between James Mayfield and Absalom Bostick revealed that a conspiracy to steal the slaves probably did exist.

Absalom Bostick and James Mayfield, business partners at the time of the shooting, subsequently became enemies. Spiess maintained that his lawyer, A. J. Hamilton, had bribed Bostick to suppress evidence at the trial, thus helping with the acquittal. This, according to Spiess, had infuriated Mayfield who was fiercely prejudiced against the German Emigration Co. and wanted to see a conviction against its chief agent, Hermann Spiess. Whatever the reason, their disagreement grew ever more heated. In the summer of 1849, the two got into a fight in the local tavern and had to be pulled apart. Bostick swore that he intended to kill Mayfield the next time they met. Very shortly thereafter, he had his chance. Sitting in the tavern, he was informed that Mayfield was coming down the street. Then, in a scene reminiscent of a Western movie, Bostick stepped outside and fired his pistol at Mayfield, but missed. Mayfield raised and fired one barrel of the double-barreled shotgun he was carrying, striking Bostick and knocking him to the ground. Mayfield then calmly walked up to Bostick, placed the other barrel to his head and pulled the trigger.

On Bostick's body, according to Spiess, were documents implicating him in a criminal gang who specialized in stealing slaves and transporting them across the state line into Arkansas and farther. Spiess' version of this is corroborated by several newspaper articles of this date reporting the discovery of a gang of slave thieves in Fayette County.[104] The articles suggest that several members of the gang had met with summary justice. Spiess does not mince words. He states that upon discovering the plot, a vigilante committee was put together, which included Otto von Roeder and August Vogelsang. The vigilantes lynched, according to Spiess, at least one of the gang members implicated by the papers found on Bostick's body and drove the others from the area.[105]

Spiess claimed that Bostick and his gang had played a double game with Schubbert. They had pretended to be his friend and came to his assistance, but their secret agenda had been to steal the plantation's slaves and whisk them across the state line for resale. Thus, claimed Spiess, Schubbert in a sense also had been a victim while he, Spiess, had been justified in his preemptive approach to unseat Bostick and cohorts from the plantation, for the slaves were in danger.

In retrospect, it is astonishing how many diverse strands make up the story of the shootout at Nassau Plantation in the fall of 1847. It was, in the first instance, the dramatic and deadly culmination of the dispute between John Meusebach and Dr. Schubbert. It also reflected the distrust and enmity between the *Darmstädter*, whom Meusebach supported, and the rest of the bureaucracy in Texas, who by and large supported Schubbert. As one of the original leaders of the *Darmstädter*, Hermann Spiess' role in the shootout certainly exacerbated these tensions.

James Mayfield's involvement added another layer to the story because the plantation and the Society suddenly became a dramatic focal point of anti-immigrant sentiment in the state, which Mayfield had helped to arouse. And finally, we add to the mix the subplot of a gang of ruffians conspiring to steal slaves and spirit them across the border for resale; a plot which became known only after James Mayfield killed Absalom Bostick, his former associate, in a spectacular shootout on the streets of La Grange, and a plot which, once revealed, provoked a concerted and joint Anglo-German vigilante action to rid the area of "rowdy loafers."

In order to complete this chapter it is necessary to finish the story of Dr. Schubbert (henceforth Friedrich Armand Strubberg). Günter Sehm, a German scholar who wrote a monograph about Strubberg, maintained that he was nervous about the litigation concerning the plantation because his true identity might be revealed leading to a revival of the old murder charge from New York.[106] Since Texas had joined the Union in the meantime, this was a legitimate concern. Consequently, according to Sehm, Strubberg departed for Mexico, and remained there until the statute of limitations (six years) expired.[107] Indeed, Strubberg made the war the subject of two novels, and his depictions have a ring of veracity, as if based on firsthand experience.[108] The dates, however, do not square with this account. Mexico City fell in September 1847 and with its fall the war was essentially over, although an official peace treaty was not finalized until almost a year later. It is possible, but unlikely, that Strubberg went to Mexico after Meusebach dismissed him as colonial-director of Fredericksburg in July 1847 and before the shootout in October. It is also possible, but improbable, that he went to Mexico after the shootout and remained there until the spring of 1848.

Regardless of when or whether he spent time in Mexico, documents in the Solms-Braunfels Archives definitively place Strubberg in Galveston in the spring of 1848; in May 1848 his presence can be documented in New Orleans.[109] Here, in a parting letter to Meusebach, extraordinarily frank and aggressive in tone, Strubberg defended himself against the charges which had led to his dismissal and challenged the abrogation of his lease to Nassau Plantation. He also leveled some very serious charges against Meusebach. He stated that nothing but jealousy had been behind Meusebach's antipathy; that he, unlike Meusebach, was a man of numerous talents, greater energy, and of an engaging and sympathetic nature, all of which rendered him more effective as a leader. His most damming charge was that the shootout at Nassau was in reality a planned assassination (*Meuchelmord*), which had been conceived and orchestrated by Meusebach behind the scenes. As a final insult, Strubberg averred that he had researched their respective family backgrounds and had discovered that Meusebach's ancestors had once served as gamekeepers (*Wildfänger*) for his family. Strubberg closed by saying that their paths were destined to cross again at which time Meusebach would receive his just deserts.[110]

Fortunately their paths never crossed. With his settlement money in hand, Strubberg moved to Arkansas where he set up a profitable medical practice and became engaged to the wealthy daughter of a plantation owner. At this point one of those odd and unforeseeable events occurred that change the course of one's life: an insect stung Strubberg in the eye, and his eyesight(and his ability to aim)were threatened. Strubberg resolved to return to Europe to seek the expertise of European doctors. In 1854 he departed, never to return. Eventually he found some relief, but his eye remained covered by a gray film so that he wore a patch over the eye for the rest of his life.

In the fall of 1854, Friedrich Armand Strubberg returned to his native Kassel where his unmarried sister still lived. After some comings and goings, he took up residence with her. With his large stock of entertaining stories he became the center of considerable attention in the refined circles of Kassel. Friends implored him to convert his repertoire of adventures into book form, which he did in 1858 under the pen name of Armand with the publication of *Amerikanische Jagd- und Reiseabenteuer* (*American Hunting and Travel Adventures*).

The book was an overnight success, launching Strubberg, under the *nom de plume* Armand, on a long and profitable career as a writer of novels based on his adventures in the New World with particular emphasis on his frontier experiences in Texas.

Among many others, Strubberg wrote a novel based on his first colony in Texas entitled *An der Indianer Grenze* (*On the Indian Border*) and a novel based on his experiences as director of the Friedrichsburg colony, which he named, aptly enough, *Friedrichsburg*.

Sometimes history contains delicious ironies, which trump anything the imagination could conceive: Strubberg, who fought and shed blood in the effort to gain control of a slave plantation, is now credited as the first German author to take as the central focus of several novels the portrayal of North American slavery from a pronounced anti-slavery point of view.[111]

Strubberg took up the theme in 1859 with *Bis in die Wildnis* (*Until the Wilderness*). The novel is episodic and loosely autobiographical, depicting in fictionalized form Strubberg's stay in the United States up until the time he came to Texas. Much in the novel, however, clearly springs from the author's imagination. The story includes several complicated love stories, as do most of his books.

In this story, he treats the fact that many plantation owners consorted with their female slaves, a fact that gave rise to complicated and often tragic scenarios, especially with respect to the offspring of these liaisons, the mulattos and quadroons.

Strubberg's most ambitious effort with respect to slavery, *Schwarzes Blut oder Sklaverei in den Vereinigten Staaten* (*Black Blood or Slavery in the United States*) was published in 1862 during the American Civil War. It is actually a trilogy of three separate stories in which the absurdities and inherent injustices of slavery are dealt with through the device of hopelessly involved and complicated romantic attachments.

The characters in these stories are carefully drawn to represent the various personalities and types associated with slavery from the sympathetic but flawed plantation owner to the pathologically cruel and unbending overseer to beautiful and talented mulatto and quadroon slave girls who can find no escape from the prejudices which confront them at every turn. Likewise, many of the sordid scenarios associated with slavery, such as slave auctions, are powerfully and accurately portrayed.

Strubberg's books never attained the status of serious literature, but they did provide him with a comfortable income and a definite prominence. He was a pioneer in the emerging genre of *Abenteuerliteratur* (literally, "adventure-literature," but usually characterized in the English-speaking world as "genre literature"). Several German authors of the period—Charles Sealsfield, Friedrich Gerstäcker, Balduin Möllhausen, and, somewhat later, Karl May-drew upon firsthand (and imaginary, in the case of May) experiences in the Far West to produce an impressive body of German Western fiction which in some ways trumps its American counterpart and still enjoys popularity to this day. Some even consider the "Western" to be a German invention. Of these authors, Karl May is the best known, even though he alone among these authors had no firsthand experience with the American West. His books have sold over forty million copies making him the most popular German author of all time. Strubberg is generally credited with being an *Unterlage*, a foundation, to Karl May's novels about the American West.

Finally, what happened to the missing portfolio of the slain artist, Conrad Caspar Rohrdorf? Strubberg's first published work, *Amerikanische Jagd- und Reise Abenteuer* (*American Hunting and Travel Adventures*),[112] contained twenty-four illustrations of Texas landscapes and settings in which Strubberg credits himself as the artist. Were these depictions, in fact, the work of Strubberg, or did he plagiarize the work of the slain artist and naturalist Rohrdorf, whose portfolio he had made off with? It is the author's opinion that some, but not all, of the illustrations are in fact Rohrdorf drawings. Stylistic differences are clearly perceptible. Some of the drawings are pure landscapes of the Texas Hill Country with extremely accurate and precise renderings of the flora and fauna of the region, facts consistent with Rohrdorf as a trained naturalist and a recognized landscape artist who had been commissioned by the German Emigration Co. to do exact landscapes and panoramas of the settlement areas. Three of the illustrations in particular—a beautiful rendering of beavers in a Texas swamp setting, a Hill Country spring, and a panoramic rendering of Enchanted Rock in the Llano uplift region of Central Texas—stand out and are included among the illustrations in this book. As a contrast, one illustration that is clearly not by Rohrdorf has been included: a self-portrait of Strubberg, his horse, and his dog. The tropical banana plant in the scene is clearly out of place for a Texas scene.

The question as to who was the real artist of the drawings cannot be definitively answered for the present, but this much is certain: if Rohrdorf's original forty drawings ever do resurface, it will most likely assure him a place alongside Friedrich Richard Petri and Karl Friedrich Hermann Lungkwitz as one of the outstanding German landscape artists of frontier Texas.

Historians need not pass final judgment on the conflict between Meusebach and Strubberg. Both were strong-willed and capable men, fully engaged in a dramatic and formative period of Texas history, but they were oil and water which refused to mix. The challenges that confronted Meusebach when he assumed the reins of authority in 1845 were almost beyond resolution. It is hard to imagine that anyone could have accomplished more under the circumstances. Still, his eccentricities left a broad path of ill will, and, consequently, he, too, must shoulder some responsibility for the *Katastrophe* of Nassau Plantation, which wasted two lives needlessly and compromised the larger mission of the Society immensely.

CHAPTER 11

Otto von Roeder

Eighteen forty-eight was a rough year for the Society both in Germany and in Texas. The shootout at the plantation set into motion the series of events which culminated in the dismemberment of the plantation. Confronted with difficulties at every hand and faced with rising debts, the Society was desperate for the good will of the citizens of the state. Its fate in Texas lay in the hands of the state legislature, in various courtrooms, and with the forbearance of its creditors.[1]

The repercussions of the shootout extended to Germany. In 1848 revolution broke out across Europe. Among the German states, the unrest manifested itself quickly in the Rhineland and Hessian provinces due to their proximity to France. Here the French ideas of liberty, fraternity, and equality had taken root among the students and the middle-class *Bürger* of the cities. Revolutionaries even briefly occupied the city of Mainz, which was in a sense the birthplace of the Society. In one of the more dramatic episodes in all of Germany, a mob of 30,000 farmers, apprentices, and handworkers, armed only with pitchforks, scythes, and axes, descended upon the Wiesbaden castle of Adolph Duke of Nassau. When the duke promised reforms, the crowd peacefully dispersed.[2]

The old order in Europe was confronted with an explosion of frustration and resentment from the common man: the exclusion from political life, the denial of basic freedoms of expression and assembly, the lack of religious freedom, the absence of economic opportunity, the onerous burden of late-feudal privileges—all these factors combined to threaten the noblemen in Germany from within even as their plans from across the sea floundered. The turmoil of the revolution compromised the Society in Germany in many ways, especially in the ability to raise funds.[3]

With the backdrop of the revolution in Germany and the flood of discouraging news from Texas, the Society reorganized itself both in Germany and in Texas, and, by so doing, hoped to stem the hemorrhage in expenses. The general assembly met in April and assigned all property in Texas to Count Castell, who in turn, in May, sold all his rights to one Ludwig Martin, a prominent and wealthy counselor from Freiburg. When this deal fell through,[4] Castell stepped down as executive director; in his place a committee was set up to conduct the everyday affairs of the Society, headed by Dr. Rauscher, an accountant from Wiesbaden.[5]

In Texas, the leadership was ordered to disband the bureaucracy, which had grown to include about twenty fulltime officials and workers from accountants to cooks to teamsters.[6] In addition to the plantation, there were three regional offices, in New Braunfels, Indianola, and Friedrichsburg, headed by Lieutenant Bené, Gustav Dresel and Hans von Coll, respectively. The largest office was in New Braunfels. The officials also began the process of disposing of the Society's property, such as wagons, horses, and buildings, through public auctions. For the time being, however, the Society intended to retain the plantation and slaves despite advice to the contrary from Prince von Solms-Braunfels and Friedrich von Wrede, Sr.

The idea was this: the Society would no longer continue to underwrite emigrants to Texas in so generous a fashion, because (on paper at least) they had introduced enough to satisfy the terms of the land grant contract. They had pushed most of the settlers through to their first crop, as they were contractually required to do. A large and expensive bureaucracy, therefore, was no longer necessary.

In the wake of the *Katastrophe*, as the shootout at the plantation came to be termed, the leadership in Texas was thrown into turmoil. As a fugitive from justice, the new commissioner-general, Hermann Spiess, felt compelled to turn over authority temporarily to a committee composed of Lieutenant Bené, Gustav Dresel, and Hans von Coll, but the committee lasted a scant two weeks.[7]

During this period, the committee did manage to issue a series of orders for the reduction of costs and the dismantling of the bureaucracy. This was in line with instructions Lieutenant Bené had brought back from Germany in the fall of 1847.

Hermann Spiess reclaimed the reins of authority briefly, but in March he was forced to flee again. This time he turned the administration over to Gustav Dresel with the assistance of Lieutenant Bené. Both men felt that Spiess was too discredited to continue as commissioner-general. When he refused to step down, Lieutenant Bené tendered his resignation saying that he could no longer work for a communist. At this point the leadership in Germany appointed Gustav Dresel to be the agent in charge, but he died after catching a fever in September 1848 at the Morris farm near Gonzales while on the way from Indian Point to New Braunfels. Upon Dresel's death Lieutenant Bené assumed the reins of authority, a position he held until 1855.

The shootout released a flood of litigation. Lawsuits for debt added to the litigation directly related to the shootout. In Fayette County alone creditors filed four cases.[8] Cases were also filed in Bexar, Comal, and other counties where the Society had done business. In 1848, the monetary woes of the Society, both in Texas and in Germany, came to a head.

Into this situation stepped Otto von Roeder, a quiet but determined man who came from a large and fascinating family with deep roots in Texas history. The family, as noted in Chapter 2, arrived in waves from Germany beginning in 1834 with the appearance of three brothers, Ludwig, Albrecht, Joachim, and a sister, Valeska.[9] A few months later, the rest of the family arrived, including Otto and his wife, Pauline (von Donop) Roeder, his father and mother, three brothers, and three sisters. One of the sisters was married to Robert Justus Kleberg. Two of Kleberg's brothers and a sister had also joined the party.[10] Before the groups could join up, both Valeska and Joachim succumbed to yellow fever.

The von Roeder family is said to have made the move to Texas due to sagging family fortunes, anti-authoritarian sentiments, and the lure of cheap land. According to Robert Kleberg, the brother-in-law of Otto, Fritz Dirks' (Friedrich Ernst) celebrated letter strongly influenced the family to make the move to Texas.[11]

The impetuousness of the younger Otto may also have played a role. He reputedly took part in a duel while he was a student in which he killed a young lieutenant.[12] Although pardoned by the King of Prussia of murder charges, social pressures were unforgiving, and the younger Otto followed his brothers to Texas.

The family located on the sandy prairie between the Brazos and San Bernard Rivers close to the Austin and Colorado County line where they were issued land. Albrecht von Roeder killed a wildcat (mountain lion) on a tributary of Mill Creek, and the community that coalesced here took the name *Wildkatzen Brunnen*, which became "Wild Cat Spring," and eventually "Cat Spring."

Ludwig (Louis) received a league (4,428 acres) about two miles northeast of Cat Spring and Rudolph von Roeder received a league about four miles to the northwest toward the present-day community of New Ulm. The Mexican government issued these leagues.[13] By the time Boos-Waldeck passed through in 1843, about twenty families had settled in the area.

When Otto emigrated in 1834, he was twenty-seven years old.

He had married the twenty-six-year-old Pauline von Donop in July, and they sailed in September. Highly educated, Otto had studied law at Heidelberg and Göttingen, had passed his examinations, and was awaiting nomination as a court secretary. Little did he know to what extent he would be called upon to use his legal skills in the years ahead.

The family arrived in Texas just prior to the disturbances that culminated in the War of Independence from Mexico and the "Runaway Scrape," as the wild and disorganized retreat before Santa Anna's armies was pejoratively termed. The family was caught up in these troubles. Otto's brother, Ludwig, and brother-in-law, Robert Justus Kleberg, both served in the Texas Army and participated in the siege of Bexar and the battle of San Jacinto. Other members of the family fled their homes and gathered on the Brazos to await the outcome of the struggle. For their service, Ludwig and Robert Kleberg were awarded certificates for land. Thus, the family has the distinction of fielding the largest Texas-German contingent in the War of Independence.

Otto was said to have served but received no certificates for his service. Later, however, he obtained a certificate for a headright from the Republic of Texas for a league and labor. It was granted on January 16, 1838, in Austin County. He established a gristmill on his land, which was located on the upper reaches of Mill Creek. A settlement eventually took shape, called by the local Germans *Rödersmühle* (Roeder's Mill) and later called Shelby. He also bought a sizeable tract of land in Fayette County.[14]

Otto's wife had died at Galveston during the Runaway Scrape and left him with a young son. Otto remarried in 1844 after a scandalous episode with his deceased brother's young widow, Theodore von Sack, nine years his junior. The two openly lived together several months prior to getting married—shocking to the sensibilities of the period, but an interesting insight into what a singular personality Otto had become.

Otto von Roeder does not fit easily into any mold. He was a consummate dealmaker and irrepressible in his desire to carve a place for himself and his family in his new home. His ambitions drove him out of the narrow confines of community life into the wider world. He used his university education, especially his studies in law, to further his ambitions.

His fortunes did rise. By the outbreak of the Civil War, he was reputedly the largest Texas-German slaveholder in the state and a considerable landholder.[15] Yet he never seemed to be able to completely consolidate his gains and, in the end, he died practically a pauper.[16] He had, it seems, a flaw: like the horse trader in the Heinrich von Kleist novella *Michael Kohlhaas*, he could brook no injustice. He would not compromise when he felt he was in the right, and, in the end, this stubbornness was his undoing.

Shelby is only a few miles to the east of the Jack League on the road to Industry. Von Roeder, therefore, was in a position to follow firsthand the developments at the plantation from its earliest stages. He met Count Boos-Waldeck on his initial expedition to the area, as noted, and he later socialized with Prince Solms-Braunfels during his stays at the plantation. Like many Germans in the area, he sensed that the Society's program might offer personal opportunities.

From the time of Prince Solms-Braunfels' initial stop at the plantation, Otto von Roeder was in the background of the Society, but his role was central: as a gristmill owner, he organized shipments and supplied grain to the hundreds of incoming settlers in 1846, 1847, and 1848.[17] His direct involvement in the plantation, however, began only after the *Katastrophe* in October 1847.[18]

The bureaucracy in Texas wanted desperately to oust Strubberg and his ruffians from the plantation when they seized control in the fall of 1847. To this end, they engaged the law firm of Hamilton & Chandler in La Grange, who succeeded in getting the district court to issue an order of sequestration.[19] This meant, in effect, that the court would take over the plantation until the legal issues could be sorted out. The German Emigration Co., however, was obligated to post a bond of $40,000. Otto von Roeder succeeded in persuading ten planters[20] from the area, for the most part prominent Anglos, to sign a bond of sequestration and indemnity.[21] This suggests either that Otto von Roeder enjoyed an amazing trust or that these men in some way had a vested interest in the dispute.

While supplying grain to the settlements in 1846, 1847, and for part of 1848, von Roeder had even pressed the slaves into service on occasion to help transport these supplies.[22] As a gristmill owner, he had connections with farmers in the area, which no doubt helped him to arrange these deliveries. In this effort he did not act as a paid official or broker for the Society; rather, he bought the grain and then sold it to the Society on credit, so that he incurred debt even as the Society grew indebted to him.[23] Hence, he had to press the Society for repayment because others were pressuring him.

A list of the names of the men from whom von Roeder purchased corn in order to supply the colonies has never surfaced. It is likely, however, that some of the prominent Anglos, such as Hamilton Ledbetter, who helped Otto von Roeder post the $40,000 bond for the Order of Sequestration, mentioned above, may have contributed. This would provide a motivation other than simple altruism or friendship with Otto von Roeder: they had a vested interest in the survival of the plantation and the solvency of the Society, or, barring that, in Otto von Roeder's capacity to recoup his debts, either in cash or in the form of the plantation itself, which could be easily converted into cash.

By the summer of 1848, the Society's debt to Otto von Roeder had risen to $6,000, a considerable sum by the valuations of the period. Unable to pay, Gustav Dresel (at this moment the chief agent) gave Otto von Roeder a deed to the plantation and all the property thereon, including twenty-five slaves.

Gustav Dresel, who had spent most of his time as the agent at Indian Point on the coast, apparently was not familiar with the plantation and its worth, for he agreed to a valuation of $14,000, a figure that by any measure of comparative values was woefully inadequate. Only six months before, the value had been set at $20,000 in a civil suit.[24] In an inventory of the Society's assets in Texas put together in 1848, the plantation is valued at $30,000.[25]

Once filed of record, however, the figure became legally binding. The mortgage, consisting of two parts, was drawn up on July 28, 1848, but was not filed of record until the following year.[26] The first part deeded the plantation to von Roeder in consideration of $14,000, from which, of course, the $6,000 owed to von Roeder would be subtracted. The second part was an indenture, or writ of reversion, whereby von Roeder agreed to deed the plantation and all its possessions back to the German Emigration Co. upon the payment $6,000 owed to him, if this money were paid back on or before July 28, 1849, or in exactly one year. In other words, von Roeder would get full title to the plantation in one year if the Society did not pay him what they owed, but if he did take over the plantation, he would have to pay the Society an additional $8,000.

With the Order of Sequestration in November 1847 a respected Anglo planter from the Round Top area, Hamilton Ledbetter, was appointed by the district court in La Grange to administer the plantation, but Otto von Roeder took his place early in 1848.[27] He also took up residence at the plantation, presumably in the *Herrenhaus,* where he could personally direct the slaves in their everyday tasks.

The Society was not able to pay back von Roeder the following year and asked for an extension, which he granted. Von Roeder's patience ran out in January 1850, when the debt once again fell due and the Society could not come up with the money. With respect to this matter, the committee in Germany had sent Lieutenant Bené the following communication:

> *Concerning the farm you will have received our decisions, funds for the redemption of the farm will be impossible for us to put at your disposal by the deadline, January 1st. We trust, therefore, that you will have taken care of the matter in the most favorable fashion possible.*[28]

In the meantime, the amount owed von Roeder had grown substantially. Several lawsuits had been filed in Fayette County against the German Emigration Co. for debt, and each of these sought a partial attachment against the property of the plantation.[29] Otto von Roeder paid these debts and settled these claims, since they directly involved the plantation and compromised his claims. He did so apparently on a discounted basis, but he presented these instruments for payment in full to the Society.[30] Left to his own devices and compelled to adjust for the changing numbers, Lieutenant Bené renegotiated the whole agreement with Roeder in a complicated document finalized on February 25, 1850.[31]

The terms were basically these: in exchange for the plantation and everything that went with it, von Roeder agreed to surrender and forego all his claims, debts, and encumbrances against the Society, and, moreover, to discount the dollar value of these significantly. This reduced his claim from the $10,857 to $8,491. To get title to the plantation, he had to make up the difference between what was owed him and what they had agreed the plantation was worth, which was $14,000. This difference amounted to roughly $5,500. Von Roeder agreed to pay the difference within eighteen months, and to back this up he mortgaged his gin and 526 acres near Shelby and 1,000 acres of the plantation. By this agreement, von Roeder took a step closer to complete and unencumbered ownership of the plantation, or so he thought.

Lieutenant Bené, at the moment, the acting general agent for the Society, justified this agreement to the leadership in Germany as follows:

Even if we had the means at hand to redeem the plantation, we would be faced with another judicial attachment, and a third and a fourth, etc., each with increased costs for the Society, and these costly attachments would continue until the last dollar had been expended. It is therefore by a wide margin the best policy of the Society to put an end to this expensive possession, which has never yielded a profit.[32]

Bené went on to point out that the total deal was worth over $20,000 to the company because von Roeder also agreed to surrender a lien on valuable property in New Braunfels worth $3,750, a lien that Gustav Dresel had also given him in exchange for corn deliveries.

Von Roeder at first was willing to consider another extension, but because his creditors were pressing him, he insisted on a resolution.[33] As of January 1, 1850, he considered the matter settled: the property was now his to deal with as he pleased. He immediately put up parts of the plantation for sale. The Society continued to press for an accommodation, but von Roeder refused. On February 22, 1850, Lieutenant Bené surrendered the Deed of Reversion to von Roeder.[34]

There was one other complication. In the wake of the disturbances in Europe and the troubles in Texas, the noblemen in Germany assembled for a meeting in the spring of 1848. Their purpose: to cut expenses drastically and, if possible, divest themselves of the whole venture. To expedite the latter, they deemed it necessary to put all the properties in Count Castell's name. In May 1848, Count Castell wrote to Cappes that a provisional deal with a group of investors, headed by one Dr. Ludwig Martin from Freiburg, had been struck in May 1848.[35]

Ludwig Martin traveled to Texas in the summer of 1848 to inspect the properties that he and his investors had provisionally bought.[36] He was given the title of Inspector General and Agent of the Society. One of his first acts was to file the sale agreement of record in Travis and Fayette Counties.[37] He also registered his new corporation, which he named the German Colonization Society of Texas, and began offering shares in the company.

Martin turned up in Fayette County in August 1848 to inspect the plantation only to find it occupied by Otto von Roeder. The appearance of Martin on the scene created another distraction in an already hopelessly complicated situation. Since he had his sale recorded before von Roeder and Dresel recorded their instrument, Martin insisted that his purchase took precedence over the agreement between Otto von Roeder and Gustav Dresel.

Martin found an ally in Charles Fordtran. Fordtran also had claims against the Society that had gone unpaid. He had also been granted power of attorney in matters concerning the plantation by Count Boos-Waldeck before he departed, and subsequently by Prince Solms-Braunfels. He had refused to surrender this instrument to Solms-Braunfels upon his dismissal. He was also still in possession of many documents and records of the Society. Martin deemed this important. He paid off Fordtran's claims against the Society and in return received the power of attorney and the papers. He thought he could outmaneuver von Roeder with these instruments, but in this he was frustrated. Von Roeder insisted on the validity of his claims and stayed at the plantation.

Martin also challenged Fischer and Miller. By the agreement signed in September 1845, Fischer had withdrawn from active participation in the Society, but he had not relinquished his claims to 250,000 acres of bonus lands as stipulated in the land grant contract. Martin challenged this claim, and a panel of two federal judges arbitrated the case. Not only did they rule in favor of Fischer and Miller, but they also adjudged that the Society was in breach of its contract and ordered a $14,000 judgment.[38]

Eventually Martin left Texas in despair that the affairs of the Society could ever be disentangled to the point that the deal could work. In 1852, he sold his shares in the German Colonization Society to a consortium of German investors, F. Roehr, J. W. Ubaghs, and M. W. Settegast, who in turn initiated a fresh round of litigation. This hopelessly complicated mess dragged on for many years; in fact, it was not completely resolved until 1872, and the final disposition did not include the plantation in any of its terms. Meusebach's deposition in the case formed the basis of his celebrated "Answer to Interrogatories," which is regarded as his most definitive statement about his role in the history of German emigration to Texas.

In retrospect, the von Roeder clan had to be one of the most energetic, unconventional, and fascinating German families to come to Texas. Their energy was too stifled by the hidebound Germany of post-Napoleonic Europe, so they moved *en masse* to Texas where they found a wide-open field for their collective vigor. Despite many harsh setbacks and defeats, they seemed meant for this formative phase of Texas, and Texas was receptive to them. In later life, Otto von Roeder always spoke with pride of his and his family's heritage as early settlers and as participants in the war for independence from Mexico.[39]

Above all, they seemed driven by the desire to acquire land. How fitting, therefore, that Robert Kleberg, Jr., Otto's nephew, married the daughter of Richard King, thus becoming part of the largest private landholding in Texas, the King Ranch.

Of all the clan, Otto von Roeder emerges as the most intriguing. Many are unaware of what an important role he and, by extension, the plantation played in the survival of the settlers during the dreadful winter and spring of 1846-47, and thus in the ultimate successful transition by thousands of German emigrants to a new life and community on the Texas frontier. Through the combination of the plantation and Otto von Roeder, the *Adelsverein* was able to keep the struggling settlements of New Braunfels and Fredericksburg fed, alive, and afloat until these settlements consolidated enough to supply their own needs. Otto von Roeder organized the grain and beef shipments, but the plantation, as the most substantial asset owned outright by the Society in Texas, supplied the reservoir of credit needed to finance these food shipments. Without these shipments, surely hundreds more would have perished, and the whole venture could have faced a *Götterdämmerung* far in excess of the desperate situation faced by the hundreds of emigrants on the beaches of Lavaca Bay in 1846. The whole venture, in fact, had narrowly averted a complete debacle—a debacle which could have led to a mass, disorganized, and chaotic retrenchment to more settled areas of the state on the part of the thousands of German emigrants introduced by the *Adelsverein* into the Hill Country of Texas.

By the close of 1852, Otto von Roeder had successfully cleared his debts and consolidated his ownership of the plantation and its slaves. His efforts in arranging for and supplying grain to the colonists in New Braunfels and Friedrichsburg appeared to have been motivated principally by genuine concern for the plight of his countrymen. Through his association with the *Adelsverein,* however, Otto von Roeder also clearly expected to advance his own fortunes. It turned out to be a deadly embrace.

CHAPTER 12

Nassau-Rosenberg

The von Rosenberg family was a prominent German family who spent the formative stage of their move to Texas at or near Nassau Plantation. Their extensive correspondence, published as *Ancestral Voices*, offers fascinating insight into the process of assimilation and establishing a new life in a new world, which included coming to terms with slavery.

Of the von Rosenbergs, it is safe to say that Germany's loss was Texas' gain. The family proved to be a clan of energetic and cultivated individuals, many of whom subsequently pursued professional and business careers, rising to positions of prominence. As a group they were also extremely civic-minded. They established schools, churches, and clubs in many communities across the state.

They were also prime participants in an unpleasant but fascinating episode concerning the plantation; they left an extensive record of their move to and assimilation in their new country; and, finally, their presence in the Round Top area acted as a magnet to other educated Germans so that the small town and surrounding community eventually emerged as one of the more refined German settlements in Texas.[1]

The record they left is generally in the form of letters; most, but not all, translated and published by the family.[2] Collectively, this correspondence offers a rich, absorbing, and multifaceted record of the trials and tribulations, as well as the simple joys and pleasures, of frontier (or quasi-frontier) life in Texas in the 1850s with particular reference to Nassau Plantation. Additionally, Amanda Fallier, the wife of Peter Carl, described life from a woman's point of view.

In 1849 Peter Carl von Rosenberg was the aristocratic master of Eckitten, an estate on the banks of the Memel River in East Prussia. He was fifty-six years old and a former officer in the Prussian cavalry who had served with Field Marshal Blücher against Napoleon in the decisive battle of Waterloo. His first wife, Amanda Dorothea (Fröhlich), had died at the young age of twenty-nine after the birth of their fourth child, Johannes Carl. In addition to taking care of the children from the first marriage, his second wife, Amanda Fallier (1806-1864), gave birth to five more children, four of whom lived to adulthood. She and her husband also adopted an orphaned niece.[3]

In this most conservative region of Germany, Peter Carl von Rosenberg nourished attitudes distinctly out of tune with most of his countrymen. He was a *Freidenker*, a freethinker, who had been sympathetic to those antiauthoritarian ideas that had been simmering under the surface for decades in all parts of Germany and that finally erupted in 1848.[4] His oldest surviving son from his first marriage, Carl Wilhelm (1821-1901), who had risen to the position of court architect in Berlin, was outspoken in his views. This was an untenable and unforgivable attitude for a prominent member of the Prussian aristocracy. In the backlash of the collapsed 1848 revolution, he was dismissed from his post, forced to resign from his commission in the reserves, and banned from professional activity.

This proscription led Carl Wilhelm (henceforth, William) to the decision to emigrate. At first his father remonstrated, but the idea took root and eventually the whole family decided to join him and emigrate *en masse*. In 1849, Peter Carl put Eckitten, his beloved estate, up for sale and with the proceeds liquidated his debts to finance the move to Texas. Moved by the spirit of adventure, Peter Carl's older brother, Ernst, had come early to Texas and had participated in the Long expedition.[5] In the aftermath of this filibustering misadventure, he was executed in Mexico. His connection with Texas, however, influenced the von Rosenbergs in their choice of a destination.[6]

The eleven members[7] of the von Rosenberg family departed Germany in October 1849 on the *Franziska*[8] under Captain Hagedorn and arrived in December after an uneventful passage. Although all were related by marriage or blood, it is best to consider the group as a collection of separate families, for the three older children (two sons and a daughter) were married (or soon to be), and each couple set up their own farmstead with their own resources.

While in Galveston, Captain Hagedorn hosted a ball for his passengers. Shortly thereafter, the party traveled overland to Velasco at the mouth of the Brazos River in two coaches, one they had brought with them from Germany and the other, a regular mail coach. For a good part of this trip they travelled along the beaches, which necessitated fording several "cuts" that were similar to small streams creating moments of anxiety for the ladies. At Velasco, they boarded the steamship *Washington* for the trip up the Brazos River to San Felipe. The *Washington*, with its stately commons, fancy windows and glass doors, made quite an impression on the family, especially the ladies.[9]

In San Felipe the party found temporary quarters for four weeks with the Meier family.[10] Frau von Rosenberg described the city as "elend [miserable]," which she attributed to the fact that it had been put to the torch during the war and had not quite recovered. She was encouraged to find, however, that most people were courteous and honest and they never lost any of their belongings to theft.

Leaving the family behind, Peter Carl and his older son William ventured into the interior to search for suitable homesteads. Like most of their fellow countryman, they headed west where the wet prairies gave way to uplands. They traveled as far as Bastrop, but while in La Grange, Peter Carl made the acquaintance of Otto von Roeder, who happened to be there on business. Otto von Roeder helped Peter Carl look for a suitable farm, but when none could be found, he offered him his Washington County gristmill and farm, located four miles to the east of Nassau Plantation. When Peter Carl declined this offer, he then offered a portion of Nassau Plantation. Peter Carl related that Otto von Roeder needed money to complete the deal with the German Emigration Co. by which he had obtained the plantation. Together with Otto von Roeder, he inspected the land, and because it had a nice house, they soon reached an agreement.[11]

Von Rosenberg doubtless felt confident that in dealing with a fellow German nobleman, he would avoid the problems associated with unscrupulous land speculators. Otto von Roeder, for his part, most likely was warmed by the thought of settling other German families of similar class and background nearby. The letters show that Otto von Roeder subsequently took an almost paternal interest in the well-being of the von Rosenberg clan, helping them to set up homesteads, plow fields, and arrange purchases. In general, he shared the experience of his years in Texas and kept an eye out for their welfare.

On February 16, 1850, the sale was completed "to von Rosenberg's complete satisfaction,"[12] and the deed was recorded in the Fayette County courthouse.[13] By the terms of the sale, Peter Carl von Rosenberg bought 800 acres of the original plantation for $1,809, of which $1,009 was for the *Herrenhaus* and other improvements and $800 was for the land. Interestingly, the land had shown only modest appreciation in value—from 75 cents an acre to $1.00 per acre—over the seven years since Boos-Waldeck had originally purchased the Jack League. The 800 acres lay east of Jack's Creek and had not been farmed up to that point, but it did include the *Herrenhaus* with its barn, garden, and orchard. Otto von Roeder moved his family to the overseer's house in the compound on the west side of Jack's Creek where he continued to farm the original fenced and plowed fields.[14]

In his quest to find a suitable homestead, Peter Carl von Rosenberg had been absent from his family for over three weeks. All were happy when he returned to San Felipe with news of his successful purchase. The families quickly packed their belongings and set out for the Round Top area in three vehicles. The trip from San Felipe to Nassau turned out to be quite an adventure. A ferocious Texas "norther" blew in with a strong wind, rain and cold. These northers, a typical and recurring meteorological phenomenon for Texas in winter and spring, made quite an impression on the family.[15] The temperature dropped dramatically, the roads turned to mud, and the streams began to swell.

The first night was spent in Industry, most likely with Friedrich Ernst, who had established an inn at his farmstead. A young German immigrant, Herrmann von Biberstein,[16] had offered to drive the lead wagon, and he pressed on even after dark, attempting to complete the trip by the evening of the second day. One of the wagons became separated from the others in the stormy darkness, but all were reunited the following day.

In the end, on January 28, 1850, all arrived safe and sound. The two older sons, William and Johannes, with the help of Otto von Roeder subsequently bought farms in the neighboring James Winn League from Crockett Peery and John Stirper respectively.[17] William, who had married shortly before departing Germany,[18] bought a 200-acre farm that included a house, stable, and corn crib. Also twenty acres had already been fenced with sixteen acres put into cultivation.[19]

The older daughter, Johanna (Hännchen) Carolina had become engaged to Herman Hellmuth, a close friend of William, before their departure from Germany. They married upon their arrival in Galveston. Hellmuth purchased a farm with "cattle, horses and all appurtenances" for $760.[20] Johannes Carl bought a farm of seventy acres with a new log house for $170, but it contained no cultivated land.[21] Later, in the fall, he married Julie Wilhelmine Gross, whose family had settled nearby. He then set up a common household with his sister and brother-in-law since their farms adjoined.

Thus, only the elder Peter Carl von Rosenberg located within Nassau Plantation proper: his two sons and his daughter established farms close by, but outside the Jack League.

Peter Carl and his wife, three younger children, and adopted niece moved into the *Herrenhaus* and set up residence. In her first extensive letter back to her sisters in Europe, Frau von Rosenberg seemed quite pleased with the house: "You also have no idea of what one calls a house in Texas—a rectangular room, high and airy, with a good roof is called here a house. Among these a structure like ours, six years ago the best and still among the best, is called a fort, a castle, a prince's house, a manor house. Our house is called these things in jest, but it is indeed pretty and, I may add, romantic. . . ."[22]

Frau von Rosenberg's enthusiasm, however, was tempered by acute arachnophobia, an unfortunate malady in Texas, since spiders are ubiquitous.[23] She also had an inordinate fear of snakes. Her family and friends tried to allay her worries, but the situation was not helped when she discovered a chicken snake in her daughter's doll box one day.

Once settled in the new residence Peter Carl wasted little time in outfitting his farm. He acquired eight horses, two oxen, ten cows with calves, ten pigs, forty-five chickens, four ducks, four dogs, and four cats.[24] The last were considered essential because of the prevalence of mice. His most important purchase, however, was a Negro man, Toms, ($800) and a Negro woman and child ($700) for the household work. Otto von Roeder helped him with these purchases. Later, the elder von Rosenberg added a flock of sheep to his purchases and the sale of wool became an important source of income.[25]

In this early stage, all seemed happy and satisfied with their new life in Texas.[26] In a letter to his brother Otto in Germany, Peter Carl characterized Texas as a place "where one lives happy and content . . . , free as a human being."[27] He went on to describe his daily routine: "At sunrise I get up, wash myself, then the pipe is lit, and while my Negro Toms and Franz, my German helper, with the children milk the cows, I feed the chickens and chop some kindling for the iron cook stove, as much as I need. While we are finishing that, my wife with one of the children cooks coffee and warms milk. With bread and butter our table is set. Franz eats with us; Toms takes his food to his room or to the kitchen, which is built at the west end of the house. We drink and discuss the day's work. I don't work in the garden or field, but Axel, Eugen and Walther do: they plant corn, thin out the seedlings, weed and chop."[28]

The elder von Rosenberg was a man of many talents who surprised his neighbor, Otto von Roeder, by his versatility: he alternately demonstrated ability as a mason, a cabinetmaker, a cooper and a saddler. Moreover, he enjoyed doing these various jobs.

William, the older son, wrote in a similar vein about his new life in Texas: "My life is so simple and uniform that one day goes like the other. I get my two horses early and feed them eight ears of corn each, help my wife milk the cows, get several buckets of water from a flowing spring some fifty steps from the yard, wash myself, eat breakfast, harness the horses and go plowing. At half-past eleven I unhitch, water and feed the horses, eat dinner, take a nap and plow until evening. Thus, one day passes like the other . . . ."[29]

In the letter in which he explained his routine William included a sketch of the layout of his farm and fields.[30] He had a fenced area of about twelve acres, half of which he rented out and half of which he planted in cotton. Of the six acres of cotton, half was to be his. In another field, which Otto von Roeder had helped him plow, he planted three acres of corn. He also put in a garden with melons, pumpkins, onions, Irish potatoes, sweet potatoes, shallots, and beans. He also kept three beehives. His residence included a house and yard, a kitchen, smokehouse, stable and a cow pen. A nearby spring provided water throughout the summer.

At what point does the frontier cease to be frontier? When Count Boos-Waldeck bought the Jack League in January 1843 the region could certainly still claim this label. Even though the Indian threat had receded by 1843, the area was only partially settled and infrastructure in the form of roads, schools, etc., was embryonic. By 1850 much had changed. Peter Carl von Rosenberg wrote that the area had become "quite civilized," with fifteen farms of various sizes (ten of which were German) within two miles, and with all kinds of craftsmen available for employment, usually at the rate of one dollar per day.[31]

Thus, by 1850, northern Fayette County had ceased by most markers to be frontier; this had shifted nearly two hundred miles to the west. Still, many of the hardships and deprivations common to the frontier continued to make life challenging for the settlers in the area, especially those from refined backgrounds. The absence of theater, music and the arts was especially hard on those who had once known these pleasures. William von Rosenberg addressed this point in one of his letters when he wrote, "Here effort and work await everyone who comes; no theater, no musical entertainment . . . in short, all recreations are absent."[32]

Despite the absence of theaters and fancy balls, the von Rosenbergs soon settled into an active social life among peers in their new home. The von Roeder and von Rosenberg families matched up in almost every category: in age, in social background, and in education. The bonds deepened as the families came to know each other.[33]

The summer of 1850 gave occasion for much socializing because in the space of one week three engagements were announced. Wilhelm von Roeder, the younger brother of Otto von Roeder, became engaged to Theodore (Dorchen) Sack, his cousin and a newfound friend to Lina von Rosenberg. A week before, Johannes von Rosenberg announced his engagement to Julie Wilhelmina Christine Gross, the daughter of Carl Apollo Gross, who had immigrated with his large family in 1848 and purchased a 210 acre farm in the Jack League from Otto von Roeder.[34] The third engagement was between Amanda Karolina (Lina) von Rosenberg, the eighteen-year-old daughter of *Herr* and *Frau* von Rosenberg and Arthur Meerscheidt, a young titled officer, who had been persuaded to settle in the Round Top area by

Franz Jäntschke, who had also purchased a small farm from Otto von Roeder.[35]

In August 1850 the families made a joint trip to Millheim where they stayed with the Ferdinand Enkelking family. In order to make the trip, Frau von Rosenberg, who suffered from a series of phobias in addition to fear of spiders and snakes, had great difficulty in gathering up enough courage to make the trip, but with the help of Frau von Roeder, who prodded her along with a combination of gentle encouragement, cheerfulness, and good-natured mockery, she finally consented.

The party travelled in two wagons supplied by Otto von Roeder, the ladies and gentlemen in one wagon, driven by Otto; the children and servants in another, driven by Butler, the erstwhile Nassau slave who had once run away from the plantation but had chosen to return. Frau von Rosenberg praised his abilities as a cook and said that he had served as Prince Solms' personal cook when the prince stayed at the plantation.

His abilities as a teamster, however, did not match his talents as a cook, leading to one of the more frightening adventures of the trip. The region between Nassau Plantation and the settlement of Millheim is quite hilly in places. Coming down one hill, Butler was not able to control the team of mules pulling his wagon. The wagon threatened to overtake and collide with the lead wagon, driven by Otto von Roeder. At the last moment Butler pulled his team hard to the side to avoid collision, causing the wagon to overturn and eject the children riding in it. Luckily they were thrown clear and the wagon and gear suffered no permanent harm.

It was a two-day trip and the weather was obliging. The party spent the night at Friedrich Ernst's guesthouse in Industry. The next day they arrived safely at Millheim, where they stayed at Ferdinand Enkelking's spacious and comfortable (*gemütliches*) house.

Frau von Rosenberg was quite taken with the personality, presence, and charm of Enkelking, who had also married one of the ubiquitous Ploeger-Sack sisters, thus being part of the wider von Roeder/Kleberg sphere of influence in this part of the state. He was, according to her description, extremely tall with striking blue eyes. He projected a carefree attitude about life and seemed unmotivated by excessive ambition, but this belied a drive and purpose that had led him to provide one of the more comfortable and cleverly designed homesteads for his family in the area. He was always charming, witty, and straightforward in his dealings with people. He had been educated in law in Germany and ran a store in Millheim where he had installed gymnastic equipment, which became the basis of a local *Turnverein* (gymnastic society). His eccentricity was genuine and he was known, beloved, and respected throughout the wider area.

Frau von Rosenberg used her description of Enkelking as an opportunity to draw a contrast between him and Otto von Roeder and in so doing has provided one of the few firsthand accounts we have of the presence of this important, but neglected, Texas-German. She described Herr von Roeder as more reserved and formal in demeanor but impressive in his own way. He was a refined and witty conversationalist, contributing his part to the general atmosphere of lighthearted but refined levity, common to their society. She praised his character and determination and was impressed with how many people he knew and the general respect and esteem with which he was universally received. Her descriptions make clear, however, that Herr von Roeder had a distant and enigmatic side.

Not so with Frau von Roeder. On at least five different occasions in her letters, Frau von Rosenberg singled out Otto von Roeder's wife for praise, writing that "When Frau von Roeder comes it is though a fairy has waved a magic wand. Everyone admires her and greets her with love, but her shining wit, who wouldn't worship this spirit."[36]

Frau von Roeder's presence was a serendipitous event for Frau von Rosenberg, easing her transition to a new life in the hinterland of Texas by her experience and good cheer and helping her to better cope with her numerous phobias and anxieties by a mixture of reassurance and good-natured ribbing.

Otto von Roeder's mother was also named Sack, thus his wife was also his first cousin, a socially acceptable arrangement for the period. The Sack sisters' father had been a man of importance in Prussia, serving as *Geheimrat* (privy counselor) to the King of Prussia. His real talent, however, seems to have been in the fathering of children. He was reputed to have produced twenty-two children by two different wives, a sobering consideration when it came to providing the numerous daughters with a *standesgemäss* (socially acceptable) existence. The effect was a stream of daughters finding their way to Texas as they came of age. They were universally praised, these Ploeger-Sack daughters, for their combination of attractiveness, refinement, adaptability, good cheer and pluck. But of all of them, Otto von Roeder's wife, Theodore, stood out.

Although at least eight German families who could count as cultured and educated lived in the immediate area of Nassau,[37] *Frau* von Rosenberg restricted her social life almost exclusively to visits to her neighbors, the Otto von Roeders, and to her own family members. This was due in large part, she confessed, to her phobias, which made it difficult for her to leave the house. Nassau-Rosenberg, as the homestead was now termed, became her pride and joy, on which she focused her energy and time. The old *Herrenhaus* underwent a series of refinements adding greatly to its livability and appeal. The windows, which were large by the standards of the day, were fitted with panes. Curtains, a *sine qua non*, for a German *Frau* were quickly sewn and attached. Next, *Herr* von Roeder had the walls whitewashed with a mixture of lime and water, a common practice of the period before paint became readily available. The practice was also believed to discourage insect infestation and retard rot.

The house was also enlarged. The north porch was enclosed to provide an additional two rooms. The German carpenters engaged to perform the work completed their task a scant two days before the wedding of Lina and Arthur in December 1850. Meerscheidt wrote that the house was built of the beautiful cedar and that two large windows, one to the north and one to the east, gave free range to an impressive view of prairie and forest.[38]

As a good German *Hausfrau*, Amanda Fallier von Rosenberg kept her house immaculately tidy and clean. She lamented when the heavy spring downpours turned the soil into temporary quagmires leading the men and children to track mud across the porches and into her house, which she then attacked with ferocity. Nassau-Rosenberg became her refuge in this new and strange land.

Even as Peter Carl von Rosenberg and his family were settling in to the routine of a simple farm life, another former member of the German nobility was also starting a new life in the Jack League. Arthur Carl Wilhelm Gustav Anton Archibald von Meerscheidt-von Hullesem, to use his full name, had also purchased a small farm from Otto von Roeder at almost the same time. Meerscheidt's life would shortly blend with that of von Rosenberg's in a substantial way.

Before he made the move to Texas, Meerscheidt (1827-1887) had already packed quite a life of adventure into his twenty-three years. He had started a career as an Austrian officer, but was caught up in the revolutionary fervor that swept Europe in 1848-49. Although aristocratic by background, he was clearly sympathetic to the spirit of change sweeping the continent.

This spirit had quickly taken on nationalistic overtones. In Hungary, where Meerscheidt was stationed, it took the form of revolt against Austrian suzerainty. Meerscheidt switched sides and joined the nationalist forces, led by Lajos Kussuth, as did many idealists from across Europe. He participated in several battles and was wounded near Czegedin. After a few initial successes, the revolt was firmly crushed when Russia intervened on the side of Austria to uphold the *status quo*. Meerscheidt was forced to flee for his life, and, after many adventures, made his way via Turkey and France to Germany and safety. Here he chafed under the reactionary forces who had regained the upper hand. He resolved, in October 1849, to leave Europe for the New World.

Meerscheidt arrived in New Orleans in January 1850. Here he fell in with a young German emigrant by the name of Franz Jäntschke who had emigrated the previous year, met, and married a younger sister of Otto von Roeder's wife and had purchased on time a small tract of land north of the Jack League. Jäntschke was returning from Europe and had brought along with him another Sack sister, Dornchen.

Jäntschke persuaded Meerscheidt to accompany him and his sister-in-law to the Round Top area to make the area his new home. In the first of many letters back to his mother in Germany, Meerscheidt described his move and recorded his initial impressions. Jäntschke's wife impressed him deeply by her determination and good cheer. Along with her two-year-old daughter, she had stayed behind with a relative while her husband made the journey back to Europe.[39]

Once settled, the two families decided to pool their resources, farm together, and build a common house. Despite the hard physical labor required by such an endeavor, labor to which he was unaccustomed, the dominant tone of Meerscheidt's early letters is enthusiastic. His move coincided with the outbreak of spring and he enthused about the attractiveness of the landscape and the magnificence of the wildflower displays.

In a decision characteristic of many German emigrants, Jäntschke and Meerscheidt decided to build a house of a more substantial nature than the norm. Similar to the *Herrenhaus*, they dressed down the logs with adzes to form more refined surfaces, an extremely time-consuming activity. These "planked" logs were then carefully notched and fitted. Once chinked, they enclosed a sturdy, weatherproof space. The Anglo settlers, Meerscheidt remarked, all seemed driven by the need to get as much land in cultivation as soon as possible. Consequently, they often put up makeshift structures, which offered minimal protection from the elements.

Meerscheidt offered his own analysis of this tendency, conceding that it was not necessarily the wisest course of action, since it took time away from fencing the fields and preparing the soil for the first year's cash crop. To his way of thinking, however, the psychological benefits of a good house outweighed other considerations.

In the meantime the party lived in a tent under the spreading branches of a giant live oak tree. All the items that constitute a household were spread around the compound while a campfire for cooking burned in one corner. Amanda Karolina (Lina) von Rosenberg wrote that it presented an almost idyllic picture.[40]

In general, Meerscheidt's letters portray poignantly a process of psychological and physical adaptation to a new life in Texas. As such, his feelings are representative of those of many of his class and background. Naturally, at first he desired to put a good face on the situation. Touching are the many letters to his mother asking, even pleading, for her to join him in his new home. He highlights the positive aspects of his new life—the freedoms, the simple joys of working the soil and building a house. He points out that many refined and educated people from Germany have settled in the area. He enthuses about the beauty of springtime in South Central Texas. On the other hand, he downplays the negatives: the capriciousness of the weather, the distance from centers of civilization and culture, the sense of isolation, and the everyday hardships. The one thing that troubles him, he reported, is his loneliness in respect to the opposite sex.

This situation was soon remedied. He struck up a friendship with Amanda Karolina von Rosenberg (Lina), the seventeen-year-old daughter of Peter Carl and Amanda. This friendship quickly blossomed into love. Before the summer of 1850 was out, the two became engaged. Meerscheidt gives a touching description of his awkwardness when he asked her father for her hand. Peter Carl, however, was quick to approve the engagement, but he set the wedding for two years down the road. Although he fully understood the rationale, Meerscheidt was disappointed at this prolongation. He needed to become more established in his household and his farming operation before he could hope to support a wife and family.

The elder von Rosenberg soon realized that the young couple's passion for one another was incompatible with such a long wait and he adjusted his requirement accordingly. The wedding was advanced to November 9, 1850. The celebration became an important social event, with over forty people in attendance from the local and surrounding communities.[41] Meerscheidt was not far enough along by this point to provide shelter or financial support. Consequently, Peter Carl invited the couple to live with him and his wife at the *Herrenhaus*. To accommodate them, he started an addition to the house, described above.

With his marriage to Lina in 1850, the Meerscheidts become an integral and important strand of the von Rosenberg story in Texas. The Meerscheidts in time were blessed to see six of their thirteen children grow to maturity and these in turn to marry and produce large families.

William was the first of the von Rosenbergs to realize that his education and background ill-suited him to life of a farmer. In 1850 the citizens of Fayette County decided to build a new courthouse. William, as a trained architect, became involved in the project. He drew up the plans and the quality of his work led to such general approbation that it led to an appointment as Chief Draftsman in the General Land Office. In 1855 he sold his farm and moved his family to Austin where he soon settled into a role as a leader in the growing German community and a man of respect and prominence in the wider society.

The year 1855 also saw a change for Peter Carl and his wife. The family patriarch had husbanded his resources frugally and wisely. He decided that he could withdraw as active participant in the everyday activities of the farm and, by renting it, afford to retire and move to Round Top, where services and social life were closer at hand. Consequently, he deeded 100 acres of the original 800 acres of his farm to Arthur and Lina and made a similar gift to his eldest son (with Amanda), Eugen. He commissioned a house in Round Top, still standing today, and in October 1856 made the move.

Over the years, frustration and disappointment begins to creep into Meerscheidt's letters. The weather was either too dry or too wet and commodity prices too volatile to get ahead financially, which, as his family grew, became an ever more pressing consideration. By training and upbringing, Meerscheidt, like William von Rosenberg, was ill prepared to be a farmer. Despite his initial enthusiasm, he never completely adapted to his new profession. He began to consider other things to do. In 1853 he had experimented with making and selling bricks. He met with only limited success in this venture and quickly abandoned the effort.

With the change in circumstances brought about by the departure of Peter Carl and his wife, Meerscheidt decided to set up a socialist experiment. He had read about the attempt by the French socialist, Victor Prosper Considerant (1808-1892)[42] to set up a socialist commune in Texas and believed that the ideas underlying his experimental farm might, in modified form, find application to Nassau. Consequently, in 1856, he entered into an agreement with a couple of other men,[43] but the experiment was unsuccessful and short-lived due to personality conflicts.

Still, Meerscheidt considered the idea of socialism "great and true." He wrote that "only thereby is general cultural betterment possible. Only through this can poverty and its attendant vices be alleviated. This is the task that humanity must set for itself, even if it takes several centuries of struggle to realize. It must be attained or humanity fails."[44]

The years of 1855–1856 proved to be watershed years for the extended von Rosenberg family on a number of counts. William sold his farm and moved with his family to Austin; Peter Carl and Amanda moved to Round Top; and, Otto von Roeder sold his remaining interest in the Jack League and moved with his family many miles to the south to a new farm in Mission Valley along the banks of the Guadalupe River in Victoria County, a move which might well have contributed to the von Rosenberg's decision to leave Nassau-Rosenberg.

The year 1856 also saw the death of the first of the von Rosenberg children, Johann Caroline, Peter Carl's daughter by his first wife, who died in childbirth in August 1856. Together with her husband, Herman Gustav Hellmuth, the couple, had set up their own farmstead on a plot of land close to Nassau, but far enough removed that only occasional visits took place. Here the young couple quickly had five children, two of whom died in infancy. With Johanna's death, Herman Hellmuth became a widower with three young children.

Establishing a new life as farmers had not been easy for the young couple. Herman Hellmuth, highly educated in Berlin, like Arthur Meerscheidt, had not shown himself particularly adept at farming. With the death of Johanna and the departure of the elder von Rosenbergs to Round Top, Arthur Meerscheidt invited his widowed brother-in-law to set up a separate household near Nassau-Rosenberg and together with another man set up a cooperative field association. In a reflection of Meerscheidt's socialist leanings, the three households, though separated, would unite in a common agricultural effort.

After Peter Carl and his wife made the move to Round Top, the plan was put into practice. In the meantime Herman Hellmuth had become engaged to Libussa Fröhlich, the adopted niece of Peter Carl who had made the move with the family in 1850. The two were married in October 1857 and from this union four children survived to adulthood.

Like Wilhelm von Rosenberg, Herman Hellmuth eventually came to the realization that he was not cut out to be a farmer. In 1859 he disposed of his farm and moved with his family to Round Top where he established a school. Over the course of the rest of his life he continued as a teacher and also as a highly accomplished musician. He established several musical societies throughout his long and active life and spent much of his time entertaining and conducting the societies.[45]

Arthur Meerscheidt was the last one to throw in the towel. In 1859 he purchased three lots in Round Top, sold his interest in Nassau to Georg Weyand, and established a store. By building on his knowledge of agriculture, however, he eventually achieved a position of comfortable affluence for his family. One of his sons, Alexander (1853-1921), studied law and became an extremely successful business man in San Antonio, where he is credited with, among other achievements, the development of the famous King William District. The Meerscheidt name spread across Texas and everywhere was received with approbation.

By any criteria, the von Rosenberg family's move to Texas must be considered a success. The family had set for themselves the goal of building a new life in a new land where they could be free of the oppressive encroachment of official authority in all aspects of their lives. They found that freedom in Texas and responded by rewarding the state with an astonishing family whose seed continued to multiply and enrich the state socially and culturally over the generations, a story which spread beyond the scope of Nassau Plantation and thus beyond the scope of this book.

Initially all attempted to build their new lives as simple farmers in their new home at Nassau-Rosenberg (or close proximity). Some of the family continued in this tradition but most eventually realized that in temperament and background they were better suited for professional careers. This process of adaptation and psychological transition enriches the legacy of the plantation.

Their success, it should be remembered, was in a real sense also the success of Otto von Roeder. He had sold them the land, offered guidance and counsel, provided them with a social life, and (finally) sealed the relationship through the marriage of his sister-in-law with Peter Carl and Amanda Fallier's first son, Eugen. The service Otto von Roeder provided, he also provided to many other fresh emigrants, not only by parceling off Nassau Plantation, but also his holdings in Austin County near Shelby, the town that he had founded in 1837.

The decade of the 1850s was a favorable period. Drought, a general shortage of money, and wild swings in commodity prices muddied the waters from time to time, but in general, it was a period of consolidation and stability and, above all, it was a period of sustained peace and social tranquility. Storm clouds, however, were gathering on the horizon from two different directions in the form of Otto von Roeder's legal problems and the first rumblings of the Civil War, and both would soon break over the family with a fury, the subject of the final two chapters.

CHAPTER 13

The Adelsverein, the Plantation, and Slavery

It has become accepted usage to refer to the military conflict between the Northern and Southern states in the period 1860 through 1865 as the "Civil War." This terminology, especially as it applies to Texas, is unfortunate because it is inaccurate and misleading. For Texas, the conflict represented a Second War of Secession. The First War of Secession had seen a successful struggle on the part of the Anglo colonists (with some support from disaffected Mexicans) to separate from Mexico. The preservation of the institution of African slavery in the colonies was undoubtedly an important underlying factor in this rebellion, but other important considerations played roles as well.

It is the belief of this author that the unsuccessful Second War of

Secession was above all about slavery. The slaveholding power elite in Texas joined with the other Southern states to withdraw from the Union for the primary purpose of maintaining and expanding slavery when it had become clear to them that they would not be able to take their slaves with them into the new territories of the West which were then opening up.

To be sure, Texas (as did two other Southern states) held a referendum on the question of secession and close to 70 percent of the male population cast their vote in favor. This left a substantial minority, however, including the governor of the state, Sam Houston, who were opposed to secession, and this produced a cauldron of seething tension, hostility and, at times, naked violence, representing the true "Civil War" for Texas of the period. Indeed, with the surrender of the Confederacy at Appomattox on April 9, 1865, the bloodshed did not come to an end in this other civil war. Rather, it ushered in another phase where the "lost cause" became a pretext and cover for terror and lawlessness, rendering Texas the most violent state in the Union for a decade after the war had ended.

It is clear that the German element in Texas, although joined by many Anglos and Hispanics, stood in the forefront of this other conflict. The true position of the Germans in Texas in relationship to slavery and secession has, therefore, been the object of a tremendous amount of scholarly and lay interest. The point of emphasis here has been almost exclusively on the settlers themselves, while little attention has been given to the role of the organization which brought most of them over, namely, the Society for the Protection of German Emigrants in Texas and to their first possession in Texas, the slave plantation Nassau.

It will be the purpose of this chapter to discuss the role of Nassau Plantation and the Society for the Protection of German Emigrants in Texas in the contemporary debates about slavery, immigration, and secession. Though not disputing the fundamental assertion that a substantial portion of the German settlers in Texas were opposed to slavery and/or secession, it will be the purpose of this chapter to show the variety of responses among the emigrants and to explore the complexity of the situation. The anomaly of Nassau Plantation provides a convenient forum for doing this.

Despite authoritarian traditions, the various states that made up Germany in the nineteenth century, unlike England, France, Belgium, Spain, or Portugal, had no history of association with slavery, either through colonial activities or through commerce and trade. Germans, therefore, had to confront a system that was alien to them, and this confrontation demanded painful choices and compromises. The noblemen who came together in the spring of 1842 to consider forming a company to underwrite and promote emigration to Texas obviously had not come to a consensus among themselves about slavery, and they lacked a full appreciation of the explosive significance of the issue. For Joseph Count of Boos-Waldeck and several others in the Society, the choice had been obvious: adapt the Negro slave paradigm to their own conception of hierarchy and authority. For others, especially Prince Solms-Braunfels, the firsthand confrontation with slavery led to a different conclusion. In any endeavor, conflicting goals can be a root cause of failure. This dissonance had serious repercussions for the Society.

Already by 1844, the question of slavery in North America had become a focal point of intense discussion in the German press. Hans Carove, for one, had published a series of decidedly anti-slavery articles in *Der deutsche Auswanderer* (*The German Emigrant*), one of the influential German newspapers devoted entirely to issues of emigration.[1] The Society was singled out for its association with slavery through the plantation. Count Castell became alarmed by this bad press because he feared it would deflect large numbers from joining their program and settling in Texas.

The count decided, therefore, to publicly proclaim in the newspapers in July 1844 the Society's opposition to slavery and its intention to keep the areas of colonization slave-free. The *Bekanntmachung über Sklaverei* (Proclamation about Slavery) was released to several newspapers in 1844 (reproduced as Appendix E). In addition to announcing a slave-free zone in Texas, the proclamation announced unequivocally that the only hope for Texas eventually to renounce slavery would be to introduce enough anti-slavery immigrants into an independent Texas to form a majority.

"Assuming Texas remains an independent country, then the abolition of slavery depends entirely on a great number of free citizens settling in the republic who exhibit a heartfelt aversion to slavery."[2]

The article also emphasized that the Society's anti-slavery stance had won the approbation of both England and France, both of which, by this point, had become officially anti-slavery.

The Anglo slaveholding class in Texas firmly held the reins of power and, if anything, their power increased by the day during the 1840s and 1850s as former plantation owners from all over the South abandoned their (by now) exhausted fields and flocked to Texas to establish new plantations on virgin ground. Moreover, by 1858 the first lodge (or castle, as it was termed) of the Grand Knights of the Golden Circle had appeared in Texas, a quasi-secret and stridently pro-slavery group organized as a counterpoint to abolitionist agitation in the North. The Knights rapidly grew in influence, staffing most of the senior command positions in the military and government once war was declared.[3]

These slaveholders had welcomed the English offer of recognition, for it held out the promise of a tariff-free market for their cotton, access to capital markets, and guarantee of English investment. Still, they were ever mindful that England, under the persistent parliamentary agitation of William Wilberforce[4] and his band of abolitionists, had succeeded in banning the African slave trade and abolishing slavery in the British Empire in 1807. Anything that threatened slavery threatened them, and so, they reasoned, the English needed to be regarded with suspicion, as did any person or any organization with whom they were associated.

Many intriguing statements and remarks by both Prince Solms-Braunfels and Count Castell point to an English connection. Some harbored the suspicion that the English were somehow behind the curtains in the Society's expanded plan to settle a land grant, for in several important ways the Society's goals and the English foreign office's goals in Texas coincided. Prince Solms' family connections with the English throne, his fluency in English, and his easy familiarity with the English representatives in Texas reinforced this suspicion.[5]

On the question of annexation, Prince Solms was, as were his English counterparts, unequivocal: Texas, he proclaimed, should remain independent and resist the temptation to join the Union. He felt strongly that the Society could better achieve its goal of establishing a German enclave with cultural and linguistic homogeneity in an independent republic. He also hoped that Texas could one day develop into a counterweight to the growing commercial and military hegemony of the United States in the Western Hemisphere, which he obviously resented and considered a threat.

When toward the end of his stay in Texas, it began to look as if Texas was moving toward annexation, the prince proposed a fantastic scheme to the English consul, Kennedy, whereby thousands of German soldiers, disguised as settlers and equipped with English weapons, would be introduced for the purpose of forcibly resisting annexation. Kennedy politely brushed off the suggestion by replying that he would "refer the matter to Her Majesty's Government for consideration."[6]

However developed the English connection might have been, it certainly raised a red flag. Likewise, the prince's personal opposition to slavery did not go unnoticed. In the summer of 1844, an article appeared in the *Houston Morning Star* warning of a German prince with pronounced anti-slavery views wishing to flood the republic with thousands of anti-slavery immigrants.[7] There was also fear that the English would attempt to do the same thing.[8] Likewise, James Mayfield, former secretary of state, raised the specter of a German-English conspiracy in a fiery speech before the legislature during the debate about annexation in June 1845.[9] Mayfield, as previously noted, later became deeply involved in the shootout at Nassau Plantation in 1847.

The bizarre inconsistency of the Society in regards to the question of slavery—on the one hand, a slave plantation owner; on the other hand, a promoter of an anti-slave agenda—produced a definite conundrum for the Society in Texas. From a political standpoint, Nassau Plantation had been a plus for the Society, signaling to the pro-slavery power structure that the Society was on their side. But once Prince Solms-Braunfels appeared on the scene and word of the Society's intentions concerning slavery in the Fischer-Miller grant filtered back, this goodwill began to evaporate.

Thus, for the Society, the politics of slavery intersected with questions of annexation and immigration, and once the Society's financial and organizational woes became acute after 1846, its compromised political situation did little to help when it sought redress in the Texas Legislature.

The Society, in any case, fell far short of introducing enough settlers to seriously dilute pro-slavery sentiment in Texas. It did, however, bring in enough settlers to create an area that was essentially slave-free, namely, the counties of Gillespie, Medina, and Comal, which are at the heart of the so-called Hill Country of Texas.[10] This fact rendered parts of Texas more like a border state than a core Southern state. It also led to a pronounced dichotomy between the two main areas of German settlement in the republic and (later) state, which imparted to the two areas different flavors that persist to the present.

Predictably, radical anti-slavery sentiment found a more fertile ground for growth in the isolated Hill Country settlements than in the South Central counties of Colorado, Fayette, Austin, and Washington, where Germans had settled among the dominant slave-holding class. But here, too, many Germans harbored a deeply felt aversion for a government and society based on slavery. This sentiment was especially strong among the educated Germans, many of whom emigrated after the failed revolution of 1848.

From the modern perspective, one cannot but applaud the progressive attitudes voiced by Prince Solms and given expression in the proclamation of 1844, which renounced slavery and proclaimed a slave-free area of settlement. Nevertheless, the central duplicity of the Society—slave owner, anti-slavery agenda—emerges as the lasting impression of this story. In a sense, the Society's confusion, as well as the plethora of attitudes encountered among the cast of characters at Nassau Plantation, discussed later, underscore the dilemma which the institution of slavery posed for the individual German emigrants who chose to make Texas their new home.

The stance on slavery in Texas of the German settlers, many of whom had been brought over under the auspices of the *Adelsverein*, is not so easy to characterize as some would have it, and the fact of the plantation underscores this point.[11] Regional variations (between the Hill Country settlements and the Central Texas settlements), generational distinctions (old line settlers versus newcomers), and educational/class difference among the German settlers all cloud the picture. The conventional assessment—that almost all Germans passionately opposed slavery and were ardent Unionists—requires a large footnote. Also, it is important to note that pro-Unionism was not the same thing as anti-slavery. They usually went hand in hand, but not always. Some Germans were Unionists because they had taken an oath of allegiance to the Union when they arrived, which they refused to renounce.

Several generalizations come close to encompassing the complexity of the situation: first, the closer the German settlers were to the centers of plantation culture, the more likely they were to modify decidedly pro-Unionist and anti-slavery sentiments, which most, but not all, brought with them; secondly, the longer an individual had been in the state/republic, the more likely he was to be sympathetic to the Southern cause; and finally, the more educated the settlers were, the more likely they were to voice anti-slavery and Unionist sentiments. Also, a deep grain of gratitude for Texas ran through the German communities, and the dilemma often took the form of how to reconcile gratitude with conviction when they pulled in different directions.

The high-water mark of abolitionist sentiment among the Germans in Texas came in the spring of 1854. Due to both a conscious policy of exclusion on the part of the *Adelsverein*, discussed above, as well as the natural unsuitability of the area for plantation culture,[12] the Hill Country settlements emerged essentially slave-free. The area became a nursery for pro-Union sentiment in the first instance and anti-slavery agitation in the second.

A Texas branch of the *Bund Freier Männer* (Federation of Free Men),[13] an association of restless German immigrant intellectuals, organized a meeting in San Antonio in May 1854 in conjunction with the second annual German *Sängerfest* (Song Festival). The Texas organization, which went by the name *Der freie Verein* (The Free Society), had been organized in Sisterdale,[14] a small community in the Hill Country between San Antonio and Fredericksburg. Sisterdale counted as one of the *Lateiner* communities, which means it had been organized and settled by German intellectuals, especially those who had fled Germany after the collapse of the 1848 March Revolution.

In its May meeting in San Antonio, *Der freie Verein* passed a resolution calling for a long laundry list of populist reforms of both a social and political nature. Along with such things as a call for a reduction in postal rates and the repeal of all temperance laws, the meeting passed a resolution declaring that "slavery is an evil, the abolition of which is a requirement of democratic principles."[15] The slavery plank, as worded, occasioned quite a discussion among the delegates, many of whom wanted to tone down the wording. In the end, however, the more strident voices prevailed.

Once released to the public, the proclamation provoked a storm of controversy among both the Anglo and German communities. Voices of moderation in the German communities were quick to react. Friedrich Ernst of Industry was one to raise his voice in opposition. Dr. Ferdinand Lindheimer, the editor of the *New Braunsfelser Zeitung*, used his paper as a forum for rebuttal. Several prominent newspapers, such as the *Victoria Advocate* and the *State Gazette* picked up on the story and began to ask disturbing questions, such as, were the singing societies, which had quickly proliferated among the German communities, in reality fronts for radical abolitionist sentiment? Lindheimer and others were quick to defend the singing societies, pointing out that they were completely apolitical and that it had been an unfortunate coincidence that *Der freie Verein* had met at the same time as the state singing festival. According to Rudolph Biesele, who wrote an extensive study on this topic, the whole matter would have calmed except that Adolph Douai,[16] who edited a German language newspaper in San Antonio, and a few others of his bent, refused to let the matter die.

This episode underscored the deep divisions and the vigorous nature of debate within the German community during the antebellum period. In an act that was perhaps emblematic of the complexity of the situation, August Siemering,[17] one of the founders of *Der freie Verein* in Sisterdale and a co-author of the anti-slavery proclamation, served as a lieutenant in a Confederate cavalry unit during the Civil War, thus, in the final analysis, choosing prudence over ideology.

With the outbreak of war, the naïve period of public discourse and debate ended abruptly. The war brought to the boiling point tensions which had simmered underneath the surface for a decade, tensions remaining mainly in the realm of discussion, though at times becoming quite acrimonious.

In February 1862 Ben McCulloch marched into San Antonio at the head of a military contingent of the Knights of the Golden Circle to accept the surrender of General Twiggs and Union forces. McCulloch immediately began to receive complaints from local ardent secessionists, such as Sam Maverick, about local abolitionists and Union sympathizers, not all of whom were of German descent.[18] But the German element soon enough came under suspicion. R. H. Williams, a member of Captain Duff's cavalry command, observed in 1861 that "Friedrichsburg, a town of 800 inhabitants, almost all of them German, [was] Unionist to a man."[19] This was an exaggeration, but many other sources corroborate the extent and depth of Unionist sentiment among the Germans in this region. Certain place names in the Hill Country, such as Loyal Valley and Union Hill, still call attention to this fact. Most haunting is the monument in Comfort, Texas, dedicated to those who fell and/or were murdered at the Battle of the Nueces on August 10, 1862: "Treue der Union [Faithful to the Union]." This is reputedly the only monument to the Union in a Southern state.

On April 28, 1862, General Hamilton P. Bee, military commander of South Texas, reacting to alarmist reports from his predecessor, General McCulloch, placed the district under martial law.[20] On May 30, Brigadier General Hébert, commanding general of the Western District of Texas, extended the order to include the entire state.[21] Ignorant of the German language and suspicious of the foreign born, both men interpreted the unrest among the Hill Country Germans as a brewing rebellion on the already vulnerable western border. On the same day, Bee ordered his field commander, Captain Duff, to lead his cavalry command into Kerr and Gillespie counties to compel an oath of allegiance, to enforce the conscription laws, to investigate currency abuses, and to gather a list of names of those suspected of treasonous activities. Moreover, by suspending *habeas corpus* and any recourse to civilian law, he gave Captain Duff a free hand to stamp out the imagined rebellion "by any means necessary."

Many of the more ardent German Unionists, who had organized a Union League, stubbornly refused to take the Confederate Oath of Allegiance or obey the conscription laws. One German-Texan who had been hauled before the Military Commission convened in San Antonio in July 1862 on suspicion of harboring treasonous views, put it simply but eloquently: "I was brought up in Europe and my views differ from yours. . . ." Prior to the proclamation of martial law and Captain Duff's appearance in Friedrichsburg, many had sidestepped the issue of oaths and conscription in a creative way: they had raised or joined volunteer frontier companies ostensibly to protect the border settlements from Indian raids. Such service exempted them from regular military service and allowed them to stay close to home. But when Jakob Kuechler[22] and Phillip Braubach allowed only pro-Union and anti-slavery men to join their companies, alarm bells began to go off. Ironically, these alarm bells were first sounded by other Germans in the Friedrichsburg area.[23] The governor was notified in a petition signed by Charles Nimitz, who served as enrollment officer in Friedrichsburg, and about twenty others of this situation, whereupon Governor Ireland disbanded the companies.[24]

Many took to the hills, refusing to join other units. Rumors of a large and organized party of mostly disaffected Germans somewhere in the hills west of Friedrichsburg fed the paranoia of the military authorities in San Antonio. While it is true that the men who had fled began to collect supplies and train militarily, it is not clear whether the purpose of this was to mount an insurrection or merely to prepare for an escape to Mexico: controversy on this point rages to this day.

The ill will thus generated culminated in a spectacular and bloody confrontation, the infamous and endlessly dissected Battle of the Nueces, where approximately sixty Texas-Germans and a handful of Anglos from the Hill Country communities under the leadership of Jacob Kuechler and Fritz Tegener were intercepted on their way to Mexico by a larger and better armed force of Texas partisans under the command of Lieutenant McRae, a subordinate of Captain Duff. The Germans, though surprised and outgunned, put up a fierce resistance. After fighting for several hours and repulsing numerous attacks, where they sustained over thirty casualties, the survivors felt compelled to withdraw and escape as best they could. Lieutenant McRae, who had been wounded along with twelve others in his command, made no attempt to negotiate with the party before launching his attack. Once the battle was over, to the disgust of many in the command, a subordinate executed those few who surrendered and shot the wounded. The troops continued to scour the countryside and summarily hanged on the spot those whom they succeeded in capturing.

In an extraordinary rebuff, President Jefferson Davis ordered General Hébert to reinstate civilian law in September 1862.[25] The proclamation of martial law and the suspension of *habeas corpus*, the president tersely informed Hébert, had been "unwarranted and illegal, and must be immediately rescinded." The implication of President Davis' order, clearly, was that Captain Duff and Lieutenant McRae's excesses had been war crimes. The Hill Country Germans certainly interpreted it this way, for they maintained a deep and enduring bitterness. Unfortunately, the suspension of martial law did not end the violence in the area. From this witches' brew of mutual suspicion and distrust, a protracted phase of lawlessness emerged, the so-called Bushwhacker War, which was punctuated by numerous lynchings and shootings on the part of organized gangs and thugs. Indeed, even the formal cessation of hostilities at Appomattox did not halt the bloodshed and terror. The Mason County War, which flared up during the Reconstruction years, can only be understood as an extension and continuation of this violence.

The proclamation of martial law in 1862 with its call for a loyalty oath and a tightening of the conscription laws also inflamed many Germans in the South Central Texas settlements and led to numerous tense encounters. Several mass meetings were held and petitions of protest drawn up.[26] The disaffection became so great that martial law was once again proclaimed, but this time restricted to the counties of Fayette, Austin, and Colorado. Despite this, the stresses here never erupted into large-scale violence. Isolated instances, as in the case of Joseph *Freiherr* von Emmenecker in Lavaca County, illustrate, however, that such a potential existed. The eccentric and untactful ex-nobleman was a vocal abolitionist in a region of the state where pro-slavery sentiment ran wide and deep. He crossed the line when he bravely but foolishly confronted a group of men who had gathered to discuss his outlandish behavior and attitudes. The group could not stomach the provocation of his sudden appearance in their midst. They seized and hanged him on the spot, but not before he pronounced a curse upon his executioners, eventually fulfilled to the letter, giving rise to one of the more colorful legends of Lavaca County.[27]

In the broadest terms, the South Central Texas-Germans faced the same conundrum as their Hill Country counterparts. They were caught in the nexus of three competing claims: gratitude to Texas, pride in their German heritage, and fidelity to the Union and/or opposition to slavery. These elements mixed differently to produce a wide spectrum of individual responses. But certainly, for these settlements, two factors exercised a moderating influence: proximity to slave culture and the influence of old-hand settlers who had assimilated to the Southern point of view. In this connection Nassau Plantation, through Otto von Roeder played an important role.

Speaking to this and other quandaries, each of two Texas-Germans, W. A. Trenckmann[28] and Charles Nagel,[29] has left a compelling account of the effect of the Civil War period on the German settlers in South Central Texas. Trenckmann recorded his thoughts in his autobiography, *Erlebtes und Beobachtetes* (Experienced and Observed); he also made these tensions the central theme of a novel, *Die Lateiner am Possum Creek* (*The Intellectuals of Possum Creek*).[30] Both works were serialized in his newspaper, *Das Wochenblatt,* a German-language weekly, which he published and edited in Bellville for over forty years. Likewise, Charles Nagel, who subsequently rose to a position of great prominence on the national stage, sat down in the waning years of his long and productive life to record for posterity the life of a young German boy on the Texas frontier before and during the Civil War.

Both Trenckmann and Nagel grew up in the Millheim community in Austin County less than twenty miles from Nassau Plantation. Millheim counted as one of the *Lateiner* communities. Undoubtedly a stronger strain of idealism existed in their community than in many others. Nevertheless, by both accounts, German settlers in the larger area by a wide majority opposed secession and rejected slavery, and of these two tendencies, loyalty to the Union was the dominant sentiment.[31]

Both men recollect how the settlers in the area came together for lively discussions, especially when secession was put to the vote.[32] Although opinion in the settlement (confirmed by the vote count, ninety-nine against, eight for)[33] was overwhelmingly anti-secession and anti-slavery, vigorous voices of restraint and caution could be heard. These voices came usually from the old-hand German settlers, those who had come over when Texas was still part of Mexico and whose loyalties had been forged in the travails and triumphs of the 1836 uprising. Here both Trenckmann and Nagel allude clearly to the von Roeder-Kleberg clan.

As a family, the von Roeders had suffered terribly during the war with Mexico, but they were fiercely proud of their contribution. The experience, moreover, had forged loyalties and sympathies that reached beyond their German heritage. They were proud Texans,[34] grateful to the country that had welcomed them and offered an open field for their collective energy. Simply put, Otto von Roeder, especially, had emerged from the cauldron of his experiences a Southerner through and through, and he argued vigorously from this point of view.

His argument: it was the duty of the German settlers to support the majority wishes of the state, and if the majority supported secession, then so be it; if war came, they must do their duty and shoulder arms willingly. The von Roeder sphere of influence was wide and deep in the German communities of Texas.[35] His presence was reinforced by familial and historical ties. Millheim was, as Adelbert Regenbrecht observed, "an offshoot of the settlement of Cat Spring,"[36] founded by the von Roeder and Kleberg families in 1834. Moreover, Otto von Roeder's sister, Caroline, had married Friedrich Enkelking,[37] the much esteemed storekeeper (and later judge) in the Millheim community. Robert Justus Kleberg,[38] Otto von Roeder's brother-in-law, served as justice of the peace in the area, in day-to-day life the most immediate and important link the settlers maintained with official authority.

By their active participation in the Texas War of Independence, the von Roeder clan had earned a deference and respect in the Anglo community, which, by association, had been a good thing for all: the good name of the von Roeders had redounded to the favor of all German settlers. Their opinions, therefore, carried weight, and many put aside their own convictions and followed the von Roeders' counsel,[39] leading, in many instances, to strained relations within the community.[40]

In *A Boy's Civil War Story,* Charles Nagel describes poignantly the heart-wrenching choices the war posed for his family.[41] The father, Hermann Nagel, has left his own account in the form of letters written to his brother in Germany.[42] In these, he makes it clear that the fact that the South had made slavery the foundation of the state was unacceptable to him.[43] The younger Nagel is especially adroit at capturing the psychological stress of the period. The tensions between the slaveholding class and the German settlers actually led to few violent confrontations in this part of the state. Considering the tensions, Nagel concedes, the Germans were actually shown a lot of deference. The problem was, at any point, some unforeseen, isolated event might precipitate a widespread eruption of pent-up hatreds, such as happened in the Hill Country. This sense of constant uncertainty and angst weighed in Hermann Nagel's decision to flee.

In a reflection of the decision among the Hill Country Germans that led to the Battle of the Nueces, a party of like-minded men[44] from Millheim and the surrounding area assembled in the dark of night and started their journey for Mexico, the only realistic path for escape to the North. Hermann Nagel took along his fourteen-year-old son Karl (Charles), who was approaching conscription age, but left behind his wife, daughter and younger son. Most of the others in the party lost heart and turned back when Confederate forces on the move blocked their path;[45] Hermann Nagel and his son chose to continue, but their flight was fraught with dangers and hardships at every turn, even more so in Mexico than in Texas, where anarchy, uncertainty, and peril, brought on by the revolution against the Emperor Maximilian,[46] accompanied their journey at every step. In time, they gained passage from Mexico to New York where, upon the advice of friends, Hermann moved to St. Louis. Here he resumed his profession as a medical doctor and began a new life. His wife was able to join him later, but, sadly, his younger son and daughter had in the meantime both succumbed to fevers.

Keeping a step ahead of the "Heel Flies,"[47] as the Home Guard was derisively termed, occupied the attention of many who remained in Texas but at heart stayed loyal to the Union. Some confrontations became quite tense. W. A. Trenckmann offers a chilling description of one such episode from his youth in Millheim. A dozen well-armed riders came to his father's gin when one of his older brothers, Hugo, reached recruitment age. Since the government exempted ginners, his father had installed Hugo as manager of his gin. The leader of the party, swearing profusely, refused at first to accept this and threatened the elder Trenckmann with his sword. Trenckmann stood his ground and was prepared to defend himself with his whip. A tense stand-off resulted before the recruiters finally rode off, cursing and jeering. Another prominent settler in the community, the Swiss-German Marcus Amsler, committed suicide rather than accept conscription into the army.

In another episode with faint overtones to Euripides' *Trojan Women*, the good German ladies of Industry, armed with brooms, pitchforks, and anything they could lay their hands on, chased an enrollment officer from the community and cornered his deputy, who was forced to pull his pistol in self-defense. The town of Industry, due to the agitation of Carl Seeliger, a German-Jewish merchant in the community, had become a hotbed of Unionist sentiment and opposition to conscription. Eventually, Seeliger was arrested, convicted of treason, and deported to Mexico.[48]

Despite these instances, the situation was not at all uniform, as both Trenckmann and Nagel take pains to point out. The German community in Houston apparently enjoyed an excellent reputation during the war.[49] Even in Industry, voices to the contrary could be heard. Ernst Knolle, a prominent Texas-German merchant in the area, owned six slaves. He was adamant in his support of the Southern cause, and under his influence Industry had initially voted in favor of secession.[50] In another example, Lieutenant Voigt, commander of an all-German company in Waul's Legion,[51] was so chagrined by the subsequent behavior of his fellow citizens in Industry that he refused to live there after the war.

Charles Nagel noted (incorrectly) that the German element, taken as a whole, contributed proportionately just as many men, perhaps more, to the Southern cause as their Anglo neighbors.[52] In fact, many of the younger men in the community had willingly volunteered, especially after Texas was invaded in November 1863.[53] Several of the all-German units, moreover, acquitted themselves admirably in combat.

Their fathers had been former revolutionaries and idealists. But for the younger generation coming of age during the Civil War period, the formative years had been spent in Texas listening to the stories of heroic resistance against Mexican oppression. For reasons of simple patriotism, many found it difficult to resist the call to serve. The elder Nagel, against his own intellectual opposition, could not suppress a sense of pride and envy as he looked into the faces of the eager young German volunteers from his community who stood before him to say good-bye.[54]

Despite the German contribution, a pall of suspicion and mistrust divided the communities. This mistrust was compounded by the fact that many of the settlers clung tenaciously to their German ways, thus inviting suspicion. The appearance of substantial numbers of Union forces off the Texas coast and the subsequent surrender of Brownsville in the winter of 1863-1864 threw the state into a panic. Many feared a full-scale Union invasion, with a thrust from Brownsville to San Antonio. This fear fanned tensions so much that the South Central Texas counties of Colorado, Fayette, and Austin were placed once again under martial law in January 1863.[55]

In the vastness and freedom of sparsely populated Texas, little communities with names like Millheim, Cat Spring, Piney Point, Industry, New Ulm, Mentz, Post Oak Point, Latium, Frelsburg, Shelby (Rödersmühle), Biegel, Round Top, etc., arose as almost self-contained islands of transplanted German culture in a sea of Southern tradition. Although large slave plantations dominated the bottomlands of the Brazos River only a few miles to the east and the Colorado River to the west and south, slavery was, with few exceptions, not practiced in these settlements. Millheim was thrown into an uproar, Charles Nagel noted, when Ferdinand Enkelking went against the unspoken rule of the community and purchased a Negro cook. The school children ran from the schoolhouse to gain a glimpse. Everyone engaged in agriculture to a greater or lesser extent, even shopkeepers and professional men, but this activity was, with few exceptions, on the free-labor model.

Hungry—even desperate—for settlers, the young republic (and later state) of Texas generally welcomed the German immigrants. Once established, they gained in acceptance both economically and socially. Recognized as good customers who conducted their business honestly and paid their bills on time, the Anglo business community grew to appreciate them. Acknowledged as exceptionally law-abiding and civic-minded, they became an anchor of social stability. This trait, Charles Nagel pointed out, was not without irony, for many of the settlers in the Millheim area (and in other *Lateiner* communities) had originally run afoul of the law in Germany, precipitating their move to Texas.

Still, the Germans tended to stick to themselves, organizing their own schools and founding numerous *Vereine* (associations)—singing, gymnastic, agricultural, literary—to satisfy their social needs and reinforce their cultural traditions. This story has played itself out many times in the history of this country: first-generation immigrants clinging stubbornly to a national identity and a mother tongue.

It was the "system," Nagel pointed out, not dislike of German culture and German ways, which had driven them from their homeland.[56] Their love and attachment to the fatherland and to the German language remained strong. Texas prior to the Civil War had permitted settlements such as Millheim an astonishing amount of autonomy and freedom in which to preserve and nurture their distinctness. Consequently, both Trenckmann and Nagel looked back on the antebellum era with a marked sense of nostalgia and gratitude.

The Germans of Texas, as Charles Nagel eloquently points out, saw no contradiction in the desire to be good Texans and the impulse to remain German; many Anglos did, and the less than wholehearted support for the Southern cause on the part of many Texas-Germans reinforced their suspicions. The Germans, formerly begrudgingly welcomed, now became "Damned Dutchmen."[57] For the Germans of Texas, the Civil War jarringly slammed the door on a period of cultural and linguistic innocence.

The personalities associated with Nassau Plantation reflected in almost perfect microcosm the spread of opinion about secession and slavery in the wider German community. Count Boos-Waldeck embraced the Southern plantation paradigm so wholeheartedly that he attempted to fashion a colonization program around it. Prince Solms rejected this model and declared slavery to be an affront to his humanity. In a different vein, Otto von Roeder, the largest Texas-German slaveholder in the state, had in essence become a dyed-in-the-wool Southerner, albeit with a German accent. Arthur Meerscheidt, the erstwhile Hungarian freedom fighter, was staunchly pro-Union and contemplated fleeing with his family to Nicaragua.[58] Unable to do so, he spent the war years disillusioned and embittered.

In the middle stood Peter Carl von Rosenberg and his sons. William von Rosenberg, the oldest son, early on took a pragmatic view of slavery. In a letter to his friends in Germany from April 1850, he stated that they should not be surprised how calmly he speaks about slavery because "the Negroes have it better here than the entire servant class in Germany."[59] The average slave, he continued, usually has time off on the weekends where he can earn a little money for himself. Additionally, slave owners naturally tend to provide their slaves with adequate food, clothing, and housing, since they are his property, and it would be irrational for an owner through abuse and neglect to destroy his own capital. As long as Texas remains so underpopulated, he continued, slavery will persist because of the scarcity and cost of free labor. Eventually, he predicted, it will die on its own through the democratic process, as more free labor becomes available. Carl Wilhelm's mother-in-law, Amanda Fallier, also echoed these sentiments in a long letter to her sister-in-law in March 1850.[60]

With the vote for secession and the outbreak of war, Peter Carl von Rosenberg and his sons unhesitatingly followed the lead of Otto von Roeder. Texas had welcomed both families with open arms and both felt it was their duty to put aside any reservations they might have and stand with their fellow citizens in their time of need. Peter Carl von Rosenberg, a veteran of the Battle of Waterloo, even went so far as to don his old Hussar uniform and ride up and down the streets of Round Top imploring the youth to enlist. Relying on letters and documents from the period, Dale von Rosenberg has reconstructed the rationale his great-grandfather William von Rosenberg followed when faced with the vote for secession.

"In 1861 I had to make a difficult decision. A vote was taken for Texas to secede from the Union. I decided to vote for secession for these reasons: I had left Prussia being proscribed for my political opinions; I selected Texas for my future home with full knowledge of the institution of slavery existing here; I did not come here as a reformer; I came here to live with this people who received the stranger unconditionally; and, I felt, right or wrong, my place was with the people of Texas."[61]

And serve they did, all four sons: Eugen, the oldest son of Peter Carl and Amanda Fallier, was one of the first to sign up with Waul's Texas Legion,[62] which included several all-German companies, where he participated in the defense of Vicksburg. William, who by this point had risen to be Chief Draftsman in the Texas Land Office, joined the staff of General Magruder, senior commander in Texas, as a captain and chief topographical engineer. The younger sons, Alex and Walther, joined Ernst Creuzbauer's Light Battery.[63] The battery was stationed first in Brownsville and then in Galveston. In the spring of 1864 the men saw action in Louisiana at the battle of Calcasieu Pass,[64] where a brief but bloody artillery exchange between the battery and two Union gun boats, the *Wave* and the *Granite City*, resulted in the surrender and capture of the same. The battery discharged itself exceptionally well in this battle, and several members of the company were commended for bravery and competence under fire, including the von Rosenberg brothers.

Eugen, Walther, and William survived the war, but their younger brother, Alex, did not. In an all-too-familiar story, he braved enemy action only to succumb to disease. He died in camp in Liberty, Texas, of typhus in the fall of 1864. His death was a great blow to the family and weighed heavily especially on the father, who shortly before had lost his wife.[65]

The von Rosenbergs had a stake in the outcome of the Civil War because of a lawsuit that was pending in the U.S. Supreme Court. The evidence suggests that the men of the family found little motivation in this; rather, they threw their support to the Southern cause for the reasons outlined by William von Rosenberg above, namely that this was their duty as they understood it.

Otto von Roeder, by contrast, more than any other Texas-German in the state, had a vested interest in the outcome of the war. As the largest Texas-German slaveholder in the state, a substantial portion of his wealth was tied up in slaves. But the Chandler lawsuit, to be discussed in the following chapter, represented an even greater danger, for it compromised all the sacrifices and effort he had made to consolidate and capitalize Nassau Plantation, the proceeds of which he had used to finance his holdings in Victoria County. The suit depended on the outcome of the Civil War.

As a man of action as well as words, Otto von Roeder did not shirk his duty. Though fifty-four, well beyond the legal age of enlistment, he volunteered for service and joined Company A of the Victoria Reserves as an officer. He was called to the defense of Mustang Island, where he was captured on November 24, 1863, when 3,000 Federal troops overwhelmed the hundred men defending the island.[66] He was paroled the following year.

Arthur Meerscheidt offers a strong contrast to both the von Rosenbergs and Otto von Roeder. His disillusionment was profound even as his fortunes took an unexpected and sharp rise during the war years. As the clouds of war began to gather, Meerscheidt decided to leave the country rather than serve under a government and system he abhorred, [67] this time to Nicaragua.[68] The war overtook his plans and the blockade prevented the move. In the following year, however, he received a commission to be a cotton broker for the settlers in New Braunfels. This proved to be a very lucrative business, allowing him to avoid conscription by paying for a substitute, a practice allowed by both the North and the South in the early stages of the conflict. It also gave him the freedom to travel legally in Texas and Mexico without fear.

The simple life of a farmer had appealed to Meerscheidt in the abstract, as it did initially to many educated Germans who had become disillusioned by the "system" in Germany. Meerscheidt had struggled as a farmer for a decade, barely keeping his head above water. One year it was too wet, the next year it was too dry; a string of less-than-successful harvests had enabled him to provide only the bare essentials to his growing family. As his family steadily grew—eventually he had thirteen children of whom eight survived to adulthood—his sensitivity to the deprivations of frontier life increased. Meerscheidt expressed this eloquently in a letter from 1856. "It is very hard," he wrote, "for anyone who has enjoyed the nectar of a high social position, with its enjoyments and vanities, to be satisfied in a simple, plain environment from which he must provide everything himself. There always comes a moment when one longs for the sweet pastries, as the Jews longed for the fleshpots of Egypt."[69]

How ironic then that the war, so detested, opened the door to a prosperity which his career as a farmer had denied. And prosper he did: in 1862 his wife wrote, "Arthur received a commission business in New Braunfels that does so well one couldn't have believed it." By the end of the war, Meerscheidt estimated his worth had grown to $15,000.[70]

Even with this unexpected and fortuitous shift in fortune, Meerscheidt was not very happy. He did not give up the idea of moving to Nicaragua with his family until news of the breakup of a colony of Germans there put an end to this plan. Above all, he and his wife longed for the Germany they loved but could no longer return to.

"One homeland I'll not find again. The old one, I fear, I have lost forever, for I fear I could not find my place there

again . . . The German who has no political fatherland misses it the most and seldom finds a new one; he is too much a person of emotion."[71]

Under the influence of the death of her brother Alex in 1864, Lina von Meerscheidt was even blunter:

"All my thoughts are turned toward Germany. My children shan't grow up in this terrible land. I believe the parting from here will not be difficult."[72]

When peace finally came, both rejoiced. Arthur wrote to his mother, "You will certainly have known, long before this letter reaches you that this miserable war has ended. Peace, freedom under these glorious United States, once again united, will make the people happy."[73] Lina wrote, "My happiness was unbounded when peace came and Arthur returned. All other complaints that I had now seem small and unimportant."[74] The two began making plans to travel to Europe to visit family and friends, which they were able to do the following year. The war brought an end to the commission business, but Meerscheidt had put away enough to begin a new life. He continued with his mercantile business in Round Top. In 1874, he moved with his family to La Grange after accepting an appointment from President Grant as postmaster, a position that might have come his way partially as a result of his pro-Union sentiments. If the political and ideological differences between Arthur Meerscheidt and the rest of the family led to tensions, no record of these is to be found in the correspondence.

William von Rosenberg might have been able to excuse his brother-in-law, but he could not serve under Jacob Kuechler. Von Rosenberg had resumed his position as chief draftsman in the General Land Office at the end of the war. In a poignant twist, General Magruder's former staff officer found himself placed under the authority of Jacob Kuechler, one of the leaders and survivors of the German Unionists at the Battle of the Nueces. Kuechler became a leading spokesman for Republicanism in the state after the war and was rewarded by

Reconstruction authorities with appointment as Commissioner of the General Land Office in 1870, a position he held for four years. William von Rosenberg resigned in protest.

With the passage of time and the growth of historical perspective, the Texas-Germans' *true* relationship to slavery and secession remains complex and elusive. Nassau Plantation, both in its conception and in the cast of characters it hosted, emerges starkly emblematic of this complexity. As a possession of the *Adelsverein*, it embodied a confused and contradictory stance on slavery by this organization. Later, two families associated with the plantation, the von Roeders and the von Rosenbergs, clearly helped to diffuse tensions in South Central Texas by offering voices of moderation and restraint in a volatile situation. This is an important legacy because their actions helped the German communities in South Central Texas to avoid the violent confrontations that the Texas Hill Country communities experienced—confrontations which left a trail of mistrust and bloodshed that persisted even after the war ended.

It is not difficult to imagine the hardships and challenges that accompanied the majority of German settlers as they moved to a new life in Texas. Despite all the frustrations they had experienced in Germany, it had to be a heart-wrenching decision to sever familial and cultural ties, usually permanently, to make the move. For those who chose Texas, slavery and the war it spawned posed for many the single greatest challenge to assimilation in their new homeland.

CHAPTER 14

A Clouded Title

"From 1850 on the affairs of the Society suffered very much due to a combination of factors. Many lawsuits were filed against the Society in 1847, 1848, and 1849, and judgments entered. The Society's property, which according to an inventory of 1847 would have had a value of approximately $250,000, was sold, mortgaged, lost, wasted and gradually disappeared until almost nothing was left. Its claim on money owed it in Texas, estimated to be $75,000, was blocked by the statute of limitations. Its right to lands in the grant, namely to the half-shares to come from the emigrants were lost from view and prejudiced in every conceivable way. Their debts did not diminish; rather they increased through such things as the cost of litigation until it would be almost impossible to say exactly what the Society owed. The worst thing about the whole affair was that neither the Society, nor its creditors, nor the emigrants derived any benefit from this situation, since the first quickly lost, one after the other, all their property as well as their right to property in the grant, and the creditors received no payment for their demands. Indeed, the prospects for it grew slimmer by the day. Only Fischer and Miller were partially satisfied on account of a judgment in 1848 they had against the Society for a substantial amount.

"And for the majority of emigrants in respect to the grant and the prospect of finally obtaining valid titles, they were led astray by speculators and ended up selling their certificates at artificially low prices. The largest number of these certificates were bought up in the districts of San Antonio, Comal, and Gillespie by speculators, who, after at first having shown little sympathy for the plight of the emigrants by acquiring their certificates at a price far from their true worth, and not satisfied with this, casting an eye over the entire land, sought to prejudice the rights of the Society and the creditors of the same to the half-shares due them from the emigrants through an act of the legislature and other means."[1]

The above summation by Henry Francis Fischer gives a grim but accurate picture of the situation of the German Emigration Co. in Texas after 1850. This process of disintegration cast a cloud over the plantation even though, ostensibly, it had passed out of the Society's hands in 1850 when the Society signed it over to Otto von Roeder.

Once Otto von Roeder gained complete ownership, he began selling it off to defray the debts he had incurred. The sale of 800 acres to Peter Carl von Rosenberg was followed in March 1850 by the sale of 361 acres to Hamilton Ledbetter, one of the more prosperous Anglo farmers in the area. Otto von Roeder also sold several smaller tracts to fresh German immigrants and financed the transactions. Hamilton Ledbetter may well have provided some of the grain that Otto von Roeder had delivered to New Braunfels in 1845, 1846, and 1847,[2] and the land in question may have served as partial or complete payment for this arrangement.

In April 1853, he sold 1,400 acres of undeveloped land to John R. Robson[3] for $3,600 and in May 1854, 1,600 acres to J. A. and W. F. Wade for $15,000.[4] The rest of the plantation was sold off in smaller tracts to newly arriving German immigrants. By 1859 Otto von Roeder had divested himself entirely of the acreage comprising Nassau Plantation.

With the sale to the Wades, Otto von Roeder vacated the plantation, for this tract included the overseer's house in which he and his family had resided since 1850, as well as other improvements. Von Roeder took his family and slaves south, moving to DeWitt County near Meyersville where his brother, Albrecht, and his brother-in-law, Robert Justus Kleberg, had located in 1847.

In May 1855, with all his debts paid off, cash in his pocket, and a coffle of thirty slaves—the original Nassau slaves and their increase plus five slaves received from Wade in partial payment for the land—von Roeder purchased 1,100 acres in the José Maria Escalara survey adjoining the Mission League about 12 miles north of Victoria on the west side of the Guadalupe River. He purchased the land from Abner Kuykendall, his old friend from Fayette County.[5]

Here over the next ten years on his Guadalupe valley plantation, both his personal wealth and his family increased. By the census of 1860, von Roeder was fifty-two years of age, with a wife and six children, a man in the prime of his life and at the top of his game, with a net worth of over $33,000, making him one of the wealthier men in the area. When he died in 1877, however, von Roeder had relinquished his Guadalupe River farm, and his fortunes had fallen precipitously. In the census of 1870, he is listed as a sheep farmer on the King Ranch, and when he died he was buried in a pauper's grave. How did this dramatic change in fortune take place?

Perhaps von Roeder intended from the very beginning to completely sell off Nassau Plantation, but there is reason to suspect that necessity rather than desire led him to divest and relocate, especially after the 1853 appearance of a young lawyer by the name of James A. Chandler. Chandler's involvement precipitated litigation in both federal and state courts challenging Otto von Roeder's ownership of the plantation and by extension the titles of those who had bought land from him.

Chandler represented one threat, but Henry Francis Fischer represented another, for the deal by which von Roeder acquired the plantation had come under intense criticism from many quarters. There were, after all, many creditors to the German Emigration Co., and by 1850 most of them in Texas had, with the encouragement of Fischer, joined together to press their claims collectively.

Prince Solms had demanded that Henry Francis Fischer withdraw from active management and participation in the Society's affairs in 1845. Fischer yielded on this point (with compensation), but he did not relinquish his claim to a share in the potential profits of the Society, which by Fischer's estimate, amounted to 250,000 acres of land. Fischer, therefore, continued to have a very real interest in the success of the venture; when things began to fall apart, starting in 1848, self-interest drove him to intervene and try to rescue the venture.

To accomplish this several things needed to happen, all of which needed to be carefully coordinated. First and foremost, the Society needed to reach some sort of accommodation with its creditors. To facilitate this Fischer compiled a list of all the creditors and then got them (that is, most of them) to join an association to seek a common agreement in which all would share in proportion to their claims.

This association took the name the German and Texan Emigration Co.,[6] and Henry Francis Fischer was elected the first president. This accomplished, Fischer traveled to Europe in 1853 to meet with the leadership in Germany and to get them to sign off on an agreement in principle. This he succeeded in doing.[7] By the terms of this agreement the creditors would receive twenty cents on the dollar for their claims. Finally, he needed to get the legislature to pass a bill releasing the surveys to the settlers and compelling them to relinquish one half of each to the Society (and Fischer and Miller). All the while he needed to fend off any legal entanglements and challenges.

This was a lot to coordinate in the days when letters often took months to cross the ocean, and travel across Texas was still long, strenuous, and dangerous. Fischer took on all this with an amazing energy and drive and, astonishingly, he very nearly succeeded.

At this point, Otto von Roeder's troubles intersected with Henry Francis Fischer and his efforts. There was a universal feeling among many of the creditors that Otto von Roeder had gotten too good a deal, or that somehow the deal by which he received the plantation had been a sham, that he had been in reality an agent of the Society, and, therefore, the transfer of the plantation to him was merely an attempt to shelter assets of the Society from *bona fide* creditors.

After all, Otto von Roeder had acted as a kind of agent for the Society when he provided grain for the settlers in New Braunfels and Friedrichsburg. He had essentially received full reimbursement for his claims. Most of the other creditors, on the other hand, had received nothing for their claims, or, if they had received any relief, it was only on a drastically discounted basis.

Indeed, at this period, IOUs against the Society were trading for as much as an 80-percent markdown. The resentment against Otto von Roeder was compounded by the fact that different officials during the turmoil and constant change in leadership following the *Katastrophe,* had actually mortgaged the plantation to different people. Why should Otto von Roeder be the only one to receive compensation in full for his claims?

This sentiment is clearly articulated by Henry Francis Fischer in a report to the "Komite" in Germany, the board set up to oversee the business affairs of the Society after Count Castell stepped down as executive director in 1848. Fischer wrote, "We will make it clear to Herr von Roeder that if he doesn't agree to pay substantially more in order to justify his acquisition, we will also contest his ownership . . . ."[8]

In the spring of 1853, a young lawyer by the name of James A. Chandler showed up in La Grange, the county seat of Fayette County, with claims against the German Emigration Co. for $2,444.16. He was originally from Massachusetts and the brother of F. W. Chandler, a lawyer who had established offices both in La Grange and in Austin. He represented clients P. Bremond and W. A. van Alstyne from San Antonio. These two had refused to go along with the "arrangement," as the agreement among creditors to pool their resources and claims in the Texas and German Emigration Society was termed. Chandler had presented the claims of his clients to the district court in San

Antonio. The court issued a writ of execution, which Chandler presented to Sheriff J. Moore of Fayette County.

The sheriff acted promptly. On May 3, 1853, he held a public auction on the steps of the courthouse to sell the plantation. Apparently not too many people knew of the sale, or, if they did, they did not take it seriously, for the 4,428 acres of the plantation plus all the assets on it, including the slaves, sold for the absurdly low price of $177.76, or about five cents an acre. The buyer, and apparently sole bidder, was James Chandler. Chandler, shrewdly and perhaps unethically, bid for himself and not on behalf of his clients.[9]

Otto von Roeder, as well as most people in the area, considered Chandler's claims to be frivolous and unsustainable. In a later deposition, John Robson swore, "that Otto von Roeder and his friends assured him that the suit of the said James A. Chandler was *frivolous in its character* and only instituted as a bit of malice to vex and harass the said plaintiff." Again, "he [von Roeder] represented not only that the claim of said Chandler was totally without merit and a mere sham, which had been drummed up with a view of extorting money by way of a compromise out of him, but, likewise, that the same would, or should be, compromised, settled, or dismissed long before this defendant would be called upon to pay said promissory notes, and this defendant relying on such representations, did, thereupon, make such purchase."[10]

The sale to John Robson for 1,400 acres was concluded at essentially the same time as the sheriff's sale to Chandler with the full knowledge by Robson of the Chandler complication. Likewise, the sale to the Wade brothers of 1,600 acres from the plantation came a full year later, in the spring of 1854.

Chandler, however, was quite serious about his purchase and did not intend to let the matter drop. In an astute move, he sued Otto von Roeder as defendant and Peter Carl von Rosenberg as co-defendant[11] in federal rather than state court in the 1854 spring term. He was able to do this because of the international nature of the dispute.[12] In his suit Chandler claimed that Otto von Roeder never had a valid title to the land (and for this reason could not sell any part of it). The original title had been in the names of Counts Boos-Waldeck and Leiningen, and no record existed of a transfer to the German Emigration Co. Therefore, he argued, the document transferring ownership from the German Emigration Co. to Otto von Roeder was defective and the sheriff's sale to Chandler was legal.

When Henry Francis Fischer found out about the Chandler suit, he offered to intervene on behalf of Otto von Roeder by offering to pay for legal counsel. Success for Chandler would remove the plantation from the claims of the creditors represented by Fischer. His offer, therefore, was a mixed blessing for Otto von Roeder, and there is no indication that he accepted.

Knowledge of this suit caused immediate concern for Peter Carl von Rosenberg and his family, for John Robson, for the Wade brothers, and for all others connected directly or indirectly with the parceling off of the plantation by Otto von Roeder—a number which eventually grew to thirteen individuals.

Otto von Roeder had financed the sale of land to both Robson and the Wade brothers. The immediate effect for Otto von Roeder was that (first) John Robson and (later) the Wade brothers ceased their payments pending settlement of the Chandler suit.

Otto von Roeder responded angrily to this action in February 1856 by filing suit in state district court against John Robson[13] and in the fall term against J. A. and William F. Wade[14] for non-payment of debt. In the case of the Robson suit, after several continuances, pleas and cross pleas, judgment was rendered in favor of Otto von Roeder in December 1857 for $1,437.80 plus all costs. This represented the last payment due him for the land he had sold. The court ruled in favor of the money, which von Roeder had sought, but not for the land, which he also sought to repossess.

The central issue of the suit was the validity of the penal bond, for Otto von Roeder had warranted the title to the purchases of both John Robson and the Wades for an amount double the value of the purchase. Von Roeder was able to demonstrate to the satisfaction of the court that in both cases he had only to defend the title after all the payments had been made, not as soon as the original obligatory note had been executed, as is customary. Von Roeder argued successfully that the fact that someone else (James Chandler) had contested the validity of his title in the meantime justified neither Robson nor the Wade brothers in suspending payments on the promissory notes.

Both defendants appealed. In January 1860, Otto von Roeder and his wife were summoned to Galveston to answer the appeal of the Wade brothers in the Texas Supreme Court. Once again the court decided in favor of Otto von Roeder, but it is doubtful that he was able to collect in any meaningful way. The evidence is not clear. In any case, it was a Pyrrhic victory.

The lawsuits between Otto von Roeder and John Robson on the one side and the Wade brothers on the other illustrate clearly how in the course of human affairs excessive self-righteousness can become a destructive force. Otto von Roeder was convinced that Robson and the Wades were using the Chandler suit as a mere pretext to avoid paying what was due, so he sued with a fury, seeking not only to recover payment, but seeking a forfeiture of the land as well. The defendants, for their part, were understandably reluctant to continue payments on property whose title now lay under a cloud, so they countersued to find legal support for their positions.

Otto von Roeder's energies and money would have been better spent in defending his title to the plantation against the claims of James Chandler, for this is where the real danger lay. All his efforts and all his expenditures in gaining possession of the Nassau Plantation, as well as all his profits in divesting himself of the same, depended utterly on the outcome of this case. Success in the civil cases against Robson and the Wades would be meaningless without eventual success in the Chandler case.

On the surface of it, Otto von Roeder seemed to have a virtually ironclad case. The route by which he had come into possession of the plantation had taken many twists and turns, but there had been no obvious fraud. Perhaps this was his fundamental miscalculation. The court documents suggest that he turned down an offer of compromise, so sure he was of the certainty and rightness of his position.[15] A jury initially supported his position when the case came to trial in federal district court in Austin in the spring of 1860. Chandler, however, immediately appealed and the U.S. Supreme Court agreed to hear the case in the fall term.

In December 1860, the same month that South Carolina adopted an Ordinance of Secession as protest against the election of Abraham Lincoln, the Supreme Court, in a stunning reversal, overturned the ruling of the lower court.[16] After reviewing the history of the litigation, Justice Campbell, in his majority opinion, gave a brief summary of both the plaintiff's and the defendants' cases. The basis of Chandler's claim was, as before, that Otto von Roeder had in reality served as an agent of the company and that in any case his title was invalid because there was no testimony or documentation to show in what manner the German Emigration Co. had come into possession of the property. Von Roeder's case (with Peter Carl von Rosenberg as co-defendant) rested on the fact that they had enjoyed adverse and peaceful possession of the land for more than five years, making improvements and paying all taxes, and that, therefore, even if the title should be suspect, they should enjoy under law coloration of title sufficient to establish fee simple ownership

In the end, the case turned on a technicality. In the district court decision, Chandler had asked the judge to instruct the jury that von Roeder had produced no evidence in the way of deeds or documents to show how the German Emigration Co. had come into possession of the land in the first place and, therefore, Otto von Roeder's title to the land was questionable. The Supreme Court ruled that the judge in the district court had erred in not instructing the jury in this matter as Chandler had requested. The Court also ruled that the claim of adverse and peaceable possession was not allowed since five years (the required minimum) had not elapsed between the date of the transfer to Otto von Roeder in 1850 and the date of the sheriff's sale in 1853.

For von Roeder, the case had to be decided on the basis of the case files, which had been forwarded from the district court. There is no indication that he made the trip to Washington, D.C. Chandler, on the other hand, most likely appeared in Washington to argue his case in person to his obvious advantage.[17]

The court in its opinion seemed more interested in upholding and underscoring a legal principle than in deciding the true merits of the case at hand. The principle in this case was that it is a judge's responsibility to determine the "competency of evidence"; it is a jury's responsibility to determine the "sufficiency of evidence." Since the trial judge erred on this point, the decision of the jury was reversed.

James Chandler did not immediately enjoy the fruits of his

victory, and Otto von Roeder did not at once suffer the consequences of his defeat. The Civil War intervened. James Chandler, a native of Massachusetts, remained in the North for the duration. For Otto von Roeder, the outcome of the war took on an even greater significance. As a substantial slave owner, the largest Texas-German slaveholder in fact, he already had much riding on the outcome. But, additionally, Northern victory would mean the Supreme Court decision would stand with disastrous consequences; Southern victory, on the other hand, would most likely annul the decision.

Otto von Roeder did his duty in serving the Southern cause. Although over fifty, he volunteered and was mustered into Company A of the Victoria Reserves as an officer. The unit saw action, and on November 23, 1863, Colonel von Roeder was captured in the Battle of Mustang Island. He was furloughed in 1864 in New Orleans following the Red River Campaign in which his eldest son had served as a Confederate officer.[18]

With Lee's surrender at Appomattox on April 9, 1865, the Civil War came to an end. Otto von Roeder and all who had purchased land from him now had to face the consequences of the sheriff's sale which had been held on the steps of the court house in La Grange some twelve years before.

James Chandler wasted little time. In the spring of 1866, he commissioned Z. M. P. Zapp to do a fresh survey of the Jack League [19] He then served notice through his brother, F. W. Chandler, also a lawyer in La Grange, to all who had purchased land from Otto von Roeder: either repurchase the land from him or relinquish ownership. Sixteen individuals were affected by this ultimatum.

From this point on, certain parts of the story become clear from the record while other points must yield to informed speculation. Devastated by the war, Otto von Roeder obviously was not in a position to compensate all who had lost title to their holdings. He did, however, quickly react to the situation. In November 1865, he put a substantial part of his assets in his wife's name. In February 1866, he did a complicated land swap, and in August 1866, he borrowed $1,600 by mortgaging 1,000 acres of land. All this complicated maneuvering represented most certainly an effort to preserve his assets against anticipated damage suits.

The situation with the von Rosenberg family must have been especially painful. The two families had been neighbors for three years—from 1850 until 1853. During this time, they socialized frequently and happily, a situation that is touchingly documented in the letters of Amanda Fallier von Rosenberg.[20] It had been an extraordinary and fortuitous coincidence: two refined German families from the German nobility within two musket shots of each other on the Texas frontier. The children of the two families, likewise, had developed deep bonds of friendship. In December 1853, Carl Eugen (1830-1913), the first child from the marriage of Peter Carl and Amanda Fallier, cemented this relationship through his marriage to Theodore Sack-von Roeder in Round Top.[21] Theodore had come to Texas in 1849 and was widowed after a brief marriage to Wilhelm von Roeder, a nephew of Otto von Roeder. She was a sister to Otto's wife and a first cousin of Otto.[22]

It was painful all around. We sense this in Peter Carl von Rosenberg's final letters from the period—he died in the fall of 1866—embittered and beaten down, not only by the Chandler affair, but also by the death of one of his son, Carl Alexander, who succumbed to typhus in 1864 while serving with the Confederate forces near Liberty, Texas.[23] Peter Carl only made one direct reference to the situation. In February 1866, he wrote that "the lawsuit over Nassau is now expected to be settled soon. I will lose about $1,200 through it. . . ."[24]

This is an intriguing comment. Peter Carl as well as his son Eugen and his son-in-law Arthur Meerscheidt chose to surrender their holdings to James Chandler rather than buy them back. Of the original 800 acres Peter Carl had purchased in 1850, he now owned 600, but this acreage, which included the *Herrenhaus* and all the improvements, was worth far more than $1,200.[25] This suggests the possibility that Otto von Roeder, as a man of honor, attempted to compensate the von Rosenbergs for their loss to the extent that he was able. Was the $1,600 loan from August 1866 raised for this purpose? Perhaps, but this must remain speculation for there is no documentary or anecdotal basis to substantiate it.

It is clear, however, that by 1870 Otto von Roeder's assets had vanished. The 1870 census lists him as a sheep farmer on the King Ranch. Presumably, this arrangement came about as a result of the fact that his nephew, Robert Justus Kleberg, Jr., had married the daughter of Captain King, the founder of the ranch.

Otto von Roeder died in 1877 broken in fortune and estranged from part of his family. His old war comrades gathered to bury him with full military honors, but they did so in an unmarked grave in the Old Bay View Cemetery in Corpus Christi. It was a sad but touching end to the extraordinary life of an extraordinary man whose contributions to the welfare of hundreds of stranded immigrants has largely gone unnoticed.

Meanwhile, for the next few years James Chandler made a profession of reselling land in the Jack League. In the end Chandler parlayed his $177 investment into a $25,000 return.

Some stories just do not end right. Nassau Plantation seems to fit this bill. From the beginning, the plantation symbolized false starts, unreal expectations, and dashed dreams. Still, with respect to the fascinating story of German immigration in Texas, a story with all the elements of an epic, both in the scale of its failures as well as the eventual size of its success, Nassau Plantation played a central role.

The plantation served above all as a reservoir of value that could be parlayed into food and other desperately needed supplies. In this role, with Otto von Roeder as facilitator, the plantation probably saved hundreds of lives, especially during the dreadful period of 1846-47 when hundreds of immigrants were stranded on the beaches of Lavaca Bay. The Society mortgaged the plantation to supply food when no other monies or sources of credit were available.

It would have been a more fitting end, therefore, if somehow those who had been more directly involved in the story eventually found reward through the plantation for their vision, sacrifice, and effort. James Chandler was a wily and persistent lawyer, but he was essentially a parasite whose larval greed drove him to enrich himself at the expense of the misfortune of others.

Unfortunately, the story of Nassau Plantation reflected the demise of the German Emigration Co. in Texas. Land speculators, for the most part, reaped the rewards for the titles that were issued in the grant area. Henry Francis Fischer struggled to put the pieces together, but in the end the task was too formidable. The German Emigration Co., *aka* the Society for the Protection of German Emigrants in Texas, in the end realized nothing but financial loss for its efforts in Texas.

POSTSCRIPT

On March 30, 1870, President Ulysses S. Grant signed the act that readmitted Texas to the Union and ended Congressional Reconstruction. Once the turmoil and disruption of Reconstruction finally subsided and the Chandler suits had ended, the Jack League and the surrounding landscape settled into a new phase, a phase of bucolic tranquility and measured change.

In the space of less than thirty years the land had gone from sparsely settled frontier to a patchwork of family farms dotting the landscape. The average size of the holdings grew smaller as the old leagues broke up and as it became easier to homestead[1] upland areas due to the dual innovations of barbed wire for fences and windmills for water.[2] A family really needed only as much land as the father, his sons, and one or two day laborers could work—fifty, sixty, at the most a hundred acres with enough surrounding acreage to pasture the draft animals and milk cows. Houses and barns sprang up on the new farmsteads and the old log houses began to give way to buildings of planked construction as sawed lumber became less expensive and more readily available.

Most of these family homesteads aimed at self-sufficiency. A few head of cows, pigs, and (perhaps) sheep plus a well-tended garden and an established orchard satisfied most of what a family required.

Still, cash was needed for cloth, food staples, and other odds and ends. There were taxes to pay and perhaps a mortgage on the land to defray. Cotton and corn served as the cash crops. Cotton was the mainstay, underpinning the economy in this part of the state for decades until the devastation of the boll weevil and the reality of low prices forced a new model. The pest first appeared in 1898 in Austin and Fayette counties. At first it confined itself to river bottoms, but after a while spread to the upland farms.[3] It reached a high-water mark of destruction in 1921 with an estimated 34 percent reduction in the crop.[4] Cotton, however, lingered as an important crop, with production peaking in the early 1950s. The introduction of mechanical tillage and chemical fertilizers allowed production to rise for many years even as the total acreage declined.

In support of the cotton economy, regional centers of commerce began to coalesce in the 1850s, 1860s, and 1870s, usually located on transportation hubs—Brenham to the north, La Grange to the south, Giddings to the west, Bellville and Sealy to the east. With the help of government incentives, the railroad grid expanded rapidly throughout the state in the 1870s and 1880s, stitching the state together and joining the rural areas to the cities. The final placement of a railroad meant either a death sentence for towns bypassed or a ticket to economic vitality for those selected. In his autobiography, W. A. Trenckmann gives a poignant account of how railroads affected the town of Bellville.[5] The Santa Fe ushered in a period of boom when it came through in 1880, but a few years later, when the Missouri, Kansas & Texas opened up a competing line to the west, the town faced a crisis. Another community, High Hill, in Fayette County, decided to move its entire business district in 1873 when the Galveston, Harrisburg and San Antonio Railway surveyed its proposed route two miles to the south at Schulenburg.

For the Round Top area, Brenham was the closest railhead. Consequently, the town could not hope to develop into a large regional center of cotton exchange and agricultural supply. Rapid growth, however, can often be a curse. Round Top never boomed over the decades, but neither did it bust; with a few stores and businesses, it satisfied local needs for generations, and this enduring stability imparted to the little town much of its charm.

The population was predominantly white in northern Fayette County and of these a substantial percentage had German surnames. By the turn of the century, Germans formed the majority, as they did in many communities throughout South Central Texas.[6] This was ironic. The organized efforts by t*he Society for the Protection of German Emigrants in Texas* to introduce German settlers had collapsed in failure and bankruptcy; through the door they opened, however, thousands of German emigrants continued to pass for generations.[7]

As the first immigrants became settled and (within the modest expectations they had set for themselves) prospered, they wrote back to the fatherland, setting into motion a process that continued on its own, without any kind of organized guidance, until the disruption of the First World War brought it to an end. The high-water mark of German immigration into the United States (and Texas) was actually the decade of the 1880s—a fact often lost because it occurred under less dramatic circumstances.[8] This progression, as it applied to Texas, led the historian John Hawgood to characterize the efforts of the *Adelsverein* as the greatest tragedy, but ultimately the greatest triumph, in the story of German emigration in the nineteenth century.[9]

Nassau Plantation, or what was left of it, followed this pattern. Otto von Roeder sold off the plantation in mostly large tracts, but these quickly subdivided so that by 1870 the plantation contained over fifteen farms, most of which were owned by fresh German immigrants.[10]

Islands of African American settlement coalesced in the area, remnants of the freed slaves. Certainly many of the early settlers owned slaves, but this area had never been plantation country to the extent that the Colorado and Brazos river bottoms had been, where the slaves had outnumbered their masters by a wide margin.

After emancipation, black people became a fringe presence in Northern Fayette County, tending to cluster in their small communities, usually of one or more extended families. Social life centered on church activities as new denominations, such as the Missionary Baptist Church, spread rapidly throughout the emancipated South. A few blacks managed to acquire land, but most eked out meager livings either as sharecroppers or as agricultural day laborers. Some even learned to speak German as their employers were predominantly German.[11]

The land itself had begun to undergo a profound transformation. The virgin black prairie gave way to pastures for domestic livestock while the densely wooded bottomlands yielded to cleared fields of cotton and corn. Wildfires, which for eons had played such a determinative role in the ecology of the area, holding the balance between prairie and woodland, no longer ranged freely. The introduction of cheap fencing in the form of barbed wire in the 1870s was a revolutionary innovation with profound ecological implications.

Plowing and road building brought about environmental degradation. The new roads interfered with the natural patterns of drainage, causing the water to concentrate and eat at the land. Plowing laid the soil bare, exposing it to the erosive power of water and wind. Ugly scars on the land began to appear where shortly before none could be seen. The native prairies, with horse-high stands of big and little bluestem, Indian, and switch grasses, began to fragment and dissolve into ever smaller islands, like the breakup of floe ice in the far north during the summer thaw.[12] The bottomlands, with thick and richly diverse stands of hardwood and cedar, retreated before the ax and plow. The land was virgin no more.

Infrastructure in the way of roads and schools slowly improved. Local settlements crystallized into recognizable towns with charters and elected officials. Various businesses sprang up to serve the needs of the predominantly agricultural economy. Communities erected schools[13] to educate their children and founded churches to serve the spiritual needs of the population. Interestingly, some of the *Lateiner*[14] communities, such as Millheim in Austin County, took a different approach. They voted to not allow churches in their towns on the grounds that their presence would serve to divide rather than unite the community.[15]

German communities throughout South Central Texas continued the venerable German tradition of formalizing their social life within various *Vereine* (societies). In this connection the area soon had a *Schützenverein* (shooting club), a *Sängerverein* (choral society), and a *Turnverein* (gymnastic society). Two of these societies exist to the present day, with the *Schützenvereinhalle* (rifle hall) continuing as one of the main venues in the area for weddings, dances, and other social events. The whole area in and around Round Top began to take on the demographic coloration of the German settlers, many of whom came to regard the decade of the 1880s as a Golden Period for Texas-Germans:[16] the bad memories had faded, the many sacrifices had been redeemed, and a promising future was there to enjoy.

By the 1880s, Georg Weyand had become the largest landowner in the Jack League. In 1861, Peter Carl von Rosenberg relinquished his remaining interest in the Jack League to Georg Weyand (1825–1896). Georg Weyand and his wife Justine (Becker) Weyand had in 1851 emigrated from a small area in the *Rothaargebirge* (Red Hair Mountains) of Germany in Westphalia.[17] In fact, a group of families from this same general area who were interrelated made the move, and many of these families ended up purchasing land in the old plantation. The names of these families—Wolff, Birkelbach, Voelkel, Becker, Menn, Kaiser, Muesse, Geise—are familiar names in the area to this day.[18]

Although the first recorded deed documenting a purchase by Weyand in the Jack League dates to 1866,[19] the tax rolls confirm that Weyand assumed ownership responsibilities in 1861.[20] Weyand, no doubt, was familiar with the Chandler lawsuit, so it is safe to assume that this was somehow factored into the sales agreement between Peter Carl von Rosenberg and Georg Weyand. The 1866 recorded purchase by Weyand was from James Chandler for 601 acres. It was located within Peter Carl von Rosenberg's previous holdings in the Jack League.

Georg Weyand most likely set up residence for his family in the old *Herrenhaus* in 1861. Like most men eligible for the military, he was called to service when the Civil War broke out. He joined an all-German artillery company of Waul's Legion[21] in 1862 and saw service in Louisiana and in the defense of Galveston. The company he joined integrated many others from the Round Top area, including Carl Wilhelm von Rosenberg. Except for this interlude, Georg Weyand lived at the *Herrenhaus* with his family for thirty years until 1891 when the farm was sold to Otto Neumann.[22] After the sale, Weyand and his wife moved to Round Top where he died in 1896. One of Weyand's daughters, Emma, married Alex von Rosenberg, a son of Peter Carl von Rosenberg. The Weyand cemetery is located in a grove of live oak trees close to the old *Herrenhaus,* and is still maintained by the family.

During Georg Weyand's tenure, the family farmstead became a lively center of community activity. Weyand was an enterprising man of action whose fortunes rose modestly but steadily. In addition to his own farming operation, he opened a store and a post office.[23] Five tenant farmers and their families also resided on the property. On Saturday and Sunday afternoons locals would gather to drink beer, socialize, and roll balls along the *Kegelbahn* (German bowling alley) that he set up for this purpose.[24]

Weyand appeared to follow a pattern of entrepreneurial initiative which was repeated by several prominent families in South-Central Texas, namely old-line immigrants making a business of catering to the needs of new waves of immigrants, often with a "one-stop shopping" approach. Enterprising individuals among these families often established grocery and hardware stores and they usually speculated in land, especially after barbed wire and windmills made it feasible to settle the upland areas. They located and sold farms to newcomers, provided the tools and implements needed, furnished groceries on credit and, with their knowledge of both German and American ways, otherwise acted as agents and intermediaries. If the newcomers could not afford to purchase farms outright, they would often settle them on their own farms as tenant farmers or finance the sale of farms. The business conducted along these lines was for the most part honest, aboveboard, and of mutual benefit, putting money into the pockets of the entrepreneurs while providing a real and necessary service for the fresh immigrants.

Georg Weyand's son-in-law, Alex von Rosenberg, continued this formula, and in the course of his career, bought and sold many farms, either selling them outright or placing tenants on them.[25]

This continued influx of Central European immigrants was, however, not without tensions. In many counties former planters had seen their lands fall into the hands of German settlers, while they themselves became more and more dependent on the goodwill of these newcomers to Texas. As office seekers, they had to court their vote by assuring their German fellow citizens of their esteem and respect; as businessmen, they had to cultivate the German clientele and cater to their needs. Under these circumstances a certain amount of bitterness on the part of the native Anglo population was understandable.

Nothing accentuated the differences more or influenced the German element to take a more active part in politics than the question of prohibition. The "dry" movement reached back to the days of the republic, but the movement gained steam in the 1880s and 1890s. It found its greatest strength in the northern and eastern areas of the state which had been settled for the most part by Protestant Anglos from the South. The issue came to a head when then Governor James S. Hogg instructed county attorneys to enforce the Sunday Law in 1895.[26] Many Germans considered this to be an abuse of power and an affront to their culture and traditions where alcohol was an accepted part of life and Sunday a principal day of trade.

The First World War brought tensions between the two groups to the fore. In the early phase, before the United States declared war on Germany, many Texas-Germans were openly sympathetic to their countrymen across the sea. In Colorado County, a local Texas-German farmer, in a fit of patriotic fervor, is said to have hoisted the Imperial German Flag on the flagpole on the courthouse square.[27] Once the United States entered the war, the situation changed abruptly. Texas-Germans, by a large majority, suppressed their internal conflicts, and put loyalty to their new country first.

The antipathy among some Anglos toward Germans as a people and toward German as a language, fed by wartime propaganda, spread an atmosphere of suspicion and mistrust over the region, which echoed unnervingly the tensions of the Civil War period.

Just as during the Civil War many Anglos suspected that their German neighbors harbored pro-Union sentiments, now, too, many suspected that they secretly sympathized with the German cause. This atmosphere contributed to the suppression of the German language, especially in public settings. German language newspapers began to disappear and public use of the German language diminished. Nevertheless, German continued to be spoken in the home and in rural venues such as church picnics, dance halls, and country beer joints. Amazingly, pockets of diglossia have endured, as if in a museum, to the present.

These tensions persisted after the First World War. The wave of anti-immigrant hysteria which spread across the country as a whole in the 1920s found an ugly advocate in the revived Ku Klux Klan. The Klan adopted an openly hostile posture and demanded that the public use of German be stopped. The Klan also threatened many business owners and elected officials with German surnames who refused to be intimidated. In one example, known to the author anecdotally, the Klan sent an ultimatum to John Wegenhoft, the sheriff of Colorado County: either resign or face the consequences. The sheriff, who had six grown sons, gave to each a Winchester rifle and a Colt revolver of matched .44-40 caliber. He then sent word to the Klan leaders, who were known to him, that each of his sons had a note with one name on it and instructions to kill that person should he be assassinated. He was deadly serious and the Klan backed down.[28]

In another sad but revealing instance, a member of the Klan stopped at a small beer joint in Oldenburg on the road from La Grange to Round Top. Upon overhearing two local farmers speaking what he took to be German, he ordered them to stop. They responded that they were not speaking German, but rather *Plattdeutsch* (Low German). Showing his ignorance, the Klan member excused himself and said that that would be okay.[29]

As tensions mounted, cooler heads on both sides pleaded for restraint. The most spectacular example of this was a giant "reconciliation" barbecue and baseball tournament held in Brenham Texas in 1923 sponsored jointly by the Klan and local German leaders.[30] Over ten thousand people were said to have attended. An accommodation of sorts was reached whereby the Germans, for their part, agreed not to speak German within the city limits of Brenham or in other public venues.

The war and its aftermath were a very trying period for the Germans of Texas. Almost as one, spokesmen and leaders in the German communities in Texas had followed Carl Schurz'[31] advice, to whit, the best way to be a good American was to be a good German. The traditions and values they brought with them were seen as a positive complement rather than a negative distraction to core American ideals of democracy, free expression, and tolerance. To their minds there was nothing inconsistent with practicing German customs, culture, and language in their new homeland, on the one hand, while regarding themselves, on the other, as thoroughly loyal, responsible, and patriotic American citizens. That this attitude was now viewed as a threat came as a shock and the readjustments, forced by wartime hysteria and nativist sentiments, carried to the utmost extreme by the Ku Klux Klan, were deeply resented and never fully digested. A bad taste lingers to this day.

By the end of the 1920s, the Ku Klux Klan's influence as a social and political movement went into rapid decline. With the collapse of the stock market in 1929 and the onset of the Great Depression the harsh new economic reality became the dominant concern for the majority of the people in the area, whether of German, Anglo, or Afro-American descent. Those farmers and businessmen who were debt-free managed, for the most part, to hold on to their possessions. Others were not so lucky, and a wave of foreclosures and business failures swept over the land.

Survival became the operative word as commodity prices fell, the monetary supply shrank, and credit disappeared. A bunker mentality set in, and for a full generation people attempted to make do. When things broke, they were patched together rather than properly mended or replaced, with the ubiquitous baling wire as the mending tool of choice. Barns fell into disrepair, houses received no new paint, and businesses invested in very few capital improvements of any kind. A kind of seediness settled in from which the countryside only emerged after the Second World War. For those who grew up in the postwar era, the transformation from the 1950s to the present has been truly astonishing. The dilapidated, rundown character of much of the countryside, known to us as children, the legacy of the Great Depression, has given way to a glitzy newness as everywhere new fences, barns, and houses spring up.

With the slow demise of cotton's supremacy beginning with the boll weevil and exacerbated by the precipitous drop in commodity prices during the Great Depression, the agricultural economy of the region sought to diversify. Improved transportation and refrigeration gave a boost to the livestock industry. With the introduction of the auction barn system in the 1950s, farmers could henceforth easily and inexpensively bring their livestock to market.

The early settlers had often remarked that this part of Texas was ideally suited to livestock production. The area has now reached its forecast potential in this respect. Livestock production after the Second World War began to supplant farming as the principal agricultural activity. Tens of thousands of acres went out of farming and back into pasturage. Today the region is home to one of the largest concentrations of cattle in the United States in the form of cow/calf operations.

The large influx of Central European emigrants (including Czech and Wendish settlers) eventually reached such proportions that it imparted a definable cultural flavor to the larger area comprised of (roughly) Fayette, Colorado, Washington, and Austin counties (and to a lesser extent Lee and Lavaca counties). This flavor, which consists of an interesting blend of Central European, Anglo, and African-American elements, persists to the present and provides marked contrast with other regions of the state.

The painted churches of High Hill, Shelby, Praha, Dubina, etc., represent one of the more prominent outward manifestations. Not surprisingly, they have become, by some accounts, the number one tourist attraction within the state. Church picnics, country dance halls, attractive meat markets, clean and orderly towns also characterize the region. Approximately half the Germans and nearly all the Czech immigrants were Catholic, thus imparting to this area of the state a religious plurality absent from East and North Texas.

Less obvious, but of even greater significance, the Central Europeans brought with them an entirely different mentality. They seemed, depending on one's point of view, wonderfully oblivious or wickedly indifferent to puritan attitudes common to many of the Anglo settlers from the South, an attitude which holds that earthly pleasures are sinful. The Czechs and Germans were unabashed beer drinkers, dancers and music lovers. The beer joints they patronized and the dance halls they erected still dot the countryside. Indeed, the beer joints, especially, became an important social institution, and any politician who neglected to visit them during a close campaign did so at his own peril. Opposition to prohibition was, of course, a natural consequence of these attitudes.

Miss Ima Hogg (1882-1975), the wealthy daughter of former Governor James Stephen Hogg, was one of the first to notice the charm of the Round Top area.[32] In the 1960s she began spending time in the community, collecting furniture and old farm buildings from the area. Eventually, she purchased the Wagner farmstead just north of the Jack League where she moved her purchases. Prior to Joseph Wagner's acquisition of the property, this had been the homestead of Samuel Lewis, discussed in an earlier chapter of this book. Miss Hogg began the restoration of the so-called Stage Coach Inn, a substantial two-story structure with interesting interior wall decorations by a local German artist. The building also shares some proportional similarities with the old *Herrenhaus* of Nassau Plantation.

Eventually, Miss Hogg bequeathed her property with its collections to the University of Texas. The compound took the name the Winedale Historical Center and is now administered by the Center for American History at the University of Texas at Austin. Her furniture collection became the basis of an acclaimed book by Lonn Taylor on pioneer Texas furniture.[33] For years the center sponsored a spring festival and other events which seemed to celebrate the unique cultural heritage of the area. In addition to a juried craft show, the festival included goose-plucking, soap making, blacksmith demonstrations and songs by members of the local *Sängerverein* (German Choral Society). The Center, however, never seemed to settle on a focus and is still struggling to define its purpose. This is unfortunate, because one can easily envisage how the center could have evolved as a focal point to showcase the unique cultural flavor of South-Central Texas and thus to help raise, define, and solidify consciousness not only for visitors, but for the local citizens as well.

Curiously, Miss Hogg's early interest in pioneer artifacts became (most certainly unintentionally) the genesis for the most well-known happening of the area, namely the annual spring antiques show and sale. Others took up her interest, and eventually dealers and traders set up shop along the highway in Round Top, Warrenton, Oldenburg, and other communities. The yearly event has now mushroomed into one of the largest events of this kind in the United States with tens of thousands of people descending on the area every year clogging the small roads for miles around. The trade in nostalgia has become big business.

Round Top is also the home of Round Top Festival Institute, a nonprofit organization devoted to the furtherance of classical music. The 1500-seat concert hall forms the centerpiece of a compound of buildings, many eccentric and whimsical in design, and is reputed to be one of the finest acoustically in the United States. The whole owes its existence to the vision and determination of James Dick, a renowned concert pianist, who also has a special talent for raising money from foundations and wealthy individuals. It is fitting that such an astonishing and enriching facility should be located in Round Top, for it appears to be a natural succession and outgrowth to the legacy of musical appreciation in the little town, a legacy that goes back to the musical conservatory founded by Herman Helmuth and the tradition of musical appreciation common to the von Rosenberg family.

Now a historical marker on the road between Round Top and Shelby near the Winedale turnoff marks the location of the plantation. In the distance, on the crown of the most prominent hill in the area, one can still see two large, two-story barns. One of these most likely dates to Nassau Plantation and, as such, represents the sole surviving structure; Georg Weyand probably erected the other. Both offer wonderful examples of post and beam construction: the rafters and beams are all hand-hewn from cedar and live oak. Mortise and tenon joints held together by pegs attest to the craftsmanship of the builders. The barns were made to last and they have withstood all the elements could throw their way for a hundred and fifty years. The present owners, Roy Randolph Rather and his wife, Mary Belle, prize the buildings and maintain them well.

Unfortunately the *Herrenhaus* has not survived. Its demise is anecdotal.[34] Otto Neumann bought the house and surrounding property from Georg Weyand in 1891, but his ownership was brief.[35] In 1907 he sold 194 acres to Michael Wolff. Wolff's new bride, the story goes, refused to live in the old house, which, by this point, was over sixty years old. Bedbugs, apparently, had infested the house and, in the days prior to modern insecticides, could not be easily dislodged. Wolff tore down the old house and used the disassembled logs for sheds and other structures around the farm: an ignominious end to what was once considered one of the finest houses on the frontier. As a replacement, Wolff had built for his bride a new two-story house of planked construction on the exact spot where the old house had so long stood, a house now occupied by the Rathers as their permanent home.

Profound changes are at present sweeping the area. Fed by the wealth of nearby cities, new economic forces have spread a veneer of prosperity over the land such as never existed before. The painted and planked fences that now snake through the countryside serve as an insistent reminder of these changes. Fences, once a purely functional necessity, designed to keep livestock in or out, now serve in the first instance to advertise wealth and status, and in the second instance to confirm that recreation has now displaced agriculture as the primary use of the land, or, to put it another way, that agriculture has now become a recreational activity. The land that was Nassau Plantation has not escaped this trend.

Drawn by the beauty of the area, the mildness of the climate, and the quaint charm of the communities that arose organically over generations, the well-to-do from the cities have flocked to the region, on the surface to the benefit of all since they have infused large quantities of cash into the area. But, one wonders, has not something of value being lost in the process? Old connections and relationships, of people to the land and of people to each other, connections from which the community drew sustenance for generations, have been altered and undermined in fundamental ways. *Pantha re*, everything flows. For better or worse, soon we will be left to our imaginations to recall how it was.

The study of history can be a wonderfully enlarging experience. Certainly much history has unfolded on the plot of land that was once Nassau Plantation. Standing on the hill where the *Herrenhaus* once stood with its beautiful, panoramic view of the surrounding countryside, it takes only a slight effort of the imagination to travel back to the days when a German count struggled through the labor of Negro slaves to fence fields for cultivation and to erect rudimentary houses of logs; when slaves fled into the unknown in the quest for freedom; when a German prince reveled with his band of followers in the shadow of the *Herrenhaus*; when officials of the German Emigration Co. struggled with the daunting task of housing and feeding thousands of fresh emigrants; when competing parties fought a deadly gun battle for control of the plantation; when a displaced German nobleman matched wits with a wily lawyer for ownership of the plantation in the highest courts of the land; when an eminent aristocratic family from East Prussia endured trials and celebrated triumphs in setting up a new life in Texas at Nassau-Rosenberg. Less dramatic, but equally significant, we can also visualize the generations of farmers who, in the comfort and security of the community to which they belonged, quietly, simply, honorably raised their families and lived out their lives close to the land they worked.

APPENDIX A:

Boos-Waldeck Purchases

(Boos-Waldeck Receipts, Verein Collection, Center for American History Studies, University of Texas, Austin)

Goods (New Orleans)

One barrel iron, two bars steel, 2 boxes mdse., one saddle and one bale saddelry, one bundle tools, one band axe handles, one tin kettle, one doz. buckets, two casks tinware, two ploughs, two fry pans, One bram and two pieds, one bellows, one doz. hames, twelve pieces castings, one crate, one box, three wagons, five casks merchandise, one ditto, five fire dogs, one anvil, one smithy vice, one shovel, one bundle saws, two bundle horse collars, one box axes, four boxes glass, five kegs nails, one small cask hardware, one keg ore, one keg tar, one can oil and nine bars iron.

 Bill of Lading of goods shipped from New Orleans February 14, 1843, on steamboat *Neptune* by Clark Day, Frank Day/Stouffer & Co. from New Orleans to Galveston, Texas.

Slaves

PURCHASED IN NEW ORLEANS, February 1843

Men

Richard	(50)	$250
Henry Carvan	(23)	$650
Georg Butler	(23)	$600
Hark Bedford	(19)	$650
Washington	(20)	$650
Joshua	(20)	$650
	Subtotal for men	$3,450

Women

Rachael	(28)	$500
Elise Allen	(19)	$500
Margaret	(19)	$500
Hanna Hurley	(14)	$500
Mary	(?)	$500
	Subtotal for women	$2,500

PURCHASED IN HOUSTON, February 1843

Family

James	(34)	$1,306
Patience	(30)	
Martha	(11)	
Anna Amanda	(7)	
	Subtotal for family	$1,306

Girls

Charlotte Valley	(16)	$252
Emily	(16)	$375
	Subtotal for women	$627
	Total for all the slaves	$7,883

APPENDIX B:

Bourgeois d'Orvanne Inventory, July 1844

(Complete inventory by Bourgeois d'Orvanne, July 15, 1844, SBAt XLIII, 166-171; XLVIIIa, 135-139.)

Acreage

100 acres of plowed and fenced land (wooden barrier) valued at $10 an acre	$1,000
4,330 acres of unplowed land at 75 cents an acre	$3,285

Manor House

A two-story house, below an office and above two rooms. The structure is not finished. Dwelling consisting of two rooms and a kitchen on the ground floor and two rooms in the second story. Although not finished it still has a worth of $1,200.

Structure with a kitchen and the necessary room for a servant	$60
A stall	$40

These buildings are surrounded by a fence.

Buildings of the farm

Dwelling of the overseer	$150
Kitchen for the Negroes	$30
Smokehouse for the meat	$30
Barns and Stalls	$200
Blacksmith shop	$50
Coal shed	$10
Six slave houses at 20 Dollars	$120

Slaves

Georg Butler	$600
Henry Carvan	$650
Hark Bedford	$650
Charlotte Valley	$500
Hanna Hurley	$500
Rachael Titus	$500
Elise Allen	$500
James (Blacksmith)	$1,300
Patience	$400
Martha	$300
Anna Amanda	$225
Richard	$250
Emily	$500
Mary	$500
Margareta	$500
	($8,375)

Horses

An American horse in good condition	$100
Two American horses in bad condition	$70
Two Spanish ponies in bad condition	$60
Five mules of which three are in bad condition	$100

Cattle

21 work oxen, each pair valued at $25	$262.50
63 head of cattle as cows, bulls, yearlings, calves at $3.50	$220.50

Swine

60 pigs and feeder pigs	$120

Poultry

A chicken coop composed of English chickens, ducks and chicks	$20

Farm implements

Two heavy plows	$30
16 common plows	$96
8 hand-discs	$6
Various implements	$150

Smithy

Blacksmith tools	$70

Wagon and harness

A harvest wagon with harness	$120
Horse harness and chains	$52
Yokes for the oxen	$20
Subtotal	$15,647

Movables

Movables in the house of the overseer	$10

Kitchen implements

Kitchen implements of the farm	$50

Provisions

The provisions on hand will be sufficient until September. Therefore they will not be noted here. No salted meat for a long time now.

Supplies in general

Shoes, shirts, socks	$22.75
14 hats	$17.50
98 yards of rough household linen	$9.80
134 yards of ¾ wide Lowel woolen material	$16
27 yards blue half linen	$5.95
1 piece with 11 yards Kersey*	$16
35 ¾ yards grey linen	$4.95
Various	$30
Medicine chest	$50

Objects belonging to the Farm

Two wagons	$200
Ox chains	$39

Weapons belonging to the Farm

Double-barreled shotgun	$40
Two small pocket pistols	$2

Household items of the Manor House

Kitchen items	$40
Porcelain dishes	$60
Table wares	$60
Bedding, Linen sheets, cabinets	$120
Objects not specified in the inventory such as saddles, books, p.p.	$<u>250</u>

Summa

$16,740.95

There are, in addition to the items specified above, other properties, some of which belongs to Count Boos and some of which to Count Leiningen. An exact list (*Verzeichnis*) of each individual object will be handed over to Mr. Fordtran, so that he will be able to give the same to the Dr. when he arrives.

The present inventory was put together by Mr. Fordtran and the overseer Mr. Denmann. Subsequently, each supervisor will assemble an inventory each year and send it to the committee. The inventory will be done stricter and in greater detail.

For colonial service we will take:

Two American horses
A Spanish horse
Two mules
The four wheel wagon
Three saddles
Two hammocks

We discovered several reference works about Texas, which we deposited in the archives of the society.

Nassau Plantation, July 15, 1844

Signed on the original: Bourgeois d'Orvanne

It becomes clear from this inventory that a considerable sum has been wasted. This year's harvest in relation to the cost of planting will result in a considerable loss. I am of thee firm opinion that the plantation is in need of a watchful eye. Without it the plantation will suffer losses year in and year out.

The result of this inventory:

We found a surfeit of unnecessary items. This year's harvest will result in a heavy loss.**

Notes:
*A coarse cloth used to make serviceable garments for yeomen, tradesmen and later army uniforms. The cloth was exported from Kersey (Suffolk) England and hence the name.
**Complete inventory by Bourgeois d'Orvanne, July 15, 1844, Solms-Braunfels (transcripts) XLIII, 166-171; XLVIIIa, 135-139.

APPENDIX C:

Inventory, December 1847

(Fayette County Complete Records C, 28, 29)

"3 Cots and 2 Bed Steads, 8 Mattresses, 9 Pillows, 3 German Blankets, 4 Pine Tables, 2 pr And Irons, 1 Looking Glass, 1 Candle Stick, 1 pr Snuffers, 1 Candle Shade, 2 Ewers, 4 Bowls, 2 Chamber [pots?], 2 Small Tumblers, 1 French Coffee Pot, 4 Small Glass Jars, 6 Dishes—6 Bowls, 2 Tea Pots, 3 Sauce Dishes, 1 large Dish, 1 Doz. Cup Plates, 1 Sugar Dish, 1 Cream Pitcher, 1 Sprinkler, Lot Empty Bottles, 2 Small Demijohns, 1 lot wire, 1 pr Small Scales, 1 Box window Glass, 1 Pistols, 3 Skillets, 1 Oven, 1 Frying Pan, 1 pr Waffle Irons, 1 Tea Kettle, 4 Water Buckets, 1 Churn, 7 Stone Jars, 3 Tin Pans, 3 Glass Tumblers, 3 Dishes, 1 Tea Pot, 1 Sugar Bowl, 6 Tea Spoons, 3 Kitchen, 3 Spoons, 1/2 Set knives & Forks, 1 pr Candle Moulds, 1 pr Shovel & Tongs, 2 Wash Tubs, 1 Water Barrel, 1 Grind Stone, 1 Keg Nails, 9 Carpenters' Planes, 7 Wood Clamps, 15 lbs. Tobacco (damaged), 30 lbs. Steel, 1,000 lbs. Iron, 100 chickens, 28 Ducks, 15 Turkeys, 12 Geese, 11 Pigeons, 1 pr. Steelyards, 1 Coffee Mill, 1 Milk Pigging, 1 pr Flat Irons,

1 Sieve, 2 Weeding Hoes, Log Chain, 3 Wagons, 2 Stacks Prairie Hay, 9 Ox. Yokes, 2 bedsteads, 1 pr Large Balancer, 1 Set Measures, 1 Steel Mill, 1 Grind Stone, 1 Froe, 5 Weeding Hoes, 1 Mill Peck, 8 Cow hides, 18 Turning Plows, 8 Shovel ploughs, 3 Cultivators, 3 Harrows, 1 Iron Tooth Harrow, 1 Set Blacksmith Tools, 2 Grass Scythes, 7 Ox Chains, 11 Yoke Oxen (Old), 3 Yoke Oxen, 4 Mares & Colts, 4 Work Horses, 3 Mules, 1 Stallion, 100 Stock Hogs—68 Head Stock Cattle, 13 Stacks Fodder, all the corn belonging to the Nassau Farm, 1 Cross cut-Saw, 1 Whip Saw, 10 Old Axes, 2 Hand Axes, 6 Drawing Knives, 8 Augers (Apt), 4 Common Planes, 11 Chisels, 1 Broad Axe, 125 lbs. Iron, 25 lbs. Steel, 9 pr. Plough Gear, 1 League of land including the Nassau Farm. Twenty-four Negro Slaves, to whit—Jim, Patience, Martha, Amanda, Emily & two children, Rachael & two children, Charlotte & two children, Eliza & two children, Elizabeth & Two children, Dick, Henry, Butler, Hockley & Hannah, and Forty-four pounds (more or less) seed cotton this 21st December 1847."

APPENDIX D:

Slave Inventories

July 15, 1844	December 15, 1847	July 8, 1848
complete inventory by d'Orvanne (SBAt XLIII, 166-171; XLVIIIa, 135)	Order of Sequestration (Fayette County Complete Records C, 29)	Bill of Sale by German Emigration Company (Dresel) to Otto v Roeder (Fayette Deed Book E, 113)
James	Jim	Jim, aged 39
Patience	Patience	Patience, aged 35
Martha	Martha	Martha, aged 16
Anna Amanda	Amanda	Amanda, aged 12
Emily	Emily two children	Emily, aged 20 two children
Charlotte Valley	Charlotte two children	Charlotte, aged 20 three children
Rachael Titus	Rachael two children	Rachael, aged 33 two children
Elise Allen	Eliza two children	Eliza, aged 24 two children

Margaretha	Elizabeth two children	Elizabeth, aged 24 two children
Richard	Dick	Dick, aged 55
Henry Carvan	Henry	Henry, aged 28
Georg Butler	Butler	Butler, about 28
Hark Bedford	Hockley	Hockley, about 24
Hanna Hurley	Hannah	Hannah, about 18
Mary		

5 men	5 men	5 men
7 women	9 women	9 women
3 children	10 children	11 children
15 slaves	24 slaves	25 slaves

APPENDIX E:

Proclamation Concerning Slavery

(*Frankfurter Journal,* No. 196, July 17, 1844, reproduced in Solms-Braunfels Archives (transcripts) V, 207, 208.)

"The rejection by the Senate and House of Representatives of the United States of North America of the bill to annex Texas confers to the Society for the Protection of German Emigrants in Texas a greater hope for a favorable prospect . . . [discussion of England and France's efforts to abolish slavery] . . . From this fact alone it is therefore no more than natural to expect complete support in every respect from the English as well as the French governments as the society undertakes to establish a colony of free German farmers in Texas with the complete exclusion of slavery, and we can document from authentic sources that we have received firm assurances in this matter.

"If Texas remains an independent country, then the abolition of slavery depends solely on the prospect of large numbers of free citizens being settled therein, who in heart and soul are opposed to slavery and who through the nature of their obligations bind themselves to not tolerate slavery in their settlements. The exclusion of all forms of labor based on slavery will be the guiding principle of the society, which is well aware, that it would dishonor itself in the eyes of all Europe if it were ever to consider sending over free Germans as slave overseers or in any way to tolerate slavery within its settlements . . . and we hope, moreover, that their project, with the full support of the German people, will soon become a national enterprise; above all, however, that the irresponsible accusations on the side of one part of the German press against the founders of the society will not shake their noble and praiseworthy resolve in this human endeavor."

APPENDIX F:

Descriptions of the Herrenhaus

Description 1, Amanda Fallier von Rosenberg:
"The house is composed of two square rooms made from oak logs. These rooms, however, are separated by a wide intervening space, something like how the threshing floor in a [German] barn unites the separate rooms. Over everything spreads a wide roof that rests in the front and the back, to the north and to the south, on columns that provide shade for two magnificent porches. When one wants to enter the house, he must go up either three or four steps, whether in the front or in the back, on to the wonderful, wide porch which runs the length of the house. Both porches have balustrades three feet high and, as mentioned, are covered by a roof supported by columns. The porches are joined by a passage, or in-between space. In this space a narrow, but decorated stairway leads to the second story where, likewise, a passage joins two rooms, one for Eugen and the other as a store room. These top rooms only have 'Texas windows,' that is, just slits in the wall. The bottom rooms, however, have real windows. Each room has two, one to the north with fifteen panes and one to the south, somewhat wider, with twenty panes. The most beautiful feature of the house, however, is the chimneys. They are built of stone that have been beautifully dressed and shaped (a rarity here); they are truly

magnificent. Using large logs, I have used them for cooking and they have yet to smoke. Now, dear friends, imagine this house so clean and neat like a jewelry box, these magnificent porches with their cedar floors . . . The entire house has only four doors, two above and two below—to the west [there is] a recent addition which one enters from the south gallery; in this room, made airy and bright by several 'Texas windows,' I now have my stove for cooking. . . . Rosenberg intends to board in the north gallery in order to gain two more rooms, also he intends to mount doors in the breezeway which can be opened in the heat and closed during storms. We also plan on whitewashing the walls with lime. What are the disadvantages you might ask? And here I would answer water; to be sure, we have an extraordinarily deep well, which cost a lot of money, but it yields bad water; sulfur water. That plus the fact that it takes so much effort to hoist up water, we hardly use it at all. . . . We haul water daily from the creek." (Frau von Rosenberg an ihrer Schwägerin Fallier [Frau von Rosenberg to her sister-in-law, Fallier], Nassau Farm, March 29, 1850, Von Rosenberg Collection, Center for American History Studies, University of Texas, Austin, 67.)

Description 2, Amanda Fallier von Rosenberg:
"You also have no idea of what one calls a house in Texas—a rectangular room, high and airy, with a good roof is called here a house. Among these a building like ours, six years ago the best and still one of the few best, is called a fort, a castle, a prince's house, manor house. Our house is called these things in fun. But it is pretty and, I might add, romantic. . . ." (Amanda Fallier von Rosenberg to Auguste und Emilie, May 25, 1850, *Ancestral Voices*, 25.)

Description 3, Peter Carl von Rosenberg:
"Now the description of my estate: the manor house, sometimes called the prince's house because a Prince von Solms, as an agent of the Adelsverein in Texas, had lived here a year or two, has two rooms downstairs with a big space in-between which connects the north and south galleries; there are two rooms upstairs connected by a lofty open space. I now sit on the south gallery writing. It is

the most convenient place for us to stay; some forty steps to the left there is a shed with three rooms: first, a harness room for me; second a room for my German laborer; and third a room for my Negro Toms. Behind the house is a stable with four partitions for horse stalls, chickens, and cow stalls. Galleries are attached to all these buildings, but not finished. I shall close these with split oak or cedar boards in country fashion, and use them as sheep, calf, and pig pens, although they can only be used in a norther for our entire livestock . . . On the extreme left, 40 paces from the house, stand some 100 oak trees; farther right on the same side of the adjoining buildings are 10 to 70 oaks and one pigeon house with four pillars. Opposite the south Gallery, some 150 paces there are several oaks and a garden [field?] planted with corn and sweet (Kunst) potatoes. The space between belongs to the horse pasture. However, this is to be reversed—the garden to the front, the pasture to the rear, at this time still in joint use with v. Roeder. To the right, next to the north garden, I am now having the ground opened up for cotton (here called breaking). This is done with six oxen, four are mine, two are Roeder's. From the north gallery one goes directly into the garden, where there are Irish potatoes, which we have been for eighteen days, peas, beans, and such, and also a small flower garden. Of trees, peaches are quite full, figs without fruit, and also some oaks near the house; such are also on the south side near the gallery and give us still more shade. . . . On the east boundary, at the corner of the south boundary, my son has his farm of two hundred acres, bought for 500 hundred dollars, and about a 1/2 [German] mile from the second brook on the La Grange Rd., Hellmuth has a farm with cattle, horses and all appurtenances for $750. Next to it, Johannes has bought a farm of 70 acres with a quite new log house, but no cultivated land for $170." (Peter Carl to his brother Otto, Rosenberg-Nassau, May 25, 1850, *Ancestral Voices*, 37.)

Description 4, Arthur Meerscheidt

"It is only a log house but better and larger than usual. It has six rooms. . . . Two rooms added to the house . . . one of these large rooms, which we will occupy, is finished entirely of the nicest red cedar wood; two windows—one to the north, one to the east. . . ." (Meerscheidt to his mother, September 18, 1850, *Ancestral Voices*, 131, 132)

Description 5, Maria Peters née Isslieb

"Whell [well], my dear Friends, I will let you know what I know yet from the Nassau Home sted [stead]. First of all they got a big yard right in the yard next to the gade [gate] was that country store. Right hand side. It was everything in was [that] the Puepels [people] need, such as matieral [material] for all kind, and Crsory [groceries] too and drings [drinks] such as Whiskey & beer. And about 10 feet from the first one was the next house on the West side. It was a log house. That's whare they Live in. That one got a cister nunderneed. they got all thair drinking Whater out thair. Right in front those houses was a big garden and side thegarden was a store hous [house] and a platform—read this in German—wo die jeden Sonntag haben Kegel gespielt [where every Sunday they bowled], with those wooden Balls. Those Balls they bin [been] setten [setting] on they [their] other End. When they threw the balls down, if they hit one or non [none] or all, that ware they try thair [their] look [luck]. And those first years we whare [were] thair [there] they Weyands Buildin 2 big Barns one side the other for the cows to crawl in by cold wether [weather]. I thing they are thair [there] no more. Its long ago I was but 8 years old when they bin build and now I am 86. They must bin rotted down long ago. They was built on the fence towards they Family cemetery. The boss man sold the Place and moved to Round Top. He lived but a couple of years their [there], then he died, but his folks braugh [brought] him back to his Old Home to his Family Cemetery. thair [there] he is barried [buried], and some more. He got a Post Office right in his store whare [where] he picktup letters and sent of at the same time they got a man riding a hors [horse]. He carred them Every day. That owner that ows [owns] the Nassau Plantation ows som [owns some] cattle too about 50 or 60 heads. Some what got little calvers they bin milked Every day and they all bin Pennet [penned] every Evening too. When we came from Germany I was but 8 1/2 years old, but we setteld down close to Shelby, but my father ditent like it their [didn't like it there]. He bin hanging around and then he Found the Nassau Plantation and he muved thair and we staid thair for 16 years in one stratch. We kits growd up all thair. I sure wish I could go thair for once more my mother bin buried thair on the Nassau Simetary [cemetery]. My Father never baugh [bought] her a Toomstone, but I dond know if I will find my mothers grave. I know from other graves what got a Toomstone whare she is barred close to them. Im the last one what is living yet from the whole Famley. We whare the 5 Famley what lives on the Nassau home Sted. All the others homs on the Nassau home stedt that ware but sheks [shacks].

(Story related by Mary Peters née Isslieb, an old lady who died about 1972 at the age of 86. She had grown up at Nassau. Document is in possession of Randolph and Mary Belle Rather, the present owners of the land where the *Herrenhaus* stood.)

A Note on Sources and Abbreviations

This study relies heavily, but not exclusively, on reports, letters and documents contained in the Solms-Braunfels Archives and related collections (Verein, Wied, Strubberg). The name is misleading. The Archives are the official business records of the *Verein zum Schutze deutscher Einwanderer in Texas* (Society for the Protection of German Emigrants in Texas), also called the *Adelsverein* (Society of Noblemen). The documents found a home at one point in the castle of the Solms-Braunfels family and hence the name. The documents languished unknown to American scholars until the 1930s when Dr. Rudolph Biesele, author of the seminal work, *History of the German Settlements in Texas*, became aware of them. Prior to World War II, he led a team that transcribed and indexed the thousands of reports, letters and documents into typewritten German, rendering them accessible and useable to a much wider audience. Interestingly, Dr. Biesele himself did not have the benefit of the Archives when he wrote his book on the German settlements in Texas. Indeed, none of the foundation works about the *Adelsverein* (von Rosenberg, Benjamin, Tiling) had access to the resources of the Archives, and the authors appeared not to have been aware of their existence.

During the disruption of the Second World War, parts of the Archives went missing, the most important part being the papers of Friedrich Armand Strubberg. The various parts eventually resurfaced and came up for auction in New York. Both the University of Texas and Yale University were keen to acquire the collections, but Yale had the deeper pockets, ending up with the original documents of the Solms-Braunfels Archives as well as the Strubberg Collection, both of which are now housed in the Beinecke Rare Book

Library. Small parts of the original Archives did end up at the Center for American History at the University of Texas at Austin (formerly the Barker Center); namely, the Verein and Wied Collections. The Verein Collection was especially helpful for this study because it contains the original receipts of purchases made for the plantation by Joseph Count of Boos-Waldeck in 1843.

The Center for American History at the University of Texas in Austin has a copy of the Archives in transcribed and indexed form. So too, does the Texas State Library in Austin and the Sophienburg Museum in New Braunfels, Texas. Because the original documents were written in the old German script (*Sütterlin*) and are often faded and difficult to decipher, most scholars must rely on the transcriptions, even if they know German. Except for the Verein and Wied collections, I have relied exclusively on the transcriptions and have henceforth abbreviated them as SBAt, as I do in the endnotes.

The SBAt encompasses seventy volumes and many thousands of pages. Although indexed, it is organized poorly. I have copied all of the relevant official reports and correspondence in the SBAt for myself and have made them more user-friendly by rearranging everything in chronological order.

In general, the seventy volumes of the SBAt represent a treasure trove of original source material about Texas in the 1840s and 1850s. In proportion to their significance, it is astounding how little they have been used.

For the chapter on the *Adelsverein*, I cite letters by Counts Christian von Leiningen, Carl von Castell, Joseph von Boos-Waldeck, Prince Carl von Solms-Braunfels, and others in the SBAt. Especially informative, the "Allgemeiner Bericht über Entstehen, Zweck und Ziel des Vereins [General Report on the Origin, Purpose and Goals of the Society]," July 28, 1845, SBAt XXX, 148; also various committee minutes (Aussschuss-Sitzungen-Protokolle) and General Assembly minutes (Generalversamlungen-Protokolle).

I have found the articles in the *New Handbook of Texas* by Louis Brister about the various officials of the *Adelsverein* to be excellent without exception. Anders Saustrup reconstructed from many sources the intricate family connections of the various officials of the *Adels-*

verein, especially Prince Solms and *Fürst* Leiningen. He generously shared this information as well as many other insights before his untimely death in 2008. The best treatment of the question of subsidies and how this related to the delicate diplomatic balancing act on the part of Prussia to avoid alienating Mexico, on the one hand, and still build a relationship with the new Republic of Texas, on the other, is the article by Manfred Kossok, "Prussia, Bremen and the Texas Question." For the complete citation on this and other works see the Select Bibliography.

The role of the *Standesherren* is vital for understanding of the *Adelsverein*, yet it is a connection that has gone largely unnoticed. Anders Saustrup explored this connection thoroughly and convincingly in an unpublished essay, which he shared with me before his death. I rely on this as well as the book by Heinz Gollwitzer, *Die Standesherren*.

Count Boos-Waldeck wrote several lengthy reports back to Germany, all contained in the SBAt. They detail the negotiations with officials of the Texas Republic, as well as the process by which the count decided to buy the Jack League in northern Fayette County, and his progress in setting up the plantation. Original receipts for Boos-Waldeck's purchases in New Orleans as well as the bills of lading are found in the Verein Collection at the Center for American History at the University of Texas at Austin.

The chapter on the runaways is based almost exclusively on the detailed reports of Charles Fordtran, the society's Texas-German supervisor, contained in the SBAt.

Much has been written about Carl Prince of Solms-Braunfels, but I concentrate on the many official reports and letters of the prince found in the SBAt and compare these with his diary entries, which were translated and published by Wolfram Von-Maszewski. Also, the reports of Bourgeois d'Orvanne, Friedrich von Wrede, Sr., Johann Otto *Freiherr* von Meusebach, Lieutenant Bené, Hans von Coll, Charles Fordtran, Philip Cappes, and Henry Francis Fischer are helpful in providing a contrast to the prince's observations. I cite an article that appeared in the *Houston Chronicle*, August 10, 1930, as an example of the legend of extravagant partying at the plantation by the prince and cohorts. Remarks in letters by Amanda Fallier von Rosenberg, published in *Ancestral Voices*, corroborate this activity.

Reports by Count Boos-Waldeck, Charles Fordtran, and Prince Solms-Braunfels all document the manor house at Nassau Plantation, the so-called *Herrenhaus*, which came in for much comment from observers of the period. Later, Amanda Fallier and Peter Carl von Rosenberg gave detailed descriptions in their correspondence. Dr. Ferdinand Roemer also described the house in his book about Texas. A post-Civil War description comes from Maria Peters, whose family lived at the plantation once it came under the control of Georg Weyand. This document, which included a drawing, was provided by Randolph and Mary Belle Rather, present owners of the site of the house. They have been very generous in sharing their knowledge of the plantation as well as artifacts from the site. Two barns are still extant. Knowledge about the eventual demise of the *Herrenhaus* is anecdotal, but I rely heavily on an interview with Nolan Schmidt, grandson of Michael Wolff, who tore down the old house and built the new one on the site around 1900. The new house is believed to rest on beams from the old.

Friedrich Von Wrede, Sr., wrote several lengthy reports found in the SBAt. They are without exception thoughtful and conscientious. His descriptions of the various personalities he encountered on his frequent travels are wonderfully perceptive and entertaining.

In the chapter on agriculture I use many different reports from the SBAt, including reports from Count Boos-Waldeck, Charles Fordtran, Prince Solms-Braunfels, Friedrich von Wrede, Sr., and Lieutenant Bené. I also use the 1840 census from the Republic of Texas as well as the U.S. census reports of 1850, 1860, and 1870. The Meusebach/Strubberg lease, filed in Fayette County, is very instructive as most of the provisions of this very thorough document concern agricultural practices. I also cite Samuel Woods Geiser, *Horticulture and Horticulturists in Early Texas*, the von Rosenberg letters, and works by W. A. Trenckmann. Walter Struve's study, *Die Republik Texas, Bremen, und das Hildenheimische*, contains an excellent overview of the development of the plantation economy and the developing cotton trade between Texas and Bremen, Germany.

For the chapter entitled *"Die Katastrophe,"* the Spiess Family Papers were especially helpful. I have never seen them cited before. Copies of this important document are to be found at the Fondren Library at Rice University and the Sophienburg Museum and Archives in New Braunfels. Hermann Spiess gives a detailed personal account of the shooting as well as the Mayfield/Bostick connection, which has never before come to light. The *Galveston Zeitung* also reported two versions of the shooting. Lieutenant Bené, at the time the chief agent in Texas, also wrote a lengthy report to the leadership in Germany about the shooting.

The Fayette County (Texas) Courthouse was the second major source of primary source material. It contains scores of deeds, documents, and court files relevant to the *Adelsverein*, the plantation and the Strubberg/Meusebach controversy. The so-called *Complete Records*, Books C and D, were especially helpful. Rather than summaries of decisions, they offer entire transcriptions of the original case files, which have long since gone missing. From these came Meusebach's deposition concerning Strubberg and a complete inventory of the plantation in 1847. The disposition of the Rohrdorf drawings can also be definitively established due to litigation for their recovery. I also researched county records in Colorado, Victoria, Austin, Fort Bend, DeWitt, and Bexar counties.

The best work on Friedrich Armand Strubberg, alias Dr. Schubbert, remains the study by Preston A. Barber, "The Life and Works of Friedrich Armand Strubberg." I also make use of a German biography by Gunter Sehm. Arnim Huber also wrote a monograph on Strubberg, which concentrates on the Meusebach dispute. Leroy Woodsen provides an excellent discussion of American Negro slavery in Strubberg and other German authors of the period. Also, Walter Struve discusses Strubberg in relation to slavery in *Die Republik Texas, Bremen, und das Hildenheimische*, 82. None of these works, however, offer a complete account of the shootout at Nassau Plantation or an accurate biographical sketch of this phase of Strubberg's life.

Many of Strubberg's novels are loosely autobiographical, and help in reconstructing stages of his life. His writings, however, have to be taken with a very large grain of salt: he was prone to exaggerate, or worse. Especially relevant are *Amerikanische Jagd- und Reise Abenteuer, Bis in die Wildnis, An der Indianergrenze, Friedrichsburg,* and *Alte und Neue Heimath*. I have all these works in my personal library. The University of Texas has some, but not all, of Strubberg's novels.

For the life story of Otto von Roeder, I have used Flora von Roeder's study, "Otto von Roeder: Prussian Nobleman and Texas Patriot." The *New Handbook of Texas* does not mention Otto von Roeder, but does contain several excellent articles on members of the von Roeder and Kleberg families. Many of the case files connected with Otto von Roeder and the various civil suits that made their way to the Texas Supreme Court are housed in the Texas State Library. These were instrumental in reconstructing the controversy surrounding James Chandler and his (eventually) successful suit in the U.S. Supreme Court to gain ownership of the plantation. The von Rosenberg family correspondence, published as *Ancestral Voices,* offer a glimpse into the personal demeanor and social life of Otto von Roeder, and the respect and esteem he was afforded.

Much has been written about anti-slavery and Unionist attitudes among German settlers in Texas. I have consulted most, if not all, of this literature, but I only list in the "Select Bibliography" the works I have cited. Because it addresses the issue from both sides of the Atlantic, I single out as especially scholarly and thorough Walter Struve's study, mentioned above. My study also addresses the *Adelsverein's* stance on slavery from a trans-Atlantic perspective and reproduces as an appendix the Society's official proclamation concerning slavery. Works by W. A. Trenckmann and Charles Nagel, largely unnoticed, have been especially helpful in reconstructing the psychological stresses of the period. A master's thesis by Cornelia Küfner and an article by Bill Stein, both specific to South Central Texas, complement each other nicely. The Küfner study analyzes in depth county records and census reports; the Stein essay mines the *Official Records of the War of the Rebellion* (*O.R.*) for all references to the area from the period of the Civil War.

For the chapter on the von Rosenberg family, I have relied heavily on *Ancestral Voices,* cited above, as well as other publications by the family. Many of the original letters are in the Von Rosenberg Collection at the Center for American History at the University of Texas in Austin. Not all of the letters, however, have been translated. Dale von Rosenberg was gracious in providing one letter from his private collection that was of particular significance.

Abbreviations:

Solms-Braunfels Archives (transcripts)	SBAt
Southwestern Historical Quarterly	*SWHQ*
Official Records of the War of the Rebellion	*O.R.*

Throughout the book I alternate between "the Society" or "*Adelsverein*" as shorthand renditions of the cumbersome official title, "The Society for the Protection of German Emigrants in Texas."

German Noble Names

I have followed the convention used by Gilbert Giddings Benjamin in his book, *The Germans in Texas*, which I prefer, because it seems to convey best in English the sense and meaning of these names in German. By this convention, the first name is usually, but not always, given first followed by the title—prince, count, etc. The last word is the locality to which the title applies. The "von" translates as "of" or "from" and was legally reserved for members of the nobility. Thus, Carl Prince of Solms-Braunfels was a prince to and from the ancestral holdings of Solms and Braunfels.

Notes

Introduction

1. Hawgood, *The Tragedy of German-America,* 142.
2. Friedrich Armand Strubberg, who served as the first director of the Friedrichsburg settlement under the pseudonym Dr. Schubbert, wrote a novel based on his experiences. His novel *Friedrichsburg*, published in 1867, suffers from distortions and a tendency to self-glorification. Nevertheless, it offers one of the best literary depictions of the dire situation of the settlers. Strubberg stresses how narrowly the whole venture avoided complete collapse and the important role of the grain and food shipments in avoiding this collapse.
3. See *San Antonio Express News*, February 21, 2003, "Prince Johannes von Sachsen-Altenburg, Duke of Saxony, discovered the plan to create a German state in Texas among documents in family archives in Germany, Russia and France."
4. Remark overheard by the author at a convention of historians.
5. For reasons of variation I sometimes refer to the organization as the *"Adelsverein"* (Society of Noblemen) and sometimes as "the Society." The term *Adelsverein* is problematic, for many societies of German noblemen existed at the time. For this reason contemporaries often referred to it as the *"Mainzner Adelsverein,"* or, better yet, as the *"Fürstenverein"* to distinguish it. I prefer this second description because it conveys the idea that it was an association of the highest order of German noblemen. Nevertheless, I will use the term *"Adelsverein"* in this study because it has become thoroughly established as shorthand for the long and cumbersome official title *"Verein zum Schutze deutscher Einwanderer in Texas."*
6. Boos-Waldeck, Galveston, September 1842, *Bericht* (Report), Solms-Braunfels Archives (transcripts), hereinafter referred to as SBAt L, 190–197.
7. The Texas Congress enacted a Colonization Law on January 4, 1841. See Gammel, *Laws of Texas*, 554–557. On February 5, 1842, the president was empowered to grant provisional title to unoccupied lands to *empresarios* who promised to meet certain conditions. The law was subsequently

amended to make it more workable (Gammel, *Laws of Texas*, 777). The Republic of Texas entered into four contracts under these provisions.

8. Boos-Waldeck an Bruder Eduard (Boos-Waldeck to brother Edward), Columbia am Brazos, October 22, 1842, SBAt L, 222.

9. Benjamin makes the statement: "Von Behr believed that the purpose was to form a feudal state." (Benjamin, *Germans in Texas*, 34–37) See also Tiling, *History*, 119; Sehm, *Armand*, 13.

10. Count Leiningen returned to Europe early in 1843 leaving Boos-Waldeck and his servant, Wilhelm Etzel, as the sole representatives of the Society in Texas.

11. Prince Carl of Solms-Braunfels, Nassau, December 23, 1844, Bericht über Plantage Nassau (Report on Nassau Plantation), SBAt L, 31, 32.

12. Helen Rummel, "German Prince Once Made Whoopee on Texas Farm," *Houston Chronicle*, August 10, 1930. Also, Frau v. Rosenberg an ihrer Schwägerin Fallier (Mrs. von Rosenberg to her sister-in-law Fallier), Rosenberg-Nassau, March 29, 1850, 60.

13. Prior to becoming an official of the *Adelsverein*, von Wrede had published a book in Germany about Texas. See Friedrich von Wrede, *Sketches of Life in the United States of North America and Texas*, Translated by Chester W. Geue (Waco, Texas: Texian Press, 1970).

14. English equivalents for titles of the German nobility are often inadequate. "*Freiherr*" has no exact English equivalent. In these cases I have used the German words. For a fuller discussion of these distinctions, see Chapter 1, Note 18.

15. As the organization of the Society evolved, it adopted certain titles for various offices. Beginning with Solms-Braunfels in 1844 the chief agent in Texas carried the title "General-Kommissar," the holder of the land grant, first Bourgeois d'Orvanne and subsequently Henry Fischer, the title "Kolonialdirektor." Johann Otto *Freiherr* von Meusebach arrived in Texas as successor to Carl Prince von Solms-Braunfels on April 21, 1845 (Solon, 60; Tiling, 79).

16. See Cappes an Castell (Cappes to Castell), October 29, 1846; Blücher an Castell (Blücher to Castell), SBAt XLI, 228, 229; also Huber, 42.

17. *Jagd- und Reiseabenteuer* mit 24 von dem Verfasser selbst nach der Natur entworfenen Illustrationen. 1 Band. (Stuttgart: J. G. Cotta, 1857).

18. See Leroy H. Woodsen, "American Negro Slavery in the Works of Friedrich Strubberg, Friedrich Gerstäcker and Otto Rupius," Dissertation, *The Catholic University Studies in German*, vol. XXII, Washington, D.C.: The Catholic University of America Press, 1949.

19. See Agreement of Redemption, Projected sale of holdings of the German Emigration Society to Dr. Ludwig Martin, May 6, 1848, Fayette Deed Book E, 192; SBAt XXXII, 33, 145). Castell, who has been given the authority to supervise and approve this sale, gives Martin a Power of Attorney (SBAt XXXII, 45).

20. Biesele, for instance, in his study, *The History of the German Settlements in Texas*, 160, dismisses the activities of the Society after 1847 with the statement that after that date the Society no longer actively sponsored emigrants.

CHAPTER 1 NOTES

1. August Heinrich Hoffmann (1798–1874), or Hoffmann von Fallersleben, as he called himself after his birthplace, was one of a group of political poets of the 1840s, which included H. F. Freiligrath and Georg Herwegh. His most famous song, written in 1841, but only famous since 1870, was "*Deutschland, Deutschland, über alles*," which subsequently became the national anthem of Germany. Hoffmann was keenly interested in Texas and came close to emigrating himself. He wrote a whole cycle of songs about Texas collected as the *Texanische Lieder* (Texas Songs). The most well-known of these is *Der Stern über Texas* (The Star over Texas).

2. Protocol der Ausschuss-Sitzung (Committee Minutes), April 26, 1842, SBAt XXXI, 192; I, 12.

3. For a discussion of the various careers open to the German nobility at this time, see Gollwitzer, *Die Standesherren*, 32.

4. In March 1848, revolution broke out in Germany, thus bringing an end to the long period of stability, hence the name *Vormärz*, or pre-March.

5. "Verein für constituirt erklärt [Society proclaimed]," SBAt XXVIII, 35.

6. In a letter of June 9, 1842, Castell is addressed as "den k. k. [königlich-kaiserlichen] Hauptmann des Infanterie Rgmts. L. Mayer und Gouvernements-Adjutanten zu Mainz [regal-imperial captain of the infantry regiment L. Mayer and governmental adjutant]," SBAt I, 223.

7. Christian Graf zu Leiningen-Westerburg, Mainz, den 8 März 1842, an die Vereinsgesellschaft (Christian Count of Leiningen-Westerburg, Mayence, March 8, 1842, to the Society), SBAt I, 1-10.

8. See "A Note on Sources and Abbreviations" at the back of the book.

9. William Kennedy, *Texas: The Rise, Progress and Prospects of the Republic of Texas,* (London: R. Hastings, 1841). The first German edition, translated by Otto von Czarnowsky, appeared under the title *Geographie, Naturgeschichte und Topographie von Texas* (Frankfurt am Main: David Sauerländer, 1841).

10. For a nice summary of the life, significance, and works of Alexander von Humboldt, see Tommy Tobiassen, "Alexander von Humboldt," *Germany and the Americas,* vol. 1, 530-532.

11. "Protocoll der Ausschuss-Sitzung [Minutes of the Committee]," SBAt XXXI, 191.

12. By the exchange rate in New Orleans in June 1844 a gulden/florin

was worth slightly less than forty cents. See "*Tabelle der rhein. u. preuss. Münzorten im Vergleich zum amerikikanischen Geld* [Table of the Rhenish and Prussian Currencies in Comparison to American Money]," SBAt LXVIII, 104.

13. Solms-Braunfels Bericht (Solms-Braunfels Report), April 27, 1845, SBAt XL, 114.

14. Boos-Waldeck, Nassau, Bericht über die Plantage, an Grafen Castell (Boos-Waldeck, Nassau, report over the plantation to Count Castell), July 11, 1843, SBAt L, 250; SBAt LXI, 139.

15. Ch. Lein. an Castell (Christian Leiningen to Castell), December 2, 1842, SBAt I, 33.

16. The dried roots of ipecac, or *Cephaelis Ipecacuanha*, a shrubby South American rubiaceous plant, were used as an emetic, purgative, etc. There is no indication that the plant actually is found in Texas. This is probably taken from one of Alexander von Humboldt's pioneering studies of the physical geography of the equatorial regions of the New World. Possibly from *Vues des Cordilleres, et monumens des peuples indigenes de l'Amerique,* (*Paris*: Chez F. Schoell, 1813) or from *Atlas geographique et physique des regions equinoxiales du nouveau continent, fonde sur des observations astronomiques, des mesures trigonometriques et des nivellemens barometriques* (Paris: F. Schoell, 1814).

17. Boos-Waldeck, Nassau, Bericht über die Plantage, an Grafen Castell (Boos-Waldeck, Nassau, report over the plantation to Count Castell), July 11, 1843, SBAt L, 250; ibid., LXI, 139.

18. See letter by Leiningen, March 8, 1842, SBAt I, 10.

19. The *Handbuch des deutschen Adels*, the great reference work of the German nobility, divides the German noble houses into three basic categories, into *Fürstliche, Gräfliche,* and *Freiherrliche* houses. Both *Fürst* and *Graf* can be translated as "Count," but in the hierarchy of the German nobility, a *Fürst* outranked a *Graf*. Both categories, however, relate to ruling houses. The *Freiherr* denomination, on the other hand, suggests a house that had originally obtained its noble status through some exceptional service (usually military). A *Freiherr*, though entitled to many privileges, stood far below the other two categories in rank. All of the original members of the *Society for the Protection of German Emigrants in Texas* came from ruling houses. Johann Otto von Meusebach, the General-Commissioner in Texas from the spring of 1845 until the summer of 1847, was the first (and only) *Freiherr* admitted into the Society. He was of lesser standing; knowing this, one can begin to detect the subtle discord this occasioned. Such distinctions in rank and class, which appear so contrived and artificial to modern sensibilities, were clearly understood by all Germans of the period, and of the utmost importance to the men in question. Different gradations in rank required different forms of address and different standards of behavior. They implied different career possibilities

and social responsibilities. These men were keenly aware of their position and standing; to uphold the honor and status of the family name was an overweening motivation.

20. Karl Emich *Fürst* of Leiningen, president of the Society, was the half-brother of Queen Victoria of England and regularly attended functions of the English court. Carl Prince of Solms-Braunfels, likewise, had access to the English court. His mother, the former Princess of Mecklenburg-Strelitz, had taken for her third husband Ernest, King of Hannover, who was the uncle of Queen Victoria. These connections were to be relevant, at least in the promise they held, for the future success of the undertaking.

21. The suspicion persists that the English Foreign Office heavily subsidized the whole colonization effort of the Society, and that there was a secret agenda at play here. For a full discussion and documentation of this debate, see Chapter 14, Note 5.

22. For the minutes of these meetings, see SBAt XXXI, 192.

23. For references to the fourth general assembly, held in March, 1844, in Mainz, see SBAt XXVIII, 35+, 83, 119, 153; SBAt V, 19; Protokoll derselben (minutes of the same), SBAt XXX, 70; SBAt LXIII, 101; SBAt XLVIIIa, 34; Auszug aus derselben (excerpt from the same), SBAt XXVIII, 8; SBAt LXIII, 101.

24. See Leiningen an Castell (Leiningen to Castell), April 30, 1842, SBAt I, 14.

25. This does not necessarily mean that they were first or second cousins. Nearly all members of the upper German nobility were related to some degree and they sometimes addressed themselves as "Vetter."

26. Volume LXI of the SBAt contains several very interesting letters by Prince Solms to Count Castell that predate the prince's trip to Texas. They shed light on their relationship, which was very close. See, for instance, the letter of November 12, 1843 (SBAt LXI, 173).

27. For the best discussion of the *Standesherren*, see Heinz Gollwitzer, *Die Standesherren* (Wien: Verlag für Geschichte und Politik, 1957).

28. Karl Emich *Fürst* of Leiningen wrote of this situation in 1847. He said the *Standesherren* found themselves between two chairs, between the old order and the new, and they needed to create a new role for themselves so that they would be worthy of the prestige they enjoyed. See Beilage zur Allgemeinen Zeitung (insert to the newspaper), December 26, 1847, reproduced in Grollwitzer, *Die Standesherren*, 374, 375.

29. Allgemeiner Bericht über Entstehen, Zweck und Ziel des Vereins (General Report over the Origin, Purpose and Goals of the Society), July 28, 1845, SBAt XXX, 148.

30. For the dimensions of the exodus, see "Statistische Angaben über die Stärke der Auswanderung aus der verschiedenen Hafen, 1836-46 [Statistical figures over the strength of emigration from various harbors, 1836-46]", in SBAt LXIX, 95.

31. According to the U.S. Bureau of the Census statistics (reproduced in Wolfgang Glaser, *Deutsche und Amerikaner*, 121), the official count was 4,991,741.

32. See "Allgemeiner Bericht über Entstehen, Zweck und Ziel des Vereins [General Report over the Origins, Purpose and Goals of the Society]" prepared for the Generalversammlung (general assembly), Wiesbaden, July 28, 1845, SBAt XXX, 146-157. See also *ad acta* No. 770, February 7, 1846, letter by Christian Leiningen and Count Castell in which they review the goals of the Society and the progress since 1843 toward these goals, SBAt V, 307+.

33. For a thorough discussion of this point based on newly released material from the Prussian Archives, see Kossok, "Prussia, Bremen and the Texas Question," 227-269.

34. Barker, ed., *A Comprehensive, Readable History of Texas*, 363.

35. Under the *empresario* system of Spanish and Mexican rule, a married man of good character could apply for a first class head right. If he applied as a rancher he received a league (4,428 acres); if he applied as a farmer, he received a labor (177 acres). Needless to say, many more declared themselves to be ranchers than farmers. The practice of giving away public lands to individuals continued under various forms from the date of independence, March 1836, until the public lands were exhausted. In 1836, Texas had approximately 216,000,000 acres of unappropriated lands; by 1840, the number had dropped to 190,000,000 acres; and by 1898, none was left. The Republic, nearly bankrupt and desperate, revived in February 1841 the *empresario* system whereby individuals could contract for conditional title to vast tracts of land. The condition was that they introduce in a set time period specified numbers of settlers into the area of the grant, which was invariably on or beyond the frontier and hence the domain of the Comanches, Kiowas, or Apaches.

36. The possibility of amassing vast wealth through land grants intoxicated entrepreneurs the world over; the practical difficulties, if not impossibilities, of carrying out the terms of the contracts did not seem to sober their enthusiasm. The speculative fever engendered by the revival of the *empresario* system extended to the noblemen in Germany, as Leiningen's letter of March 1842, clearly shows (SBAt I, 1-10). For a complete discussion of the Texas land situation, see Miller, *The Public Lands of Texas, 1519-1970*.

37. "Sitzungs Protocoll des Ausschusses am 4. May 1842 unter Zuziehung u. Einstimmung der in der Nähe sich aufhaltenden Hrn. Actionärs [Minutes of the Committee from May 4, 1842, with Consultation and Agreement from the Stockholders who are Close By]," SBAt XXXI, 193-196.

Chapter 2 Notes

1. Instruktion für den Grafen Boos-Waldeck und Grafen Viktor von Alt-Leiningen-Westerburg (Instructions for Count Boos-Waldeck und Count Viktor von Alt-Leiningen-Westerburg), SBAt L, 225–227.

2. Wilhelm Ötzel was born June 24, 1820, in Wehrheim, Nassau, and died September 18, 1889 in Round Top. He is buried in the Becker Cemetery, a family cemetery adjacent to the north boundary of the Jack League. Although he came over as the manservant to Joseph Count of Boos-Waldeck, he was trained as a cabinetmaker in Germany and continued to practice that trade in Texas (Geue, *A New Land Beckoned*, 22). He subsequently put his carpentry and cabinetmaking skills to use in the construction and outfitting of the manor house (*Herrenhaus*) at Nassau Plantation. The University of Texas Winedale Historical Center has a cedar china cabinet by him in their collection, which is reproduced in Taylor, *Texas Furniture*, 248.

The German *umlaut* vowels "ö," "ü," and "ä" are difficult for English speakers to pronounce, leading to a tendency to anglicize them to the nearest English sound, which in the case of "ö" would be "e." Hence "Ötzel became Etzel. Texas–German dialects have dropped the *umlaut* vowels for the most part.

3. Other than the information given in Count Boos-Waldeck's report, little is known about Johann Schwind.

4. See Chapter 1, note 8.

5. Le Havre, France, emerged in the second half of the nineteenth century as a port whose principal product was the transportation of emigrants to the New World. After 1847, it enjoyed rail connection with Paris.

6. In 1842 only one company offered passenger service between Bremen and New Orleans, the firm of D. H. Waetjen & Co. By 1844, twelve German ships from Bremen fully occupied themselves with the Galveston trade. The area where they loaded and unloaded had even come to be called "Bremen" street. The Prussian government established a consulate in Galveston and named D. H. Klaener as consul. Klaener, who would later serve as an agent of the Society in Galveston, become the focal point of much criticism and misunderstanding. He had expressed himself favorably concerning a colonization initiative in Texas. His chief reservation was the primitive state of communication between Texas and Germany.

7. William (Wilhelm) Kobbé was born in Idstein, near Wiesbaden, in the Duchy of Nassau, and represented that country in New York until it was absorbed by the Kingdom of Prussia in 1866. Kobbé married the daughter of a prominent New England family. His son Gustav gained prominence as a prominent music critic in New York. (Hamersly *et al., Who's Who in New York [City and State]*, 353).

8. Morgan L. Smith (1802-?) rose steadily in prominence and wealth in Texas from the 1840s until the outbreak of the War Between the States. A former colonel in the New York Seventh Regiment, he had come to Texas in 1838 where he engaged in merchandizing with Thomas J. Pilgrim, John Adriance, and a succession of others. Abigail Curlee, in "A Study," 76, describes him as "An energetic man of business with an inexhaustible driving power. . . ." Tax records from Brazoria County reveal the astonishing rise in his personal fortune. In 1843, he owned 700 acres valued at $2,800. He had no slaves. By 1851, he possessed a total of 3,616 acres in Brazoria County valued at $54,280. In addition the rolls list him with seventy-six slaves valued at $30,400. This yields a personal taxable estate of $84,688. These figures do not include the value of his property outside of Brazoria County, or the value of his partnership interests, both of which were substantial.

9. G. A. Scherpf: see Chapter 1, note 8.

10. Boos-Waldeck an den Herzog zu Nassau (Boos-Waldeck to the Duke of Nassau), July 31, 1842, SBAt XXX, 208.

11. Eduard Ludecus observed: "Dieses Land ist jetzt der Anziehungspunkt der Nordamerikanischen Länderspekulanten. . . . [Texas is now the focal point of North American land speculators. . . .]" (Ludecus, *Reise im Jahre 1834*, 57) Similarly, Hermann Achenbach wrote of the excitement among German emigrants in New York caused by news from Texas. Friedrich Ernst's (Fritz Dirk's) famous letter was apparently making the rounds of emigrant groups in New York in 1833. Achenbach reproduces the letter in his guidebook for emigrants published in 1835. (Achenbach, *Reiseabentheuer*, 132ff.)

12. Ibid., 209.

13. Swante M. Swenson is regarded as the first Swedish immigrant to the state. His story is one of remarkable business success. In the 1840s he ran a mercantile business in Houston, but he later moved to Austin and expanded his interests. His greatest interest lay in land, which he succeeded in accumulating in vast quantities through the trade in Texas railroad land certificates. *Handbook of Texas Online*, s.v. "Swante M. Swenson," (accessed February 27, 2007).

14. Boos-Waldeck, New York, 23.7.42 an den Herzog von Nassau, Bericht der Reise nach New York (Boos-Waldeck, New York, July 23, 1842, Report on the Trip to New York), SBAt L, 198-204; see also General Bericht des Grafen Jos. Boos-Waldeck (General Report of Count Joseph Boos-Waldeck), SBAt L, 150.

15. Two communities developed close to the mouth of the Brazos River in southeastern Brazoria County: Velasco on the east bank and Quintana on the west bank. They became ports of entry for many thousands of immigrants, especially after riverboats began making their way up the Brazos River to San Felipe and beyond.

16. Probably James Campbell McNeill, son-in-law of Levi Jordan, prominent plantation owner in the area. See *Handbook of Texas Online*, s.v. "James Campbell McNeill," (accessed April 18, 2007).

17. Boos-Waldeck an den Herzog zu Nassau, Sept 42 (Boos-Waldeck to the Duke of Nassau, September 1842), SBAt L, 190.

18. Auszug, datiert Galveston 5.9.42 aus Brief des Grafen Boos Waldeck, New York, 31.7.42 an Herzog zu Nassau, Reisebericht New York-Texas (excerpt, dated Galveston September 5, 1842, from the letter of Count Boos-Waldeck, New York, July, 31, 1842, to the Duke of Nassau, Travel Report), SBAt L, 213.

19. Waldeck an Nassau (Waldeck to Nassau), September 1842, SBAt L, 190.

20. Morgan Smith owned (or controlled) a plantation in southern Brazoria County called "Waldeck Plantation." Apparently Joseph Count of Boos-Waldeck visited the plantation in 1842, and his presence was sufficiently imposing that thereafter the plantation was named after him. Whether or not he had any ownership interest is a matter of dispute. One writer, Strobel, *Old Plantations*, 17, claims he did through a management firm, a claim repeated in Weyand and Wade in *Early History*, 108. Curlee, "A Study," 83, discusses the plantation at length, but never mentions any ownership interest by Waldeck. By contrast, Davis in *The Historic Towns of Texas*, 29, asserts that Boos-Waldeck did not purchase an interest in the plantation. There is an intriguing entry in the Solms-Braunfels Archives (L, 223) in which Boos-Waldeck intimates that he has bought 1,000 acres for the Duke of Nassau on the lower Brazos. Was this an interest in Waldeck plantation? In any case neither the count nor the duke had a direct involvement in the management of the plantation. An examination of the tax and deed records of Brazoria County, moreover, does not corroborate the assertion that Boos-Waldeck was part owner of the plantation. His name never appears. Morgan Smith subsequently built the plantation into one of the finest sugar plantations in Texas.

21. He stayed at the E. H. Hall boardinghouse for two months and eleven days recuperating—until January 10, 1843. (Boos-Waldeck, General-Bericht [Boos-Waldeck, General Report], SBAt L, 151) There is a good chance, of course, that the equestrian abilities of both Wilhelm Schwind, Leiningen's servant, and Wilhelm Etzel, Boos-Waldeck's servant, were as deficient as their hunting skills: practice in either of these avocations in Europe was reserved for men of standing.

22. Flora von Roeder, *These are the Generations,* 113.

23. The famous Texas folklorist J. Frank Dobie included the legend in *Tales of Old-time Texas* as "The Planter who Gambled away his Bride." Dobie credits Sigmund Enkelking who lived in Comfort, Texas, at the time, but whose family had originally settled at Millheim near the von Roeder family. The legend rests on a letter by Caroline Luise Baronin von Roeder

reproduced by Flora von Roeder in her book, *These are the Generations*, in which this tale is related. The letter refers to the protagonist as "Sigismund," but I assume she meant Otto von Roeder. No other corroboration for this story exists, and since Otto von Roeder was already married at the time, the story is most certainly an embellishment.

24. *The New Handbook of Texas*, Vol. 2, 884.

25. There is disagreement on this point. If it was published, a copy has never been found.

26. Detlev Dunt, who wrote one of the first accounts of Texas in German (*Reise nach Texas*) in 1834, begins his book with a discussion of the importance of the letter. He reproduces a complete text of the letter. The purpose of his book, he maintained, was to see firsthand if the glowing portrayal of Texas, as presented in the letter, was true. For the importance of the letter to the von Roeder family, see Flora von Roeder, *These are the Generations*, 27.

27. For a nice discussion of Charles Fordtran, see Brown, *Indian Wars and Pioneers of Texas*, 524, 525.

28. *The New Handbook of Texas*, Vol. 2, 1076.

29. Friedrich Ernst was interested, especially, in the cultivation of tobacco, which had not enjoyed the success in Texas that many had hoped for. Ernst experimented successfully with Cuban varieties and shared his experiences in several articles in the Galveston newspaper. He continued to raise tobacco and sell cigars made from his crop for many years. See Richter and Lindemann of Industry, *Historical Accounts of Industry*.

30. 1850 Census, Fayette County, Slave Schedules.

31. Boos-Waldeck, General-Bericht (Boos-Waldeck, General Report), SBAt L, 153.

32. Horatio Chriesman surveyed many of the headright grants in South Central Texas. It was the recipient's responsibility and requirement to have his land surveyed. Very often the surveying fee was paid in kind so that a surveyor might take, say, half or a quarter of a headright for the service of surveying it. Men like Chriesman profited handsomely as surveyors. Chriesman was the surveyor of the Jack League upon which Nassau Plantation was established. My family still owns a substantial part of the Cunningham League in Colorado County, which has passed down through inheritance since it was granted in 1833. Among the family papers is the original survey done by Horatio Chriesman.

33. William von Rosenberg first made this claim in 1894. See Rosenberg, "Kritik," SWHG 85, No. 2 (October, 1981), 179. The charge was then repeated in subsequent studies. See, for instance, King, *John O. Meusebach: German Colonizer in Texas*, 33; also Biesele, *History*, 67; also Tiling, *The German Element in Texas*, 61.

34. Boos-Waldeck, General-Bericht (General Report), SBAt L, 152.

35. SBAt L, 155.

36. Boos-Waldeck's instructions specified, as we have seen, that he was only to purchase land from the government.

37. Boos-Waldeck, Anlage zum General-Bericht (Exhibit to General Report), no date, SBAt L, 170.

38. Ralph A. Wooster. "Notes on Texas' Largest Slaveholders, 1860," *Southwestern Historical Quarterly* 65 (July 1961): 73-77.

39. Mills speculated in land in other counties besides Fayette. In examining the chain of title to the "Home Place" in the Gilliland League where I grew up in Colorado County, I was surprised to discover that Robert Mills had owned the land briefly. Alex von Rosenberg, who has a direct connection to Nassau Plantation, had also owned it for a number of years.

40. Fayette County Deed Book B, 351.

41. March 19, 1831, Wm. H. Jack is issued a *sitio* of land. Surveyed by Horatio Christsmann [*sic*: Chriesman] (Land Office Records 3: 282; Book 8, 140; Record of Surveys, transcribed, A, 117; N, 158). Biesele, *A History*, 68, incorrectly gives the date as 1833.

42. Most accounts of Nassau Plantation either falsely assume that the property was purchased as an intact plantation complete with slaves and buildings or they sidestep the issue.

43. Fayette County Deed Record Book C, 205-206.

44. General-Bericht des Grafen Boos-Waldeck: Reise u. Kauf der Plantage Nassau (General Report of Count Boos-Waldeck over trip and purchase of Nassau plantation), SBAt L, 150-163.

45. SBAt L, 173.

46. See Geiser, *Naturalists of the Frontier*, 95-131, for an informative biography of Louis Cachand Ervenberg, a fascinating and tragic character, who was also an amateur naturalist.

47. Boos-Waldeck, Anlage zum General-Bericht (Exhibit to General Report), SBAt L, 170.

Chapter 3 Notes

1. Bollaert, *William Bollaert's Texas*. 135.

2. By 1842 moneychangers in the United States had drastically discounted the interest-bearing notes issued by the republic, whereas the non-interest-bearing notes, the so-called "red backs" had become practically worthless. Barter had replaced currency in many activities, and the currency that was acceptable was often issued by private businesses. Boos-Waldeck was quick to notice these things. (SBAt XXX, 53) By mortgaging slaves or lands, one could obtain certificates of credit from certain private firms such as McKinney and Williams in Galveston or the Mills Brothers of

Brazoria. These certificates enjoyed widespread confidence and became a *de facto* currency in the areas around Galveston and Brazoria, a fact that Boos-Waldeck had noted when he judged Robert Mills to be a reputable man. A developed and orderly system of credit and finance is a prerequisite for economic development and the growth of capital. The absence of such a system in the Texas of the 1840s was a real hindrance. See Carlson, *Monetary and Banking History of Texas*.

3. See Palmer, "Published Passenger Lists: A Review of German Emigrants and Germans to America."

4. W. Steinert gives an excellent picture of New Orleans. See Gilbert Jordan, "Notes and Documents: W. Steinert's View of Texas in 1849." Translated and edited by Gilbert J. Jordan. Serialized translation of Steinert's book, which appeared in the July 1976, October 1976, January 1977, April 1977, and July 1977 issues of *Southwestern Historical Quarterly*.

5. Beginning in 1837, several schooners, sloops and steamboats began to make regular runs between New Orleans and Galveston. The *New York*, the *Neptune*, the *Cuba* and the *Galveston* were all steamboats that made the trip. The *Neptune* could accommodate about thirty cabin passengers and forty steerage passengers. (Hogan, *The Texas Republic*, 6-9.)

6. SBAt XXX, 42.

7. We do not know the exact cost of the New Orleans slaves. However, an inventory from the following year (see Appendix A) assigns all the slaves a value, and it can be assumed that these values reflect the purchase price.

8. Bill of lading on the *Neptune* by Stark, Day, Stouffer & Co., February 14, 1843, New Orleans, Boos-Waldeck original receipts, Verein Collection, Center for American History, The University of Texas at Austin.

9. A German "Zentner" was equal to 110.23 pounds; an American "Centner" was twice that amount. I assume he meant a German one.

10. Boos-Waldeck receipts, Verein Collection: #32 Mule for $30, Mr. Woodsen, 24 Feb '43; #33, yoke of oxen $40 from Vickery, 25 Feb '43, Buffalo Bayou; #34, yoke of oxen $50, Houston, 25 Feb.'43, Killenny; #37, bought of Nath Townsend two yoke of oxen and a large road wagon for $200, no date, yoke of oxen for $40.

11. SBAt L, 211.

12. Boos-Waldeck an Lieber Freund Castell (Boos-Waldeck to his good friend Castell), April 29, 1843, Nassau am Cummings Creek, SBAt L, 231.

13. No independent source found for Bryan. William Joel Bryan mentioned as an overseer on Perry's plantation from 1836 through 1839 (Curlee, *A Study*, 103), but this was most certainly someone else, for according to the *Handbook of Texas* (s.v. William Joel Bryan), William Joel Bryan was married with several children at this time. See Curlee, *A Study*, 103.

14. Boos-Waldeck an Lieber Freund Castell (Boos-Waldeck to his good friend Castell), April 29, 1843, Nassau am Cummings Creek, SBAt L, 231.

15. SBAt XXX, 43.

16. Blue norther: A meteorological peculiarity of Texas that occurs in the winter and early spring months. A rapidly advancing line of blue clouds in the north signals the approach of cold, windy, and wet weather, which can sometimes drop the temperature 30 degrees or more in a matter of minutes. The "northers" made quite an impression upon the Germans. Charles Nagel (*A Boy's Civil War Story*, 143) gives one of the best descriptions of their onset.

17. Fordtran Bericht (Fordtran Report), Mill Creek, November 1843, SBAt L, 1, 2.

18. Boos-Waldeck Bericht, April 1844 (Boos-Waldeck Report), SBAt XXX, 46.

19. Boos-Waldeck an Lieber Freund Castell (Boos-Waldeck to his good friend Castell), April 29, 1843, Nassau on Cummings Creek, SBAt L, 231.

20. SBAt L, 167.

21. Bené, SBAt XLIV, 353. For a description of Nassau fences, see *Ancestral Voices*, 44, "Die Fens wird wie folgt gemacht [the fence is made in the following way]," Frau v. Rosenberg an ihre Schwägerin Fallier (Frau von Rosenberg to her sister-in-law Fallier), Nassau, March 29, 1850, 64–68; see also Boos-Waldeck describe fence, SBAt L, 167.

22. Frau von Rosenberg, *Ancestral Voices*, 64–68. For an excellent discussion of the Texas German dialect, see Hans C. Boas, "Texas German Dialect," *Germany and the Americas*, 1029–1035.

23. SBAt L, 167.

24. "To plow twenty acres of land would cost eighty dollars for it costs four dollars to break an acre . . . To work up the native prairie requires a strong and peculiarly constructed breaking plow. The cost of one of these is between fifteen and twenty dollars," Leutnant Bené, SBAt XLIV, 353.

25. Boos-Waldeck Bericht (Boos-Waldeck Report), May 1844, SBAt XXX, 44.

26. d'Orvanne Tagebuch (Diary), SBAt XLVIIIa, 158.

27. SBAt XXX, 46.

28. SBAt XXX, 46.

29. In a letter from Prince Solms to Count Castell from July 15, 1844, the prince remarks: "It is clear to me that the famous Negress Emily, well-known in Wiesbaden and other port cities, contributed much to Boos-Waldeck's illness." SBAt XL, 155.

30. Boos-Waldeck an den Grafen Castell (Boos-Waldeck to Count Castell), April 29, 1843, SBAt L, 228.

31. Ibid., 230.

32. Boos-Waldeck Bericht (Boos-Waldeck Report), May 1844, SBAt XXX, 43.

33. Boos-Waldeck, Brief an Castell (Letter to Castell), May 26, 1843, SBAt L, 236.

34. Boos-Waldeck an Castell (Boos-Waldeck to Castell), SBAt L, 243.

35. Boos-Waldeck an Castell, SBAt L, 249.

36. Rutersville is on State Highway 159 five miles north of La Grange in central Fayette County. John Rabb and other members of the Methodist Episcopal Church founded it for the purpose of establishing a college in 1839 on the La Bahia Road. A post office opened in 1846. By 1884, the town had two general stores, two blacksmiths, three gin-gristmills, a harness maker, a wagon maker, a carpenter, a physician, and a population of 150. *Handbook of Texas Online* s.v. "Rutersville," (accessed June 14, 2007).

37. Boos-Waldeck Bericht (Report), SBAt XXX, 55, 56.

38. Could Boos-Waldeck's illness be connected to his infatuation for Emily, the young and beguiling slave girl? Could he have contracted syphilis from her? We do not know. The comment by Solms-Braunfels about Emily concerning her availability for sexual favors, cited above in Note 29, is certainly intriguing. Boos-Waldeck's disease could also have been brought on by contaminated water. From the report we know that Boos-Waldeck had a well dug, but the water tasted bad and went dry from time to time. They then had to fetch water from the creek. Subject to animal waste and runoff, it was certainly less than wholesome.

39. Boos-Waldeck an Lieber Castell (Boos-Waldeck to Dear Castell), SBA L, 251.

40. Fordtran Bericht (Fordtran Report), Mill Creek, February 14, 1844, SBAt L, 18; ibid LI, 128, 129.

41. Castell an Boos-Waldeck (Castell to Boos-Waldeck), May 24, 1843, SBAt I, 77.

42. Boos-Waldeck an Castell (Boos-Waldeck to Castell), November 15, 1848, SBAt L, 254-257.

43. Boos-Waldeck Belege (Boos-Waldeck receipts), Verein Collection.

Chapter 4 Notes

1. See, for instance, Leutnant Coloredo Mannsfeld an Castell (Lieutenant Coloredo Mansfeld to Castell), January 26, 1843, SBAt I, 54; also, April 24, 1843, SBAt I, 70; also, Graf von Walderdorff an Castell [Count von Walderdorff to Castell], February 2, 1843, SBAtI, 63.

2. Castell an Boos-Waldeck (Castell to Boos-Waldeck), May 24, 1843, SBAt XXVIII, 35; also, June 1, 1843, SBAt I, 80.

3. Castell has the power of attorney for Karl Eberhardt von Leiningen, Solms-Braunfels, Graf zu Neuleiningen-Westerburg,, Landgraf zu Hessen-Homburg, and Graf Renesse, SBAt XXX, 88.

4. SBAt I, 80.

5. For this reason, the date of the founding of the Society is sometimes given as June 1843.
6. Boos-Waldeck had requested 20,000 fl.
7. See Chapter 5, Note 45.
8. SBAt XXX, 101, 102.
9. Ibid, 103-105.
10. See Dangerfield an Castell (Dangerfield to Castell), October 8, 1843, SBAt I, 108.
11. See Solms an Castell, "Teilnahme deutscher Regierungen" (Solms to Castell, "Participation of German Governments"), February 3, 1844, SBAt LXI, 156.
12. See SBAt I, 117ff. for an interesting but anonymous, "Beschreibung der Tex. Verhalt [Description of the circumstances in Texas]," December 15, 1843. It offers a very sober evaluation of the prospects of Prussia benefiting from a colonization initiative to Texas, especially from the standpoint of trade. Also of interest is a letter from Eduard Boos-Waldeck, the brother of Joseph von Boos-Waldeck, to Count Castell, dated October 29, 1843, informing him that Alexander von Humboldt is against the matter. The King of Prussia gave him an audience, he relates, but the king remarked that the Society needed a harbor. SBAt LXI, 172. For the most comprehensive discussion of Count Castell's request for subsidies (and von Humboldt's rejection), see Kossok, "Prussia, Bremen and the Texas Question," 240-245.
13. According to Caroline Ernst, d'Orvanne owned a store at San Felipe and bought tobacco from her father, Friedrich Ernst. See Caroline von Hinueber, "Life of Early German Pioneers in Texas." *Quarterly of the Texas State Historical Commission*, Vol. II, no. 3 (Jan. 1899).
14. Solon, "A History," 11; Gammel, *Laws of Texas*, II, 777; SBAt XLVIIIa, 33-39.
15. Vertrag (Contract), SBAt XLVIIIa, 33.
16. Sehm, *Armand: Biographie und Bibliographie,* 14; Solms-Braunfels, *Voyage to North America*, 9.
17. Vertrag zwischen dem Verein and Orvanne (Contract between the Society and d'Orvanne), SBAt XLVIIIa, 33-39.
18. Dangerfield to Castell, October 8, 1843, SBAt LXI, 109.
19. SBAt I, 110.
20. This is the date given by Biesele (*History of the German Settlements*, 66), and clearly this is the name they used after this date. According to Henry Francis Fischer, however, the Society only officially incorporated itself under this name in Wiesbaden on October 16, 1847. See "Agreement between Fischer and Ludwig Martin (Inspector General)," February 4, 1849, Henry Francis Fischer Papers, Verein Collection, Center for American History, University of Texas at Austin. We note, however, by 1845 most in Texas referred to the Society as the German Emigration Co. while the

Society eventually incorporated itself in Texas officially as the Lavaca, Guadalupe, and San Saba Railroad by act of the Texas Legislature on May 8, 1846. At one point the Society had seriously considered building a railroad from Carlshafen on the Lavaca Bay to Friedrichsburg following along the watershed of the Guadalupe River. The rails were to be made of wood and the cars pulled by mule.

21. Protocol (Minutes), SBAt XXX, 82-87.

22. Protokoll derselben (Minutes of the same), SBAt XXX, 70; SBAt XLVIIIa, 34; Auszug aus derselben (Excerpt from the same), SBAt XXVIII, 8; SBAt LXIII, 101; SBAt V, 19.

23. "Bericht des Grafen von Boos-Waldeck über die Resultate seiner Mission nach Texas [Report about the Results of his Mission to Texas]," April 1844, SBAt XXX, 39-69.

24. See Solon, "A History," 37, which refers to the Colonization Papers in the Texas State Library; see also Seele, *The Cypress and other writings of a German Pioneer in Texas,*" 19; Sehm, *Armand: Biographie und Bibliographie*, 14; and "Offizieller Aufruf der Mainzer Vereinsdirektion [Official Proclamation of the Mayence Society]," April 9, 1844, SBAt XXVIII, 119.

25. SBAt XXVIII, 119

26. Ibid., 119-123.

27. Gammel, *Laws of Texas*, II, 958.

28. SBAt XXX, 158

29. See Vertrag (contract), SBAt LVIII, 3-7.

30. Biggers, *German Pioneers in Texas*, 25, 26.

31. Tiling, *A History of the German Element in Texas*, 73.

32. Castell an Solms (Castell to Solms), Mainz, June 25, 1844, SBAt LIX, 146-7.

33. SBAt LIX, 148.

34. Castell an Solms (Castell to Solms), Mainz, June 25, 1844, SBAt LIX, 151.

35. "Agreement of February 4, 1849," Fischer Papers, Center for American History Studies, University of Texas at Austin.

Chapter 5 Notes

1. Fordtran Bericht (Fordtran Report), Mill Creek, November 15, 1843, SBAt L, 1-8.

2. Fordtran Bericht (Fordtran Report), Mill Creek, November 15, 1843, SBAt L, 1.

3. Holman Plantation: Plantation established by John Holman, who married the daughter of Jesse Burnam, one of Stephen F. Austin's original colo-

nists and the owner of an important ferry joining the La Bahia road to the Gonzales road on the Colorado River south of La Grange. The community of Holman, located approximately halfway between La Grange and Weimar on Texas 155, takes its name from the plantation. *Handbook of Texas Online*, s.v. "Holman Plantation," (accessed June 15, 2007).

4. Ward & Cazello: apparently cotton traders who had set up an office in La Grange. No other references found.

5. John Murchison: The 1840 census for Fayette County, or rather general inventory, made by each county in the republic in preparation to a direct tax, lists a John Murchison. He has 1,150 acres of land, 30 head of cattle, a two-wheel cart and three slaves. Census of the Republic of Texas, 1840, Fayette County, 39. He was a native of South Carolina and settled with his young wife in Texas in 1836. He served as a justice of the peace and a short time in the Congress of the Republic of Texas. He was also a prominent Mason. See Weyand and Wade, *An Early History of Fayette County*, 31.

6. Fordtran an Boos-Waldeck (Fordtran to Boos-Waldeck), Nov. 15, 1843, SBAt L, 1.

7. Namenliste der Sklaven auf der Plantage Nassau (List of the names of the slaves at the plantation), SBAt XLIII, 167; SBAt XLVIIIa, 135; Inventory of July 15, 1844, SBAt XLIII, 166.

8. Boos-Waldeck, Brief an Castell (Letter to Castell), May 26, 1843, SBAt L, 238.

9. See Jordan, "W. Steinert's View of Texas in 1849."

10. See Curlee, "A Study of Texas Slave Plantations, 1822–1865," 62.

11. Boos-Waldeck an Lieber Freund (Castell) (Boos-Waldeck to dear friend), April 29, 1843, Nassau on Cummings Creek, SBAt L, 228)

12. Boos-Waldeck Bericht (Report), April 1844, SBAt XXX, 48.

13. Boos-Waldeck an Castell (Boos-Waldeck to Castell), July 11, 1843, SBAt L, 248, 249.

14. Ibid., 253.

15. Boos-Waldeck, Brief an Castell (Letter to Castell) May 26, 1843, SBAt L, 242.

16. Fordtran an Boos-Waldeck (Fordtran to Boos-Waldeck), Mill Creek, February 14, 1844, SBAt L, 12.

17. Dresel and Spiess families' records, 1785-1914, MS 239, Woodson Research Center, Fondren Library, Rice University, 27.

18. Prinz Solms an den Verein (Prince to the Society), July 15, 1844, SBAt XL, 2.

19. Stevens Farm: most likely James Stevens who had bought land from Nate Townsend on the La Bahia road. See Fayette County Deed Book A, 390.

20. Hermann Spiess wrote: ". . . Brown [*sic*: Bryan] died (it was alleged he was poisoned by the slaves)." See Dresel and Spiess families' records, 27.

21. "Dropsy" is a symptom rather than a disease *per se*. It is characterized by swelling due to water accumulation, usually in the legs. It suggests a heart or kidney problem.

22. See Note 36 in Chapter 3. Rutersville was, and still is, a small community on the La Bahia road, present-day Texas 159, between La Grange and Round Top.

23. The Biegel farm was on Baylor and Cedar creeks in the Joseph Biegel League, eight miles east of La Grange in central Fayette County. It is considered to be the second-oldest German settlement in Texas. Joseph Biegel, a German immigrant from Alsace-Lorraine, received his league, originally granted to F. W. Johnson, from the Mexican government on November 29, 1832. He sold one-quarter of the league to Bernard Scherrer, 1,872 acres to Christian Wertzner, and smaller parcels to others. By 1845, Biegel owned only 400 acres of his original 4,428. In 1974–75 the Biegel League was acquired by the Lower Colorado River Authority, and a coal-fired generating plant and reservoir were constructed there. Several buildings and family cemeteries were moved to various locations in Texas. The Biegel home, built of twenty-foot logs, was moved to the Winedale Historical Center. See Norman C. Krischke, *Biegel Settlement; also, Handbook of Texas Online*, s.v. "Joseph Biegel," (accessed February 28, 2007).

24. Holloway: Fordtran spells it Alloway, but it was most likely John A. Holloway who came to Fayette County from Person County, North Carolina with his wife, four children, and nine Negroes in the early 1840s and thereafter located on a farm eight miles below La Grange on the Colorado River. He died in 1846. His widow married P. J. Shaver who is reputedly the founder of Fayetteville, Texas.

25. They were probably in the river bottom near the present community of Ellinger located on Highway 71 about halfway between La Grange and Columbus.

26. Coyer: identity unknown.

27. This puts Fordtran at a spot very close to the area where I grew up. I am familiar with the Colorado River bottom at this point and can appreciate how difficult it was to find the escapees in the dense undergrowth and difficult terrain.

28. Higgenbotham: possibly R. T. Higgenbotham, listed in the 1840 census as a landowner in Bexar County. Census of the Republic of Texas (1840), Bexar County, 14.

29. Leal: identity unknown.

30. McDonald: possibly A. J. McDonald listed in the 1840 census as owning 640 acres of land in Colorado County. Census, 29.

31. Butler's Farm: no references found. Perhaps Fordtran meant John Baylor who owned an 840-acre farm in the vicinity.

32. Amanda Fallier von Rosenberg to her sister, Rosenberg-Nassau, August 24, 1850, *Ancestral Voices*, 51.

33. Murchison: see note six above.

34. Schneider: most likely George Schneider who had purchased several tracts of land in Fayette County.

35. Unfortunately not all issues of newspapers from this period survive. I have not been able to locate Fordtran's announcement.

36. Lewis: possibly Sam Lewis, but the information is too vague to say who this Lewis might have been.

37. Stephen Townsend: a member of the Townsend family who came to Texas from Florida in 1826 and acquired choice land in Fayette County. He was 44 years old at this time and by the census of 1850 was worth $6,000 and owned six slaves, which counted him as one of the more prosperous settlers of the area. His homestead was two miles south of the present town of Round Top, which at one time was referred to as Townsend's settlement. Several members of the Townsend family had farms in and around Nassau Plantation at this time. See Weyand and Wade, *An Early History of Fayette County*, 30.

38. Toni: most likely James Toney listed on the 1850 census as a farmer, aged 59, married with eight children, but also possibly a poor transcription (common with Fordtran) for William Jones, who is listed on the 1850 slave schedule as owning two slaves in the immediate vicinity of Nassau Plantation.

39. See note 27 above.

40. Solms-Braunfels, Bericht über Nassau (Report over Nassau), July 15, 1844, SBAt XL, 2.

Chapter 6 Notes

1. See Chapter 1, note 1.

2. *Texanische Lieder* (Texas Songs) 1845, by Hoffmann von Fallersleben. See <http://www.von-fallersleben.de/fallerslebenarchiv-6.html>.

3. Rummel, "German Princes Once Made Whoopee," 5.

4. See *Handbook of Texas Online*, s.v. "Kleberg, Rosalie von Roeder."

5. Somervell: Alexander Somervell (1796-1854) was an entrepreneur, soldier, and leader of the Somervell expedition, an aborted punitive raid into Mexico after the Mexican incursions into Texas in 1842. See *Handbook of Texas Online*, s.v. "Somervell".

6. See, for instance, Green, *Memoirs of Mary A. Maverick*, 87: "General Somerville [*sic*: Somervell] was a noted laugher—he saw the Prince's two attendants dress his highness, that is lift him into his pants, and General Somerville was so overcome with the sight that he broke out into one of his famous fits of laughter, and was heard all over the point. The Prince and suite were all very courteous and polite to us. They wore cock feathers in their hats, and did not appear quite fitted to frontier life."

7. See Caroline Ernst von Hinüber, "Life of German Pioneers in early Texas," *Texas State Historical Quarterly*, vol. 2, no. 3 (January 1899), 227-232.

8. As an example of his anti-Anglo bias: "And concerning Hays and his company as well as all other Americans and foreign elements, I implore you, once and for all, to keep them all out of the settlements...." (Author's translation) Solms Brief an Fischer (Solms letter to Fischer), Aqua Dulce, January 6, 1845, SBAt XL, 100

9. SBAt XXX, 158.

10. d'Orvanne an Castell (d'Orvanne to Castell), May 18, 1844, SBAt XLVIIIa, 26.

11. See Solms-Braunfels, *Voyage to North America*, 22; SBAt XXX, 158

12. "Eine Salve von 21 Kanonenschüsse begrüsste den Prinzen von Solms bei seiner Ankunft [A salvo of twenty-one cannon shots greeted Prince Solms upon his arrival]." d'Orvanne Tagebuch (diary), SBAt XLVIIIa, 153.

13. Armand Ducos was Bourgeois d'Orvanne's partner in the land grant contract. This was his first appearance.

14. d'Orvanne Tagebuch (diary), SBAt XLVIIIa, 154.

15. Ibid, 156.

16. The report says Lessley, but this has to be a mistake of transcribing the written German in German script (*deutsche Schrift*) to typewritten form. It was surely Etzel.

17. Nassau, July 15, 1844, SBAt XXX, 1-9.

18. d'Orvanne Tagebuch (diary), SBAt XLVIIIa, 158.

19. Prince Solms wrote, "... kann nur aus vollen Herzen versichern, dass diese Negerwirtschaft eine des Vereins durchaus unwürdige Sache, ein wahrer Schandfleck für die menschliche Gesellschaft ist, und dass mir diese Sache besonders, so wie die ganze Farm, mehr Ärger, Sorge und Unannehmlichkeit, als alle die Gefahren, Entbehrungen und Strapazen, welche ich im Interesse der deutschen Colonisation bisher erlitten, zusammen genommen [I can only stress from the bottom of my heart that this business with Negro slaves is a matter totally unworthy of the Society; it is a true stain on human society, and that this matter, as well as the whole farm, has cost me more aggravation, worry and unpleasantness than all the dangers, discomforts and aggravations I have suffered up to this point]."(Aus den Lager bei La Vaca [From the camp at La Vaca], December 23, 1844, SBAt L, 32).

20. "Ich erinnere dich an die Uhr des Herrn Fordtran. Graf Boos hatte sie ihm versprochen, der Nachfolger [Solms] wollte sie ihm nicht geben, da er sich nicht für gebunden hielt, Graf Boos ihn dafür auf Pistolen, da er sein Wort compromittiert habe ... [I will remind you of the watch of Mr. Fordtran. Count Boos had promised it to him; the successor (Prince Solms-Braunfels) did not want to give it to him; Count Boos challenged him to pistols since he saw his word compromised ...]." Castell an die Comite

des Texas Vereins (Castell to the Committee of the Texas Society), January 9, 1850, SBAt LXII, 63.

21. The man was Lieutenant von Bauer from the 7th Hanoverian Regiment. He later assumed command of Prince Solms' militia. See Solms-Braunfels, *Voyage to North America,* 78.

22. See Geiser, *Naturalists of the Frontier,* Chapter VII.

23. See Solms-Braunfels, *Voyage to North America,* 79.

24. Ibid., 65.

25. Ibid., 41.

26. In his diary d'Orvanne says the Dr. Meyer was newly arrived in Texas, had served in the Dutch army, but was Swiss by nationality. He reported that he was lively and sociable, but otherwise little was known about him. D'Orvanne Tagebuch (Diary), SBAt XLVIIIa.

27. See *Voyage to North America,* 41. The abbot's name was Jean Pierre Ogé; the hunters had the last names Wangen and Tory; the cook was named, appropriately, Anton Kueck.

28. The grant included the present day counties of Medina, Uvalde, Real, and Bandera.

29. See Solms, *Voyage to North America,* August 11, 1844, 53.

30. Friedrich Wilhelm von Wrede, Jr. (1820-?) and his father, Friedrich, Sr. (1786-1845), both play important roles in this story. "Von Wrede" is a very prestigious name in German military history due to the exploits of Karl Philipp von Wrede (1767-1838), an extremely successful field commander in the Bavarian army during the Napoleonic Wars, first as an ally, then as an opponent of Napoleon. A bronze statue commemorates his achievements in the *Feldherrenhalle* (Hall of the Field Commanders) in Munich. The family hailed from Westphalia and supplied members of the *Ritterkurien* (Knight's cura) for many generations. One branch can make the extraordinary claim of having occupied continuously the same manor house, Haus Amecke, since 1338, a period of over 600 years. The elder von Wrede, a veteran of the battle of Waterloo, traveled extensively in the United States and published an account of his travels upon return to Germany in 1844 (see bibliography). Both returned to North America as officials of the Society. His son became a close confidant and secretary for Prince Solms while the father served as the Society's agent in New Orleans and later the supervisor of Nassau Plantation. Indians killed the elder Von Wrede in October 1845 while he was camped at Live Oak Springs south of Austin. *The New Handbook of Texas,* vol. 6, p. 1088.

31. Bericht des General Commissairs (Report of the Commissioner-General), August 26, 1844, SBAt LX, 29.

32. See Solms-Braunfels, *Voyage to North America,* note 50, 73, 74.

33. SBAt XXX, 159; XL, 124.

34. Solms Bericht (Report), September 20, 1844, SBAt XL, 43.

35. A comparison of the inventories reveals that it was Mary who died. Apparently the "deserter" returned, for Mary is the only change from 1844 to 1847.

36. Sutton: William Sutton, local plantation owner and slaveholder who lived in the vicinity of Nassau Plantation. By the 1850 census, he is listed as 67 years old, married with several children. His farm has a modest value of $2,000, and he owns five slaves.

37. Amanda Fallier von Rosenberg wrote five years after these events that the prince had thrown a party costing over 15,000 Thaler (dollars). (Frau von Rosenberg an ihrer Schwägerin Fallier [Frau von Rosenberg to her sister-in-law, Fallier], Nassau Farm, March 29, 1850, Von Rosenberg Collection, Center for American History, University of Texas at Austin, 60.) This figure seems unlikely, but it suggests that the legend must have some basis in fact.

38. See Gilbert J. Jordan, "W. Steinert's View of Texas in 1849," 80-81. Steinert recounts that three wagonloads of empty wine bottles had to be removed from the plantation.

39. Otto von Roeder had killed a young lieutenant in a duel in Germany.

40. Charles Fordtran recounts a horse-race contest between the von Roeder brothers and the Townsends in which the von Roeders bet heavily and lost heavily. Fordtran Bericht (Fordtran Report), Mill Creek, February 14, 1844, SBAt L, 17.

41. See Biesele, "Prince Solm's Trip to Texas, 1844-1855," 1-23.

42. Prince Solms's reports the following exchange: "D'Orvanne: Oh, this matter of nationality! It is only a word. . . ." Solms: "Yes, perhaps for you, but not for me, and not for the *Verein*." (Author's translation) Solms *Bericht* (Report), Agua Dulce, August 20, 1844, SBAt XL, 13.

43. See Prince Solms' report of March 5, 1845, SBAt XL, 82-0.

90. Prince Solms is much chagrined with Fischer whom he accuses of fomenting distrust and unrest with his ideas of liberty and freedom. He mentions that their three blacksmiths have put together fourteen wagons and mounted one cannon from their own means.

44. SBAt XXX, 160.

45. Fordtran an Schubbert (Fordtran to Schubbert), Castle of Indolence, January 20, 1847, SBAt XLI, 276. See also Peter Carl von Rosenberg to his brother Otto, Nassau, May 28, 1850, *Ancestral Voices*, 37.

Chapter 7 Notes

1. SBAt L, 15

2. See Friedrich von Wrede, *Lebensbilder aus den Vereinigten Staaten von Nordamerika und Texas* (Kassel, 1844; English ed., *Sketches of*

Life in the United States of North America and Texas, as observed by Friedrich W. von Wrede, comp. Emil Drescher, trans. Chester W. Geue [Waco: Texian Press, 1970]).

3. By one account. Johann Otto von Meusebach's ancestors had been ennobled as a result of helping Charles XII during his epic flight. William von Rosenberg took exception to this claim. See von Rosenberg, "Kritik," *SWHQ* 85, no. 3 (January 1982): 303, 304

4. Friedrich von Wrede an Euer Erlaucht (Friedrich von Wrede to his Grace), Galveston, February 1, 1845, SBAt L, 34-42.

5. Billburg: identity unknown. Often names were written phonetically in the reports so that one has to guess at the true spelling.

6. Tres Palacios Bay is the northeastern arm of Matagorda Bay in Matagorda County. The Colorado River empties into Matagorda Bay.

7. Friedrich von Wrede Bericht (Report), Indian Point, March 24, 1845, SBAt L, 52.

8. S. A. Durand: dates and age unknown; former employee of Hardin R. Runnels, a rich planter who had moved to Texas in 1841 and set up a plantation in Brazoria County. In 1856 Runnels defeated Sam Houston for the governorship.

9. Vertrag (Contract), SBAt L, 73.

10. Friedrich von Wrede an die General-Direktion zum Schutze deutscher Einwanderer in Texas zu Mainz (Friedrich von Wrede to the Executive Office of the Protection of German Emigrants in Texas), Galveston, May 20, 1845, SBAt L, 47.

11. Friedrich von Wrede Bericht (Report), SBAt L, 65.

12. Ibid., 67.

13. Friedrich von Wrede an die General-Direktion zum Schutze deutscher Einwanderer in Texas zu Mainz (Friedrich von Wrede to the Managing Office of the Protection of German Emigrants in Texas), Galveston, May 25, 1845, SBAt L, 75-82.

14. Ibid., 79.

Chapter 8 Notes

1. Roemer, *Texas*, 160-165.

2. Von Wrede Bericht (Report) #2, Galveston, May 20, 1845, SBAt L, 69.

3. Amanda Fallier von Rosenberg to August and Emma Fallier, May 25, 1850, *Ancestral Voices*, 25.

4. Wilhelm von Rosenberg, *Ancestral Voices*, 17.

5. Roy Randolph Rather and his wife Mary Belle, the present owners of the land where the *Herrenhaus* stood, have some timbers from the old house. The beams are about 4x10 inches, flattened with a dovetail joint.

6. See Jordan, *Texas Log Buildings*, 72, 73.

7. Fordtran Bericht (Fordtran Report), February 14, 1844, SBAt L, 18.

8. There are several receipts for planked lumber in this time period. For instance, receipts from May 1843 show that Boos-Waldeck purchased over 1,500 hundred feet of pine flooring from L. M. Rodermel and Crockett Peery. The going rate seemed to be around three dollars 100 board feet delivered. See Boos-Waldeck Receipts, Verein Collection, Center for American History, University of Texas at Austin, #50, May 10, 1843, received from Boos-Waldeck for 1,000 feet pine flooring $27.50 and two dollars fifty cents more having no change, [signed] L. M. Rodermel; #56, May 1843, twelve dollars and seven bits for payment for 500 feet of plank from Crockett Peery.

9. Amanda Fallier von Rosenberg, *Ancestral Voices*,

10. Bourgeois d'Orvanne Inventarium (inventory), SBAt XLVIIIa, 135.

11. Frau von Rosenberg an ihrer Schwägerin Fallier (Frau von Rosenberg to her sister-in-law, Fallier), Nassau Farm, March 29, 1850, Von Rosenberg Collection, Center for American History, University of Texas at Austin, 67.

12. See Lonn Taylor and David Warren, *Texas Furniture*, 248, 291.

13. This was most likely the son of the noted Austin colonist and Indian fighter by the same name. He appears on the 1850 regular and slave census for Fayette County. In 1844 he was 37 years old, married with seven children and seven slaves. (1850 Census, Fayette County, Schedule 2, Slave Inhabitants of Fayette County, Texas, 411.) For a biography of the elder Abner, see J. H. Kuykendall, "Reminiscences of Early Texas," *Texas State Historical Quarterly* vol. 6, no. 4 (January 1903): 314.

14. Fordtran Bericht (Fordtran Report), February 14, 1844, SBAt L, 16.

15. Frau v. Rosenberg an ihre Schwägerin Fallier Nassau (Mrs. von Rosenberg to her sister-in-law Fallier), March 29, 1850, 67.

16. Arthur Meerscheidt, who subsequently bought land in the plantation, gives a good description of how quickly the basic structure of a log house could be erected. See Arthur Meerscheidt to his mother, February 4, 1850, *Ancestral Voices*, 120.

17. D'Orvanne inventory, July 15, 1844, SBAt XLVIII, *Herrenhaus* 135.

18. See inventory, Appendix A.

Chapter 9 Notes

1. See *Inventory of the County Archives of Texas, Fayette County No. 75*, "Historical Sketch," San Antonio: Texas Historical Records Survey, 1940, 7.

2. An analysis of the 1850 agricultural schedule shows that 12.36 percent of the farmland was "improved," meaning it was fenced and in cultivation.

3. All figures taken from the 1850 and 1860 federal census for Fayette County.

4. See Nagel, *A Boy's Civil War Story*, 234.

5. Gotier's Trace, also known as Goacher's Trace, was a pioneer trail built by James Gotier in 1831 or 1832 under the authority of the *ayuntamiento* of San Felipe. The road, which connected San Felipe and Bastrop, probably followed a curved route to take advantage of an easier crossing of Cummins Creek. As settlement progressed, the course of the trace may have been moved slightly to the south to follow a more direct route. A branch of the trace may have connected Bastrop with Washington-on-the-Brazos. *Handbook of Texas Online*, s.v. " Gotier's Trace," (accessed July 1, 2007).

6. The name of the firm was Ward & Cazello. Charles Fordtran mentioned the firm in one of his reports. See Fordtran an Boos-Waldeck (Fordtran to Boos-Waldeck), Nov. 15, 1843, SBAt L, 1.

7. Shuffler, 6.

8. Compiled Tax Records 1850

9. The barn that now serves as the theater at the Winedale Historical Center contains timbers from the original Lewis gin. Interview with H. H. Howze, former curator of the museum, July 7, 2007.

10. Peter Carl von Rosenberg wrote, for example, "The farmers of the Brazos and lower Colorado . . . use very many mules; they are said to be better than horses and oxen." (*Ancestral Voices*, 44) Apparently Sam Lewis' donkeys roamed the area. He wrote that a herd of sixteen paid him a visit several times a week and greeted them with their "outrageously offensive" cries.

11. Rechnung von Georg Vogt (Bill of Georg Vogt), Mainz, October 20, 1840, SBAt L, 86.

12. Boos-Waldeck Bericht (Report), April 44, XXX, 52; Boos-Waldeck an Lieber Freund (Castell) (Boos-Waldeck to his dear friend), April 29, 1843, Nassau am Cummings Creek, SBAt L, 230.

13. Wilhelm von Rosenberg to friends in Germany, Pryry's Place, April 21, 1850, *Ancestral Voices*, 21.

14. See note 390 below. For the best study of the German contribution to viticulture in Texas, see Samuel Wood Geiser, *Naturalists of the Frontier*.

15. Mustang Grape: This is the common name given to a grape (*vitis mustangensis*) native to Texas, especially to the south central area of the state where it is found in abundance.

16. Peter Carl von Rosenberg, *Ancestral Voices*, 44.

17. Johann Leyendecker (1803-1869) came over with his wife in 1843 from Neuhäusel in the Rhenland Palatinate and settled on the Zimmerscheidt League in northern Colorado County, which had been obtained by his father-in-law, probably in 1828. Leyendecker's son, Johann Friedrich (Fritz) Leyendecker (1838-1908) subsequently founded a nursery on the family land. He became a prominent horticulturist in the state and is credited with, among other things, with developing and introducing several new varieties of peaches. He also published several articles in *Texas Farm and Ranch* on

grapes. Several catalogs from this nursery are still extant. For more information, see Samuel Woods Geiser, *Horticulture and Horticulturists in Early Texas* (Dallas: Southern Methodist University Press, 1945), 59, 60.

18. The interest in viticulture in Texas began with European immigrants. The native Anglos had little knowledge or interest. Most of the varieties of grapes they brought with them, however, were ill-suited to the climate and so they began to experiment with the native mustang grape (*vitis mustangensis*). W. A Trenckmann discusses the importance viticulture held for many Germans in South Central Texas. See Trenckmann, "Experiences and Observations," 57, 58.

19. Many forests in Germany have been owned or controlled since time immemorial by the nobility and, to this day, many are. The noblemen were very solicitous of their forests and often employed *Jägermeister* (game wardens) to patrol them and keep out poachers and wood thieves. Resentment over aristocratic control and limited access to the forests contributed (at least among the peasants) to the 1848 revolution.

20. Boos-Waldeck General-Bericht (General Report), SBAt XXX, 54.

21. Mein lieber Freund, Neu Wied in Texas, den 14. November 1849 (My dear friend, Neu-Wied, Texas, November 14, 1849), reproduced in SBAt XLIV, 300–326.

22. Winter wheat has become one of the state's most important cash crops. A comparison of statistics shows how quickly wheat increased in importance. In 1850 the wheat crop was less than 50,000 bushels, but by 1867 it reached 6,000,000 bushels with a market value of a dollar a bushel. For an excellent discussion, see *The Handbook of Texas Online*, s.v. "wheat."

23. General Bericht (Comprehensive Report), Solms-Braunfels (transcripts), XXX, 151.

24. Nachschrift (Postscript), Solms-Braunfels (transcripts), I, 121.

25. The standard Anglo diet seemed to consist of variations of cornbread and pork and pork and cornbread. Friedrich Schlecht, W. A. Trenckmann, and Amanda Fallier von Rosenberg, to name a few, all comment on the monotony of the American diet.

26. Established in 1854, the Society exists to this day. The Society published a journal in which local farmers spoke of their experiments and observations. Their meeting hall, an unusual octagonal structure, is a landmark and still used for many community events.

Chapter 10 Notes

1. S. Schulz an Castell (S. Schulz to Castell), January 21, 1848, SBAt LVI, 224.
2. Bené an Castell (Bené to Castell), February 24, 1848, SBAt XLIV, 34.

3. His real name translated more like "Big Buffalo Balls." Victorian sensibilities caused his name quite early to be sanitized to "Buffalo Hump," and it is this form that usually appears in history books. (Schilz, *Buffalo Hump*, note 2.)

4. King, *John O. Meusebach*; Porter, *El Sol Colorado*.

5. In April 1846 Meusebach wrote to Castell, "... wir nun wirklich bei Ausführung des Grants die Aussicht haben, wenigstens eine Million und eine Masse Grundbesitz zu gewinnen, bedauere ich, dass in dem Augenblick, wo man nahe dran ist, die Früchte grosse Aufopferung zu ziehen, die Sache durch Geldmangel zu Grunde gehen sollte [. . . now that we are on the point of carrying out the terms of the grant and at the least will get a million and a large amount of land to boot, I regret, that in the moment when we are able to pluck the fruit of all the sacrifice, the whole thing will fail because of a lack of money.]." Meusebach an Castell (Meusebach to Castell), April 17, 1846, SBAt LII, 173, 174.

6. Seele, *The Cypress and Other Writings*, 29.

7. For a graphic report of 1846 and a scathing indictment of Meusebach see Coll Bericht (Coll Report), February 5, 1847, SBAt XLIII, 98.

8. Strubberg, alias Dr. Schubbert, made this very charge. Schubert an Meusebach (Schubbert to Meusebach), New Orleans, May 14, 1848, SBAt XLI, 379.

9. In October 1845, Count Castell wrote Kläner, the Society's agent in Galveston, "... seit dem 10. Juli ohne alle Nachrichten von Meusebach sind . . . [. . . since the 10th of July we have heard nothing from Meusebach . . .]." Castell an Kläner (Castell to Kläner), October 26, 1845, SBAt LVI, 10.

10. "Organisation des Vereins in Deutschland" (Organization of the Society in Germany), SBAt XXVIII, 159.

11. In 1846 Alwin Sörghel visited New Braunfels. What he saw led him to write his book, *Für Auswanderungs-lustige*, a bitingly satirical *Veriss* (critique) of the Society and its leaders. In 1847 he returned to New Braunfels from his farm near Nassau Plantation and reported on the great change for the better that had occurred in the meantime. He published his views in *Neueste Nachrichten aus Texas*. He also accepted employment from the Society.

12. Meusebach resorted to the extreme measure of advertising the plight of the colonist by placing an announcement in the German press. The Society's agent in Galveston, D. H. Kläner, helped him. King, *John O. Meusebach*, 82; Meusebach, Answer to Inquiries, 20.

13. Meusebach Bericht (Meusebach Report), Friedrichsburg, January 19, 1847, SBAt XXVIII, 184.

14. William von Rosenberg discusses these accusations in length. ("Kritik," *SWHG* 85 no. 3 [January 1982]: 308-310.) He attributes the story to Dr. Ferdinand Roemer. Roemer's report, however, was mild compared to

the judgment of Hans von Coll, the Society's accountant in New Braunfels. See Von Coll, Indian Point, February 5, 1847, "Ausführlicher Bericht über die elenden Zustände in der Kolonie [Comprehensive Report over the Horrible Conditions in the Colony]," SBAt XLIII, 88-1170).

15. Ibid., 98.

16. Meusebach defended his conduct while at the plantation the following year. Meusebach Bericht (Report), January 19, 1847, SBAt XXVIII, 187, 188.

17. Schubbert to Cappes, January 29, 1847, SBAt XLIII, 85.

18. Colonization Contract, Fischer and Miller and the Republic of Texas, General Land Office, Austin, Texas.

19. Huber, "Frederic Armand Strubberg," 47, refers to Cappes to Castell letter of November 29, 1847, SBAt LVI, 44.

20. Meusebach an Castell (Meusebach to Castell), March 6, 1846, SBAt, LII, 138; Huber, 41

21. Meusebach/Schubbert Lease, Fayette Deed Book D, 536-42.

22. Ibid.

23. Darstellung (Portrayal), June 13, 1847, SBAt XXVIII, 73.

24. Huber, "Frederic Armand Strubberg," 45.

25. Julius Splittgerber has left a lively account of the formative period in Friedrichsburg, including an account of Schubbert's expedition. (Penninger, *Fredericksburg*, 29-37) Several personality conflicts arose during the trip which led to several challenges and at least one duel between Lieutenant Bené, whom Dr. Schubbert had replaced as director of the Friedrichsburg settlement, and Victor Bracht, who later wrote an informative book about the physical geography, agricultural prospects and social statistics of Texas (Bracht, *Texas in 1848*). Dr. Schubbert and Bené also had a serious disagreement, which, according to Splittgerber, almost resulted in a fight. Dr. Schubbert was recognized as an excellent shot and when he refused to duel under handkerchiefs (to level the field), Lieutenant Bené prudently reconsidered. These episodes underscore that, for whatever reason, violence seemed never to be far from Dr. Schubbert and that duels were a determinative factor for several of the personalities associated with this story, including Dr. Schubbert, Lieutenant Bené, and Otto von Roeder. Hans von Coll, who served as the Society's accountant under Prince Solms and Meusebach, was later killed in a duel in Friedrichsburg.

26. Schubbert to Cappes, January 29, 1847, SBAt XLIII, 85.

27. Fordtran to Schubbert, January 20, 1847, SBAt XLI, 124.

28. Schubbert to Cappes, January 29, 1847, SBAt XLIII, 85.

29. Hermann Spiess, for example, later wrote that Schubbert had set himself up as a kind of "Pasha," who curried favor by dispensing supplies from the commissary and organizing festivals at public expense. (Spiess recollections, 24, in: Dresel and Spiess families records, 1785-1914, MS 239, Woodson Research Center, Fondren Library, Rice University.)

30. In his novel *Friedrichsburg*, Strubberg wrote about the Mormon settlers and how his initial prejudice had given way to unbounded admiration on observing their industry and individual subordination to the welfare of the whole. See Strubberg, *Friedrichsburg*, 177-181.

31. Meusebach was in many ways the exact opposite of Prince Solms-Braunfels in attitude. His disagreement with Dr. Schubbert about the degree to which the Society should support the colonists in Friedrichsburg underscored their differences. Count Castell, Prince Solms and others in the Society were imbued with a kind of paternalistic attitude toward the German people. They felt that most Germans were incapable of doing things for themselves and looked to the German nobility to take care of them. Indeed this attitude was one of the guiding sentiments behind the organization. Prince Solms revealed how deeply ingrained this attitude was in a report from July 28, 1845. Referring to the disagreements with Henry Francis Fischer, who took issue with the prince displaying the Austrian flag and continuing to play the role of a prince on the Texas frontier, the prince wrote that Fischer "was not able to shake the innate trust [*das angeborne Vertrauen*] of Germans for a German Prince, even in a faraway, wild country that had fallen victim to the hogwash about freedom." (Prince Solms Bericht [Report], July 28, 1845, SBAt XXX, 161.) Meusebach, on the other hand, had come to despise this attitude. He had been impressed by the self-sufficiency and imitative he had encountered in many Americans whom he had met. Moreover, he understood separation of church and state to be "das grosste Prinzip der Vereingten Staaten [. . . the most important precept of the United States]," and thought the organization of churches should be an entirely private affair. (Meusebach Bericht [Meusebach Report], Galveston, January 20, 1846, 108.) Dr. Schubbert's paternalistic and communal policy, Meusebach felt, undermined the effort to wean the settlers from a habituated attitude of dependence. They needed to learn to stand on their own feet. Likewise, the construction of a church at the Society's expense violated the principle of separation of church and state. In 1867 Friedrich Armand Strubberg, *aka* Dr. Schubbert, published a novel, *Friedrichsburg*, which is a fictionalized account of his role as colonial director in Fredericksburg. The novel glorifies the role of Schubbert and strays from the truth in many areas. Nevertheless, it is an important work, which throws light on the Meusebach/Schubbert controversy from the Schubbert point of view.

32. Schubbert an Meusebach (Schubbert to Meusebach), July 5, 1847, SBAt LXI, 246-253.

33. In July 1846 Meusebach wrote in a report to Count Castell that "Luckily, Dr. Schubbert, well versed in indigenous diseases, was able to make a favorable diversion in a short period of time." (SBAt LII, 218).

34. Reproduced in Barber, "Strubberg," 47, 48.

35. Meusebach an Castell (Meusebach to Castell), Friedrichsburg, January 19, 1847, SBAt XXVIII, 179.

36. In 1851 Friedrich Schlecht from Bunzlau travelled through Texas. In a published account of his travels, he relates an episode that illustrates the effectiveness of the Meusebach treaty with the Comanches. Travelling alone in the Hill Country two day's ride west of the Medina River, he blundered into a camp of Comanche Indians. Through signs he made it known that he was German whereupon he was made to be welcome. The chief made it clear, however, that had he been Anglo, he would have had his throat cut and been scalped. (Friedrich Schlecht, *Ausflug nach Texas*, 73, 74.) As a further example, the *Telegraph and Texas Register,* May 24, 1859, a full twelve years after the treaty was concluded, made the following report: "The Comanche chiefs, Cotemseh and Buffalo Hump, with a large band of warriors visited Fredericksburg a short time ago, and expressed the warmest friendship for the whites . . . They abandoned Fredericksburg as if panic stricken, as soon as the news was received that the cholera had appeared in Bexar . . ."

37. Meusebach an Cappes (Meusebach to Cappes), SBAt XLI, 156.

38. There was substance to this suspicion. By the terms of the agreement with the *Darmstädter* this group had the right to claim ". . . either 500 hundred acres of the Society's property on the Pedernales or the Nassau farm, whichever they choose, to be given to the group, should the settlement on the Llano fail." (Vertrag [Contract], no.10, SBAt XXVIII, 9-17); for the correspondence in question, see Schubbert an Cappes (Schubbert to Cappes), Friedrichsburg, April 28, 1847, SBAt XLI, 207-209; reproduced in Huber, "Frederic Armand Strubberg," 57; also: Schubbert an Cappes, Bericht über Kolonieverhältnisse (Schubbert to Cappes, Report over the colonial situation), SBAt XLIII, 146-150.

39. Apparently word got out about the real identity of Dr. Schubbert through a settler by the name of Bernstein. "Bernstein had knowledge of Schubbert's earlier life and from him we learned that his name was Strubach [*sic:* Strubberg] not Schubbert." (Splittgerber, "The Second Train," in Penninger, *Fredericksburg*, 35.)

40. Von Coll to Meusebach, July 17, 1847, reproduced in Huber, "Frederic Armand Strubberg," 58.

41. In the opening chapter of Friedrich Armand Strubbergs' adventure novel, *An der Indianergrenze* (*On the Indian Border*), Strubberg gives a vivid self-portrait of himself. According to Günter Sehm, Strubberg's biographer, it was an accurate description.

42. Sehm, *Armand,* 3.

43. Most accounts state that it was on the Leona River, a tributary of the Rio Grande, west of San Antonio (Sehm, 9; Barber, 35). Strubberg states unequivocally that this was the location in the opening page of his first novel, *Amerikanische Jagd- und Reiseabenteuer,* where he gives a pre-

cise description of the location. But it is clear that Strubberg often has exaggerated, and, occasionally, has fabricated episodes in the book, even though it purports to be based on real experiences. The same holds true for another novel, *An der Indianergrenze*. It seems extremely unlikely that Strubberg could have founded a "colony" on the Leona River at this time. Another scholar puts his settlement on the San Gabriel River near its confluence with Brushy Creek in present day Milam County, and this appears to the author to be more probable, if, indeed, he ever had a colony at all. (Huber, "Strubberg," 41).

44. "Ich stehe auf dem Sprunge mit dem Dr. Schubbert (Baron von Bruckennau??), einen sehr praktischen und energischen Mann . . . [I am in negotiations with Dr Schubbert (Baron von Bruckennau??), a very practical and energetic man . . .]", Meusebach Bericht (Meusebach Report), SBAt LII, 138.

45. Reichstein, *German Pioneers*, 21.

46. Ludwig Feuerbach(1804-74) was an important professor of theology in Germany and the author of several influential works. He believed that man created God in his own image rather than the other way around and that mankind projects intelligence upon the God we imagine that we should rather use for ourselves. He also believed that Jesus was an important historical figure, but was not divine. Many of the educated Germans of the period, especially those who settled in the so-called *Lateiner* settlements, had been deeply influenced by Feuerbach and, in fact, often referred to themselves as *Feuerbachianer* (devotees of Feuerbach).

47. Sörghel, *A Sojourn*, 32.

48. Ibid., 22.

49. See Castell an Cappes, (Castell to Cappes), SBAt XLIX, 189; also Graf Castell an Ew. Hochwohlgeboren (Count Castell to His Excellency), February 15, 1847, SBAt LII, 477.)

50. Agreement between Castell, Spiess and Herff, February 11, 1847, SBAt XXVIII, 1-17.

51. Dr. Herff's mother was a von Meusebach.

52. Reichstein, *German Pioneers*, 50.

53. Bené an ein hohes Comite (Bené to the High Committee), SBAt XLIVt, 150.

54. Bené an Castell (Bené to Castell), February 22, 1848, SBAt XLIV, 149.

55. Spiess Family Papers, 23.

56. Bené Bericht (Bené Report), November 25, 1847, SBAt XLIV, 104-113.

57. Splittgerber, "The Last Wagon Train," in Penninger, *Fredericksburg*, 36.

58. Many men of importance in Texas were Freemasons, and not a few Texas-Germans, especially Protestant Germans, joined the organization as a means of connecting with the influential. The Masons had a strong

presence in Fayette County. No record exists to show that Strubberg was a Mason, but, in view of his ambitious nature, it would not be surprising to learn that he was. It would explain, at least partially, the presence of Captain Somers, who was, according to the reports of his funeral, a well-known and respected Mason. James S. Mayfield of La Grange, former secretary of state and legislator, was implicated by Hermann Spiess (Spiess family Papers, 37) in encouraging and helping Dr. Strubberg in his forceful takeover of the plantation. Mayfield, records indicate, was also a prominent Freemason. (Walter Freytag to J. A. Newsome, January 14, 1959, Freytag Papers, James Mayfield File, La Grange Library, La Grange, Texas).

59. The harvest in 1847 was significant. The plantation had on hand over 70,000 pounds of cotton and 3,500 bushels of corn. See *German Emigration Co. v. Frederick Schubbert*, Fayette County Complete Records C, 23.

60. Ibid., pro-Schubbert report.

61. See note 11 above.

62. *Galveston Zeitung*, November 10, 1847; *The State of Texas v. Absalom Bostick*, Assault and Battery, Fayette County Complete Records C, 186.

63. The names are taken from a subsequent indictment. Fayette County Case File Book E, 383. In addition to Spiess, there were Ernst Sörgel; Adolph Benner, a bookkeeper; Georg Ulrich; Henry Flagge, a saddlemaker; Krauskopf, a carpenter, and Feuermann. For a list of the Society officials in New Braunfels, see Center for American History, University of Texas at Austin, Verein Collection, 3c32, Texas Verein Account Books.

64. M. A. Dooley (dates unknown) was elected the first chief justice (county judge) of Comal County (New Braunfels) when the county was incorporated in 1846. He had energetically come to Meusebach's defense when a mob of disgruntled settlers threatened him in January 1846. (Biesele, "Early Times in Comal County," *SWHQL*, 83) Dooley, a lawyer of Pennsylvania Dutch ancestry, was fluent in both German and English and thus well positioned to referee the two cultures. He moonlighted as the Society's lawyer both in respect to the Nassau Plantation litigation and in respect to the legal entanglements associated with the Fischer-Miller grant and by any standard was a competent advocate who often served *pro bono*. Dooley was a master of legal procedure and often resorted to technicalities to defeat or frustrate lawsuits against the Society.

65. H. Spiess, *Neu Braunfels Herald-Zeitung*, July 15, 1853, no. 36.

66. Spiess is inconsistent on this point. In his report to the newspaper (*Neu Braunfels Herald-Zeitung*, July 15, 1853, no. 36) he maintained that Dooley got lost; in a later account (Spiess family records, 29, 30), he

maintained that Dooley was present at Sörgel's house the night before the shootout.

67. Spiess later wrote, "At the moment when the breakfast table was set in the mansion, I wanted to enter the mansion with Zobel, Krauskopf and Rohrdorf quietly, and then face Strubberg, requesting him to surrender the plantation and in the case of his refusal, to go away calmly and protect the Negroes during the four days until the court convened. Please keep in mind: I do not relate this as if it were a story, no indeed, it was sworn to in court by Dooley, Ledbetter and Lorch, one of my companions whom they captured and turned into a state's witness; at the same time they gave evidence under oath with regard to my definite instructions only to make use of firearms in case of necessity. . . . If I had ordered a siege of the plantation, it would have been impossible for me to have been acquitted. . . . The gangsters, we later learned, had heard of our arrival and had posted guards." (Spiess Family History, 31) Hermann Krauskopf, a saddler for the *Verein* in New Braunfels, was recruited by Hermann Spiess in New Braunfels to be one of the attacking party. Krauskopf was taken prisoner by Strubberg and his men and he gave the names of all who had taken part to the authorities. He also testified against Spiess during his trial. In 1853 he wrote a letter in the *New Braunfels Herald-Zeitung*, accusing Hermann Spiess of being a trigger-happy aggressor in the affair. Spiess replied with a lengthy and spirited defense of his actions. He maintained that his intentions had been peaceful, with no thought of forcing Strubberg and his party out with firearms. *New Braunfels Herald-Zeitung,* July 15, 1853.

68. SBAt LVI, 207–210.

69. *Erster Bericht* (First Report), published in *Der Deutsche Auswanderer (The German Emigrant),* no. 15, 1847, reproduced in SBAt LXVIII, 115+, 126, 128. Report also given in SBAt LVI, 207–210.

70. ". . . kam im Frühjahr an, erforschte die Natur der Faulheit [. . . came in spring, researched the nature of laziness]." (Sörgel, *A Sojourn*, 307).

71. The original is housed in the Texas State Library in Austin.

72. Rohrdorf's work is sometimes referred to as *Kupferstiche* (copper plates) and sometimes as drawings. It is possible that they were facsimile drawings designed for transfer at some stage to copper etchings, which then of course, could be used to make prints.

73. Spiess Family Papers, 29.

74. Ibid.

75. By one source von Zabitsch and his family had made the trip from Friedrichsburg to La Grange with Schubbert. See Splittgerber, "The Last Wagon Train," in Penninger, *Fredericksburg*, 36.

76. The most extensive account of the shooting appeared in the *Galveston Zeitung*, November 10, 1847. It included two detailed, but

anonymous, firsthand accounts; one sympathetic to Hermann Spiess and the other not particularly partial to Strubberg, but definitely contra Spiess. Lieutenant Bené also wrote an extensive report to Count Castell (Bené an Castell, November 25, 1847, SBAt XLIV, 102-113). Bené's report, as might be expected, very much took Spiess' side in the affair.

77. See note 47 above.

78. Bené an den Grafen v. Castell, betr. Farm Nassau u. Finanzlage der Colonie (Bené to Count Castell concerning Nassau Plantation and the financial situation of the colony), Neu Braunfels, November 23, 1847, SBAt XLIV, 2-11.

79. Fayette County District Court Minutes ABCD, 383.

80. Ibid., 401.

81. Spiess Family Papers, 33.

82. Ibid. 36.

83. Narrett, "A Choice of Destiny," SWHQ, no. 100 (January 1997): 272-301.

84. Ibid., 301.

85. Spiess Family Papers, 36.

86. Hogan, "Rampant Individualism," *SWHQ* XLIV, no. 4, 460.

87. In the summer of 1842 Mayfield had led a contingent of volunteers from Fayette County to retake San Antonio from the Mexican general Adrian Woll. For military reasons, he refused to allow his contingent to come to the aid of the Dawson party, which had been surprised and overwhelmed by a much larger Mexican force. Burleson and others had charged cowardice, which led to the challenge by Mayfield. The two were only prevented from carrying out the duel by a preventative arrest.

88. Fayette County Case File 188, April 22, 1848.

89. *German Emigration Co. v. Schubbert et al.* Fayette County Complete Records C, 23-31.

90. Bené Bericht (Report), Wiesbaden, May 12, 1851, SBAt XXXVII, 112.

91. August Vogelsang: Vogelsang came over with the *Darmstädter* and lived for s short period with them at Bettina on the Llano (SBAt XXXIX, 81; LVI, 104). Later he moved to the vicinity of Nassau Plantation. W. Steinert identified him as the operator of a horse-drawn mill at Nassau in 1849. (Jordan, "Notes and Documents," 37)

92. "Dr. Schubbert soll in Galveston mit einer Entschädigung von $3000 abgefunden [Dr Schubbert is said to have settled in Galveston with a damage award for $3,000.]." Cappes Bericht (Report), New Orleans, April 22, 1848. SBAt LVI, 275.

93. Fayette County District Court Minutes E, 8, 22.

94. *Wilke v. Schubbert*, Fayette County District Court Minutes E, 89, case #297; Fayette County Complete Records C, 159.

95. Fayette County Complete Records C, 161, April 48, Demurral filed by Strubberg to Wilke suit.

96. In her college term paper, Meusebach descendant Miss Christine Pool of San Saba, discovered and wrote that Strubberg took the original Peace Treaty document along with Rohrdorf's sketches with him to Kassel in 1854. Miss Pool also relates that Strubberg developed an abiding friendship with Princess von Hesse-Kassel, a close friend of Prince Herman of Wied. Prince Herman had in his possession some official archives of the *Adelsverein* and other Texas *Verein* records that had come to Germany. Somehow Strubberg documents had come into the possession of a descendant of Strubberg, Miss Elisabeth von Strubberg. She is said to have received the archives from her father, The Prussian General Otto von Strubberg. Miss von Strubberg sold her documents, including the Peace Treaty of 1847, to Simon Goldberg, a Jewish antiques dealer. In 1938 Goldberg fled to Ecuador in South America. In 1953 Goldberg sold the Peace Treaty and other materials about Strubberg and the *Adelsverein* to a German journalist, Arnim O. Huber. It was from Arnim O. Huber that John Meusebach's granddaughter, Irene Marschall von Bieberstein King bought the Peace Treaty in 1970. The treaty was placed and resides today in the Texas State Library in Austin." (Quoted from Ken Knopp, "Friedrichsburg's Infamous "Doctor" Schubbert," 62, from a paper presented at the international Karl May Symposium, Texas Tech University, September 2000. Reproduced in *The Journal of the German-Texan Heritage Society*, vol. 22, no. 3 (Fall 2000, 53–65.)

97. Memorandum, March 1848, SBAt XLIV, 43

98. Hermann Spiess had ordered that the slaves were never to be whipped at Nassau. Apparently word of this proscription had leaked out and caused some dissatisfaction.

99. Fayette County District Court Minutes E, 139.

100. Spiess Family Records, 35.

101. Ibid. E, 420.

102. Ibid. D, 387, 388, 401.

103. Ibid. E, 192.

104. "A few weeks since a desperado named Bostick was killed in La Grange by General Mayfield in self defense. An examination of his letters and papers disclosed an organized gang of Negro thieves extending from Missouri to the Rio Grande. Several of these have been taken and some of them summarily executed; others remain in confinement awaiting trial . . ." (*Northern Standard* [Clarksville], September 1, 1849). Again, "We learn that the citizens of Washington County have detected several more of the Negro and horse thieves that infested the line of counties from the Red River to the Colorado during the last year or two. Several of this gang, it is said, reside near La Grange and have hitherto been regarded as

respectable. The informer could only be induced to disclose their names when the halter was about this neck . . ." (*Telegraph and Texas Register*, July 5, 1849).

105. Hermann Spiess described how they dispatched the gang member. They put him on the back of a gentle donkey without a bridle with a rope around his neck under a giant spreading live oak tree. Then they left. When the donkey emerged from the overhanging limbs they knew that the deed had been done. (Spiess, Family Papers, 37)

106. Gunter Sehm, *Armand, Biographie und Bibliographie*, (Lauretum Verlag: Wien, 1972), 25, 26

107. Gunter Sehm, "Armand, Abenteuer und Dichter: Grundri seines Lebens," *Magazin für Abenteuer-, Reise- und Unterhaltungsliteratur*, 31/3, Quartal 81, 19, 20.

108. In *Alte und Neue Heimath*, Strubberg has one of the characters, Albert Werner, 237-264, join Hays contingent of Texas Rangers. Several battles are depicted in great detail as if they were witnessed firsthand. *Scenen aus den Kämpfen der Mexikaner und Nordamerikaner* also contains many descriptions of the campaign. It also contains a description of the fall of the Alamo.

109. Schubbert an Meusebach (Schubbert to Meusebach), New Orleans, May 1848, SBAt LVI, 285.

110. Ibid.

111. See Struve, *Die Republik Texas, Bremen, und das Hildenheimische*, 82; also Woodsen, "American Negro Slavery in the Works of Friedrich Strubberg, Friedrich Gerstäcker and Otto Rupius," 42-157.

112. *Jagd- und Reiseabenteuer mit 24 von dem Verfasser selbst nach der Natur entworfenen Illustrationen* (*Hunting and Travelling Adventures with 24 Illustrations done by the Author himself According to Nature*),1 Band, Stuttgart: J. G. Cotta, 1857.

CHAPTER II NOTES

1. Bené Bericht (Bené report), SBAt XLIV, 46.

2. The March Revolution of 1848 in Germany was a complicated affair. In the broadest sense, the unrest represented the inability of the old political order to adapt in any meaningful way to the new historical reality brought on by four factors: population growth, the Industrial Revolution, the rise of nationalism, and growth of the middle class. Various governments brought forth initiatives from time to time to address the growing pauperism among the working classes through the establishment of relief funds or the introduction of savings accounts. These efforts, however, only addressed the symptoms, not the root causes of the problem. The program of the Society for the Protection of German Emigrants in

Texas can be understood in part as a rather naïve program to address overpopulation and pauperism. The noblemen failed to acknowledge that the system of late-feudal privileges, which they as a class enjoyed, was a root cause of the unrest. The fact that 1848 was not a unified revolt, but three different revolts by three different groups—the educated/bourgeoisie, the handworkers/tradesmen, and the farmers/peasants—helps to explain its eventual failure. This fact also elucidates important tensions and divisions within the bureaucracy and the German emigrant community in Texas, which separated roughly along class lines.

3. Fischer Bericht (Fischer Report), October 1858, SBAt XLIII, 250-261.

4. The story is actually quite complicated. Martin organized his company as the German Colonization Society of Texas. In 1852 he sold his shares to M. Settegast and assigns, who then turned around and sued the Duke of Nassau *et al.* in the spring term of Travis District Court (April 1853). The complete and original text of the suit is in the colonization files (4) of the State Land Office.

5. Bericht Generalversammlung (Report of the General Assembly), SBAt XXX, 261.

6. See Pro Memoria des Comites (Committee Retrospect), January 23, 1848, SBAt LXVIII, 117-132.

7 Bené an das hohe Comite (Bené to the high committee), March 23, 1848, SBAt XLIV, 45.

8. See, for example, *E. J. Hirt & Co. v. German Emigration Co.*, Fayette County District Court Minutes E, 200; *also, Henry Rohde v. Duke of Nassau et al.*, ibid., 287.

9. *Handbook of Texas Online*, "Roeder, Albrecht von," (accessed March 7, 2008).

10. Flora von Roeder, *These are the Generations*, 30.

11. Ibid., 27.

12. By one account, he killed a Prince of Prussia. See Flora von Roeder, *These are the Generations*, Prologue, xii.

13. Emilie von Roeder, letter, Center for American History Studies (Barker), 3C155.

14. On January 9, 1847, Otto von Roeder bought a league and a labor from John Vanderwerth (Fayette Deed Book K, 483).

15. Ralph Wooster, "Notes on Texas' Largest Slaveholders."

16. Flora von Roeder, *These are the Generations*.

17. William von Rosenberg, in a position to know from firsthand accounts, states that over time Otto von Roeder supplied over 10,000 bushels of corn to the colonists in New Braunfels and Fredericksburg, largely on his own credit. He also supplied wagons for the delivery of the same. See William von Rosenberg, "Kritik," translated by Louis Brister, *SWHQ* 85 no. 3 (January 1982): 316.

18. The best summary of Otto von Roeder's role is to be found in an official report by Lieutenant Bené. See Ad Acta 34, "Den Verkauf der Farm

Nassau betreffend [Concerning the Sale of Nassau Farm]," L. Bené, May 12, 1851, Wied Archives, Center for American History, University of Texas at Austin.

19. See A. W. Hamilton to the Agent of the German Emigration Co., December 20, 1847, SBAt XLIV, 102.

20. The ten were H. Ledbetter, William Henct, Oliver Suton, Davis Shelby, John Murphy, D. C. Thomas, Abner Kuykendall, Stephen Townsend, Joel Robinson, and Crocket Peery. See Bond for Sequestration, December 15, 1847, Fayette County Complete Records C, 27.

21. See Bené Bericht (Bené Report), SBAt, 169.

22. Ibid.

23. Amanda Fallier von Rosenberg explains this relationship clearly in a letter from 1850. See Frau von Rosenberg an ihrer Schwägerin Fallier (Frau von Rosenberg to her sister-in-law, Fallier), Nassau Farm, March 29, 1850, von Rosenberg collection, Center for American History, University of Texas at Austin, 60.

24. *German Emigration Co. v. Schubbert*, December 1847, Fayette County Complete Records C, 23, 24.

25. See Vermögens- und Schulden Übersicht (Overview of Assets and Liabilities), SBAt XXXIX, 112-115.

26. Fayette County Deed Book E, 113.

27. Ibid. Bené report, note 18 above.

28 Comite an Bené (Committee to Bené), February 7, 1850, SBAt XLIV, 335.

29. The suits were *Sinks & Reynolds v. German Emigration Co.*, April 1848, Fayette District Court Minutes E, 22; *Levi Young v. Otto von Roeder*, September 19, 1848, Fayette District Court Minutes E, 91; and *Henry Rohde v. German Emigration Co.*, September 25, 1849, Fayette District Court Minutes E, 287.

30. According to Amanda Fallier von Rosenberg, this amounted to 700,000 Thaler, which is surely an exaggeration. See Frau von Rosenberg an ihrer Schwägerin Fallier (*Frau* von Rosenberg to her sister-in-law, Fallier), Nassau Farm, March 29, 1850, von Rosenberg collection, Center for American History, University of Texas at Austin, 61.

31. Fayette County Deed Book G, 133-134.

32. Bené an das Komite (Bené to the committee), March 7, 1850, SBAt XLV, 39.

33. Ibid. Bené report, note 18 above.

34. Biesele, *A History*, 68.

35. Castell an Cappes (Castell to Cappes), May 8, 1848, SBAt XLVII, 257.

36. Martin made his offer contingent on the following conditions: (a) that everything be there; (b) that all employees be terminated with the exception of the chief agent; (c) that the payment schedule be as follows:

March 15, 1849-54 at 4 percent; (d) that the payments go to the agent in Texas for the liquidation of debts there.

37. "Sales Agreement," Fayette County Deed Book E, 192-198.

38. See Bené and den Verein (Bené to the Society), August 1, 1849, SBAt XLIV, 210-220.

39. W. A. Trenckmann speaks of this pride in his autobiographical sketch "Experiences and Observations."

CHAPTER 12 NOTES

1. Her name was Charlotte Wilhelmine Libussa Fröhlich (1839-1918).

2. See Alma von Rosenberg, compiler, *The von Rosenberg Family of Texas*, 17.

3. The Long expedition, named for its commander, James Long, was an early attempt by Anglo-American filibusterers to wrest Texas from Spain.

4. In 1821 Ernst von Rosenberg joined Long's expedition, which subsequently captured la Bahía at Goliad. When Long's forces could not hold the presidio, the Mexicans allowed them to settle peacefully. Ernst von Rosenberg joined the Mexican army with the rank of colonel. He went to Mexico City, where he became a supporter of the emperor Iturbide. Some years later, when the emperor was overthrown, Ernst was shot and killed. (Dale von Rosenberg, "A Free Man," a narrative written in 1995 as might have been told by his great-grandfather, Carl Wilhelm von Rosenberg.)

5. Several German settlements in Texas were founded by educated Germans, especially those who left Germany in the wake of the failed revolution of 1848. These were generally referred to as "Lateiner" settlements because in those days all educated people had been schooled in Latin. Rudolph Biesele in his study of the German settlements in Texas listed five such settlements: Millheim in Austin County, Latium in Washington County, Bettina in Llano County, and Sisterdale and Tusculum in Kendall County. Millheim is located eight miles south of Bellville in central Austin County and was in many ways a companion settlement to Cat Spring, established in 1834 by the von Roeder/Kleberg clan. Round Top emerged slightly later as a center of German learning and culture in Texas, but in the scope of what the town offered—in music, in schools, and in *Vereine* (social clubs)—Round Top in many ways eclipsed the others.

6. The originals to these letters are housed for the most part in the von Rosenberg collection at the Center for American History, University of Texas at Austin.

7. They were Peter Carl von Rosenberg (1794-1866); his wife, Amanda Fallier (1806-1864); sons from the first marriage, Carl Wilhelm (1821-1901) and his wife, Auguste Anders; Johannes Carl (1826-1906); daughter from the first marriage, Johanna Caroline (1824-1856); children from

the second marriage, Carl Eugen (1830-1913), Amanda Karoline (1832-19110, Carl Alexander (1833-1864), Carl August Walther (1839-1903); and adopted niece Charlotte Wilhelmine Libussa Froelich (1839-1918).

8. The *Franziska* was a well-known three-masted bark built in Germany in 1845 with a capacity of 440 tons. She made several trips carrying emigrants over a ten-year period.

9. Frau von Rosenberg an ihrer Schwägerin Fallier (Frau von Rosenberg to her sister-in-law, Fallier), Nassau Farm, March 29, 1850, von Rosenberg collection, Center for American History, University of Texas at Austin, 55.

10. Maier family: a family of German immigrants who owned a farm near San Felipe. They opened their house as a kind of inn to travelling Germans. *Ancestral Voices*, 13

11. Peter Carl von Rosenberg to brother Otto, Nassau, May 28, 1850, *Ancestral Voices*, 37.

12. Frau von Rosenberg an ihrer Schwägerin Fallier (Frau von Rosenberg to her sister-in-law), 59.

13. Fayette Deed Book G, 111.

14. It is actually not clear if Otto took up residence initially in the *Herrenhaus* or in the overseer's house. The evidence seems to suggest that he did put his family in the *Herrenhaus*, probably in 1848.

15. *Ancestral Voices*, 73.

16. Herrmann von Bieberstein, an early settler in the community of Latium in Washington County.

17. Fayette Deed Book G, 104, 107.

18. Carl Wilhelm married Auguste Franziska Anders on September 5, 1849, in Herzberg. *The von Rosenberg Family of Texas*, 16.

19. *Ancestral Voices*, 14.

20. Peter Carl to his brother Otto, Rosenberg-Nassau, May 25, 1850, *Ancestral Voices*, 38.

21. *Ancestral Voices*, 37.

22. Amanda Fallier von Rosenberg to Auguste und Emilie, May 25, 1850, *Ancestral Voices*, 25.

23. *Ancestral Voices*, 27. (Frau von Rosenberg, 71) Her fears were not altogether irrational. Texas is indeed home to many species of spiders, most of which are harmless. Even the large and fearsome-looking tarantula is not particularly dangerous. Two spiders common to the area, however, are dangerous: the black widow and the brown recluse. The recluse's bite produces a festering wound that refuses to heal, resulting, in the most serious cases, in blood poisoning and death.

24. Frau von Rosenberg an ihrer Schwägerin Fallier (Frau von Rosenberg to her sister-in-law, Fallier), Von Rosenberg family papers, Center for American History, University of Texas at Austin, 62.

25. *Ancestral Voices*, 21.

26. "Essentially my family is content with the new environment."

Peter Carl von Rosenberg to his brother Otto, May 28, 1850, *Ancestral Voices*, 41.

27. Peter Carl von Rosenberg to his brother Otto, Rosenberg-Nassau, May 25, 1850, *Ancestral Voices*, 39

28. Ancestral Voices, 39.

29. Wilhelm von Rosenberg to friends in Germany, April 1850, *Ancestral Voices*, 20.

30. Ibid.

31 Peter Carl von Rosenberg to his brother Otto, Nassau-Rosenberg, May 28, 1850, *Ancestral Voices*, 39.

32. *Ancestral Voices*, 21.

33. Adolphine von Roeder is Libussa's best friend, *Ancestral Voices,* 47.

34. Carl Apollo Wilhelm Gross (1794–1882) moved to Texas as a widower with eight children in 1848. Otto von Roeder sold him a small farm in the Jack League, most likely on credit. Gross appears on the Fayette County tax rolls in 1850 with a 210-acre farm in the Jack League, but there is no recorded title, leading to the supposition that Otto von Roeder had sold him the land on credit and, according to standard practice, had not recorded a title until the final payment. Gross' farm was perhaps the first divestiture by Otto von Roeder of lands which had comprised Nassau Plantation.

35. Meerscheidt Briefe (Meerscheidt Letters), 119.

36. Amanda Fallier to August and Emma Fallier, Nassau-Rosenberg, May 25, 1850, *Ancestral Voices*, 27, 30; August 24, 1850, 48.

37. *Ancestral Voices*, 61

38. Meerscheidt Briefe (Meescheidt Letters), November 15, 1850, 118.

39. Meerscheidt Briefe (Letters), Von Rosenberg Archives, Center for American History, University of Texas at Austin, 86.

40. Lina to August Schweinberger, Rosenberg-Nassau, April 2, 1850, *Ancestral Voices*, 8.

41 Amanda Fallier von Rosenberg to Charlotte Richter, Rosenberg-Nassau, January 21, 1851, *Ancestral Voices* 54.

42. See Arthur Meerscheidt to his mother, *Ancestral Voices*, 157; *Handbook of Texas*, "Considerant, Victor Prosper," vol. 2, 281.

43. The names of the men are not mentioned. See *Ancestral Voices*, 150.

44. *Ancestral Voices*, 156, 157.

45. *The von Rosenberg Family of Texas*, 54

Chapter 13 Notes

1. There is a reproduction in the SBAt LXIX, 66, 79, 87, 88, 92, of a discussion in *Der deutsche Auswanderer,* a leading German newspaper devoted solely to issues of emigration, of Friedrich Wilhelm Carove's book,

Gegen die Sklaverei in den Nordamerikanischen Freistaaten (In Opposition to Slavery in the North American Free States).

2. "Bekanntmachung über Sklaverei," *Frankfurter Journal* no. 196, July 17, 1844 (Reproduced in SBAt V, 207, 208.)

3 The Grand Knights of the Golden Circle had military, financial, and political degrees. The organization pursued an aggressive pro-slavery and expansionist agenda, looking first toward northern Mexico as an area for future expansion and then toward the Southwestern United States. Once Texas seceded, the higher military positions in Texas were staffed initially almost exclusively by members of the military order of the society. The Order did not look kindly on those opposed to secession. For an important discussion of the Knights and their role in the secession see Linda S. Hudson, "The Knights of the Golden Circle in Texas, 1858-1861," in Howell, ed., *The Seventh Star of the Confederacy,* 52-67.

4. William Wilberforce (1759-1833): Prominent abolitionist, who eventually succeeded after many frustrations and setbacks in getting Parliament to abolish the slave trade.

5 This suspicion rests on two facts: first, on the family connections mentioned in Chapter 1, note 19; second, on the common hope that Texas would remain a viable republic and eventually develop into a counterweight to the growing commercial influence of the United States in the New World, which both England and the various Continental Powers regarded as threatening. The introduction of large numbers of Central European settlers would, if successful, certainly promote the goal of keeping Texas independent. See Benjamin, *The German Texans,* for a discussion of these suspicions. William von Rosenberg, whose father purchased 800 acres of Nassau Plantation in 1850, wrote the first objective and research-based study of the Society in 1894 (*Kritik der Geschichte des Vereins zum Schutze der deutschen Auswanderer nach Texas,* [Austin, 1894]). His study was largely in reaction to an article, appearing in a Chicago periodical, *Der Auswanderer.* The author of this article made many unsubstantiated claims, one of which was that the British Foreign Office was a secret partner in the Society's colonization scheme. Louis Brister, who translated von Rosenberg's study, states the following in a footnote (page 410): "The author of the allegation that England had supported the Society financially seems without a doubt to have been August Siemering. According to Frederick Law Olmstead, Siemering had claimed as early as 1857 in a study on the Germans in Texas that there had been a contract between the Society and the British." See "William von Rosenberg's *Kritik.* A History of the Society for the Protection of German Emigrants in Texas," translated and edited by Louis E. Brister, SWHG 85, no. 2 (October 1981), no. 3 (January 1982), and no. 4 (April 1982). Mr. Brister offers a nice overview of the English controversy in his introduction.

6. See Chapter 1, note 20.

7. *Houston Morning Star*, July 9, 1844.
8. *Houston Telegraph and Texas Register*, July 24, 1844.
9. Narrett, "A Choice of Destiny," *SWHQ* no. 3 (January 1997): 299, 300.
10. By the 1850 tax rolls, Gillespie County (Fredericksburg) had no slaves, while the other counties of German presence in the Hill Country, i.e., Comal and Medina, had relatively very few.
11. According to Struve, *Die Republik Texas, Bremen, und das Hildenheimische,* 84, Frederick Law Olmstead's *A Journey through Texas* contributed greatly to the myth that all Germans in Texas opposed slavery.
12. Harking back to arguments of Walter Prescott Webb, who stressed the importance of physical geography (climate, latitude, etc.) on the spread of social institutions, some have argued that slavery never would have taken root in the Hill Country of Texas in any case. There is undoubtedly an element of truth in this argument. The way things turn out must necessarily be a response to all the variables at play. The difficult and elusive task of the historian is to assign weight to the various strains of influence. Certainly the fact that there was a conscious, deliberate policy of exclusion of slavery rather than a vague, generalized sense of opposition among the settlers (a point that many historians are unaware of) must be seen as a determinative factor.
13. Two great migrations of German intellectuals have enriched this country. The first was in the wake of the failed March Revolution in Germany in 1848; the second, and perhaps the greatest transfer of intellectual talent in the history of the world, occurred prior to World War II with the persecution by the Nazis of the (largely) Jewish intelligentsia. The 1848 wave of *"Lateiner"* organized themselves into the *Bund Freier Männer.* They promoted a quasi-socialistic, progressive, and populist program. On the question of slavery they were staunch abolitionists and free-soilers.
14. Sisterdale was established by Nicholas Zink in 1847. Zink had served as Prince Solms' engineer in 1844, but his stormy temperament created problems. The town was situated about twelve miles north of Boerne in a quintessential Texas Hill Country setting. Several educated refugees from the failed March Revolution of 1848 settled in the town, and it quickly gained a reputation as one of the *Lateiner* communities (see chapter 12, note 5). It attracted such men as Ernst Kapp, Ottmar Baron von Behr, Julius Fröbel, and Edgar Edler von Westphalen, all of whom were *Freidenker* (freethinkers or agnostics) in matters of religion and radical Republicans in matters of politics. Ernst Kapp was *ex-officio* leader, but other notables such as Adolph Douai and August Siemering found a home there. If there was an epicenter of abolitionist and pro-Union sentiment among Germans in Texas, it was Sisterdale.
15. Biesele, "The Texas State Convention of Germans in 1854," SWHQ 33, 217–266.

16. After spending a year in prison because of his participation in the failed revolution of 1848, Carl Daniel Adolph Douai (1819-1888) emigrated to Texas with his family in 1852. He settled first in New Braunfels, where he founded a school. He moved the following year to San Antonio to serve as the editor of the newly founded San Antonio *Zeitung*. Douai used the paper as a forum for his outspoken abolitionist views, arousing thereby not only the enmity of many pro-slavery Anglos, but many Germans as well. See *Handbook of Texas*, s.v. "Douai, Carl Daniel Adolph," vol. 2, 683.

17. August Siemering (1830-1883) arrived in Texas in 1852 as one of the "Forty-Eighters." He spent his first ten years as the first teacher at the newly established school in Fredericksburg and subsequently as a teacher at a German school in Sisterdale in Kendall County. Siemering helped to organize the Texas branch of the *Bund freier Männer* (see note 14 above) and he also co-authored the anti-slavery resolution passed in San Antonio in May 1854. When the Civil War broke out, Siemering served the Confederacy as a lieutenant in Taylor's Batallion of the First Texas Cavalry. After the war Siemering founded a newspaper, the *San Antonio Freie Presse für Texas,* a leading voice of Republican sentiment in Texas. He also founded the *San Antonio Express News,* which continues to this day.

18. "We the undersigned believe Wm W. Gamble to be a disaffected person opposed to the government of the Confederate States and should be confined as being dangerous to its welfare and credit. That we believe he is an agent of the Abolitionists of the North placed here for the purpose of distributing such books as are dangerous to the institutions of Southern people. Signed S. A. Maverick." Reproduced in Barr, "Records of the Confederate Military Commission," *SWHQ* 70, no. 2, 289.

19. *War of the Rebellion* (henceforth referred to as *O.R.*), vol. IV, series 2, 585.

20. H. E. McCulloch, commanding general of the sub-district of the Rio Grande wrote in the spring of 1862: Since I wrote you respecting the filling up of the mounted regiment I think I have discovered a pretty considerable under-current at work through this country against our cause...it may amount to something in the end which will require force to be used. Men have been heard to say when we (the Confederates) lost a battle that "We (the Union men) have won a battle..." General McCulloch to Major Davis, San Antonio, Texas, March 3, 1862, *O.R.*, vol. IX, series 1, 701, 702.

21. General Orders No. 3, Sub-Military District of the Rio Grande, April 24, 1862, *O.R.*, series 1, vol. 9, 708, 709.

22. Jacob Kuechler (1823-1893) came over under the auspices of the *Adelsverein* as one of the *Darmstädter* in 1847. He was an amateur scientist and is credited with being one of the founders of the science of dendrochronology, or the science of analyzing tree rings. Kuechler was ardently pro-Union. He joined German Unionists attempting to flee to Mexico and survived the Battle of the Nueces. He remained in exile in Mexico during

the rest of the war and worked as a surveyor in the northern Mexican states until the end of 1867. Upon his return to Texas he was appointed deputy collector of customs at San Antonio. He was elected a delegate to the state Constitutional Convention of 1868-69 and became a leading spokesman for Germans in the Republican Party during Reconstruction. He was appointed Commissioner of the General Land Office in 1870 and served for four years.

23. See Alwyn Barr, ed. "Records of the Confederate Military Commission," *SWHQ* 71, 262.

24. See Barr, "Records of the Military Commission," 262, 263. Charles Nimitz was the grandfather of Admiral Chester Nimitz of World War II fame.

25. *O.R.*, series 1, vol. IX, 735-736.

26. See Bill Stein, "Distress, Discontent, and Dissent: Colorado County, Texas, during the Civil War," in *The Seventh Star of the Confederacy*. Kenneth W. Howell, ed. Denton: University of North Texas Press, 2009. 301-316.

27. This and other fascinating tales from Lavaca County are related by Judge Paul Boethel in the (rare) *Sand in Your Craw*, 111-116. A signed and dedicated copy of the book from 1959 is a prized possession of the author.

28. William A. Trenckmann (1859-1935) grew up in Millheim, a famous *Lateiner* community in Austin County. He was a noted educator and editor. He published *Das Wochenblatt*, a German-language weekly newspaper, for over forty-two years, until it was sold in 1933. He and Charles Nagel, who also grew up in the Millheim community, have left excellent accounts of the tensions of the Civil War period. Trenckmann addresses them in his autobiography, "Experiences and Observations," and also in a novel, *Die Lateiner am Possum Creek*. He serialized both of these works in his newspaper.

29. Opposed to both slavery and secession, Hermann Nagel, a medical doctor and early settler at the Millheim community in Austin County, fled with his son Charles to Mexico in 1863. They later traveled by ship to New York, thence to St. Louis in 1865 where his mother joined them. From humble beginnings in Texas, Nagel's son Charles (1849-1940) rose to become, by most accounts, the most prominent of the Texas-Germans from this period at the national level. Charles Nagel attended country schools in Texas, completed high school in St. Louis in 1868, and graduated from St. Louis Law School in 1872. He is credited as the founder of the U.S. Chamber of Commerce and he served as Secretary of Commerce and Labor in the Taft Administration. In 1934, as an old man, he wrote *A Boy's Civil War Story*. See *Handbook of Texas*, s.v. "Nagel, Charles," vol. 4, 931.

30. The novel was serialized in Trenckmann's weekly, *Das Bellville*

Wochenblatt. It began in the December 25, 1907, issue and continued in forty-nine installments, concluding in the November 19, 1908, issue.

31. When the vote for secession came up, ninety-nine votes were cast against secession, eight for secession at the Millheim-Cat Spring box (Regenbrecht, 30).

32. In fact, several mass meetings were held, even after war was declared. Several hundred German-Texans met at Shelby near Nassau Plantation in 1862, and also another meeting was well attended at Biegel's settlement east of La Grange. See Stein, "Distress, Discontent, and Dissent: Colorado County, Texas, during the Civil War."

33. Ibid.

34. As an example, Robert Justus Kleberg, a veteran of the Battle of San Jacinto, had the words "Remember the Alamo" engraved upon his tombstone, which was shaped like a soldier's tent.

35. On the occasion of a visit to Millheim in 1850 with Otto von Roeder and family, Amanda Fallier von Rosenberg wrote, "...where in all of Texas is (Otto) von Roeder not known and loved?" (*Ancestral Voices*, 50.)

36. See Regenbrecht, "The German Settlers of Millheim before the Civil War," 28-34.

37. Ferdinand Friedrich Enkelking (1810-1885) studied law in Germany. He came to Texas as a young man and is credited with being one of the earliest settlers of Millheim. He married the youngest sister of Otto von Roeder, Carolina. He was instrumental in founding the first school in Millheim, conducted for many years by Gustav Maetze. His large home and store became centers of German culture in the area. He even set up gymnastic equipment in his store, reminiscent of the *Turnvereine* (gymnastic societies), which had played an important role in German student life and in which some of the first nationalistic stirrings had taken root. Amanda Fallier von Rosenberg described him as follows: "...highly cultured, intelligent man, who is indescribably simple in his needs and who is governed by the precept of living in the greatest possible simplicity in the most agreeable way; witty, cheerful, piquant, he is always the most charming host..." (Amanda Fallier von Rosenberg to her husband's sister, Charlotte Richter, Nassau Rosenberg, November 1850, *Ancestral Voices*, 52.)

38. Robert Justus Kleberg (1803-1888) came to Texas as part of the von Roeder clan. He was married to Rosalie von Roeder, eldest sister of Otto von Roeder and daughter of Lt. Ludwig Sigismund von Roeder. Kleberg was educated in law in Germany and continued in the profession in Texas as justice of the peace and chief justice of Austin County (1846). He was a man of strong will and character who, according to Charles Nagel (*A Boy's Story*, 197) stood out among men. Although short in stature, he projected force of will and manly strength combined with extraordinary good looks. He had fought in the battle of San Jacinto, a fact of which he was very

proud. He ardently supported the cause of the Confederacy, raising a company of militia to support the cause. His youngest son, also named Robert Justus Kleberg, married the daughter of Capt. Richard King, the founder of the legendary King Ranch.

39. Gustav Maetze, who taught school at Millheim for more than twenty-five years, illustrates this sentiment nicely. He joined the Democratic Party, but was opposed to secession and so abstained from voting. When secession passed, he submitted to the will of the people and became a loyal Confederate. He entertained no bitterness against the South or Southerners, but he was glad the Union was preserved. (Regenbrecht, 34)

40. See note 422 above. Maetze's qualified support for the South chilled relations between the two families. (Nagel, *A Boy's Civil War Story*, 209).

41. Trenckmann, *Experiences and Observations*, 41.

42. See Kamphoefner, *Germans in the Civil War*.

43. Ibid., 395, "Hermann Nagel to his brother," Millheim, April 28, 1861.

44. The party included Meissner, Langhammer, Soder, and Kluever. (Nagel, *A Boy's Civil War Story*, 239.)

45. The whole state was thrown into an uproar if not panic by the appearance of large number of Union forces off the Texas coast between Matagorda Bay and Brownsville in the latter part of November 1863. General Magruder, commander of Southern forces in Texas, was not sure of the enemy's intentions, fearing an invasion of western Texas, with the eventual goal of capturing San Antonio. In November 1863, 7,000 Union soldiers commanded by General Banks landed at the mouth of the Rio Grande and captured Brownsville, cutting the important trade between Texas and Mexico. Banks then sent one wing of his army upriver to capture Rio Grande City and another column along the coast to capture Corpus Christi, Aransas Pass, and the Matagorda peninsula. General Magruder called upon state and Confederate authorities for additional forces to halt the advance. (See Allen Ashcroft, "Union Occupation," in *Texas Military History*.) The activity occasioned by the Federal advance meant that a traveler between Columbus and San Antonio was much more likely to encounter units of Confederate soldiers on the move. Because of the Union advance, Hermann Nagel and his son had to travel from San Antonio to Eagle Pass, across from Piedras Negras, instead of to Brownsville to seek asylum in Mexico. This, in turn, occasioned a much more difficult and lengthy trip to Matamoros, from where they hoped to get passage to New York.

46. The Austrian archduke, Ferdinand Maximilian, denied a share in the imperial government of the Austrian Empire, negotiated with Napoleon III of France to become Emperor of Mexico. Maximilian was persuaded to accept the crown. In 1864 he sailed to Mexico. The empire was a failure from the start. Maximilian, who had no real understanding of Mexico,

found most of the country hostile to him and loyal to Benito Juárez. Eventually he was captured and shot.

47. During the Civil War, the so-called Home Guard in Texas spent a good deal of time and energy hunting able-bodied men to conscript. They exercised their "authority" in a way that made them odious to the populace, whether of Anglo or German ancestry. John Warren Hunter wrote "Such was the high-handed, outrageous conduct of the Home Guards, not only in a few sections, but throughout the state generally, that they obtained the sobriquet of "Heel-Flies" on account of the similarity of their course to the tortuous proclivities of a pestiferous insect so well known to cattlemen all over Texas. No class of men, or rather striplings, in our great state has ever been the recipient of more righteous contempt heaped upon them by patriotic men and women of Texas—than these Home Guards" (*Frontier Times*, vol. 1, no. 8, May 1924). One of the most colorful and instructive accounts of the role of the "Heel Flies" is given by Judge Boethel, *Sand in Your Craw*, 120ff. Official correspondence of the period reveals what serious problems desertion and the avoidance of conscription were. See, for instance William G. Webb, Brigadier-General of the Texas State Troops to Col. H. L. Webb, La Grange, Texas, November 26, 1863, *O.R.*, vol. XXVI, series I, part II, 455, 456.

48. See Boethel, *Big Guns of Fayette County*, 15, 16.

49. On January 14, 1854, the German community in Houston organized a *Turnverein* (gymnastic society), which became the focal point of social life in the city. Robert Voigt (see note 25 below) was a charter member of the Society. A contemporary observer wrote, "When war was talked of, the famous military company was organized composed entirely of members of the *Verein*.... The people of Houston really do not realize what the *Turners* have done for Houston and the state" (Young, *Houston and Houstonians*, 214).

50. Boethel, *Big Guns of Fayette County*, 15, 16.

51. Waul's Texas Legion was raised in and around Brenham in the spring of 1862 by Thomas Neville Waul. A legion was somewhat akin to a present-day division in that it was a combined command composed of infantry, cavalry and artillery units. Three companies out of the eighteen companies in the legion were composed almost exclusively of Germans from nine different counties. Captain Robert Voigt, who had emigrated from Germany in 1850 and who had become a prosperous store-owner in San Felipe and Industry, was elected to command Company C infantry. He has left us with many letters describing his experiences. (Kamphoefner, *Germans in the Civil War*, 403–426) The legion was assigned originally to Arkansas, Louisiana, and Mississippi (Vicksburg). Many Texas-Germans from South Central Texas, including the Round Top area, served in Waul's Texas Legion in all-German companies. Georg Weyand, who bought Peter Carl von Rosenberg's remaining interest in the Jack League, also served

with Waul. For a sense of the importance of the all-German companies, see Boethel, *Big Guns of Fayette County*.

52. Statistics do not corroborate this assertion, but it is interesting that he should have felt this to be a fact.

53. To cite an example of this tendency, the son of Gustav Maetze, the Millheim school teacher opposed to secession, volunteered for Sibley's Brigade (Regenbrecht, 34); see also Charles Nagel, *A Boy's Civil War Story*, 207.

54 Hermann Nagel to "My dear Brother," Millheim, April 28, 1861. Reproduced in Kamphoefner, *Germans in the Civil War*, 395.

55. The first proclamation of martial law dates to May 30, 1862, and covered the whole state (*O.R.*, series 1, vol. IX, 716). The law imposed an oath of allegiance and made it easier for the authorities to enforce the conscription laws. President Jefferson Davis, however, in an unusual rebuff of General Hébert, rescinded martial law in Texas in September 1862. General Hébert's declaration and conduct, he stated, were an "Unwarrantable assumption of authority and as containing abuses against even a proper administration of martial law" (*O.R.*, series 1, vol. IX, 735-736). In January 1863 German resistance to conscription led to a renewed imposition of martial law in Fayette, Austin, and Colorado Counties. See Kerby, *Kirby-Smith's Confederacy*, 96; also, "German Attitudes Toward the Civil War," *Handbook of Texas*, vol. 3, 138, 139.

56. Nagel, *A Boy's Civil War Story*, 30.

57. In Texas the German settlers were uniformly called "Dutchmen" by the Anglos. The confusion comes from the German word for German, "Deutsch," which sounds like "Dutch" to the Anglo ear.

58. Nicaragua attracted the attention of some German colonists in the 1850s, especially in the highlands around Matagalpa where coffee was grown. Emigration on a large scale never took place.

59. Wilhelm von Rosenberg, "To Friends in Germany," April 21, 1850, *Ancestral Voices*, 18.

60. "Die Sclaverei ist im ganzen das nicht, was man in Europa denkt [Slavery is totally not what Europeans think...]." (Frau von Rosenberg an ihrer Schwägerin Fallier [Mrs. von Rosenberg to her sister-in-law Fallier], Nassau Farm, March 26, 1850, Von Rosenberg Family Papers, Center for American History, University of Texas at Austin, 76.) Citing attitudes such as these, one scholar has argued that far from uniformly opposing slavery, Biedermeyer sensibilities actually inclined many German emigrants to accept slavery. (Cornelia Küffner, "Texas-Germans Attitudes Toward Slavery: Biedermeyer Sentiments and Class-Consciousness in Austin, Colorado and Fayette Counties," Master's Thesis, University of Houston, 1994.) The term Biedermeyer refers to many things, but in this context it is understood to be a frame of mind that arose in the German lands during the nineteenth century. Deprived of political expression and religious freedom and stul-

tified by oppressive police states watching their every move, many Germans, especially those of the middle classes, retreated into the comfort and security of home, family, and the ubiquitous apolitical social clubs, for which Germans have become famous. This resulted in a sort of collective passivity with respect to the *status quo*, which, according to this scholar, translated into acquiescence, or even acceptance, of slavery on the part of many new immigrants. This scholar specifically pointed out Carl Wilhelm (William) von Rosenberg's letter as an example of such an attitude. This analysis suffers from several shortcomings, especially when applied to the von Rosenbergs. They came from a part of Germany (East Prussia) and were of a class (landed nobility) least affected by Biedermeyer sensibilities. Her analysis also ignores the determinative influence of Otto von Roeder, whose pro-slavery sentiments most certainly did not derive from Biedermeyer attitudes.

61. See "A Narrative of the Life of William von Rosenberg," included in "Six Documents of Interest of the von Rosenberg Family," compiled by Dale von Rosenberg.

62. See note 24 above.

63. The artillery battery was split off and sent first to Brownsville then to Galveston. Later it distinguished itself in the battle of Calcasieu Pass in Louisiana in which two Union gun boats were compelled to surrender after a ferocious artillery duel. See Boethel, *Big Guns of Fayette county*; Hasskarl, *Waul's Texas Legion, 1862-1865*; "Handwritten Report of Walther von Rosenberg" included in "Six Documents of Interest of the von Rosenberg Family," compiled by Dale von Rosenberg.

64. Battle of Calcasieu Pass: a largely forgotten battle, which took place May 5, 1864, involving Creuzbauer's light battery. The battery was rushed from Sabine Pass to intercept two Union gunboats, the *Wave* and the *Granite City*, making their way up the Louisiana inlet in support of Union raiding parties. Both sides received about an equal number of casualties. On the Texas side, W. Kneip, F. Fahrenhold, and Private Foersterman were killed. Several other soldiers received serious wounds. The Union boats were so severely damaged by the accurate fire from Creuzbauer's battery that they were compelled to surrender or face total destruction. Prior to the engagement, Captain Creuzbauer had been summoned to appear before a military commission to answer charges of incompetency. The outstanding performance and courage of his men in this engagement put all such suspicions to rest. For the best account of the battle, see Boethel, *Big Guns of Fayette County*.

65. "Alexander was his [Peter Carl von Rosenberg's] favorite and the pride of the family...." (Lina Meerscheidt to her mother-in-law, January 30, 1854, *Ancestral Voices*, 168). Amanda Fallier von Rosenberg passed away April 22, 1864, in Round Top.

66. Three thousand Union soldiers landed on the island and over-

whelmed the garrison of 100 men and three guns. For an official report of the battle, see *O.R.*, vol. XXVI, series I, part II, 454, 455. One of Otto von Roeder's sons also served in the Confederate Army. Ludwig von Roeder served as a Lieutenant in Company C, Fourth Texas Cavalry. He saw action with Sibley's Regiment in the New Mexico campaign, participating in the Battle of Glorieta Pass, and also in the battle to recapture Galveston. (Flora von Roeder, *These are the Generations*, 121, 122)

67. "Arthur wants to go to Nicaragua; I, too, our entire family, even the parents, like many Germans, partly because of the poverty, Arthur principally because of *political conditions*." (Lina von Meerscheidt to her mother-in-law, Round Top, 1861, *Ancestral Voices*, 162.)

68. The first documented German in Nicaragua was a man known simply as "Don Alemán (the German)." He established an export business in 1810. In order to develop coffee production, the government of Nicaragua made various attempts to encourage emigration from European countries in the nineteenth century, including Germany, but the volatile political situation was always an impediment. In 1852 two Germans, Janssen and Reichardt, established a plantation in the state of Chontales, an upland plateau area noted for its salubrious climate. Here they planned a German colony of farmers with the aid of a colonization company in Hamburg. Reichardt eventually returned to Germany declaring colonization in Nicaragua a foregone failure, while Janssen apparently remained. It is not known if this is the endeavor to which Meerscheidt refers, but this is the only organized colonization attempt by Germans in Nicaragua uncovered by the author. See Güetz Von Houwald, "Los Alemanes in Nicaragua," s.v. "Deutsche in Nicaragua," http://www.inwent.org/v-ez/lis/nic/seite5.htm, accessed March 3, 2008.

69. Arthur von Meerscheidt to his mother, August 12, 1856, *Ancestral Voices*, 157.

70. The story of the cotton trade in Texas during the war is fascinating, and it has a German component. Because of the Union blockade, cotton from all over the South had to be transported to northern Mexico by way of Texas. Some of the many Texas-Germans who fled to Mexico to avoid conscription became involved in the trade. (Tyler, *Santiago Vitaurri*, 64.) Cotton became the *de facto* currency of the South during the war, and there was much abuse. Clever speculators and cotton traders developed many schemes for defrauding the government and the planters. The most common scheme was to sell cotton for gold and reinvest in devalued Confederate currency, which planters were legally compelled to accept as payment for more cotton. The authorities were aware of the problem and considered it serious, but their efforts to curtail it were ineffectual. (W. A. Broadwell, Lt. Col., to Hon C. G. Memminger, Shreveport, La., December 26, 1863, *O.R.*, series 1, vol. XXVI, part II, 535-541.) Many fortunes were made during this period, including that of Captain Richard King of the King Ranch. It is probable that Arthur Meerscheidt had been engaged by the German cotton

brokers in Monterrey to buy cotton from the German farmers in the New Braunfels area.

71. Arthur von Meerscheidt to his mother, July 16, 1865, *Ancestral Voices*, 168.

72. Lina von Meerscheidt to her mother-in-law, Round Top, July 18, 1865, *Ancestral Voices*, 170.

73. Arthur von Meerscheidt to his mother, *Ancestral Voices*, 165.

74. Lina von Meerscheidt to her mother-in-law, Round Top, January 30, 1865, *Ancestral Voices*, 167.

Chapter 14 Notes

1. Fischer an die Aktionäre (Fischer to the stockholders), SBAt LIII, 159.

2. Hamilton Ledbetter, as earlier noted, helped post the bond for sequestration after the 1847 shootout. This suggests strongly that he had a direct interest in Otto von Roeder's ability to gain control of the plantation.

3. On April 20, 1853, Otto von Roeder sold 1,400 acres to John R. Robson for $3,600. Otto von Roeder supplied Robson with a penal bond for double the purchase price in the event he could not supply a good title. (*Texas Reports* 20, 755)

4. On May 18, 1854, Otto von Roeder entered into contract with J. A. and W. F. Wade for the purchase of a tract of land containing 1,600 acres and embracing his homestead for $15,000. Upon signing the Wade brothers signed over five Negroes valued at $5,100; a promissory note for $4,900 was due December 25, 1854; the final payment for $4,000 was due December 25, 1855.

5. Victoria County Deed Book 7, 266.

6. With the formation of the abovementioned association of creditors, we encounter after 1850 three organizations in Texas with somewhat similar names connected to the situation: the German Emigration Co. (the old *Verein*), the German and Texas Emigration Co. (association of creditors in Texas), and the German Colonization Society of Texas (the company set up by Ludwig Martin and later taken over by, Ubagh, Settegast, and Rohrbach).

7. SBAt LIII, 161.

8. Fischer an das Comite (Fischer to the Committee), September 19, 1855, SBAt LIII, 64.

9. Fayette Deed Book I, 426, 427.

10. Affidavit, December 3, 1857, in *Otto von Roeder v. John Robson*, Fall Term 1857, Case 1049, Texas State Archives, M-2938.

11. Chandler only named those as co-defendants who had bought land from Otto von Roeder prior to the sheriff's sale in 1853.

12. Count Boos-Waldeck had had his title to the Jack League transferred to the Society in New Orleans prior to his departure in 1843 and he requested that Count Leiningen have the same done in Germany.

13. *Texas Reports* XX, 755.

14. See J.A. Wade v. Otto v. Roeder, May 17, 1858, State Archives Case File M-4148; also, Otto v Roeder v. J.A. & W.F. Wade, filed January 12, 1860, from Fayette County Case File 1342, State Archives Case File M-4121.

15. See Affidavit, December 3, 1857, in *Otto von Roeder v. John R. Robson*, Fall Term 1857, Case 1049, Texas State Archives holding M-2938, 18.

16. U.S. Supreme Court, December 1860, *Chandler v. von Roeder*, 65 US 224 (1860).

17. This is speculation, but a close reading of the court's decision leads to this inference.

18. Flora von Roeder, *The History and Heritage of Victoria County*, vol. 2, Austin: Nortex Press, 2000.

19. Fayette Deed Book J, 507.

20. *Ancestral Voices*, 48.

21. *The von Rosenberg Family of Texas*, 97, 98.

22. Otto von Roeder's second wife, Adolphine Auguste Theodore Ploeger Sack, was also his first cousin. His mother had been a Sack. See *These are the Generations*, Otto von Roeder.

23. *The von Rosenberg Family of Texas*, 92.

24. Peter Carl to Wilhelm von Rosenberg, *Ancestral Voices*, 76.

25. In 1855 Peter Carl von Rosenberg gifted 100 acres each to his son Eugen and his son-in-law Arthur Meerscheidt. (Fayette Deed Book K, 157, 160).

POSTSCRIPT NOTES

1. During the Reconstruction administration of Governor Davis, the legislature passed two homestead laws to encourage immigration and farm expansion. This was necessary because, unlike most other states west of the Mississippi, Texas owned its own lands; the federal homestead laws, therefore, did not apply. The Texas law echoed the federal law: it allowed 160 acres of state land for each head of a family who did not already possess a homestead. In turn, the homesteader had to occupy the land for three years and pay processing fees.

2. Before the introduction of windmills to Texas, inhabitable land was confined to areas where a constant water supply was available. Windmills began to become generally available in the 1870s. The intro-

duction of barbed wire, also in the 1870s, rendered the fencing of the prairie and uplands, bypassed by the earlier settlers, economical and feasible.

3. Trenckmann, "Experiences and Observations," 68.

4. *Handbook of Texas*, s.v. "Boll Weevil," Vol. 1, 628.

5. See W. A. Trenckmann, "Experiences and Observations," 51, 52.

6. See Cornelia Küffner, "Texas-Germans' Attitudes Toward Slavery: Biedermeyer Sentiments and Class-Consciousness in Austin, Colorado and Fayette Counties," Master's Thesis, University of Houston, 1994.

7. The Shelby community a few miles to the east of Nassau Plantation became, according to W. A. Trenckmann ("Experiences and Observations," 41), one of the most solidly German communities in the area. Most of the settlers had originally come over under the auspices of the *Adelsverein*. Upon hearing of the fate of the New Braunfels settlement, they preferred to seek a new home near the old German settlements in Austin and Fayette counties.

8. According to the U.S. Bureau of Census, 1,445,181 Germans immigrated to the United States from 1880 to 1889. The next largest influx was from 1850 to 1859 with 976,072. Statistics reproduced in Wolfgang Glaser, *Deutsche und Amerikaner*, 121.

9. John A. Hawgood, *The Tragedy of German-America: The Germans in the United States of America during the Nineteenth Century and After,* (New York: Putnam, 1940).

10. This can be reconstructed from the deed records and tax rolls from Fayette County.

11. Küffner, "Texas-Germans Attitudes," 65.

12. W. A. Trenckmann ("Experiences and Observations," 42) described the changes that occurred to the prairie between Industry and Shelby in the 1880s. The broad, grass-covered prairie, which he remembered from his youth, had been fenced in.

13. For a thorough and excellent discussion of the development of education in the German communities of the area, see W. A. Trenckmann, "Experiences and Observations."

14. *Lateiner* communities: see chapter 13, note 5, above.

15. W.A. Trenckmann, "Experiences and Observations," 6.

16. Ibid., 54.

17. Personal correspondence with J. T. Koenig, descendant of G. Weyand, January 2008.

18. Ibid.

19. Fayette County Deed Book Z, 99, 100.

20. Otto von Roeder disappears from the tax rolls of the Jack League in 1853. Peter Carl von Rosenberg disappears in 1860. Georg Weyand appears for the first time in the Jack League in 1860 with 140 acres valued at $1,400 and the following year with 540 acres.

21. Waul's Legion: see chapter 14, note 43.

22. Fayette Deed Book 43, 325.

23. The Groos family served as postmasters at Nassau until February 26, 1887, when the Nassau Post Office was moved to nearby Shelby in Austin County. (J. G. Banik speech, reproduced in the *Congressional Record*, vol. 14, no. 101, June 13, 1968.

24. Maria (Isslieb) Peters came to Texas from Germany when she was eight years old. Her father toiled many years as a tenant farmer for Georg Weyand. Before she died in 1972, she wrote a brief account of her childhood at Nassau. Much of what is known about Georg Weyand during this period derives from this account.

25. An examination of the deed records shows that Alex von Rosenberg owned the farm where I grew up in Colorado County for about ten years. He leased it out to several tenant farmers and eventually sold the land to a German immigrant family.

26. The "Sunday Law," also termed the "Blue Law," which restricted the sale of alcohol and required all businesses to be closed on Sundays, was an offshoot of the prohibition movement and was deeply resented and widely ignored by immigrants of Central European ancestry, who continued to observe Sundays just as they had in their homelands. For them, Sunday was a principal trade day, and the many festivals, where beer was sold, were usually held on Sunday. All businesses and all saloons were wide open. James S. Hogg, governor from 1891 to 1895, insisted that county governments enforce the Sunday laws. The German element in Texas held this edict to be an abuse of power and refused to comply. Local officials, conscious of the German vote, balked at enforcing the laws, so that the Sunday Law became a dead letter among an otherwise law-abiding citizenry. For a greater elaboration, see Trenckmann, "Experiences and Observations," 66.

27. Story the author has heard many times.

28. Story related by Travis Wegenhoft, grandson of the sheriff.

29. Story related by Norman Wied, whose family has lived in the area for many generations.

30. See "Bootleggers, Baseball and Barbecue: Brenham in the 1920s," *Texas Co-op Power*, January 2008, 12-15.

31. Carl Schurz, one of the most celebrated German Americans, was born on March 2, 1829, in Liblar near Cologne, and died on May 14, 1906, in New York. In 1929, on the 100th anniversary of his birth, Germany's Foreign Minister Gustav Stresemann characterized him in the following way: "Carl Schutz managed to combine his love for Germany with a loyalty to his American homeland in a marvelous unity reflecting the striving of his great personality which, here as well as there, was concerned with profound moral goals that are not restricted to a single nation, but apply to all mankind." Information quoted from the German

Corner Homepage, s.v. "Schurz, Carl," germanheritage.com, accessed April 24, 2008.

32. The author was privileged to meet Miss Ima at Winedale as a graduate student in 1975, the year of her death.

33. Lonn W. Taylor, *Texas Furniture: The Cabinet Makers and Their Work* (Austin: University of Texas Press, 1975).

34. Information about the demise of the house was obtained in an interview with Nolan Schmidt, grandson of Michael Wolff, on January 21, 1996.

35. Fayette Deed Book 43, 325.

Select Bibliography

Books and Journals

Achenbach, Hermann. *Reiseabentheuer und Begebenheiten in Nord-Amerika im Jahre 1833; kein Roman, sondern ein Lehr- und Lesebuch für Auswanderungslustige und gemütliche Leser.* Düsseldorf: gedrückt auf Kosten des Verfassers und in Kommission bei G.H. Beyer & Comp., 1835.

Adams, Ephraim Douglas. "British Correspondence Concerning Texas," *Southwestern Historical Quarterly* 18, no. 3 (January 1915): 309, 310.

"Andeutung über den politischen Einfluss der Slaverei in den Vereinigten Staaten von Nord Amerika." *Der deutsche Auswanderer.* Reproduced in Solms-Braunfels Archives (transcripts) LXX, 57.

Appleyard, C. *Texas: A Patriotic Song.* Austin: William von Rosenberg, 1902.

Barber, Preston A. "The Life and Works of Friedrich Armand Strubberg." Vol. 16. *Americana Germanica.* Publication of the University of Pennsylvania. New York: Appleton & Co., 1913.

Benjamin, Gilbert Giddings. *The Germans in Texas: A Study in Immigration.* Austin: Jenkins Publishing Co., 1974.

Biesele, Rudolph Leopold. *The History of the German Settlements in Texas.* 1930. Reprinted, Ann Arbor: McNaughton & Gunn, 1987.

———. "The First German Settlement in Texas." *Southwestern Historical Quarterly* 34 (April 1931).

———. "The Germans and the Indians in Texas, 1844-1860." *Southwestern Historical Quarterly* 31 (October 1927).

———. "Texas Collection." *Southwestern Historical Quarterly* 50 (July 1946).

———. "The Texas State Convention of Germans in 1854." *Southwestern Historical Quarterly* 33, no. 4 (April 1930): 217-266.

———. "Prince Solms's Trip to Texas, 1844-1855," *Southwestern Historical Quarterly* 40 (July 1936): 1-23.

Biggers, Don H. *German Pioneers in Texas.* Fredericksburg: Hoffmann, 1925.

Boas, Hans C. "Texas German Dialect." *Germany and the Americas.* Edited by Thomas Adams. Vol. 1. Santa Barbara: ABC-Clio, 2005. 1029-1035.

Boethel, Paul. *The Big Guns of Fayette County.* Austin: Von Boeckmann-Jones, 1965.

———. *Sand in Your Craw.* Austin: Von Boeckmann-Jones, 1959.

Bollaert, William. *William Bollaert's Texas.* Edited by W. Eugene Hollen and Ruth Lapham Butler. Norman: University of Oklahoma Press, 1956.

Buenger, Walter L. "Secession and the Texas German Community: Editor Lindheimer and Editor Flake." *Southwestern Historical Quarterly* 82 (1979a): 379-402.

Campbell, Randolph B., and Lowe, Richard G. *Wealth and Power in Antebellum Texas.* College Station: Texas A&M Press, 1977.

Campbell, Randolph B. *An Empire for Slavery: The Peculiar Institution in Texas, 1821-1865.* Baton Rouge and London: Louisiana State University Press, 1989.

Carlson, A. L. *Monetary and Banking History of Texas: The Mexican Regime to the Present Day, 1821-1929.* Fort Worth: Texas Christian University Press, 1930.

Carove, Friedrich Wilhelm. "Gegen die Sklaverei in den Nordamerikanischen Freistaaten." *Der deutsche Auswanderer.* Reproduced in Solms-Braunfels Archives (transcripts) LXIX, 66, 79, 87, 88, 92.

Creighton, James. A. *A Narrative History of Brazoria County.* Angleton, Texas: Brazoria County Historical Commission, 1975.

Curlee, Abigail. "The History of a Texas Slave Plantation." *Southwestern Historical Quarterly* 27 (1922): 79-127.

Dielmann, Henry B. "Dr. Ferdinand Herff, Pioneer Physician and Surgeon." *Southwestern Historical Quarterly* 57 (1953-1954).

Dobie, J. Frank. "The Planter Who Gambled Away His Bride." *Tale of Old-Time Texas,* 6th printing. Austin: University of Texas Press, 1994. 173-177.

Elliot, Claude. "Union Sentiment in Texas, 1861-1865." *Southwestern Historical Quarterly* 50 (1947): 449-477.

Dunt, Detlef. *Reise nach Texas, nebst Nachrichten von diesem Lande; für Deutsche, welche nach Amerika zu gehen beabsichtigen.* Bremen: Carl W. Wiehe, 1834. (In my personal papers I have an unpublished translation of Dunt's book by Anders Saustrup along with an eighty-page biography and historical sketch by the same.)

Frizzell, Isabel. *Bellville: The Founders and their Legacy.* New Ulm, Texas: New Ulm Enterprise, n.d.

Geiser, Samuel W. *Naturalists of the Frontier.* 2nd ed. Dallas: Southern Methodist University Press, 1937.

———. *Horticulture and Horticulturists in Early Texas.* Dallas: Southern Methodist University, 1945.

Geue, Chester William and Ethel Hander. *A New Land Beckoned.* Waco: Texian Press, 1966.

Gollwitzer, Heinz. *Die Standesherren.* Wien: Verlag für Geschichte und Politik, 1957.

Gorman, John W."Frontier Defense: Enlistment Patterns for the Texas Frontier Regiments in the Civil War." In *The Seventh Star of the Confederacy.* Edited by Kenneth W. Howell. Denton: University of North Texas Press, 2009. 70-84.

Goyne, Minetta Altgeld. *Lone Star and Double Eagle.* Fort Worth: Texas Christian University Press, 1982.

Green, Rena Maverick, ed. *Memoirs of Mary A. Maverick.* San Antonio: Alamo Printing, 1921.

Gurasich, Marj. *A House Divided.* Ft Worth: Texas Christian University Press, 1994.

Hasskarl, Robert A. *Waul's Texas Legion, 1862-1865.* Ada, Oklahoma: Book Bindery, 1976.

Hawgood, John A. *The Tragedy of German-America: The Germans in the United States of America during the Nineteenth Century and After.* New York and London: G.P. Putnam's Sons, 1940.

Hinueber, Caroline von, "Life of German Pioneers in Early Texas." *Texas State Historical Quarterly* 2, no. 3, (January 1899): 227-232.

Hoffmann, David R. "A German Pioneer Remembers: August Hoffmann's Memoirs." *Southwestern Historical Quarterly* 102 (1999): 487-509.

Holbrook, Abigail Curlee. "A Glimpse of Life on Antebellum Slave Plantations in Texas." *Southwestern Historical Quarterly* 76 (April 1973).

———. "Cotton Marketing in the Ante-Bellum South." *Southwestern Historical Quarterly* 73 (1970): 431-455.

Huber, Arnim O. "Frederic Armand Strubberg, Alias Dr. Shubbert, Town-Builder, Physician, and Adventurer, 1806-1889." *West Texas Historical Association Yearbook.* XXXVIII. (1962).

Hudson, Linda S. "The Knights of the Golden Circle in Texas: An Analysis of the (First) Military Degree Knights." In *The Seventh Star of the Confederacy.* Edited by Kenneth W. Howell. Denton: University of North Texas Press, 2009. 52-67.

Hunter, John Warren. *Heel Fly Time in Texas: A Story of the Civil War Period.* Bandera, Texas: Privately Published, 1930.

Jaeger, Henry C. *The History of Early Pioneer Families of Winedale.* Brenham, Texas: Herrmann Print Shop, 1990.

Jordan, Terry G. *German Seed in Texas Soil: Immigrant Farmers in Nineteenth-Century Texas.* Austin and London: University of Texas Press, 1966.

———. *Texas Log Buildings.* Austin: University of Texas Press, 1978.

Jordan, Gilbert J., ed. and translator. "W. Steinert's View of Texas in 1849." *Southwestern Historical Quarterly* 80-81 (July 1976-July 1977).

Kamphoefner, Walter D., and Wolfgang Helbich. *Germans in the Civil War.* Translated by Susan Carter Vogel. Chapel Hill: University of North Carolina Press, 2002. Originally published in German with the title *Deutsche im Amerikanischen Bürgerkrieg: Briefe vom Front und Farm, 1861-1865* (Paderborn: Schöningh, 2002).

———."New Perspectives on Texas Germans and the Confederacy." *Southwestern Historical Quarterly* 102 (1999): 441-455.

Kennedy, William. *Texas: The Rise, Progress and* Prospects of the Republic of Texas. London: R. Hastings, 1841. The first German edition, translated by Otto von Czarnowsky, appeared under the title *Geographie, Naturgeschichte und Topographie von Texas* (Frankfurt am Main: David Sauerländer, 1845).

Klotzbach, Kurt. *Wagenspur nach Westen.* Göttingen: Fischer Verlag, 1973.

King, Irene Marschall. *John O. Meusebach: German Colonizer in Texas*. London and Austin: University of Texas Press, 1967.

Kossok, Manfred. "Prussia, Bremen and the Texas Question." *Texana* 3, no. 3 (Fall 1965).

Krischke, Norman C. *Biegel Settlement*. Schulenburg: Norman C. Krischke, 1999.

Kubena, Sadie Redmond. "Schulenburg Builded on Pioneer Faith." *San Antonio Express*, October 29, 1929.

Kuykendall, J. H. "Reminiscences of Early Texas." *Texas State Historical Quarterly* 6, no. 4 (January 1903): 314.

Ludecus, Eduard. *Reise durch die Mexikanischen Provinzen Tamaulipas, Coahuila und Texas im Jahre 1834*. Leipzig: Johann Friedrich Hartknoch, 1837.

Lich, Glen E., and Donna B. Reeves, eds. *German Culture in Texas: A Free Earth; Essays from the 1978 Southwest Symposium*. Boston: Twayne Publishers, 1978.

Lynn, Jodye, Dichson Shilz, and Thomas F. Schilz. *Buffalo Hump and the Penateka Comanches*. Southwestern Studies, no. 88. El Paso: Texas Western Press, 1989.

Marten, James. *Texas Divided: Loyalty and Dissent in the Lone Star State, 1856-1874*. Lexington: University Press of Kentucky, 1990.

Merck, Frederick. *Slavery and the Annexation of Texas*. New York: Alfred A. Knopf, 1972.

McGowen, Stanley S. "Battle or Massacre? The Incident on the Nueces, August 10, 1862." *Southwestern Historical Quarterly* 104, no. 1 (2000): 64-86.

McKay, Seth Shepard. *Texas Politics, 1906-1944: With Special Reference to the German Counties*. Lubbock: Texas Tech Press, 1952.

Meusebach, John O. *Answer to Interrogatories*. Austin: E. von Boeckmann, 1894.

Miller, Thomas Lloyd. *Bounty and Donation Land Grants of Texas, 1835-1888*. Norman: University of Oklahoma Press, 1972.

Nagel, Charles. *A Boy's Civil War Story*. St. Louis: Eden Publishing House, 1935.

Narrett, David E. "A Choice of Destiny: Immigration Policy, Slavery, and the Annexation of Texas." *Southwestern Historical Quarterly*, no. 3 (January, 1997): 272-301.

Newton, Melba. "Round Top, Rich in Texas Traditions, Heroes." *Houston Post*, April 28, 1936.

Olmsted, Frederick Law. *Journey through Texas.*

O'Rear, Mary Jo. "Reckoning at the River: Unionists and Secessionists on the Nueces, August 10, 1862." In *The Seventh Star of the Confederacy*. Edited by Kenneth W. Howell. Denton: University of North Texas Press, 2009. 85-109.

Penniger, Robert. *Festausgabe zum 50 jährigen Jübilaum der Gründung der Stadt Friedrichsburg*. Fredericksburg, Texas: Robert Penninger, 1896. Reprinted and translated from the German text by C. L. Wisseman under the title F*redericksburg, Texas: The First Fifty Years* (Fredericksburg, Texas: Fredericksburg Publishing Co., 1971).

Porter, Jenny Lind. *El Sol Colorado*. Austin: Southwest Classics Press, 2001.

Ramsdell, Charles W. "The Natural Limits of Slavery Expansion." *The Southwestern Historical Quarterly* 33, no. 2 (October 1929).

Raunick, Selma Metzenthik. "A Survey of German Literature in Texas." *Southwestern Historical Quarterly* 33, no. 2 (July 1929): 134-159.

Regenbrecht, Adelbert. "The German Settlers of Millheim before the Civil War." *Southwestern Historical Quarterly,* no. 1 (July 1916): 28-34.

Reichstein, Andreas V. *German Pioneers on the American Frontier: The Wagners in Texas and Illinois*. Denton: University of North Texas Press, 2001.

Reinhardt, Louis. "The Communistic Colony of Bettina." *Quarterly of the Texas State Historical Association* 3 (July 1899): 33-40.

Richter, William, and Ann Lindemann, and James Lindemann. *Historical Accounts of Industry, Texas, 1831-1986*. New Ulm, 1986.

Roeder, Flora von. "Otto von Roeder: Prussian Nobleman and Texas Patriot." *The Journal* (German-Texan Heritage Society) 33, no. 2 (2001): 137-143.

———. *These are the Generations*. Houston: Baylor College of Medicine, 1978.

Roemer, Dr. Ferdinand. *Texas with Particular Reference to German Immigration and the Physical Appearance of the Country*. Translated by Oswald Mueller. 1935. Reprint, San Antonio: Texian Press, 1983.

Rosenberg, William von. *Kritik der Geschichte des Vereins zum Schutze der deutschen Auswanderer nach Texas.* Austin: Boeckmann, 1894. Edited and translated by Louis E. Brister. *Southwestern Historical Quarterly* 85, no. 2 (October 1981): 161-186; no. 3 (January 1982): 299-318; and no. 4 (April 1982): 409-422.

Rosenberg-Tomlinsen, Alma von, compiler. *The von Rosenberg Family of Texas.* Boerne, Texas: Toepperwein Publishing, 1949. Reprint, [Mount Pleasant, Texas]: Nortex Press, 1986.

Rummel, Helen. "German Prince Once Made Whoopee on Texas Farm." *Houston Chronicle,* August 10, 1930.

Sansom, John W. *The Battle of Nueces River in Kinney County, Texas,* April 10, 1862. San Antonio, 1905.

Scherpf, G. A. *Entstehungsgeschichte und gegenwärtiger Zustand des neuen, unabhängigen, amerikanischen Staates Texas. Ein Beitrag zur Geschichte, Statistik, u. Geographie dieses Jahrhunderts. Im Lande selbst gesammelt von G. A. Scherpf. Mit zwei Karten von Texas, Rio Grande und dem West-Land am stillem Ozean.* Augsburg: Verlag der Math. Augsburg: Rieger'schen Buchhandlung, Druck von Reichel, 1841.

Schlecht, Friedrich. *Mein Ausflug nach Texas.* Bunzlau: Voigt, 1851. Reprint, Manor, Texas: Indio Bravo Press, 1998.

Sehm, Günther. *Armand: Biographie und Bibliographie.* Wien: Lauretum-Verlag, 1972.

———. "Armand: Abenteurer und Dicter; Grundri seines Lebens." *Magazin für Abenteuer-, Reise und Unterhaltungs-Literatur* 31/3, Quartal 81, 2-53.

Seele, Hermann. *The Cypress and Other Writings of a German Pioneer in Texas.* Translated by Edward C. Breitenkamp. Austin and London: University of Texas Press, 1979.

Shook, Robert W. "The Battle of the Nueces." *Southwestern Historical Quarterly* 66, no. 1 (July 1962): 31-42.

Shuffler, R. Henderson, "Winedale Inn at Early Texas Culture Crossroads." *Texas Quarterly* 8, no. 2 (Summer 1965): 134.

Schutze, Albert. *Diamond Jubilee: Souvenir Book of Comfort, Texas.* San Antonio, 1929.

Siemering, A. "Die lateinische Ansiedlung in Texas." *Der deutsche Pionier.* Vol. 10 (1878), 57-62.

———. *Ein verfehltes Leben; eine Novelle*. San Antonio, 1876.
Smallwood, James. "An Impending Crisis: A Texas Perspective on the Causes of the Civil War." In *The Seventh Star of the Confederacy*. Edited by Kenneth W. Howell. Denton: University of North Texas Press, 2009. 21-31.
Sörgel, Alwin H. *A Sojourn in Texas, 1846-1847*. Edited and translated by W. M. Von-Maszewski. San Marcos: German Heritage Society, 1992.
———. *Neuste Nachrichten aus Texas*. Eisleben, 1847.
Solms-Braunfels, Carl, Prinz von. *Texas, Geschildert in Beziehung auf seine geographischen, socialen und übrigen Verhältnissen mit besonderer Rücksicht auf die deutsche Colonisation*. Frankfurt am Main: Johann Davis Sauerländer, 1846.
———. *Voyage to North America, 1844-45: Prince Carl of Solms's Texas Diary of People, Places, and Events*. Translated and annotated by W. M. Von-Maszewski. Denton, Texas: German-Texas Heritage Society and University of North Texas Press, 2000.
Stammel, H. J. *Gebranntmarkt*. Hamburg: Rowohlt Taschenbuch Verlag 1980.
Stein, Bill. "Consider the Lily: The Unguilded History of Colorado County, Texas." *Nesbitt Memorial Library Journal* 7, no. 1, (January 1997): 37-50.
———. "Distress, Discontent, and Dissent: Colorado County, Texas, during the Civil War." In *The Seventh Star of the Confederacy*. Edited by Kenneth W. Howell. Denton: University of North Texas Press, 2009. 301-316.
Strobel, Abner J. *The Old Plantations and Their Owners of Brazoria County, Texas*. Brenham, Texas: Independence House Press, 1926.
Strubberg, Friedrich Armand. *Alte und Neue Heimat*. Roman in 1 Band. Breslau: Eduard Trewendt, 1858.
———. *An der Indianergrenze*. Hannover: Rümpler, 1859.
———. *Aus Armands Frontierleben*. 2nd ed. Hannover, 1868.
———. *Bis in die Wildnis*. Roman in 5 Bänden. Breslau: Eduard Trewendt, 1858.
———. *Friedrichsburg: Die Colonie des deutschen Fürsten-Vereins in Texas*. "In zwei Bänden. Seiner Hohheit, dem regierienden

Herzog von Sachsen- Coburg-Gotha, Ernst II, in tiefster Ehrfurcht gewidmet." Leipzig: Friedrich Fleischer, 1867.

———. *Die Fürstentochter*. 3 Bde. Hannover 1872. Eine deutsche Gräfin wandert während der 1840er Jahre nach Texas aus.

———. *Jagd- und Reiseabenteuer*. mit 24 von dem Verfasser selbst nach der Natur entworfenen Illustrationen. 1 Band. Stuttgart: J. G. Cotta, 1857.

———. Scenen aus den Kämpfen der Mexikaner und Nordamerikaner. Breslau: Eduard Trewendt, 1859.

———. *Schwarzes Blut oder: Sklaverei in Amerika*. Roman in 3 Bänden. Hannover: Carl Rümpler.

Struve, Walter. *Die Republik Texas, Bremen, und das Hildenheimische*. Hildesheim: Lax, 1983.

Taylor, Lonn W., and David B. Warren. Foreword by Miss Ima Hogg. *Texas Furniture: The Cabinet Makers and Their Work*. Austin and London: University of Texas Press, 1975.

Tiling, Moritz. *The History of the German Element in Texas, 1820-1850*. Houston: M. Tiling, 1913.

———. "Die Deutschen in Texas vor der Massen- Einwanderung im Jahre 1844." *Deutsch-Texanische Monatshefte* 11 (1906-1907).

Tobiassen, Tommy. "Alexander von Humboldt." *Germany and the Americas*. Vol. 1. Edited by Thomas Adams. Santa Barbara: ABC-Clio, 2005. 530-532.

Trenckmann, William A. "Austin County." Beilage zum [Supplement to] *Bellville Wochenblatt*, Bellville, Texas, 1899.

———. "Experiences and Observations." A translation by his children of W. A. Trenckmann's autobiography, which appeared in German in serialized form in *Das Bellville Wochenblatt*, Bellville, Texas, September 17, 1931-February 16, 1933.

———. *Die Lateiner am Possum Creek*. A novel about the dilemma of educated Germans in Millheim during the Civil War serialized in the *Bellville Wochenblatt*, Bellville, Texas, starting December 25, 1907, and continuing through the next forty-seven issues, concluding on November 19, 1908.

Underwood, Rodman L. *Death on the Nueces: German Texans "Treue der Union."* Austin: Eakin Press, 2000.

Urbanke, Carl, Rev. *Texas is the Place for Me: The Autobiography of a German Immigrant Youth; Carl Urbanke, Founder of Blinn College*. Translated from the German by Ella Urbanke Fischer. Austin and New York: Jenkins Press, 1970.

Von Rosenberg-Tomlinsen, Alma, compiler. *The von Rosenberg Family of Texas*. Boerne, Texas: Toepperwein, 1949.

Von Rosenberg, Charles Wilburn, compiler. *Ancestral Voices. The Letters of the von Rosenberg and Meerscheidt Families, 1844-1897*. Self-Published.

———. *The von Rosenberg Family Record, Book II*. Waco: Texian Press, 1974.

Wade, Houston, and Leonie Rummel Weyand. *An Early History of Fayette County*. Burnet, Texas: Eakin Press, 1936.

Williams, R. H. *With the Border Ruffians*. New York: E. P. Dutton & Co., 1907.

Williams, R. H. and John W. Sansom. *The Massacre on the Nueces River: The Story of a Civil War Tragedy*. Grand Prairie, Texas: Frontier Times Publishing, no date [presumably 1911].

Wilson, Joseph. "The Earliest Anglicisms in Texas German." *Yearbook of German-American Studies* 16 (1981): 103-113.

Winkler, Ernest William, ed. *Journal of the Secession Convention of Texas, 1861*. Austin: Austin Printing Co., 1912.

Woodsen, Leroy H. "American Negro Slavery in the Works of Friedrich Strubberg, Friedrich Gerstäcker and Otto Rupius." A Dissertation. Published in *The Catholic University Studies in German*. Vol. XXII. Washington, D.C.: The Catholic University of America Press, 1949.

Wooster, Ralph A. "Notes on Texas' Largest Slaveholders, 1860." *Southwestern Historical Quarterly* 65, no. 1 (July 1961): 61-71.

———. *Texas and Texans in the Civil War*. Austin: Eakin Press, 1985.

Wrede, Friedrich von. *Sketches of Life in the United States of North America and Texas*. Translated by Chester W. Geue. Waco, Texas: Texian Press, 1970.

Wupperman, Walther Otto, translator. *Emigration of the von Rosenbergs to Texas, 1849*. 3rd edition. N.p.:Published by Philip Meerscheidt, 1976.

Wurster, Ilse. *Die Kettner Briefe: A Firsthand Account of a German Immigrant in the Texas Hill Country, 1850-1875*. Edited by

Charles A. Kettner. Wilmington, Delaware: Comanche Creek Press, 2008.
York, Miriam Korff. *Friedrich Ernst of Industry*. Giddings: Nixon Publishing Co., 1989.
Young, Dr. S. O. *True Stories of Old Houston and Houstonians*. Galveston: Oscar Springer, 1913.
Zantop, Susanne M. "Kolonialphantasien im vorkolonialen Deutschland (1770-1870)." *Philologischen Studien und Quellen,* Band 158, 1999.

Reference Works

Adams, Thomas, ed. *Germany and the Americas: Culture, Politics and Tradition*. New York: ABC-Clio, 2005.
Benjamin, Steven M, ed. "The Texas-Germans. A Working Bibliography." Occasional Papers of the Society for German American Studies 8 (1980), 91-116.
Brown, John Henry. *Indian Wars and Pioneers of Texas*. Austin: L. E. Daniel, 1978.
Day, James M. ed. "Handbook of Texas Archival and Manuscript Depositories." Texas Library Monograph 5. Austin, 1966.
Gammel, H. P. N. ed. *The Laws of Texas, 1822-1897*. Austin: Gammel Book Co., 1898.
Genealogisches Handbuch des Adels. 128 Bänden in sechs Reihen. Limburg an der Lahn: Starke, ab 1953.
Gesamtverzeichnis des deutschspragigen Schriftums, 1700-1910. München: K. G. Sauer, 1985.
Hamersly, Lewis Randolph et al. *Who's Who in New York (City and State)*. New York: L. R. Hamersly, 1904.
Jenkins, John H. *Basic Texas Books: An Annotated Bibliography of Selected Works for a Research Library*. Austin: Jenkins Publishing Co., 1983.
List of Books from the New York Public Library on German Texans, from the April 30, 1909, issue of *Texas Vorwärts*.
Morrison, Richard. *Eyewitness Texana: A Biography of Firsthand Accounts of Texas before 1860*. Austin: W. M. Morrison Books, 1992.
New Handbook of Texas. In six volumes. Austin: Texas State Historical Association, 1996.

"Sklavenfrage, Die." *Die Gegenwart: eine Encyklopädische Darstellung der neuesten Zeitgeschichte für alle Stände.* Band VIII. Leipzig: Brockhaus, 1849, 181-192.

The Slave Narratives of Texas. Edited by Ron Tyler and Lawrence R. Murphy. Austin: State House Press, 1974.

Solms-Braunfels Archives (transcribed and indexed). Vols. I-LX. Center for American History, University of Texas at Austin.

Schweizerisches Künstlerlexikon. Frauenfeld: Huber, 1905.

Streeter, Thomas W. *Bibliography of Texas, 1795-1845.* Cambridge: Harvard University Press, 1960.

Stephens, Ray A., and William M. Holmes. *Historical Atlas of Texas.* Norman and London: University of Oklahoma Press, 1988.

"Tabelle der rhein. u. preuss. Münzorten im Vergleich zum amerikanischen Geld [Table of the Rhenish and Prussian Currencies in Comparison to American money]." SBAt LXVIII, 104.

Texas Reports. "Otto von Roeder v. John R. Robson." Vol. XX. Philadelphia: Kay Brothers, 1858. 754-767.

The War of the Rebellion: A Compilation of the Official Records of the Union and Confederate Armies. 70 Vols. Washington: Government Printing Office, 1880-1891.

U.S. Reports. *"Chandler v. Von Roeder et al."* Vol. 65. Washington: Morrison, 1861. 224-228.

Theses

Curlee, Abigail. " A Study of Texas Slave Plantations, 1822-1865." Ph.D. Dissertation. University of Texas at Austin, 1932.

Heinzen, Frank W. "Fredericksburg, Texas, during the Civil War and Reconstruction. Ph.D. Dissertation. St. Mary's University, San Antonio, 1944.

Küffner, Cornelia. "Texas-Germans Attitudes toward Slavery: Biedermeyer Sentiments and Class-Consciousness in Austin, Colorado and Fayette Counties." Master's Thesis. University of Houston, 1994.

Solon, Ollie Loving. "A History of the Fischer-Miller Land Grant from 1842-1860." Master's Thesis. University of Texas at Austin, 1934.

Woodsen, Leroy H. "American Negro Slavery in the Works of Friedrich

Strubberg, Friedrich Gerstäcker and Otto Rupius." A Dissertation. Published in *The Catholic University Studies in German.* Vol. XXII. Washington, D.C.: Catholic University of America Press, 1949.

Deeds, Litigation, Records

Deeds

Abner Kuykendall to Otto von Roeder, Sale, May 25, 1855, Victoria Deed Book 6, 216.
Abner Kuykendall to Otto von Roeder, Sale, May 18, 1855, Victoria Deed Book 7, 266.
Agreement of Redemption, Projected sale of holdings of the German Emigration Society to Dr. Ludwig Martin, January 10, 1849, Fayette County Deed Book E, 192.
Bené to Otto von Roeder, Release, February 22, 1850, Fayette County Deed Book G, 132-134.
Bené to Otto von Roeder, Mortgage Cancelled, May 25, 1852, Fayette County Deed Book I, 29-30.
James A. Chandler to Georg Weyand, Sale, April 2, 1866, Fayette Deed Book 2, 99-100.
James A. Chandler to J. Wagner, Sale, April 20, 1866, Fayette Deed Book K, 772.
James A. Chandler to A. Gross, Sale, April 20, 1866, Fayette Deed Book R, 770.
James A. Chandler to Theo Michaelis, Sale, April 20, 1866, Fayette Deed Book R, 771.
James A. Chandler to J. R. Robson, Sale, October 22, 1866, Fayette Deed Book S, 456.
James A. Chandler to C. Franze, Sale, April 20, 1866, Fayette Deed Book V, 58.
James A. Chandler to C. Franze, Sale, December 11, 1869, Fayette Deed Book V, 525, 526.
James A. Chandler to James A. Wade, Sale, February 20, 1869, Fayette Deed Book V, 165.
James A. Chandler to A. Kneip, Sale, January b6, 1870, Fayette Deed Book V, 791.

James A. Chandler to H. Ledbetter, Sale, February 2, 1871, Fayette Deed Book W, 501.

James A. Chandler to A. Koenig, Sale, July 5, 1870, Fayette Deed Book W, 606.

James A. Chandler to W. Werchau, Sale, January 6, 1870, Fayette Deed Book X, 90.

John O. Meusebach to Henry F. Fischer and Burchard Miller, Indenture, December 30, 1845, Fayette Deed Book D, 192-198.

G. Weyand to Otto Neumann, Sale, November 3, 1891, Fayette Deed Book 43, 325.

German Emigration Co. and Frederic Schubbert, Lease, Fayette County Deed Book D, 536-542.

German Emigration Co. and Henry Francis Fischer, Agreement, Fayette County Deed Book E, 192-198.

German Emigration Co. and Ludwig Martin, Sale, Fayette County Deed Book E, 192-198.

German Emigration Co. and Otto von Roeder, Agreement of Reversion, Fayette County Deed Book E, 321.

John O. Meusebach and A. F. Schubbert, Lease Agreement, April 7, 1846, Fayette Deed Book D, 536-542.

Lavaca, Guadalupe and San Saba Rail Road Company and Otto von Roeder, Deed, Fayette County Deed Book E, 113.

Otto von Roeder and Charles von Rosenberg, Sale, February 15, 1850, Fayette County Deed Book C, 111, 112.

Otto von Roeder and Franz Jäntschke, Sale, January 10, 1853, Fayette County Deed Book K, 546.

Otto von Roeder and German Emigration Co., Contract, Fayette County Deed Book E, 321.

Otto von Roeder and German Emigration Co., Release, Fayette County Deed Book I, 29-30.

Otto von Roeder and German Emigration Co., Deed, Fayette County Deed Book G, 130-133.

Otto von Roeder and Hamilton Ledbetter, Sale, March 19, 1850, Fayette County Deed Book G, 111.

Otto von Roeder and Heinrich Kneip, Sale, Fayette County Deed Book L, 118.

Otto von Roeder and John Robson, Sale, December 8, 1858, Fayette County Deed Book N, 129.

Otto von Roeder and W. J. & J. A. Wade, Sale, May 18, 1854, Fayette County Deed Book M, 309.
Otto von Roeder and Walther Andras, Sale, May 5, 1852, Fayette County Deed Book I, 64.
Otto von Roeder and Bruno Schumann, Sale, August 15, 1853, Fayette County Deed Book JK, 419.
Robert Mills conveys Jack League to Waldeck and Westerburg, January 9, 1843, Fayette County Deed Book C, 205.
Samuel K. Lewis, Probate of Will, Fayette County Probate Records G, 455-457.
William Jack, County of Brazoria, conveys to Robert Mills, County of Brazoria, the Jack League for $5,000, Fayette County Deed Book B, 351.
Sheriff Moore to James Chandler, sheriff's sale, Fayette County Deed Book I, 426, 427.
William Jack League. March 19, 1831. Texas Land Office: Vol. 3, 282; Book 8, 140.
W. Werchau to Georg Wagner, Sale, January 6, 1870, Fayette County Deed Book X, 91.

LITIGATION

"Chandler v. von Roeder et al." U.S. Reports 65 (1861): 224-228.
Edward Kaufmann v. The Duke of Nassau. Attachment. Fayette County District Court Minutes E, 24.
Frederick Shubbert v. Baron de Meusebach et al. Fayette County District Court Minutes E, 8.
German Emigration Co. v. Frederick Shubbert, Bostick, Breeding. Case 280, Sequestration. Fayette County Complete Records C, 23-30.
German Emigration Co. vs. Frederick Shubbert. Sequestration. Fayette County District Court Minutes E, 22.
Grand Jury returns a true bill for murder against H. Spiess, Ernst Soerghel, Adolph Beimer (Benner), Flagge-zabel-Krauskopf & Feurmann, Fayette County District Court Minutes ABCD, 383.
Henry Rohde v. The Duke of Nassau et al. Attachment. Fayette County District Court Minutes E, 287.

J. A. and W. F. Wade v. Otto von Roeder. Injunction, Fayette County District Court Minutes G, 536–537.

J. A. and W. F. Wade v. Otto von Roeder. Case Files, Texas State Archives.

Otto von Roeder v. John R. Robson. Debt, Case Files, Texas State Archives. Originally filed February 20, 1846, in Fayette County; judgment rendered by Texas Supreme Court January 1858; see also *Texas Reports* XX, "Otto von Roeder v. John R. Robson," 765–767.

State of Texas v. Absalom Bostick. Assault and Battery. Fayette County Complete Records C, 186; Fayette County District Court Minutes D, 387, 388, 401.

State of Texas v. Ernst Sörghel. Murder. Fayette County District Court Minutes E, 34, 47, 133, 138, judgment 139, 203; D, 383, 400, judgment 401.

State of Texas v. Hermann Spiess. Murder, file 56, Fayette County District Court Minutes D, 383, 400, judgment 401; Fayette County District Court Minutes E, 132, 133, not guilty 138, 139; state will not further prosecute 420.

Herman Wilke v. Frederick Shubbert. Fayette County Complete Records C, 159, 160; Fayette County District Court Minutes E, 89.

Order of Sequestration. Fayette County Complete Records C, 27–31.

E. J. Hart & Co. v. The German Emigration Co. Debt. District Court Fayette County, Fall Term (1848). Fayette County Complete Records C, 280–289.

Schubbert v. Baron de Bastrop et al., case 235, Fayette County District Court Minutes E, 8; case 252, Fayette County District Court Minutes A, 368.

Sinks & Reynolds v. German Emigration Co. Attachment. Fayette County District Court Minutes E, 23.

RECORDS

"Morgan Smith." Brazoria County Deed and Tax Records. Books B, C, and D.

"Boos-Waldeck Receipts." Verein Collection. Center for American History, University of Texas at Austin.

Census and General Inventory of the Republic of Texas (1840): Fayette, Colorado, Austin, and Washington counties.
Census of Property Owners in Fayette County (1847). Commissioners Court Minutes, Fayette County. Untitled A, 94, 95.
Seventh Census of the United States. Texas: Colorado, Victoria, Dewitt, Fayette, and Nueces counties.
Eighth Census of the United States (1860). Texas: Austin, Washington, Fayette, Victoria, and Dewitt counties.
Ninth Census of the United States (1870). Texas: Colorado, Victoria, Dewitt, Fayette, and Nueces counties.
William H. Jack League. Land Office Records 3, 282; Book 8, 140; Record of Surveys, transcribed, A, 117; N, 158.

Documents

Bliem, Milton J. "The Medical Career of Doctor Ferdinand Herff." An address delivered before the Bexar County Medical Society in 1909.
"The Duties of an Overseer." Taken from Affleck's Cotton Plantation Record and Account Book. *DeBow's Review* 18 (March 1855): 339-345.
"Plantation Rules," Tait Papers, Charles William, 1847-1875. Reproduced in Curlee, *A Study*, Appendix C.
"Bekanntmachung des Vereins über Sklaverei in Texas." Reproduced in Solms-Braunfels Archives (transcripts) V, 207, 208.
Collections
Douai, Adolph. Douai Papers, Center for American History, University of Texas at Austin.
Fischer, Henry Francis. Collected Papers. Center for American History, University of Texas at Austin.
Henkel, George August Edward. Papers, 1860-70. Center for American History, University of Texas at Austin.
Moore, John Henry. Papers, 1838-43. Center for American History, University of Texas at Austin.
Spiess Families Records, 1785-1914, MS 239, Woodson Research Center, Fondren Library, Rice University.

Thomas, Nathan. Papers. Center for American History, University of Texas at Austin.
Verein Collection. Center for American History, University of Texas at Austin.
Von Rosenberg Family Papers. Center for American History, University of Texas at Austin.
Wied Collection. Center for American History, University of Texas at Austin.

Newspaper Articles

Clarksville [Texas] Northern Standard, September 1, 1849. (Report on Bostick killing and gang of slave thieves).
Der deutsche *Auswanderer*. "Deutschlands Anteil an den Kampf gegen die Sklaverei in den Nordamerikanischen Freistaaten." Reproduced in Solms-Braunfels Archives (transcripts) LXX, 46, 53, 54, 57, 58, 65, 66, 76, 77, 83, 84.
Frankfurter Journal 196 (July 17, 1844). "Der Verein zum Schutze deutscher Einwanderer in Texas in Bezug auf die Sklavenfrage." Reproduced in Solms-Braunfels Archives (transcripts) L, 207, 208.
Galveston Zeitung, Mittwoch (Wednesday), November 10, 1847. "Aus dem Innern von Texas [From the interior of Texas]."
Houston Chronicle, August 10, 1930. Rummel, Helen. "German Prince Once Made Whoopee on Texas Farm."
Houston Morning Star, July 9, 1844. (Letter to the editor).
Houston Telegraph and Texas Register, July 24, 1844. (Letter about Solms-Braunfels).
Houston Telegraph and Texas Register, July 5, 1849. (Report on killing of Bostick and discovery of gang in Fayette County.)
Neu Braunfels Herald-Zeitung, no. 36, July 15 1853 (Spiess letter).
San Antonio Express News, February 21, 2003, "Prince Johannes von Sachsen-Altenburg, Duke of Saxony, Discovered the Plan to Create a German State in Texas among Documents in Family Archives in Germany, Russia and France."
San Antonio Weekly Herald, August 21, 1862. (Letter to the editor by G. W. Y.).

INDEX

abolitionism, 186, 189, 194
Adelsverein, 1, 263n5. *See also* Society for the Protection of German Emigrants (*Adelsverein*)
African Americans, 221-22, 227, 228
Agricultural Society at Cat Spring, 120, 293n26
agriculture
  See also livestock
  and Boos-Waldeck, 113-14, 119
  crops, 110, 114, 118, 119-20, 121, 220, 292n22
  cultivated land, 110
  and free-labor farms, 113
  German contributions to, 120
  grazing land, 110
  innovations in, 117-20
  and number of farmers, 112
  and slave economy, 112-13, 120, 121
  and success of Sam Lewis, 115-16
  sustainable agriculture, 120, 121
  and von Rosenberg family, 170-71
Albert, Prince Consort of Victoria, 77

Alstyne, W. A. van, 211
Alt-Leiningen, Friedrich, Count of, 54
Alt-Leiningen-Westerburg, Viktor, Count of, 16, 25, 49, 53-54
Altstäder, A., 138
Amerikanische Jagd-und Reiseabenteuer (Strubberg), 149, 150-51, 297n43
Amsler, Marcus, 197
Ancestral Voices, 165
An der Indianer Grenze (Strubberg), 149, 297n41
Anglos
  attitudes toward land, 111
  and austerity of frontier lands, 47
  and Central European immigrants, 225, 229
  as slaveholders, 112, 113
  and Solms-Braunfels, 34, 77, 95-96, 285n8
annexation of Texas, 187
"Answer to Interrogatories" (Meusebach), 163
antiques, 230
Arista, Mariano, 20
Arnim, Achim von, 135

artisans, 36
auction barns, 228
Austin, Stephen F., 21, 31
Austin County
  and anti-slavery sentiment, 188
  and Central European
    immigrants, 228
  and the Civil War, 194, 198
  and colonization efforts, 31
  free-labor farms of, 113
  and *Lateiner* communities, 195

banking houses, 58
barbed wire, 219
barley, 119-20
barns, 45, 106, 230-31
Battle of Calcasieu Pass, 201
Battle of Mustang Island, 202, 216
Battle of Nueces, 191, 192-93, 196
Battle of Plum Creek, 83
Bauer, J. P. von, 138
Bee, Hamilton P., 191
Bekanntmachung über Sklaverei
  (Proclamation on Slavery), 185,
  247-48
Belgium, 12, 19, 21
Bellville, 220
Bené (lieutenant)
  and *Darmstädter*, 136
  and deed to Nassau Plantation,
    160-61, 162
  leadership position of, 145, 154,
    155
  and Schubbert, 295n25
  on shootout, 141
  on Spiess, 144-45
Bettina commune, 135
Biberstein, Herrmann von, 169
Biebrich, 13, 21
Biegel, Joseph, 69, 282n23
Biesele, Rudolph, 88, 190, 308n5
Biggers, Don, 61
Billburg (judge), 95, 288n5
Bird, James, 31
Bis in die Wildnis (Strubberg), 149

Black Blood or Slavery in the
  United States (Strubberg), 150
blacksmith's shed, 42
Blücher (Field Marshal), 166
Blue Law, 225, 314n26
boll weevils, 220, 228
Boos-Waldeck, Anton, 59
Boos-Waldeck, Eduard von, 50, 55
Boos-Waldeck, Joseph, Count of,
  25-37
  and agriculture, 113-14, 119
  alternative plan of, 4-5, 33, 59
  on beauty of the Jack League, 45,
    48
  class bias of, 34, 42
  and colonization grant, 33
  on colonization plans, 3-4, 36,
    46, 47-48, 50-51, 57-58, 126
  and corporation charter, 32-33,
    51
  cultural standards of, 41
  departure from plantation, 49
  on emigrants in Texas, 35-36
  and Etzel, 84-85
  and expedition to Texas, 3-4,
    25-26, 27-28
  and financial system in Texas,
    275n2
  health of, 45, 48-49, 277n29,
    278n38
  and *Herrenhaus* (manor house),
    104, 106
  and Jack League, 34-35, 172
  and land acquisition, 54
  and land grants, 4, 5, 54
  and land speculation, 169
  and land title disputes, 212
  on livestock, 117-18
  and mistress, 45
  and potential U.S. annexation of
    Texas, 22
  provisions for plantation, 39-42,
    43, 45-46, 233
  replacement of, 46, 47, 49, 55
  reports of, 35-37, 54, 59

resignation of, 4, 311n12
return to Germany, 51
and slavery, 25, 27, 36, 113, 120, 185, 200
and slaves of Nassau, 39, 40, 41-42, 45, 47, 66-67, 234-35
and Solms-Braunfels, 81
vision for plantation, 115, 117
and Waldeck Plantation, 29, 272n20
and well, 106-7, 278n38
Bostick, Absalom
  criminal background of, 139
  death of, 147, 303n104
  and Mayfield, 146
  and pistol-whipping incident, 137, 141
  role of, 143
  and Schubbert, 139, 147
  at shootout, 123-24, 140, 141
  trial of, 145
A Boy's Civil War Story (Nagel), 196
Braubach, Phillip, 192
Brazos River, 167, 272n15
Breeding, Benjamin, 140, 143, 145
Bremond, P., 211
Brenham, 220, 221, 226-27
Britain, 12, 111. See also England
Brookfield, William, 32
Brownsville, 198
Brune brothers, 82
Bryan, William
  accomplishments of, 115
  appointed as overseer, 41
  arrival at plantation, 42
  Boos-Waldeck on, 47
  death of, 68, 282n20
  dismissal of, 79-80
  and Fordtran, 114
  responsibilities of, 49, 64
  and runaway slaves, 65-66, 68, 69, 71, 73
  treatment of slaves, 67-68, 71, 80
Buffalo Hump, 125, 293n3

Bund Freier Männer, 189-90
Burkhardt (physician), 60
Bushwhacker War, 193
Butler (neighbor), 71
Butler (slave), 65-72, 173

Campbell, John Archibald, 215
Cappes, Philip, 127, 130-31, 136, 162
Carove, Hans, 185
cash, 81
cash crops, 220
Castell-Castell, Carl, Count of
  ambitions of, 53
  on colonization plans, 50, 51, 57
  and Count Neu-Leiningen-Westerburg, 15-16
  and *Darmstädter*, 135
  donations of, 54
  enthusiasm for Texas, 5, 19, 22
  executive director appointment, 15-16, 58
  and expedition to Texas, 23, 26
  and Fischer, 61, 62
  and land grants, 5, 50, 53, 55, 115
  and Meusebach, 127, 133
  on objectives of Society, 18
  paternalism of, 295n31
  and properties of the Society, 162
  as replacement of Boos-Waldeck, 55
  and slavery, 185, 186
  and Texas properties, 154
Castro, Henri, 56
Cat Spring area, 30, 34, 156, 195
cattle, 45, 110, 117-18
Center for American History, 229
Central Europe, 12, 225, 228-29
Chandler, F. W., 216
Chandler, James A., 8, 202, 209-12, 214-17, 218, 223
chickens, 110
churches, 222-23, 228

Civil War
  and Confederates, 191, 196, 216, 217
  economic transition following, 112
  and land title disputes, 215–16
  and military service, 224
  and secession, 183–84, 195, 214–15
  and Unionists, 189, 191–92, 197, 204
  and wartime propaganda, 225–26
Claren, Oskar von, 101
class and rank distinctions, 42, 77, 85, 103, 267n19
Coll, Hans von, 136, 154, 155
colonization project
  See also emigration to Texas; Society for the Protection of German Emigrants
  audacity of, 1
  Boos-Waldeck on, 3–4, 36, 46, 47–48, 50–51, 57–58, 126
  and cultural identity, 18–19
  discontinuation of, 155, 265n20
  and land grants, 62
  recruitment of settlers, 59
  Society's emphasis on, 55
  success of, 1–2
  and trade, 19
Colorado County
  and anti-immigration sentiment, 226
  and anti-slavery sentiment, 188
  and Central European immigrants, 228
  and the Civil War, 194, 198
  free-labor farms in, 113
  and World War I, 225
Colorado River, 65
Comal County, 188, 208
Comanches
  See also Indians
  Meusebach's treaty with, 125, 132–33, 296n36
  Peace Treaty document, 139, 144, 302n96
  threat of, 83, 96
Comfort, 191
commissioners-general
  See also Meusebach, Johann Otto *Freiherr* von; Solms-Braunfels, Carl, Prince of; Spiess, Hermann
  appointment of, 6–7, 60
  resignation of, 133
  and shootout, 124, 136, 137, 155
  struggles faced by, 127
communes, 179–80
Confederate Oath of Allegiance, 192
Congress of Vienna, 13
conscription, 197
Considerant, Victor Prosper, 179
corn, 110, 111, 121, 128, 220, 292n22
cotton, 110, 111, 116, 121, 220–21, 228
courthouse, 179
craftsmen, 82
credit, availability of, 81
creditors and debts, 125, 127, 128, 155, 161
Creuzbauer, Ernst, 201
Cummins Creek watershed, 33–34, 82, 290n5
Curlee, Abigail, 66
Czech-speaking immigrants, 111, 228, 229

Daingerfield, William Henry, 55, 57
Darmstädter, 133, 134–36, 140, 147, 297n38
Das Guadalupelied (Fallersleben), 75–76, 86
Das Wochenblatt, 194
Davis, Jefferson, 193
debts and creditors, 125, 127, 128, 155, 161
democracy, 125, 200
demographic changes, 172, 222–23

Denman (overseer), 80, 85, 87, 96, 98, 114
Der deutsche Auswanderer, 138, 185
Der freie Verein, 190, 191
Deutscher Bund (German Confederation), 13
Dick, James, 230
Die Lateiner am Possum Creek (Nagel), 194
die Vierziger (Society of Forty), 135
Dobie, J. Frank, 273n23
Donop, Pauline von, 157
Dooley, M. A., 137, 141, 299n64
d'Orvanne, Alexander Bourgeois
 Boos-Waldeck on, 57
 inventory of, 237-42
 land grant of, 5, 56, 59, 60, 77-78, 82-83
 position of, 60
 and Society, 55, 56-57
 and Solms-Braunfels, 82-83, 88
 on state of plantation, 79
Douai, Adolph, 190
Dresel, Gustav, 154, 155, 159, 161
Ducos, Armand, 56, 77, 79
Duff (Captain), 191-92, 193
Durand, S. A. (overseer), 96, 97-98, 114, 128, 288n8

East Texas, 228
Eckitten estate, 166, 167
ecological damage, 222
education, 222-23, 308n5
Ein Guadalupelied (Fallersleben), 75-76, 86
Elisabeth (slave), 41
emancipation, 222
emigration to Texas
 See also colonization project; settlers
 and anti-immigrant sentiments, 124, 142, 147
 and available land, 110
 celebrated in song, 75-76

 Census reports on, 313n8
 and cultural identity, 18-19
 and Ernst, 31
 and feasibility assessment, 119
 and Indians, 99
 promotion of, 14-15, 61
 and Solms-Braunfels, 77, 82-83, 88
 success of, 1-2
Emily (slave), 41, 45, 66, 73, 277n29, 278n38
Emmenecker, Joseph *Freiherr* von, 194
empresario system, 21, 269n35
Engels, Friedrich, 58
England
 and Republic of Texas, 19-20, 21
 and slavery, 186
 and Society, 16, 17, 20, 267nn20-21
Enkelking, Caroline Roeder von, 195-96
Enkelking, Ferdinand, 173-74, 199
entrepreneurship, 224
Erlebtes und Beobachtetes (Nagel), 194
Ernst, Friedrich
 and Fordtran, 31-32, 87, 97-98
 guests in home of, 94, 95, 169
 influential letter of, 156, 271n11
 and slavery, 190
 and tobacco, 273n29
Ernst, Johann, 82
Ervendberg, Ludwig Cachand, 35-36, 54, 82, 119
Escalara, José Maria, 209
Etzel, Wilhelm
 ambitions of, 64
 and construction of *Herrenhaus*, 42, 104-5, 107, 270n2
 and expedition to Texas, 26
 furniture construction by, 106
 and Solms-Braunfels, 79, 80-81, 84-85
 working style of, 104

Experienced and Observed (Nagel), 194
eye surgery, Texas's first, 135

Fallersleben, Hoffmann von, 11, 75, 86, 265n1
Fayette County
  acreage in production, 110, 146–47
  and anti-slavery sentiment, 188
  and Central European immigrants, 228
  and the Civil War, 194, 198
  demographic changes, 172
  free-labor farms of, 113
  and railroads, 221
  slaveholders in, 112
Fayetteville, 111
feather mattress, 40, 84, 85, 86, 107
Fehrmann, 137, 141, 143
fences, 219, 222, 231
Ferry-not (schooner), 28
feudalism, 4, 15, 154, 264n9
Feuerbach, Ludwig, 135, 298n46
First War of Secession (Texas War of Independence), 30, 31, 157, 183–84, 196
Fischer, Henry Francis
  appointment of overseer, 96, 97
  arrival at plantation, 87–88
  and Boos-Waldeck, 50
  buyout of, 89
  contract with, 62, 84, 163, 280n20 (*see also* German Emigration Co.)
  court judgment for, 163
  criticisms of, 61
  and immigrants, 126
  land grant of, 50–51, 56, 60–61
  and land title disputes, 208, 210–11, 213, 218
  and Solms-Braunfels, 61, 62, 84, 85, 88–89, 288n90
  and Texas Rangers, 83

Fischer-Miller grant, 128–29, 130, 132
Fordtran (wife), 71
Fordtran, Charles
  accomplishments of, 115
  arrival at plantation, 42
  background of, 31
  and barn construction, 106
  and Bryan, 114
  claims against the Society, 162
  dismissal of, 5, 87, 96, 98
  and Ernst, 31–32, 87, 97–98
  garden of, 117
  gift to, 49, 54, 81, 87
  and Meusebach, 128
  outfitting the plantation, 39, 40
  and power of attorney, 80, 87, 162
  and rented fields, 44
  and runaway slaves, 63, 68–73, 283n27
  and Solms-Braunfels, 5, 79, 80, 83, 84, 87, 93, 115
  on state of plantation, 64–65, 84, 130–31
  supervisory appointment, 5, 49
  and treatment of slaves, 68
France, 12, 19–20, 21
Franz (helper), 171
Franziska (ship), 167
freed slaves, 221–22
free-labor farms, 113
Freemasons, 124, 136, 299n58
Friedrichsburg (Fredericksburg) settlement
  arrival of settlers in, 128, 130
  and Civil War, 191–92
  directors of, 7, 131–32, 136, 149, 295n25
  regional office in, 154
  survey of settlement, 129–30
Friedrichsburg (Strubberg), 149, 263n2, 295n31
Fröhlich, Libussa, 180
frontier lands, 47, 58, 81, 95

INDEX 343

Für Auwanderungs-lustige (Sörghel), 294n11

Galveston, 167
Galveston, Harrisburg and Railroad, 220-21
Galveston Zeitung, 138
General Land Office, 179, 204-5
German and Texan Emigration Co., 210
German Colonization Society of Texas, 162, 163
German Element in Texas (Tiling), 61
German Emigration Co.
  See also Society for the Protection of German Emigrants (*Adelsverein*)
  and deed to Nassau Plantation, 160, 168
  demise of, 218
  and land speculation, 218
  and land title disputes, 208, 210-11, 212-13, 215
  and lease dispute, 143
  and Mayfield, 142, 145, 146
  name of, 311n6
  potential profits from, 62
  and Rohrdorf's illustrations, 151
  and Schubbert, 158
  and shootout, 124, 142
  and Spiess, 124
German language, 226
German Pioneers in Texas (Biggers), 61
Germany
  and Congress of Vienna, 13
  exodus from, 12, 18-19
  nationalism in, 18-19, 22
  nobility of, 13, 17-18, 20
  revolution in (1848), 7, 85, 153-54, 265n4, 292n19, 304n2
  and *Standesherren*, 17-18
Gerstäcker, Friedrich, 150
Giddings, 220

Gillespie County, 188, 191-92, 208
Gotier's Trace, 114, 290n5
Grand Knights of the Golden Circle, 186, 191
Granite City (ship), 201
Grant, Ulysses S., 204, 219
grapes, 118
Great Depression, 227-28
Gross, Carl Apollo, 172
Gross, Julie Wilhelmine Christine, 170, 172
Guadalupe Valley, 76
guitar, 41, 107
Gürth, M., 138
gymnastic society (*Turnverein*), 174, 223

habeas corpus, 192, 193
Hamilton, A. J., 124, 142, 146
Hamilton & Chandler, 158
Hanna (slave), 40
Hawgood, John, 221
Hays (Captain), 83
Hébert (General), 191, 193
Hellmuth, Gustav, 180
Hellmuth, Herman, 169-70, 180-81, 230
Hellmuth, Libussa Fröhlich, 180
Henry (slave), 65
Herff, Ferdinand von, 135
Herrenhaus (manor house), 103-8
  chimneys in, 105
  compound surrounding, 106
  construction of, 42, 104-5, 107, 270n2
  demolition of, 231
  described, 6, 42, 104, 249-53
  and Etzel, 79, 84
  flooring in, 105, 289n8
  and Fordtran, 64
  furniture in, 106
  garden of, 117
  innovations in, 117
  kitchen for, 105
  luxuries for, 40-41, 107

Herrenhaus (manor house), (*cont.*)
  shootout at, 123–24, 137–41, 148
  site of, 42, 103, 104, 114, 232
  and Solms-Braunfels, 79
  and underground cistern, 107
  and von Roeder family, 175, 309n14
  and von Rosenberg family, 6, 8, 168–70
  and von Wrede, 98–99, 102, 103
  well for, 85, 106–7
  and Weyand family, 223–24
  windows of, 106
hierarchical social structure, 185. *See also* slavery
Hill, Isaac Lafayette, 112
Hill Country, 188, 189, 196
Hockley (slave), 73
Hogg, Ima, 229–30
Hogg, James S., 225, 229
Holman Plantation, 64, 281n3
Home Guard, 197
homesteads, 219–20
horses, 69, 117–18
Houston, 197–98
Houston, Sam
  and Boos-Waldeck, 29, 57
  and land grants, 21, 33, 50, 59, 84
  land speculation of, 27
  on secession, 184
  and Solms-Braunfels, 84
Houston Chronicle, 76
Houston Morning Star, 187
Humboldt, Alexander von, 14, 56, 119, 266n16, 279n12
Humboldt, William, 14
Hungary, 176

Indianola, 154
Indians
  Meusebach's treaty with, 125, 130, 132–33, 139, 144, 296n36
  murder of von Wrede, 6, 101–2
  and Schubbert, 130, 132
  threat of, 33, 34, 83, 96, 99, 110
Industry, Texas, 30–31, 32, 109, 197–98
ipecac, 15, 266n16
Isenburg, Count, 54

Jack, William, 35
Jack League
  and Boos-Waldeck, 34, 35, 45, 109
  ecology of, 118
  and Etzel, 81
  and land speculation, 169
  and land title disputes, 218
  post-Reconstruction era, 219
  purchase of, 35, 275n42
  as site of plantation, 9 (*see also* Nassau Plantation)
  survey of, 216
  and tax rolls, 313n20
  value of, 169
  and von Roeder, 180, 216
  and the von Rosenberg family, 170
  and Weyand, 223
Jack's Creek, 106, 169
James Winn League, 169
Jäntschke, Franz, 173, 176–77
Jim (slave), 41, 67
Johann Dethard schooner, 88
Jones, Anson, 29, 79, 87–88
Jordt, Karl, 82, 94
Joshua (slave), 65–71, 72–74, 112

Katastrophe (shootout), 123–24, 137–41, 148, 153–54, 155
Kaufmann, David, 143
Kegelbahn (bowling alleys), 224
Kennedy, William, 14, 20, 21, 187
Kentucky, 111
Kerr County, 191–92
King, Richard, 163
Kingdom of Prussia, 55, 174–75
King Ranch, 163, 209, 217–18
King William District, 181

Kleberg, Robert Justus, 156, 157, 196, 209
Kleberg, Robert Justus, Jr., 163, 217
Knights of the Golden Circle, 186, 191
Knolle, Ernst, 198
Kobbé, Wilhelm A., 26, 28, 271n7
Krauskopf, Hermann, 140
Kück, Anton, 94
Kuechler, Jakob, 192-93, 204-5
Ku Klux Klan, 226-27
Kussuth, Lajos, 176
Kuykendall, Abner, 107, 209

La Grange, 220
land
  See also Jack League; land grants
  attitudes toward land, 121
  and expedition to Texas, 26
  land fraud, 26, 59
  land speculation, 12, 15, 22-23, 26-27, 168-69, 207-18
  wooded land, 118
land grants
  and Boos-Waldeck, 4, 5, 54
  and Castell, 5, 50, 53, 55, 115
  of d'Orvanne, 5, 56, 59, 60, 77-78, 82-83
  enthusiasm for, 269n36
  and Houston, 21, 33, 50, 59, 84
  and land title disputes, 207-18, 223
  and objectives of the Society, 115
  requirements for, 128-29
  and settlers, 128-29
  Society's pursuit of, 55, 57, 62
  and Solms-Braunfels, 5, 53, 84
Lanfear & Co., 40, 96
Lateiner communities, 190, 195, 199, 222-23
Lavaca County, 193-94
Ledbetter, Hamilton, 112, 139, 143, 159, 160, 208-9
Leiningen, Christian
  arrival in Galveston, 29
  and Boos-Waldeck, 47
  and Castell, 15-16, 17
  and colonization grant, 33
  enthusiasm for Texas, 19, 26
  and general assemblies, 53
  and land purchases, 51
  and land title disputes, 212-13
  and origins of Society, 13-14, 15
  and outfitting the plantation, 39
  and participation in Society, 15-16
Leiningen, Karl Emich, Prince of, 16, 267n20, 268n28
Lewis, Sam, 44, 115-16, 229
Lewis-Wagner House, 116
Leyendecker, Johann (father), 118, 291n17
Leyendecker, Johann Friedrich (son), 118, 291n17
Light Battery, 201
Lincoln, Abraham, 214-15
Lindheimer, Friedrich, 82
liquor provisions, 131-32
literature on German settlements, 2
livestock
  on average Texas farms, 110-11, 291n10
  and fencing, 43
  of Lewis, 116
livestock industry, 228
  at Nassau Plantation, 43, 45, 64, 117-18
  of von Rosenberg family, 170, 291n10
Llano River, 129
Long expedition, 167, 307nn3-4
Loyal Valley, 191
lynchings, 193

Magruder (General), 201, 204
Mainz, Germany, 12-13, 154
Mansfeld, Collorado, Count of, 54
martial law, 191, 193-94, 198
Martin, Ludwig, 154, 162-63, 280n20

Marx, Karl, 58
Mary (slave), 84, 112
Mason County War, 193
Maverick, Sam, 191
Maximilian I, 197
May, Karl, 150
Mayfield, James S.
  and annexation of Texas, 187
  and anti-immigrant sentiments, 147
  and Bostick, 146, 303n104
  and German Emigration Co., 142, 145, 146
  as legal defense of Society, 141, 142–43
  and San Antonio, 302n87
  and shootout, 124
  on slaves, 146
McCulloch, Ben, 191
McNeill, James, 28, 272n16
McRae (Lieutenant), 193
Medina County, 188
Meerscheidt, Amanda Karolina (Lina) von (formerly Rosenberg), 172, 175, 177–78, 204
Meerscheidt, Arthur
  and the Civil War, 200, 202–4
  and farming, 179, 180, 181, 203
  and *Herrenhaus* (manor house), 251–52, 290n16
  land purchases of, 176, 181
  and land title disputes, 217
  marriage of, 172–73, 175, 178
  move to Round Top, 176–79
  and socialist commune, 179–80
Mercer, Charles, 56
Messrs. Schmidt & Co., 40
Meusebach, Johann Otto *Freiherr* von
  and "Answer to Interrogatories," 163
  challenges faced by, 124–30, 131–33
  and colonists, 125, 126, 127–28, 129, 130, 133, 294n12, 295n31
  commissioner-general appointment, 6–7
  and *Darmstädter*, 136
  and debts of Solms-Braunfels, 90
  democratic leanings of, 125
  and Dooley, 299n64
  and leadership in Germany, 127, 133
  and lynch mob, 7, 126, 127
  personal style of, 126–27
  rank of, 267n19, 288n3
  and requests for capital, 125–26, 127
  resignation of, 133
  and Schubbert, 7, 131–32, 133, 144, 148, 151
  stays at the plantation of, 128
  and treaty with Comanches, 125, 130, 132–33, 139, 144, 296n36
  and von Roeder, 128
  and von Wrede's proposals, 100–101
Meusebach-Schubbert lease, 118–19, 258
Mexico
  and *empresario* system, 21, 269n35
  Mexican-American War, 126
  and potential U.S. annexation of Texas, 20
  and Republic of Texas, 19–20, 20–21
  and runaway slaves, 65–66
  threat of invasion by, 21–22, 34, 110
  and war for Texas independence, 30, 31, 157, 183–84, 196
Meyer, Emil, 58, 85, 86, 121, 286n26
military service, 176, 197–98, 202–3, 216, 223–24
Miller, Burkhart, 50, 56, 62, 163, 208
Millheim community, 195, 196, 197, 199, 222–23
Mills, Robert, 34–35, 274n39
Missionary Baptist Church, 222

Mission League, 209
Missouri, Kansas & Texas Railroad, 220
Möllhausen, Balduin, 150
Moore, J., 212
mules, 116, 291n10
Murchison, John, 65, 281n5
music, 189-90, 230
Mustang grapes, 118, 291n15, 292n18

Nagel, Charles, 194-95, 196-97, 198, 199-200
Nagel, Hermann, 196-97
Nassau, Adolph, Duke of
  and alternative plan of Boos-Waldeck, 59
  donations of, 54
  faction led by, 60, 61
  and origins of Society, 12, 13
  as protector of the Society, 54
  and revolution (1848), 154
Nassau Plantation
  and the Civil War, 200, 205
  and colonies, 130
  and creditors, 125, 127, 128
  crops of, 65, 97, 99, 100
  deed to, 159-63, 164, 168
  division of, 3, 8, 98, 99, 221
  employment at, 82
  failure of, 113-15, 120, 121
  fencing in, 43, 44, 99
  house on (see *Herrenhaus*)
  inventory of, 44, 79, 87, 105, 107, 159, 243-44
  and land title disputes, 209, 218
  leasing proposals for, 99-100
  legacy of, 218
  and livestock, 43, 45, 64, 117-18
  location of, 1, 3, 9, 27-28 (see also Jack League)
  management of, 114 (see also commissioners-general; overseers; supervisors)
  and objectives of the Society, 115
  planting season on, 43
  plowing of, 43-44, 47, 64, 99, 277n24
  power of attorney for, 80, 87, 162
  provisions for, 39-42, 43, 45-46, 233
  purchase of, 35, 275n42
  and rented fields, 44
  and Schubbert's lease, 118-19, 130, 136-38, 139-41, 143-44, 147-48, 158, 258
  secondary status of, 58, 60
  self-sufficiency goal of, 45
  and shootout, 123-24, 137-41, 148
  significance of, 1-2
  slaves (see slaves of Nassau Plantation)
  state of, 64-65, 79-80, 84, 130-31
  structures of, 42, 44-45, 98-99, 106 (see also *Herrenhaus*)
  value of, 43, 44, 159
  and the von Rosenberg family, 168, 170, 182
  well for, 85, 106-7, 278n38
Nassau-Rosenberg house, 175-76, 181
nationalism, 18-19, 22, 176
Native American. *See* Indians
native plants, 15, 266n16
Naturforschender Verein (Society for the Research of Nature), 138
Negro Jim
  and Durand, 97
  and Etzel's departure, 84
  as overseer, 6, 89, 114, 131
  quarters for, 106
  wife of, 98
Neighbors (American Indian agent), 132
Neptune steamer, 40, 276n5
Neumann, Otto, 224, 231

New Braunfels
    and the Civil War, 203
    colonists in, 7, 88, 96, 126, 127, 128, 129, 130
    and land title disputes, 209
    regional office in, 154
    and Solms-Braunfels, 76
    Von Roeder's property in, 161
New Braunfelser Zeitung, 190
New Orleans, 39-40, 45-46, 66
newspapers, 185-86
Nicaragua, 202-3
Nimitz, Charles, 192
North Texas, 228
nostalgia, 2

Oak Valley, 32-33
oats, 119-20
Old Bay View Cemetery, 218
Oldenburg, 230
On the Indian Border (Strubberg), 149
Ordinance of Secession, 214-15
Ötzel, Wilhelm (Etzel), 26, 270n2. *See also* Etzel, Wilhelm
overseers
    See also Bryan, William; Denman; Durand, S. A.
    appointment of, 41, 96
    dismissal of, 79-80, 87, 96
    expectations of, 27, 80, 114
    house of, 42-43, 44, 107, 169, 209
    Negro Jim as, 6, 88, 114, 131
    and supervisors, 114
oxen, 64

painted churches, 228
The Panorama of New Braunfels (Rohrdorf), 139
Patience (slave), 66
patriotism, 198
Peace of Luneville, 17
"Peach Orchard" field, 44
Peery, Crockett, 169
Peters, Maria (née Isslieb), 252-53

pigs, 45, 110-11, 116, 117-18
plantation culture and system, 27, 28, 189. *See also* Nassau Plantation
planting season, 43
Plum Creek, battle of (1840), 83
Proclamation on Slavery, 185, 247-48
prohibition, 225, 229
Prussia, 55, 174-75

Rachael (slave), 66
railroads, 220-21, 280n20
rank and class distinctions, 42, 77, 85, 103, 267n19
Rather, Mary Belle, 231
Rather, Roy Randolph, 231
Rauscher (accountant), 154
Reconstruction, 193, 205, 219
Red River Campaign, 216
Regenbrecht, Adelbert, 195
regional offices, 154
Reichsdeputationshauptschlu of 1803 (Imperial Decree), 17
religion, 82, 222, 228-29
Republic of Texas
    annexation of Texas, 187
    coastal prairies of, 27-28
    and *empresario* system, 21, 269n35
    financial system of, 39-40, 110, 275n2
    frontier lands of, 47, 58, 81, 95
    geography of, 14
    hopes for, 12
    and land grants, 4, 5, 21, 22-23, 33, 36, 55, 59-60, 128-29
    land speculation in, 12, 15, 22-23, 26-27, 168-69, 207-18
    and Mexico, 19-20, 20-21
    political status of, 14
    population of, 109, 110
    and potential U.S. annexation of, 19, 20, 22
    and settlers, 21, 57, 59, 269n35

special legislative session, 32–33
and *Standesherren*, 18, 19
and Texas War of Independence, 30, 31, 157, 183–84, 196
and trade subsidies, 55
value of lands in, 14–15
Richard (slave), 40, 65, 85
Robison, J. R., 112
Robson, John R., 209, 212, 213–14, 311n3
Roeder, Albrecht von, 156, 209
Roeder, Caroline von, 195
Roeder, Ludwig (Louis) von, 156, 157
Roeder, Otto von, 153–64
  acquisition of Nassau Plantation, 9, 158–63
  and the Civil War, 195–96, 202
  death of, 218
  duel, 86, 287n39
  emigration to Texas, 156–57
  and *Herrenhaus* (manor house), 175, 309n14
  and the Jack League, 180, 216
  and land speculation, 169
  and land title disputes, 7–8, 208–18
  and legacy of the Nassau Plantation, 218
  legal problems, 182
  legendary poker game of, 30, 273n23
  livestock of, 110–11
  marriages of, 157, 312n22
  and Meusebach, 128
  military service, 202, 216
  sale of property, 221, 311nn3–4
  and settlers' plight, 158–59, 163–64, 305n17
  and slavery, 112, 113, 158, 194, 200, 201
  and Solms-Braunfels, 82, 158
  and Spiess, 145
  supervisor appointment of, 143
  and vigilante committee, 146–47
  and von Rosenberg family, 168, 169–70, 170–71, 173, 181–82
Roeder, Rudolph, 156
Roeder, Theodore Sack von, 157, 172, 174–75, 176, 217
Roeder, Wilhelm von, 172
Roehr, F., 163
Roemer, Ferdinand, 104, 105
Rohrdorf, Conrad Caspar, 7, 124, 138–41, 144, 150–51
Rosenberg, Alex von, 201, 204, 224–25, 274n39, 314n25
Rosenberg, Amanda Dorothea Fröhlich von, 166, 180, 217
Rosenberg, Amanda Fallier von
  on Butler's service, 72
  children of, 166
  on Enkelking, 173–74
  and *Herrenhaus* (manor house), 104, 105, 175–76, 249–50
  and the Nassau Plantation, 170
  and slavery, 200–201
  on von Roeder, 173–74
  on wheat compared to corn, 120
Rosenberg, Amanda Karolina (Lina) von, 172, 175, 177–78, 204
Rosenberg, Axel von, 171
Rosenberg, Carl Wilhelm von (William)
  on cultural shortcomings, 172
  daily routine of, 171
  emigration to Texas, 166–67
  and Land Office tenure, 204–5
  land purchases of, 168, 169
  and livestock, 118
  and military service, 201–2, 204, 224
  sale of farm, 180
  and slavery, 200
Rosenberg, Dale von, 201
Rosenberg, Emma von, 224
Rosenberg, Ernst von, 167, 307n4
Rosenberg, Eugen von, 171, 182, 201, 202

Rosenberg, Johanna (Hännchen) Carolina von, 169-70, 180
Rosenberg, Johannes von, 169, 172
Rosenberg, Julie Wilhelmine Christine von, 170, 172
Rosenberg, Peter Carl von
  emigration to Texas, 167
  on frontier life, 166, 170-71, 172
  and *Herrenhaus* (manor house), 6, 8, 170, 250-51
  land purchases of, 8, 168-69
  and land sales, 223
  and land title disputes, 208-9, 213, 215
  and livestock, 118
  and Meerscheidt, 178
  move to Round Top, 180
  retirement, 179
  and slavery, 200, 201
  and von Roeder, 182
Rosenberg, Walther von, 171, 201-2
Round Top
  and antique shows, 230
  and Central European immigrants, 111, 229
  Jäntschke on, 176-77
  and Meerscheidt, 204
  and military service, 224
  and railroads, 221
  and social organizations (*Vereine*), 223
  and von Rosenberg family, 166, 179
Round Top Festival Institute, 230
"Runaway Scrape," 157
rye, 119-20

Sack, Theodore (Dorchen), 157, 172, 174-75, 176, 217
San Antonio, 191, 208, 211-12, 302n87
San Felipe, 167-68
Sängerfest (Song Festival), 189-90
Sängerverein (choral society), 223, 229

Santa Fe Railroad, 220
sassafras, 15
Schenk, Friedrich, 135
Scherpf, G. A., 14, 21, 26, 27, 34
Schiller, Friedrich, 86, 107
Schleicher, Gustav, 135
Schneider's Negro, 72
schools, 222-23
Schubbert (Friedrich Armand Strubberg)
  appearance of, 133
  in Arkansas, 148-49
  background of, 134, 297n39
  and Bené, 295n25
  and Bostick, 139, 147
  criticisms of, 131-32, 295n29
  dismissal of, 133, 134, 136, 148
  and Friedrichsburg settlement, 7, 125, 129-30, 131-32, 149
  and lease on plantation, 118-19, 130, 136-38, 139-41, 143-44, 147-48, 158, 258
  and litigation threat, 147
  and Meusebach, 7, 131-32, 133, 144, 148, 151
  novels of, 149-50, 263n2, 295n31, 297n41, 297n43
  and Rohrdorf's illustrations, 7, 144, 150-51, 302n96
  and shootout, 123, 137-41, 148, 300n67
  time in Mexico, 147-48
Schulenburg, 221
Schultz, Georg, 138
Schurz, Carl, 227, 314n31
Schützenverein (shooting club), 223
Schwarzes Blut oder Sklaverei in den Vereinigten Staaten (Strubberg), 150
Schwind, Johann, 26, 30, 270n3
Sealsfield, Charles, 150
Sealy, 220
secession, 183-84, 195, 214-15
Second War of Secession, 183-84. *See also* Civil War

Seeliger, Carl, 197
Sehm, Günter, 147
self-sufficiency, 45, 110, 220, 295n31
Settegast, M. W., 163
settlers
  and agricultural opportunities, 110-11
  anti-slavery sentiments of, 3, 8, 121
  arrival of, 88, 95-96, 125, 127-28
  capital required for, 125-26
  and *Darmstädter*, 136
  discontent among, 126
  and education and religious instruction, 35-36
  and food supplies, 158-59, 163-64, 305n17
  and free-labor farms, 113
  hardships endured by, 126, 127, 294n12
  and Indian threat, 101-2
  and land grants, 128-29
  and Meusebach, 125, 126, 127-28, 129, 130, 133, 294n12, 295n31
  military escort for, 85, 86
  origins of, 111
  and Republic of Texas, 21, 57
  slave-holders among, 32, 112
  and Solms-Braunfels, 6, 77, 81-82, 82-83, 85, 88, 95-96
  and transport to settlements, 126, 127, 128, 129, 130
Shelby, 182, 313n7
shootout, 123-24, 137-41, 148, 153-54, 155, 300n67
Sisterdale, 190, 191
slavery
  See also slaves of Nassau Plantation
  and abolitionism, 186, 189, 194
  anti-slavery novels, 7, 149
  attitudes toward, 3, 5, 8, 121, 184-85, 188, 195, 199
  and ban on slave trade, 186
  and Boos-Waldeck, 25, 27, 36, 113, 120, 185, 200

  and Civil War, 112
  and emancipation, 222
  and freed slaves, 221-22
  number of slaves and slaveholders, 111-12
  and potential U.S. annexation of Texas, 20
  Proclamation on Slavery, 185, 247-48
  and shootout, 124
  and slave economy, 112-13, 120, 121
  and Smith, 27
  and Society, 8, 80, 186, 187-88, 188-89
  Texas-German slaveholders, 32, 112, 113, 158, 165, 170
slaves of Nassau Plantation, 63-74
  Boose-Waldeck's disappointment with, 47
  and Burkhardt, 60
  children of, 112
  escape of, 5, 63, 65-71, 72-74, 80, 112, 283n25, 283n27
  inventory of, 245-46, 276n7
  need for, 46
  number of, 112
  and objectives of the Society, 62
  purchases of, 39, 40, 41-42, 234-35, 276n7
  quarters for, 43, 44-45, 67, 79, 106, 107
  and rented fields, 44
  serving in leadership positions, 6, 89, 114, 131
  and shootout at *Herrenhaus*, 139-40, 146, 147
  and Solms-Braunfels, 5, 68, 72, 73-74, 79, 84, 93, 112, 173, 285n19
  teamster work of, 128
  treatment of, 67-68, 71, 80, 303n98
  value of, 66
small grains, 119-20

Smith, Morgan, 27, 28, 29, 41, 271n8, 272n20
smokehouse, 42, 43
SMS Ranches, 28
S. M. Swenson & Co., 43
socialism, 179-80
social life, 175, 181-82, 229
social organizations (*Vereine*), 199, 223
Society for the Protection of German Emigrants (*Adelsverein*)
  See also German Emigration Co.; land grants; *specific individuals*
  artist of, 138-39
  and colonization grant, 33
  and control of plantation, 50
  and corporation status, 32-33, 51, 54, 280n20
  and Duke of Nassau, 54
  and English throne, 16, 17, 20, 267nn20-21
  executive committee of, 54
  financial issues, 100-101, 125, 129-30, 154-56
  general assemblies, 13, 49-50, 51, 53-54, 57, 58-59
  impatience of, 115
  inventory of assets, 159
  and Jack League acquisition, 34-35, 36
  and land title disputes, 207-8, 218
  leadership of, 6-7, 15-17, 58, 60, 264n15
  legacy of, 221
  liquidation of property, 154-55
  membership in, 16, 17-18, 56, 267n19
  and Meusebach, 127, 133
  name of, 263n5, 280n20
  objectives of, 1-2, 4, 22, 47-48, 58, 115, 120, 127-28, 268n28, 304n2
  origins of, 12, 13-16, 21-22
  and potential U.S. annexation of Texas, 22
  reports of Boos-Waldeck to, 35-37, 54, 59
  and shootout, 124, 141-42, 153-54
  and slavery, 8, 80, 186, 187-88, 188-89
  and trade, 50
Society for the Research of Nature, 138
Solms-Braunfels, Carl, Prince of, 75-90
  accounting practices of, 89-90
  and Anglos, 34, 77, 95-96, 285n8
  appearance of, 77
  assessment of plantation, 5-6
  and Bryan, 115
  and Castell, 17
  debts of, 90
  and Denman, 114
  donations of, 54
  and d'Orvanne, 82-83, 88
  emphasis on rank, 77, 85
  and Etzel, 79, 80-81, 84-85
  and Fischer, 61, 62, 84, 85, 88-89, 288n90
  and Fordtran, 5, 79, 80, 83, 84, 87, 93, 115
  horse race, 86
  influence of, 76
  and land grants, 5, 53, 84
  and land title disputes, 210
  military escort of, 85, 86
  on need for religious services, 82
  and New Braunfels, 76
  party of, 86, 287nn37-38
  paternalism of, 295n31
  poetry and song compositions of, 86
  position of, 60
  replacement of, 125
  reports of, 77, 83
  security guard of, 82

and settlers, 6, 77, 81-82, 82-83, 85, 88, 95-96
and slavery, 5, 186-87, 200
and slaves of Nassau, 5, 68, 72, 73-74, 79, 84, 93, 112, 173, 285n19
on state of plantation, 79-80, 84, 89, 115
stays at the plantation of, 77-78, 79-83, 84-88
on Texas's independence, 22
ties to English throne, 16, 267n20
and von Roeder, 82, 158
and von Wrede, 84, 85, 94
Solms-Braunfels Archives, 2
Somers, Frederick, 123, 124, 140, 142, 145
Somervell, Alexander, 77, 284nn5-6
Song of the Guadalupe (Fallersleben), 75-76, 86
Sörghel, Alwin, 138, 294n11
Sörghel, Ernst, 124, 137, 138, 139, 141, 144-45
Spiess, Hermann
on Bostick, 143, 147
on Bryan, 282n20
as commissioner-general, 136, 155
and *Darmstädter*, 135
and murder trial, 144-46
and Schubbert, 137, 295n29
and shootout, 124, 133, 137-41, 142, 300n67
and slaves of Nassau, 68, 146, 303n98
Stage Coach Inn, 229
Standesherren, 17-18
Starkenburgia Corps, 135
State Gazette, 190
Steinert, W., 66
Stirper, John, 169
Strubberg, Friedrich Armand. *See* Schubbert
subsidies, 55, 57, 119

sugar cane crops, 65
Sunday Law, 225, 314n26
supervisors
See also Fordtran, Charles; Roeder, Otto von; Solms-Braunfels, Carl, Prince of; Wrede, Friedrich von, Sr.
appointment of, 5, 49, 96, 130, 143
dismissal of, 5, 96
and overseers, 114
turnover in, 114
surveys, 274n32
Swenson, Swante Magnus, 28, 41, 271n13

Taylor, C. H. (Kit), 112
Taylor, Lonn, 229
Tegener, Fritz, 192-93
Tennessee, 111
Texanische Lieder (Fallersleben), 75
Texas and German Emigration Society, 211-12
Texas Land Office, 201
Texas Rangers, 83
Texas Songs (Fallersleben), 75
Texas Supreme Court, 8, 214
Texas War of Independence, 30, 31, 157, 183-84, 196
The Intellectuals of Possum Creek (Nagel), 194
Tiling, Moritz, 61
tobacco, 110, 111, 121, 273n29
Toms (slave), 170, 171
Tonkawa Indians, 72
Townsend, Stephen, 73, 284n37
trade, 19, 22, 50, 55, 57
tradesmen, 36
Trenckmann, Hugo, 197
Trenckmann, W. A., 194-95, 197, 199, 220, 313n12
Turnverein (gymnastic society), 174, 223
typhus, 202

Ubaghs, J. W., 163
Union Hill, 191
Unionists, 189, 191-92, 197, 204
Union League, 192
United States
  and annexation of Texas, 187
  and Republic of Texas, 12, 19, 20, 22
University of Texas's Winedale Historical Center, 116, 229
Until the Wilderness (Strubberg), 149
U.S. Supreme Court, 8, 202, 214-16

Velasco port, 28
Vereinskirche (Society Church), 131-32
Victoria Advocate, 190
Victoria Reserves, 202, 216
Virginia, 111
viticulture, 118, 291n15, 292n18
Vogelsang, August, 143, 146, 302n91
Voigt (Lieutenant), 198
Von Roeder family, 30, 31, 195. *See also* Roeder, Otto von

Wade, J. A., 209, 212, 213-14, 311n4
Wade, W. F., 209, 212, 213-14, 311n4
Wagner, Joseph, 229
Wagner, Julius, 135
Wagner farmstead, 229
Waldeck Plantation, 29, 272n20
Wallenstein (Schiller), 86
Ward & Cazello, 65
Warrenton, 230
Washington (slave), 65-71, 72-74, 112
Washington (steamship), 167
Washington County, 113, 168, 188, 228
Washington-on-the-Brazos, 32-33, 77-78

water availability, 85, 106-7, 312n2
Waul's Legion, 198, 201, 224
Wave (ship), 201
Wegenhoft, John, 226
Wendish immigrants, 228
Western genre, 150
Weyand, Alexander, 181
Weyand, Georg, 181, 223-24, 230-31
wheat, 119-20, 292n22
Wied, Hermann zu, 49, 60, 81, 87
Wilberforce, William, 186
wildfires, 222
Wildkatzen Brunnen (Cat Spring) settlement, 30, 34, 156, 195
wildlife, 170
Wilke, Hermann, 130, 137, 144
Williams, R. H., 191
Williams, Sam, 34
windmills, 219, 312n2
Wolff, Michael, 231
wooded land, 118
wool, 170-71
World War I, 221, 225-26
World War II, 227-28
Wrede, Friedrich von, Sr., 94-102
  and agriculture, 119
  analysis and proposals of, 98-100, 155
  arrival at plantation, 97
  arrival in Texas, 94
  background of, 286n30
  death of, 6, 101-2, 103, 130
  and Durand, 97-98, 114
  experimentation of, 117
  garden of, 117
  and *Herrenhaus* (manor house), 98-99, 104, 114
  responsibilities of, 88
  and Solms-Braunfels, 84, 85, 94
  supervisory appointment, 6, 88, 96, 101
  and viticulture, 118

Wrede, Friedrich Wilhelm von, Jr., 94, 286n30

yellow fever, 28
yeoman, 36

Zabitsch, 140
Zapp, Z. M. P., 216
Zobel, 140
Zunftwesen, 121

www.ingramcontent.com/pod-product-compliance
Lightning Source LLC
Chambersburg PA
CBHW030301080526
44584CB00012B/400